Media Industries

Media Industries
History, Theory, and Method

Edited by Jennifer Holt and Alisa Perren

WILEY-BLACKWELL

A John Wiley & Sons, Ltd., Publication

Blackwell Publishing was acquired by John Wiley & Sons in February 2007. Blackwell's publishing program has been merged with Wiley's global Scientific, Technical, and Medical business to form Wiley-Blackwell.

Registered Office
John Wiley & Sons Ltd, The Atrium, Southern Gate, Chichester, West Sussex, PO19 8SQ, United Kingdom

Editorial Offices
350 Main Street, Malden, MA 02148-5020, USA
9600 Garsington Road, Oxford, OX4 2DQ, UK
The Atrium, Southern Gate, Chichester, West Sussex, PO19 8SQ, UK

For details of our global editorial offices, for customer services, and for information about how to apply for permission to reuse the copyright material in this book please see our website at www.wiley.com/wiley-blackwell.

Library of Congress Cataloging-in-Publication Data

Media industries : history, theory, and method / edited by Jennifer Holt and Alisa Perren.
   p. cm.
   Includes bibliographical references and index.
   ISBN 978-1-4051-6341-5 (hardcover : alk. paper) – ISBN 978-1-4051-6342-2 (pbk. : alk. paper) 1. Mass media. I. Holt, Jennifer. II. Perren, Alisa.
P90.M3676 2009
302.23–dc22
                                    2008041563

A catalogue record for this book is available from the British Library.

Set in 10/12pt Bembo
by SPi Publisher Services, Pondicherry, India
Printed in Singapore by Utopia Press Pte Ltd

001   2009

Contents

CONTENTS

Figures

Acknowledgments

We would like to thank all of the contributors for their innovative work and generous commitment to this book. Collaborating with every one of them was a privilege and we are sincerely grateful for all of the effort, energy, and ideas they each brought to this project. Some have contributed even more than their essays. John Caldwell, Horace Newcomb, and Tom Schatz have been brilliant mentors to us over the years, and this book is largely a product of their inspiration and teachings. Particular appreciation goes to Tom for the unwavering support, expert guidance, and friendship that he has provided throughout our careers.

We are grateful to our colleagues in Film and Media Studies at UC-Santa Barbara and the Department of Communication at Georgia State for the encouragement and thoughtful discussions. We are also indebted to numerous graduate students and faculty at UT-Austin, the place where the seeds for this project were first planted.

This book would not have existed without the input of Jayne Fargnoli at Blackwell. We thank her for enthusiastically taking a chance on us and also for her limitless patience and sage counsel. Thanks also to Ken Provencher and Margot Morse for editorial assistance.

Danielle Williams and Shane Toepfer have proven to be invaluable as research assistants. Their attention to detail and willingness to put in the extra hours toward the end helped bring this project to the finish line. Thanks also to Caroline Frick, Jennie Phillips, and Rebecca Epstein for their input from the initial idea to the final drafts.

Finally, special thanks to our families as well as to both Greg Siegel and Cully Hamner for their heroic support throughout this process.

Jennifer Holt and Alisa Perren
March 2008

Notes on Contributors

About the Editors

Jennifer Holt is assistant professor of film and media studies at the University of California, Santa Barbara. Her work has appeared in journals and anthologies including *Film Quarterly, Quality Popular Television*, and *Media Ownership: Research and Regulation*. She is currently working on *Empires of Entertainment*, a manuscript chronicling deregulation and structural transformation in the film and television industries.

Alisa Perren is assistant professor in the Department of Communication at Georgia State University. She is completing a manuscript tracing the evolution of Miramax during the 1990s as it transitioned from independent company to studio subsidiary. She has published articles on the development of niche markets in the New Hollywood as well as on the programming and distribution strategies of contemporary US television networks.

About the Contributors

John Thornton Caldwell is professor and chair of cinema and media studies in the Department of Film, Television, and Digital Media at UCLA. His books include *Production Culture: Industrial Reflexivity and*

Critical Practice in Film and Television (2008); *Televisuality: Style, Crisis, and Authority in American Television* (1995); *Electronic Media and Technoculture* (editor, 2000); and *New Media* (co-editor, 2003). He has also published articles in *Cinema Journal, Asian Film, Television & New Media*, and *Media, Culture & Society*. Producer/director of the award-winning films *Rancho California (por favor)* (2002) and *Freak Street to Goa: Immigrants on the Rajpath* (1989), and recipient of grants and awards from the National Endowment for the Arts, the AFI, and regional fellowships, his films and videos have been shown widely at festivals in Sundance, Berlin, Chicago, Los Angeles, Hawaii, Toulouse, and Mexico City, and broadcast on public television in the US and Australia.

Michael Curtin is director of global studies at the University of Wisconsin International Institute and professor of media and cultural studies in the Department of Communication Arts. His books include *Redeeming the Wasteland: Television Documentary and Cold War Politics* (1995); *Playing to the World's Biggest Audience: The Globalization of Chinese Film and TV* (2007); *Making and Selling Culture* (co-editor, 1996); and *The Revolution Wasn't Televised: Sixties Television and Social Conflict* (co-editor, 1997). He is currently working on *Media Capital: The Cultural Geography of Globalization* (Blackwell) and *The American Television Industry* (British Film

Institute). He is co-editor of the International Screen Industries book series for the British Film Institute.

Mark Deuze holds a joint appointment at Indiana University's Department of Telecommunications in Bloomington, US, and as professor of journalism and new media at Leiden University, the Netherlands. Publications comprise five books including *Media Work* (2007); guest-edited special issues of journals on convergence culture (*Convergence* 2008, *International Journal of Cultural Studies* 2009); and articles in journals such as *Information Society, New Media & Society*, and *Journalism Studies*. Weblog: http://deuze.blogspot.com.

Caroline Frick serves as assistant professor in the School of Information and the Department of Radio-TV-Film at the University of Texas at Austin. In addition, she founded and acts as executive director of the Texas Archive of the Moving Image (www. texasarchive.org). She has worked in film preservation at Warner Bros, the Library of Congress, and the National Archives and Records Administration. She has also programmed films for the American Movie Classics cable channel in New York and currently serves as a director of the board for the Association of Moving Image Archivists. Her book, *Saving Cinema*, is forthcoming from Oxford University Press.

Nitin Govil teaches comparative media and cultural studies at the University of California, San Diego, where he is assistant professor in the Department of Communication. He is co-author of *Global Hollywood* (2001) and *Global Hollywood 2* (2005) and has also published on cultural politics and media technology, media history, globalization and the culture industries, and film piracy across local and global contexts. He is currently completing a co-authored book on the Indian film industries.

Joshua Green is a postdoctoral researcher in the comparative media studies program at MIT, where he is also research manager of the Convergence Culture Consortium. His research looks at changing understandings of what television "is," the formation of the participatory audience, and television branding in the context of participatory culture. He has published work on participatory culture and the relationship

between producers and consumers, television scheduling strategies, the history of Australian television, and the construction of the cultural public sphere. He is co-author (with Jean Burgess) of *YouTube: Online Video and the Politics of Participatory Culture* (2008). He holds a Ph.D. in media studies from the Queensland University of Technology.

John Hartley is Australian Research Council federation fellow and research director of the ARC Centre of Excellence for Creative Industries and Innovation at Queensland University of Technology in Australia. He is a distinguished professor of QUT and adjunct professor of the Australian National University. He was foundation dean of the Creative Industries Faculty (QUT), and previously head of the School of Journalism, Media and Cultural Studies at Cardiff University in Wales. He is author of 18 books, translated into a dozen languages, including *Television Truths* (2008); *Creative Industries* (2005); *A Short History of Cultural Studies* (2003); *Communication, Cultural and Media Studies: The Key Concepts* (2002); *The Indigenous Public Sphere* (with Alan McKee, 2000); *American Cultural Studies* (with Roberta Pearson, 2000); *Uses of Television* (1999); and *Popular Reality* (1996). He is editor of the *International Journal of Cultural Studies*.

David Hesmondhalgh is professor of media industries at the Institute of Communications Studies and co-director (with Justin O'Connor) of CuMIRC, the Cultural and Media Industries Research Centre at the University of Leeds. His publications include *The Cultural Industries* (2nd edn. 2007) and five edited volumes: *The Media and Social Theory* (with Jason Toynbee, 2008); *Media Production* (2006); *Understanding Media: Inside Celebrity* (with Jessica Evans, 2005); *Popular Music Studies* (with Keith Negus, 2002); and *Western Music and its Others* (with Georgina Born, 2000). He is currently writing up a two-year research project, "Creative Work in the Cultural Industries," conducted with Sarah Baker and funded by the UK Arts and Humanities Research Council.

Michele Hilmes is professor of media and cultural studies and director of the Wisconsin Center for Film and Theater Research at the University of Wisconsin-Madison. She is author or editor of several books on media history, including *NBC: America's Network* (2007); *Only Connect: A Cultural History of Broadcasting in the United States* (2nd edn. 2006); *The Television History Book* (2003); and *Radio Voices: American Broadcasting 1922 to 1952* (1997).

Henry Jenkins is the co-director of the MIT comparative media studies program and the Peter de Florez professor of humanities. He is author and/or editor of 12 books on various aspects of media and popular culture, including *Convergence Culture: Where Old and New Media Collide; Fans, Bloggers, and Gamers: Exploring Participatory Culture; The Wow Climax: Tracing the Emotional Impact of Popular Culture; Textual Poachers: Television Fans and Participatory Culture; Hop on Pop: The Politics and Pleasures of Popular Culture*; and *From Barbie to Mortal Kombat: Gender and Computer Games*. He writes regularly about media and cultural change at his blog: henryjenkins.org.

Victoria E. Johnson is associate professor of film and media studies and visual studies at the University of California, Irvine, where she is also affiliated faculty in African American Studies. Her book, *Heartland TV: Prime Time Television and the Struggle for US Identity* (2008), examines the imagination of the American Midwest as symbolic heartland in critical moments in prime-time television and US social history. She has published several articles and chapters regarding the politics of place, race, and popular music in anthologies and journals including *Film Quarterly* and *The Velvet Light Trap*.

Douglas Kellner is George F. Kneller chair in the philosophy of education at UCLA and is author of many books on social theory, politics, history, and culture, including *Camera Politica: The Politics and Ideology of Contemporary Hollywood Film*, co-authored with Michael Ryan; *Critical Theory, Marxism, and Modernity; Jean Baudrillard: From Marxism to Postmodernism and Beyond*; works in cultural studies such as *Media Culture* and *Media Spectacle*; a trilogy of books on postmodern theory with Steve Best; and a trilogy of books on the media and the Bush Administration, encompassing *Grand Theft 2000, From 9/11 to Terror War*, and *Media Spectacle and the Crisis of Democracy*. His latest book is *Guys and Guns Amok: Domestic Terrorism and School Shootings from the Oklahoma City Bombings to the Virginia Tech Massacre*. Website: www.gseis.ucla.edu/faculty/kellner/kellner.html.

Jordan Levin is co-founder and CEO of Generate, a next-generation studio launched in early 2006 creating targeted content for multi-platform distribution across both traditional and digital media. Formerly CEO of The WB, he was part of the founding executive team responsible for defining series that established the network's distinctly youthful brand such as *Dawson's Creek, Gilmore Girls, Buffy the Vampire Slayer, Felicity, Smallville*, and *Everwood*, for which he also directed an episode. In addition to The WB, he oversaw Kid's WB! and established The WB's original movie division by launching the *American Girl* film franchise. Prior to The WB, he was a member of the creative group that revitalized the Disney brand in network television with properties like *Home Improvement, Ellen*, and *Boy Meets World*. He has lent his expertise as a consultant to leading digital companies and currently sits on numerous boards including nonprofit organizations, academic institutions, political advocacy groups, and media companies.

P. David Marshall currently holds a chair in new media and cultural studies at the University of Wollongong. He has also been professor and chair of communication studies at Northeastern University. His books include *New Media Cultures* (2004); *Web Theory* (with Robert Burnett, 2003); *The Celebrity Culture Reader* (2006); *Fame Games* (with Graeme Turner and Frances Bonner, 2000); and *Celebrity and Power* (1997). He has published many articles and been regularly interviewed by the media and press on new media, media and popular culture, and the public persona. His current research focuses on the shift from a "representational" media regime to a presentational media regime via new media forms.

John McMurria is currently assistant professor in the Department of Communication at the University of California, San Diego. In addition to his published articles in book anthologies and journals, he is co-author, with Toby Miller, Nitin Govil, Richard Maxwell, and Ting Wang, of *Global Hollywood 2* (2005). He is working on a critical cultural policy history of cable television in the US.

Cynthia Meyers is assistant professor of communi-cation at College of Mount Saint Vincent in New York City. Her research areas include the advertising industry, broadcast history, media economics, and new media. She is currently completing a book manuscript about the role of the advertising industry in the development of radio from the 1920s through the 1940s. Her publications include articles in *Quarterly Review of Film and Video*, the *Encyclopedia of Television*, and *Columbia Journal of American Studies*.

Toby Miller is author, co-author, or editor of *The Well-Tempered Self: Citizenship, Culture, and the Postmodern Subject* (1993); *Contemporary Australian Television* (1994); *The Avengers* (1998); *Technologies of Truth: Cultural Citizenship and the Popular Media* (1998); *Popular Culture and Everyday Life* (1998); *SportCult* (1999); *A Companion to Film Theory* (1999); *Film and Theory: An Anthology* (2000); *Globalization and Sport: Playing the World* (2001); *Sportsex* (2001); *Global Hollywood* (2001); *Cultural Policy* (2002); *Television Studies* (2002); *Critical Cultural Policy Studies: A Reader* (2003); *Television Studies: Critical Concepts in Media and Cultural Studies* (2003); *Spyscreen: Espionage on Film and TV from the 1930s to the 1960s* (2003); *Política Cultural* (2004); *Global Hollywood 2* (2005); *El Nuevo Hollywood: Del Imperialismo Cultural a las Leyes del Marketing* (2005); *A Companion to Cultural Studies* (2006); and *Cultural Citizenship: Cosmopolitanism, Consumerism, and Television in a Neoliberal Age* (2007). He is editor of *Television & New Media* and co-editor of *Social Identities*.

Philip M. Napoli is the director of the Donald McGannon Communication Research Center at Fordham University. He teaches and conducts research in the areas of media institutions and media policy. His books include *Audience Economics: Media Institutions and the Audience Marketplace* (2003) and *Foundations of Communications Policy: Principles and Process in the Regulation of Electronic Media* (2001). He has testified before Congress and the Federal Communications Commission on media policy issues, and his work has been supported by organiza-tions such as the Ford Foundation, the Social Science Research Council, the Benton Foundation, and the Center for American Progress.

Horace Newcomb holds the Lambdin Kay chair for the Peabodys and is director of the George Foster Peabody Awards in the Grady College of Journalism and Mass Communication, University of Georgia. He is editor of two editions of the Museum of Broadcast Communications *Encyclopedia of Television* and seven editions of *Television: The Critical View*. He is author of *TV: The Most Popular Art* and co-author of *The Producer's Medium*. He writes and lec-tures on topics related to television and culture.

Thomas Schatz is professor and Mary Gibbs Jones centennial chair of communication at the University of Texas, where he has been on the faculty in the Radio-Television-Film Department since 1976. He has written four books about Hollywood films, including *Hollywood Genres; The Genius of the System: Hollywood Filmmaking in the Studio Era*; and *Boom and Bust: American Cinema in the 1940s*. He also edited a recent four-volume collection on Hollywood for Routledge. His writing on film also has appeared in numerous magazines, newspapers, and academic journals, including the *New York Times*, the *Los Angeles Times*, *Premiere*, *The Nation*, *Film Comment*, *Film Quarterly*, and *Cineaste*. He is currently working on a book project with Thom Mount, former president of Universal Pictures, and serving as executive director of the UT Film Institute, a program devoted to train-ing students in narrative and digital filmmaking, and the production of independent feature-length films.

Cristina Venegas is assistant professor in film and media studies at the University of California, Santa Barbara. The focus of her research is on interna-tional media with an emphasis on Latin America, Spanish-language film and television in the US, and digital technologies. She has written about film and political culture, revolutionary imagination in the Americas, telenovelas, contemporary Latin American cinema, and regionalism. Her book, *Digital Dilemma*, about Cuban digital media since the 1990s, is forth-coming from Rutgers University Press. She has curated numerous film programs on Latin American and indigenous film in the US and Canada, and is co-founder and artistic director of the Latino CineMedia Film Festival in Santa Barbara.

Introduction

Does the World Really Need One More Field of Study?

....

Jennifer Holt and Alisa Perren

The study of media industries is a varied and diverse project, incorporating research on everything from "mobisodes" designed for iPhones and the labor force manufacturing plasma television sets in Malaysia to the Creative Commons movement and trade shows in Budapest. Such work is conducted in film and television studies, communication, law, public policy, business, economics, journalism, and sociology departments. The research about these issues is dispersed across similarly vast terrain, as the media industries have been substantively explored and discussed in numerous arenas far beyond the traditional purview of academic study. Discourses in the trade papers, the popular press, and academic publications are supplemented by writing in digital communities, online journals and the blogosphere.[1]

This range of perspectives is both a necessary component and a constitutive element of this work; after all, to explore the media industries in the twenty-first century is to engage with an extraordinary range of texts, markets, economies, artistic traditions, business models, cultural policies, technologies, regulations, and creative expression. And yet, while such an array of resources and emphases sustains an inspiring breadth of scholarly endeavors, thus far these diffuse conversations have not been united by any specific disciplinary tradition. Further, there remains a dearth of formal gatherings and conferences for those researching the media industries,[2] as well

as an absence of journals or anthologies devoted specifically to the study of media industries as a coherent discipline.

While academic organizations and cross-disciplinary conversations focused on the media industries have been in short supply, the media industries themselves have been experiencing a period of unprecedented influence, prosperity, cultural debate, and transformation. Shifts in regulatory philosophy and political power have led to dramatic clashes between Congress and the FCC, which have put the regulation of these industries on the front page and at the center of heated public discussion. Trade agreements and other economic and geopolitical alliances have led to more regional and transnational collaborations in a globalized media culture. Technological and industrial convergence has eroded old relationships between media while cultural policies have created new ones. Audiences have become newly valued and "monetized" by media industries seeking the latest user-generated content, and at the same time new modes of distribution have undercut decades of industry tradition and thrown well-established business models into disarray.

Further, as the media industries grapple with the evolution of their products and structures, they are also affected by a multitude of external developments. These include the ascendance of neoliberal economic policy, the increasing power of new global markets and trade, the growth of an international middle class (and the erosion of an American one), wars in the Middle East and Africa, dramatic Internet-induced changes in social interaction, and the changing definitions and roles of labor in the digital era. Meanwhile, shifting hierarchies of taste and value in popular culture are having a profound impact on media products and strategies; one need only consider the proliferation of television programming across digital platforms to understand how audience behavior, advertising strategies, and longstanding conceptions of "old" media are changing rapidly in the new millennium.[3]

These myriad developments have created a pressing need to bring interdisciplinary scholarship on media industries into a common dialogue. It is therefore our belief that media industry studies should be mapped and articulated as a distinct and vitally important field unto itself. This has become increasingly urgent in the present landscape of convergence, technological growth, and global exchange, and we believe that the time is right for such an intervention. To that end, we have enlisted the help of internationally renowned scholars to delineate and integrate the various traditions, historical trajectories, critical parameters, and potential paths of inquiry that define this discipline. These essays represent the early imaginings of what the field of media industry studies might look like. This book is neither a definitive blueprint nor a final statement. It is not an exploration of specific media industries in any particular locale. Rather, it is an open conceptual discussion about the many ways that media industry research has been undertaken in the past and what interdisciplinary models, methods, and visions it might embrace in the future. It is also a recognition of the fact that, while the world does not necessarily *need* another field of study, one has indeed emerged.

Defining Media Industry Studies

In this volume, we focus on film, radio, television, advertising, and digital media. This list could easily be expanded to include music, newspapers, book publishing, and even telecommunications. Scholars who write about "creative industries" and "culture

industries" incorporate all of the aforementioned as well as a host of other areas in discussing both the art and economics of media industries. Those focusing on creative industries[4] have also analyzed the realms of architecture, art and design, performing arts, fashion, and software, among others. Cultural industries scholars have included museums, art institutions, libraries, live performance, and sport in their purview.[5]

Choosing the appropriate scope for this project has been challenging. We have decided to narrow our focus to primarily audiovisual media (with the exception of radio, which is inextricably bound to broadcast and advertising histories) for the purposes of initially mapping this critical terrain. Our parameters were determined by the disciplinary cohesion and shared academic traditions of these media, as well as the degree of commonality or overlap between their cultural and institutional histories, objects of study and modes of analysis. By no means do we consider industries such as music, publishing, or telecommunications to be "outside" disciplinary boundaries or of lesser significance; they were merely beyond what could be substantively and productively addressed by this volume.

Our main objective is to articulate the diverse academic traditions and common threads defining media industry studies while also illustrating how the integrated analyses of media texts, audiences, histories, and culture could enable more productive scholarship. Another goal is to situate this discipline within a humanistic context; while some of the methodologies and models explicated here are more commonly employed by the social sciences, we believe that the textually oriented concerns of film and media studies could be enhanced and enlivened by a broadened base of analysis without threatening the larger commitment to the qualitative, critical work associated with humanist paradigms. To that end, the essays in this book attend to constructs of text and image as they relate to industrial structure and economics, connect politics and policy to issues of art and audience, and develop theoretical and methodological paradigms that not only engage with the past but also offer ways of thinking about media industries in the present (and presumably future) landscape of convergence.

In the essays collected here, the authors address several key themes and concerns, including:

- the relative power and autonomy of individual agents to express divergent political perspectives, creative visions, and cultural attitudes within larger institutional structures;
- the means by which the relationships between industry, government, text, and audience can be conceptualized;
- the need for a grounded, empirically based understanding of media industry practices, including the operations, business models, and day-to-day realities of the media industries, past and present;
- the aesthetic, cultural, economic, and social values associated with the media industries and their contents;
- the degree of diversity in both the industries themselves and the products that they create and distribute;
- the power of the media industries to shape cultural agendas in local, trans/national, regional, and/or global contexts;
- the moral and ethical issues that emerge as a result of the activities and operations of the media industries;
- the roles and responsibilities of scholar-citizens in the process of describing and analyzing the media industries.

The discussion that follows emphasizes both the historical and future importance of these issues for scholars of media industries. In looking back on the formative influences on this area of study, we have opted for a macro-level survey that sketches the diverse disciplinary roots of a media industry studies approach. Since our contributors effectively provide the background relevant to their particular topics, our goal in the next few pages is to outline the relationships between a range of scholarly traditions and to show how these traditions both inform this field at large and illuminate the dynamics outlined above. In the process, we indicate ways in which future work on the media industries can further engage in a transdisciplinary conversation about the converging global media landscape.

The Genesis of Media Industries Scholarship

The culture industry and mass communication theories

Many of the foundational ideas about the media industries emerged in critical/scholarly writing from the 1920s through the 1950s. The arrival of World War II – combined with the dominance of several forms of mass media including motion pictures and radio – contributed to the development of different strands of media industries research in both the humanities and social sciences. A key contribution to humanities-based scholarship came with the arrival of a number of German-Jewish emigrants, including Frankfurt School members Herbert Marcuse, Leo Lowenthal, Theodor Adorno, and Max Horkheimer, into the US. These Marxist theorists were previously based at the Institute of Social Research in Germany until the war led them to flee the country. As Douglas Kellner explores more fully in his essay, the ideas forwarded by the Frankfurt School influenced both political economy and cultural studies, as well as a wide range of other disciplines including philosophy and literature. For the purposes of our discussion, what is particularly significant is an essay written by Adorno and Horkheimer in 1944 entitled "The Culture Industry: Enlightenment as Mass Deception."[6]

This essay has influenced how media industries are conceptualized by scholars in a number of ways. Adorno and Horkheimer expressed concern about the extent to which mass media commodified culture. They believed the commercialized media produced within industrial structures – which they labeled "the culture industry" – contributed to the cultural and artistic bankruptcy of American society. Further, they were troubled by the potential degree to which such large-scale media industries shaped the minds of the "masses." They believed that the ideology perpetuated by mass media systems contributed to a depoliticized populace and to their willingness to accept the current social and political status quo. From their point of view, Hollywood represented the epitome of mass-produced culture;

its products cultivated superficial materialistic needs instead of leading people to see the way in which the capitalist system oppressed them and led to their continued domination by the established powers.

While many of these ideas are anathema to our current approach, they are important to understand because of the degree to which they have framed the discourses about the media industries for decades. Their work was significant in terms of raising questions about the kinds of texts produced by mass media industries and the ways these texts might impact audiences.[7] Nonetheless, from the perspective of contemporary media industry studies scholars, Adorno and Horkheimer's views become problematic for a number of reasons. First, inherent in their work was an elitist attitude toward what constituted art (e.g., such high culture activities as operas and symphonies qualified; Hollywood movies and network broadcasts did not). Second, they assumed a monolithic media industry when in fact, as Michele Hilmes and Cynthia Meyers show in their essays, even during the 1930s and 1940s there were numerous stakeholders *within* the industries that had different agendas. Though the metaphor of the "factory system" might have been applied to the Hollywood studios, for example, struggles continually took place between everyone from producers to directors to writers and cinematographers. The factory system also implied highly standardized, interchangeable products – a point that has been significantly challenged by work in such areas as film studies and cultural studies for decades.[8] Third, the vision of the industry constructed by Adorno and Horkheimer assumed a one-way flow of communication from a central industry out to a passive audience. This attributed a tremendous amount of power to the media, combined with minimal agency for individual viewers. What's more, it presumed that other social, cultural, and political institutions had little influence on movie viewers and radio listeners.

Concurrent with the rise of humanistically oriented research by the Frankfurt School, there emerged another strand of scholarship on the media industries out of the social sciences. This area, which was labeled as "mass communication" by the 1930s,[9] differed from the Frankfurt School in terms of its

politics and its methodologies. The Frankfurt School used qualitative analyses informed by Marxian critical theory; these analytical tools were designed to advance radical, polemical arguments about overhauling political and economic structures. Conversely, mass communication scholars generally used quantitative methods such as surveys and content analyses in the interest of better understanding the "effects" of mass media forms such as motion pictures and radio on the public. Their interest was less in the radical social change pursued by the Frankfurt School than in modifying the existing system in order to make it more democratic. Mass communication researchers often assumed minor modifications in media systems could contribute to a more democratic society. These views and methods made their work more amenable to government and industry funding.[10]

Notably, much mass communication scholarship viewed communication via the "transmission model" of "who says what to whom to what effect."[11] This model assumes a linear communication process with the greatest power and influence residing with the "who" (typically sectors of industry or government) and much less authority residing with the "whom" (namely, the audience). Communication scholars – as well as related fields of sociology and psychology – often focused on the ways messages (the "what") could be modified. For the government, the modification of messages was pursued largely in the interest of increasing public participation and civic involvement; for industry, the goal was to sell more of the growing number of consumer goods being produced on assembly lines. These two primary objectives contributed to the direction of much of the initial work on the media industries. Specifically, early communication-oriented studies of the media industries were frequently geared to looking at either advertising or news and information programming. To this day, researchers coming out of mass communication departments continue to focus extensively on these topics. For example, prominent books like David Croteau and William Hoynes' *The Business of Media* and Robert McChesney's *The Problem of the Media* are centered on deficiencies in news coverage and the continuing expansion of consumer culture.

These topics are framed in terms how the media industries add to – or, more frequently, constrain – democratic discourse.[12]

As these recent applications of decades-old ideas illustrate, concepts developed during the 1930s and 1940s continue to shape the research questions and approaches of scholars across the humanities and social sciences. It is precisely these perspectives that the contributors of this book are contesting, challenging, and reconceptualizing. While the ideas formulated by "mass culture" and "mass communication" researchers are valuable, they must be viewed largely as of *historical* value. The essays by Thomas Schatz and Victoria Johnson on film and television industry history reveal the degree to which such views on mass culture and mass communication were produced within specific Fordist economic, political, and social circumstances[13] (e.g., the Hollywood studio system and the classic broadcast network system).

While the "mass culture" and "mass communication" approaches may inform media industry studies, they are not central to its future development. As will be explored in the following pages, media industry studies favors different models of the media industries than those developed in the Fordist era. This means supporting analysis that more fully considers the interrelationships between industry, text, audience, and society. Further, the "industry" spoken of by media industry studies scholars is presumed to be anything but monolithic – a point underscored by Horace Newcomb in his provocative essay, which concludes this book. Rather, our approach perceives culture and cultural production as sites of struggle, contestation, and negotiation between a broad range of stakeholders. These stakeholders include not only sectors of industry and government, but also "ordinary people" (e.g., media user/consumer/viewers). In addition, media industry studies is no longer bound to old frameworks that operated predominantly in terms of nation-based media systems. Nor should we necessarily think only in terms of specific media forms. Changes in the industries, the texts they produce, and the ways these texts are consumed make media-specific formulations increasingly problematic. A number of authors in this collection, including Thomas Schatz,

P. David Marshall, Henry Jenkins, and Joshua Green explore the challenges that emerge in writing about "distinct" media, past and present, in light of industrial convergence. Thus, while this section has dealt with foundational and historical approaches to the study of the media industries, what follows is a sketch of influences and analytical frameworks that more immediately inform contemporary understandings of this discipline.

Disciplinary Influences and Analytical Frameworks
. . . .
Sociology and anthropology

Mass communication and mass culture perspectives may have been prominent from the 1920s to the 1950s, but they were not the only ways media industries research was undertaken during those years. Indeed, a handful of scholars, including sociologist Leo Rosten and anthropologist Hortense Powdermaker, initiated ethnographically oriented studies of the Hollywood community and filmmaking process.[14] Rosten and Powdermaker looked at Hollywood from the "bottom up." These individuals were among the first to employ interviews and participant observation in order to better understand the complex nature of power relations in the media industries, the tensions that arise in the process of making meaning, and the ways in which audiences are conceptualized by both executives and creative figures.[15]

In spite of the richness that such methods can provide, few media industry scholars employed these strategies until the 1970s. When this work was taken up again, it was predominantly by sociologists interested in exploring the day-to-day operations of news organizations. In the late 1970s, American sociologists Gaye Tuchman and Herbert Gans, as well as British sociologist Philip Schlesinger, undertook studies that examined the ways institutional structures variably enabled or constrained newsroom staffs.[16] A handful of studies on the production of entertainment programming emerged simultaneously. These included several works by UK-based scholars; examples include John Tulloch and Manuel

Alvarado's observation of the production of *Dr. Who* and Tom Burns' ventures down the halls of the BBC.[17] One of the few scholars to have conducted examinations of both news production and entertainment programming is sociologist Jeremy Tunstall. Over more than 30 years, Tunstall has interviewed hundreds of individuals involved in both public and commercial media systems throughout Britain and the US.[18] Of course, no survey of cultural production is complete without referring to Todd Gitlin's landmark *Inside Prime Time*, first published in 1983. This study is distinguished by the degree of access he had to prominent US television executives, writers, and producers, as well as by the depth and breadth of his analysis.[19]

The ethnographically oriented accounts above have been complemented by organizational analyses by individuals such as Paul DiMaggio and Paul Hirsch. These writers have taken a more macro-level approach in examining the "sociology of work" in the cultural industries; they evaluate cultural institutions in terms of how they deal with such issues as uncertainty and change.[20] As John Caldwell discusses in his essay, collectively these strands of sociology and anthropology strongly influence the direction taken in scholarship on cultures of production. In addition, as explored in the next section, these studies provide useful counterpoints to the kinds of institutional analyses undertaken by media economists.

Media economics and industrial analysis

In contrast to the "bottom-up" approach employed by many anthropologists and sociologists, early researchers with backgrounds in business and economics examined the film industry through a "top-down" perspective of industrial and organizational structures. This work includes *The Story of the Films*, a series of lectures at Harvard's business school in the 1920s compiled by Joseph P. Kennedy; Mae Huettig's 1944 study, *Economic Control of the Motion Picture Industry*; and Michael Conant's *Antitrust in the Motion Picture Industry: Economic and Legal Analysis* (1960). Economists have provided media industry studies with models for discussing both the macroeconomic (e.g., industrial organization and

structure) and microeconomic (e.g., operations of individual firms and agents within the marketplace).[21]

Douglas Gomery has played a pioneering role in bringing industrial and economic analysis to the study of media industries.[22] Drawing from applied neoclassical microeconomic theory, he offered a concrete framework for conducting economic analysis via a discussion of industry structure, conduct, and performance.[23] Gomery's *Who Owns the Media* (written with Benjamin Compaine, 3rd edn. 2000) represents an extraordinary effort to address matters of policy and economics across a range of media industries including newspapers, publishing, radio, film, music, and television. *Who Owns the Media* supplements its extensive survey of the media industries with an assessment of the amount of competition present both within and across sectors of the media industries.

The degree to which an industry is determined to be competitive by economists impacts the extent to which it is regulated – or deregulated. Since the late 1960s, the subject of media de/regulation has provoked debate from scholars around the world. The debates about media concentration have been conducted by "traditional" economists and political economists, as will be explored below in more detail. A significant portion of this work has focused on the arena of telecommunications,[24] but there is also dedicated work on television (e.g., Mara Einstein's *Media Diversity*, 2004) and media conglomeration (e.g., Marc Cooper, ed. *The Case Against Media Consolidation: Evidence on Concentration, Localism and Diversity*, 2006)[25] that illustrates how productive economic analysis can be for media industry scholarship. The humanist aversion to statistics has loomed large in the somewhat strained historical relationship between media studies and economics, but recent work on the economics of creative industries (most notably that of Richard Caves) suggests how this disciplinary divide can be overcome with artful analysis and an emphasis on conceptual issues.[26] In his essay, Philip Napoli productively bridges this historic divide, outlining possible ways in which media economics can be applied to a study of the media industries that are sensitive to cultural, political, and aesthetic issues.

Political economy and cultural studies

One of the most prominent ways in which the media industries have been studied is through the lens of political economic analysis. While initial concepts in political economy were formulated by "classical" political economists such as Adam Smith and David Ricardo in the eighteenth and nineteenth centuries, its present-day "critical" orientation developed in the post-World War II period.[27] The dramatic social, political, and cultural transformations around the world provided the backdrop through which many of these early ideas were formulated. Vincent Mosco's comprehensive *The Political Economy of Communication* indicates the range of political economic approaches as well as the diverse means by which this framework has been applied globally. Though there are significant distinctions between approaches in Europe, North America, and the "Global South" (e.g., Latin America, Asia, and Africa), Mosco describes political economy as broadly concerned with the "study of the social relations, particularly the power relations, that mutually constitute the production, distribution, and consumption of resources."[28] A central interest is with the way in which resources are allocated, how they favor some at the expense of others, and how greater equity can be obtained throughout society. As Napoli discusses in his essay, these approaches tend to find "traditional" economic analyses problematic for the degree to which they are seen as sustaining and supporting dominant modes of power and existing capitalist structures.

There are various strands of critical political economy, and each has contributed to scholarship on the media industries in notable ways. The European strand described by Graham Murdock and Peter Golding is "holistic, historical, and centrally concerned with the balance between capitalist enterprise and public intervention."[29] The primary objective of scholars working out of this tradition involves the pursuit of social justice. Social justice is a central goal of several contributors in this collection as well, including John McMurria, Toby Miller, and David Hesmondhalgh. However, while the European-based political economic perspective influences these contributors' research, they all note

that the approach is not sufficient in and of itself. Rather, each author identifies ways that a media industry studies approach might be integrated with other modes of cultural and institutional analysis.

The "Global South" approach to critical political economy emerged most prominently in Latin America, though a growing body of work has developed in Africa and Asia as well. This perspective, which emerged during the 1960s and 1970s, has been shaped by the specific political, cultural, and economic inequalities that these regions have faced in relation to the "Global North" (e.g., Western Europe and the US). Early discussions here were framed largely in terms of "cultural imperialism" and "media imperialism."[30] These terms broadly suggested a coercive unidirectional flow of western – and especially American – media into developing nations. Members of less powerful and wealthy nations maintained that the "dumping" of Hollywood products (and western consumerist ideologies) prevented the development of their own local or regional media industries. The indigenous cultures and values of many of these regions and countries were seen as threatened by the arrival of American media. These views helped motivate local activism and impact policy-making in many countries around the world – a point Cristina Venegas explores in depth with her essay.

Along with Venegas, Michael Curtin and Nitin Govil acknowledge the continuing influence of the cultural/media imperialism framework. As they make clear, in spite of the fact that discussions of cultural imperialism have been replaced and complicated by more complex culturally based theories about global flows, these early political economic frameworks often serve as the baseline from which later analysis proceeds. Significantly, it was not only writers in developing nations who spoke about – and to varying degrees, continue to speak about – cultural imperialism. In fact, this perspective is also prominent in the North American strand of critical political economy as forwarded by scholars such as Herbert Schiller, Ben Bagdikian, Robert McChesney, and Edward Herman.[31] It should be underscored that many of the early North American critical political economists began writing during the same historical moment, and within the same economic, social and political climate as those writing in the Global South.

Such work initially explored the expansion of (what were then) US-based media companies around the world; as the companies themselves transformed into multinational media conglomerates, scholarship shifted to address this development. However, as David Hesmondhalgh discusses in his essay, the underlying nature of this strand of scholarship has not changed significantly; individuals speaking from the "Schiller–McChesney" perspective, as he calls it, remain predominantly concerned with the ways in which a handful of media corporations have a homogenizing influence on media culture around the world. This line of research is criticized by authors in this collection for being reductive, simplistic, and too economistic, and many political economists working in North America have since taken more nuanced approaches to analyzing the structures and business strategies of major media companies.[32]

Scholarly efforts to incorporate political economy and cultural studies have been widely attempted in the last couple of decades. This "integration" generally has been conceived of as uniting political economy's interests in ownership, regulation, and production with cultural studies' interest in texts, discourse, audiences, and consumption.[33] Supposed oppositions between these two approaches have been largely collapsed during the last two decades as a broad range of scholars including Douglas Kellner, Thomas Schatz, and Michael Curtin have reinforced how many of the same theoretical and political goals drive both perspectives.[34] It is our belief that one of the many virtues of a media industry studies approach is that it marks a further step beyond the discussions of "how to blend political economy and cultural studies." Indeed, that the integration of these two perspectives is vital to any productive analysis of the media industries in the twenty-first century is effectively axiomatic for authors in this collection (and fully explored by Kellner in his essay). The challenge, then, is to provide the most sophisticated models with which to undertake an inherently interdisciplinary and multi-methodological project. Any such undertaking must, from the outset, acknowledge the complexity and contradictions of media

texts as well as have a respect for media audiences consuming these texts. Further, such a project must understand the histories of specific media – along with the ways that they have been studied previously – in order to fully engage with present discourses circulating about contemporary media industries.

Ideas developed by the Centre for Contemporary Cultural Studies (CCCS) at the University of Birmingham in the 1960s and 1970s prove particularly useful for an emergent media industry studies. Several individuals influencing or affiliated with the Centre, including Richard Hoggart, Raymond Williams, E. P. Thompson, and Stuart Hall, helped develop scholarship that was taken up in the study of the media industries during the 1980s. A central contribution of this strand of cultural studies to media industry studies is its interest in the ways that cultural power is produced and reproduced, mediated and negotiated, circulated and consumed. Meaning is made – and by extension, cultural power is exercised – throughout the processes of making texts ("encoding") *and* interpreting texts ("decoding").[35] Historically, cultural studies scholars have more readily examined the "decoding" process, considering the ways that audiences can read mass-mediated texts in unanticipated, potentially liberating ways.[36] They have shown how, even if texts largely reproduce dominant ideologies (as per the Frankfurt School model, and a point of contention in itself), the ways that audiences interpret and respond to these ideologies differ widely depending on factors such as race, class, gender, sexuality, age, ethnicity, and national identity.

While the "decoding" process has been of central interest to cultural studies scholarship for several decades, a number of scholars recently have applied cultural studies' view of culture as a site of struggle, contestation, and negotiation to the industry itself.[37] This shift in emphasis to cultural production (referring here to everything from production itself to distribution, marketing, and exhibition practices) has helped foreground the role of individual agents within larger media structures and further challenged notions of a monolithic industry, past or present. More recent work in the "cultural studies of production" has increasingly rendered this divide outdated.[38] Meanwhile, other media scholars, including Elana Levine and Julie D'Acci, have continued to refine Hall's encoding/decoding model (as well as Richard Johnson's "circuit of culture") in pursuit of more integrated approaches to media studies. These studies indicate how scholarship has further moved away from earlier linear or top-down models. In addition, recent discussions of the "circuit of media study" help to promote work that more fully brings together discussions of cultural production, artifacts, reception, and sociohistorical context.[39]

Journalists and activists

More "traditional" scholars based in academe are by no means the only ones to explore the role of media industries in a cultural context. A range of individuals – from trade publication writers and members of the popular press to journalists and scholars – offer valuable alternative perspectives on how the media industries operate and how they deal with change. Their articles, books, blogs, and websites are often used to nuance understandings of contemporary debates and to provide a sense of the prominent discourses circulating among various stakeholders at given historical moments. Given the proprietary nature (and extreme expense) of much industry data, these publications have proven especially valuable to media industries scholars. The essays by Thomas Schatz, Victoria Johnson, and Cynthia Meyers are examples of how such data can be effectively employed in constructing historical analyses.

Members of the popular press have published a wealth of material on the media industries. The access granted to journalists, as well as the financial resources available to them to conduct their research, often far exceeds what is available to scholars. A prominent example of this work is Ken Auletta's *Three Blind Mice* (1991), which provides a look inside media corporations and the operations of their news divisions during a period in 1980s when they were in the midst of a radical structural transformation. Other journalists to have written extensively on various dimensions of media companies include

Alex Ben Block on the formation of the Fox Network, Edward Jay Epstein on the transformation of the film industry in the late 1990s and early 2000s, and Scott Donaton on the complex negotiations taking place between the advertising and entertainment industries in the early twenty-first century.[40] These projects have been complemented by a range of first-person narratives from executives and creative figures who have worked in the industry.[41]

A variety of public intellectuals – activist scholars and journalists – have also taken a critical approach in their examination of the products, institutions, policy and power attached to media industries. As global media corporations have wielded more cultural and economic influence, critical voices emerging from a number of activist scholars and journalists have become more prominent. Notable work comes from Naomi Klein and David Bollier, who look at the growing prominence of brand management by global conglomerates; Eric Alterman and Eric Klinenberg, who analyze the conglomerate control and political bias of news; and Jeff Chester, who investigates the threat posed by new media policy to democracy.[42] Media consolidation also contributed to the return of semi-retired journalist Bill Moyers to PBS. *Bill Moyers' Journal* regularly explores such topics as concentration of ownership and bias in news reporting from a liberal perspective.

Though ownership and concentration remain concerns to many scholar-activists, with the rise of digital media many have shifted their focus to a wider menu of issues including intellectual property rights, network neutrality, democratic Internet access, and privacy protections for consumers.[43] Stanford law professor Lawrence Lessig's role in the formation of the Creative Commons movement is an example of how those studying the media industries can expand the impact of their research and influence broader cultural conversations. Lessig as well as media scholar Siva Vaidhyanathan have recently generated a great deal of academic and public discussion about the intersection of digital technologies and intellectual property law with their work, demonstrating how researchers can serve as public intellectuals while at the same time making scholarly interventions.[44]

Film and television studies

The humanities-based study of film and television has offered industry analysis far more than merely an object of study or a disciplinary residence from which to work. In fact, film and television studies have produced, developed, taught, and promoted a great deal of the research and work on media industries in the academy. Contributions to media industry studies have come from industrial historians as well as textual critics and theorists. As it would be impossible to discuss all the relevant work emanating from this field in such limited space, Michele Hilmes' chapter is dedicated to exploring this more fully. Here we limit the discussion to a brief overview of some prominent ways in which methods and frameworks developed in film and TV studies have been directed toward the study of the media industries. As the other sections of this introduction indicate, film and television studies have also drawn from other areas (e.g., political economy, cultural studies) and applied those areas to a study of different media forms.

A central site of analysis for film and television studies remains the text. As a methodology or focal point, textual analysis has not been associated with industry studies per se. However, many foundational studies have examined the intersection between industrial/economic factors and *style*. Out of cinema studies, a pioneering work was Bordwell, Staiger, and Thompson's *The Classical Hollywood Cinema: Film Style and Mode of Production to 1960* (1985).[45] Justin Wyatt's *High Concept* (1994) was notable for examining the interrelationship between motion picture marketing practices and New Hollywood aesthetics.[46] In television studies, John Caldwell's *Televisuality: Style, Crisis and Authority in American Television* (1995) showed how shifting production practices affected the kinds of programs aired on US television in the 1980s and 1990s.[47]

Studies of *authorship* represent another significant way that film and television studies have probed the relationship between industrial organization and individual agency while also retaining a close attention to the textual dimensions of these media. In their essays, Hilmes and Schatz both note how a central interest of humanities-based media industry studies lies in the creative input of directors, producers, writers, or studio executives. In film studies, the auteur theory has been applied most extensively toward exploring the relative influence of the director; with television studies, scholars have focused more on the role of the writer-producer. However, the idea of authorship has been applied by both film and television studies scholars at the institutional level as well.[48]

The relationships between industrial structures, cultural conventions, and textual practices have also been directly linked to *genre* analysis. There is a rich tradition of work in film studies that explores how a range of players – from industry to audience, critics to filmmakers – interact to shape genre conventions over time.[49] Recent forays into genre study have looked at television as a means of addressing how industrial and textual practice combine to create strategies for reducing risk, ritualizing production, managing audience expectations, and codifying marketing practices.[50]

Industrial histories have yielded the largest volume of film and television studies scholarship thus far. These include media-specific surveys of particular companies and institutions, interactions between cultural regulators and industry, and examinations of the launch of new technologies.[51] What distinguishes these projects from other forms of regulatory and policy analysis discussed here is the degree to which these studies address the specific textual and industrial histories of film and television. A defining study for film historiography at large and media industry studies in particular was Allen and Gomery's 1985 book, *Film History: Theory and Practice*.[52] This book proposed an interdisciplinary approach to studying the medium, offering a model that encouraged scholars to integrate textual analysis with sociocultural, technological, and industrial/economic analysis of films. The essays in the first section of this collection continue the project of integrating these varied dimensions to the analysis of different media forms.

Cultural policy studies

In the late 1980s and early 1990s, a number of scholars coming out of cultural studies became involved in cultural policy studies. As developed by individuals such as Stuart Cunningham and Tony Bennett, cultural policy studies marked an attempt to "make cultural studies more relevant."[53] A great deal of debate ensued about precisely how closely scholars should align themselves with dominant political systems. Though the political perspectives of individual scholars have varied immensely, work done in cultural policy studies has marked a crucial moment in reintegrating matters of policy and industry into humanities-based projects.[54] Projects in cultural policy studies have employed a range of methods, from analyzing contemporary policy documents to interviewing representatives from local film commissions to mining archives for memos between government and industry.[55]

While work in this area has flourished in many places around the world, its application in the American context has remained noticeably limited. The paucity of cultural policy studies work in the US context can be seen in part as a function of the degree to which mainstream voices dismiss the idea that *there is* cultural policy in the US. Of course, as Miller and colleagues note in *Global Hollywood*, local, regional, and national governments implement media policies on a regular basis.[56] Indeed, everything from intellectual property laws to favorable trade policies to decisions about media preservation (a matter explored by Caroline Frick in her essay) are matters of cultural policy. However, many Americans' resistance to the idea that culture is regulated by the government – combined with the extent to which the media industries themselves formulate policy in the US – have made it difficult to successfully adapt a cultural policy studies approach in the American context.

Meanwhile, the deregulation of media industries around the world have made cultural policy studies difficult to sustain as an approach in other regions. As Toby Miller discusses in his essay, changes in leadership in many nations, continued privatization, and the rise of new technologies have contributed to a move away from cultural policy discussions and toward discourses about "creative industries" or "creative economies." However, this does not mean that an explicitly *critical* cultural policy studies does not have a place within media industry studies research. Miller's essay illustrates how and why such an approach remains relevant and vital to those desiring a progressive model for analyzing the intersection of government and media institutions.

Converging Media/Converging Scholarship

The convergence of entertainment, communication and information technologies in the early part of the twenty-first century has motivated a flurry of speculation and discussion by scholars, creative figures and executives about what the future might hold. As P. David Marshall, Mark Deuze, Jordan Levin, Joshua Green, and Henry Jenkins explore in their respective essays, the concept of convergence carries a variety of meanings and potential consequences. These authors investigate the implications of convergence for media aesthetics, institutions, labor, production, markets and regulation as well as culture and identity. Meanwhile, Michael Curtin, Cristina Venegas, and Nitin Govil explore how convergence occurs at the levels of the national, regional and global. All suggest ways we can continue to update our frameworks and methodologies for the study of the media industries.

Because convergence is occurring in media industries, forms, and technologies, it is the responsibility of scholars across a range of humanistic and social scientific disciplines to converge intellectually as well. As the historic divisions between media products, industries, audiences, and cultures become less and less recognizable, there are new opportunities to unite what have often been disconnected conversations. As Caroline Frick shows, new possibilities of media distribution force us to rethink the role and relationship of archivists to the media industries; for John Hartley, these same possibilities, as manifested in social networking, indicate the possibilities for a reorganization of relations between industry and user/producer/viewer.

As will become apparent in reading these diverse essays, sometimes ideas overlap; often sources do as well. Sometimes there are dramatic differences of opinion regarding what "media industry studies" has been, what it is, and what it could be. We do not presume to offer the definitive answer here. Rather, this book is designed to jump-start the conversation about what has contributed to this emerging area of study in the past and what theories, methods, and models might be employed in future research. It was in this spirit that contributors were asked to articulate how their specific topic relates to the field of media industry studies. You will find very distinct interpretations and answers in these pages. Many of these essays also point out just how much research remains to be done in this complex and often contradictory arena.

This returns us to the themes outlined earlier in the introduction and to the point that we can engage with media industry studies in widely divergent ways. At the same time that we celebrate these possibilities, we also recognize a common call across the essays in this anthology for more integrated scholarship in this area. To that end, *Media Industries* is designed to encourage and promote cross-disciplinary conversation about the field as it has developed thus far, as well as to provide a "road map" for those just entering into the discussion.

Notes

1 At this writing, online venues discussing the media industries include TV Decoder, http://tvdecoder. blogs.nytimes.com; Nikki Finke's Deadline Hollywood Daily, www.deadlinehollywooddaily.com; Cynopsis Media, www.cynopsis.com; Media Bistro's TVNewser, www.mediabistro.com/tvnewser; the Media Access Project, www.mediaaccess.org; Free Press, www. freepress.net; and The Hot Blog, www.mcnblogs. com/thehotblog. Websites accessed March 14, 2008.

2 Although that has started to change in recent years, with a pre-conference at the 2008 International Communications Association devoted to media industry study, large components of the semi-annual Media Reform Conference focused on industry scholarship and a growing number of panels on this topic at the annual gathering of the Society for Cinema and Media Studies. There is also NATPE's Educational Foundation outreach to academics researching the television industry through their annual faculty fellowship program, www.natpe.org/educationalactivities/fellowshipprogram; and various opportunities for students and faculty offered through the International Radio & Television Society Foundation (IRTS), www.irts.org/programs/programs.html, and the Television Academy Foundation's Education Program, http://cdn.emmys.tv/foundation/education.php, accessed March 14, 2008.

3 For a discussion of the rapid transformation of television in the post-network era, see Lotz, A. (2007) *The Television Will Be Revolutionized*. New York University Press, New York.

4 John Hartley and Stuart Cunningham are widely regarded as pioneering this field. Another notable text employing economic and sociological analysis

of the creative industries is Caves 2000. Hartley, J. (ed.) (2005) *Creative Industries*. Blackwell, Malden; Cunningham, S. (1992) *Framing Culture: Criticism and Policy in Australia*. Allen & Unwin, Sydney; Caves, R. E. (2000) *Creative Industries: Contracts Between Art and Commerce*. Harvard University Press, Cambridge.

5 An exploration of the cultural industries can be found in Hesmondhalgh, D. (2007) *The Cultural Industries*, 2nd edn. Sage, London. For additional applications of the "cultural industries" approach, see McRobbie, A. (1998) *British Fashion Design: Rag Trade or Image Industry?* Routledge, London; Toynbee, J. (2000) *Making Popular Music: Musicians, Creativity and Institutions*. Net Library, New York; Born, G. (2004) *Uncertain Vision: Birt, Dyke, and the Reinvention of the BBC*. Secker & Warburg, London.

6 Horkheimer, M. and Adorno, T. (2006) Culture industry: enlightenment as mass deception. In Durham, M. and Kellner, D. (eds.) *Media and Cultural Studies: Keyworks*, 2nd edn. Blackwell, Boston, pp. 41–72.

7 Given the particular historical context within which Adorno and Horkheimer composed their essay, along with their status as refugees from fascism, it is easier to understand their fear that mass media systems were encouraging passivity and working against democratic ideals.

8 For example, see Schatz's (1989) discussion of the complexity of the Hollywood studio system. Schatz, T. (1989) *The Genius of the System: Hollywood Filmmaking in the Studio Era*. Pantheon, New York. Also see Scott, A. J. (2005) *On Hollywood: The Place, The Industry*. Princeton University Press, Princeton.

9   See McQuail, D. (1994) *Mass Communication Theory: An Introduction*, 4th edn. Sage, London, p. 13.

10 A classic example is Frank Stanton, who earned a doctorate studying audience effects and then put this work to use first for the US government during World War II and then as longtime president of CBS. See www.museum.tv/archives/etv/S/htmlS/stantonfran/stantonfran.htm, accessed March 14, 2008.

11 Lasswell, H. D. (1948) The structure and function of communication in society. In Bryson, L. (ed.) *The Communication of Ideas*. Harper, New York, pp. 37–51.

12 See Miller (1990); McQuail (1994); McChesney (2004); and Croteau & Hoynes (2006). Croteau, D. and Hoynes, W. (2006) *The Business of Media: Corporate Media and the Public Interest*. Pine Forge, Thousand Oaks; McChesney, R. W. (2004) *The Problem of the Media: US Communication Politics in the Twenty-First Century*. Monthly Review Press, New York; Miller, M. C. (1990) *Seeing Through Movies*. Pantheon, New York.

13 The term "Fordism" literally refers to Henry Ford and the assembly-line system of mass production and mass consumption, which he initiated with the manufacturing of cars during the early twentieth century. However, the label has been expanded by scholars to refer more broadly to the assembly-line process of manufacture of standardized products prominent in many western nations from the post-World War II period to the early 1970s. Other key components of Fordism include a division of (unionized) labor, a large-scale production of highly homogenous products, and a concentration of capital, labor, and manufacturing in a limited number of locales. See Harvey, D. (1989) *The Condition of Postmodernity: An Enquiry into the Origin of Cultural Change*. Blackwell, Cambridge. In addition, for an application of post-Fordism to the media industries, see Curtin, M. (1996) On edge: culture industries in the neo–network era. In Ohmann, R. (ed.) *Making and Selling Culture*. University Press of New England, Hanover, pp. 181–202.

14 Rosten, L. (1941) *Hollywood: The Movie Colony, the Movie Makers*. Harcourt, Brace, New York; Powdermaker, H. (1950) *Hollywood: The Dream Factory: An Anthropologist Looks at the Movie-Makers*. Little, Brown, Boston.

15 For more on the roots of this research in anthropology and sociology – as well as precise means of proceeding with this form of analysis, see Deacon, D., Pickering, M., Golding, P., and Murdock, G. (1999) *Researching Communications*. Oxford University Press, New York.

16 Gans, H. J. (2004) *Deciding What's News*. Northwestern University Press, Chicago; Schlesinger, P. (1980) Between sociology and journalism. In Christian, H. (ed.) *The Sociology of Journalism and the Press*. Rowman & Littlefield, New York, pp. 341–69. Also see Fishman, M. (1980) *Manufacturing the News*. University of Texas Press, Austin.

17 Burns, T. (1979) *The BBC: Public Institution and Private World*. Palgrave Macmillan, London; Tulloch, J. and Alvarado, M. (1983) *Dr. Who, the Unfolding Text*. Macmillan, London. For an example of a US-based study, see Newcomb, H. and Alley, R. S. (1983) *The Producer's Medium: Conversations with Creators of American TV*. Oxford University Press, New York.

18 Examples of Tunstall's prolific output include (1973) *Journalists at Work: Specialist Correspondents: Their News Organizations*. Sage, London; (1993) *Television Producers*. Routledge, London; and his edited collection (2001) *Media Occupations and Professions*. Oxford University Press, Oxford.

19 A number of studies of cultural production flourished from the 1990s onward, especially in terms of television studies. These include Gripsrud, J. (1995) *The Dynasty Years: Hollywood Television and Critical Media Studies*, Routledge, London; Shattuc, J. (1997) *The Talking Cure: TV Talk Shows and Women*. Routledge, New York; and Dornfeld, B. (1998) *Producing Public Television, Producing Public Culture*. Princeton University Press, Princeton.

20 Thanks to John Caldwell for his thoughts on this topic. Examples of literature on the sociology of work include Hirsch, P. M. (1972) Processing fads and fashions: an organization-set analysis of cultural industry systems. *American Journal of Sociology* **77**, 639–59; Becker, H. (1973) *Art Worlds*. University of California Press, Berkeley; DiMaggio, P. (1982) Cultural entrepreneurship in nineteenth-century Boston. Part 1: The creation and organization of an organizational base for high culture in America. *Media, Culture & Society* **4**, 33–50.

21 Notable economic surveys include Harold Vogel's (2007) comprehensive *Entertainment Industry Economics: A Guide for Financial Analysis*, 7th edn. Cambridge University Press, Cambridge; Noam, E. (2008) *Media Ownership and Concentration in America*. Oxford University Press, New York; Hoskins, C., McFayden, S., and Finn, A. (2004) *Media Economics: Applying Economics to New and Traditional Media*. Sage, London; Alexander, A., Owers, J., Carveth, R., Hollifield, C. A., and Greco, A. N. (eds.) (2004)

Media Economics: Theory and Practice, 2nd edn. Lawrence Erlbaum, New York; Doyle, G. (2008) *Understanding Media Economics*, 2nd edn. Sage, New York.

22 Gomery has not only surveyed all of the media industries, but he has also examined the histories and programming practices of specific sectors (for example, see Gomery, D. (1986) *The Hollywood Studio System*. St. Martin's Press, New York; Gomery, D. and Hockley, L. (2006) *Television Industries*. British Film Institute, London).

23 See Gomery, D. (1989) Media economics: terms of analysis. *Critical Studies in Mass Communication* **6**, 43–60.

24 For outstanding examples, see Horwitz, R. B. (1991) *The Irony of Regulatory Reform: The Deregulation of American Telecommunications*. Oxford University Press, New York; and Aufderheide, P. (1999) *Communications Policy and the Public Interest: The Telecommunications Act of 1996*. Guilford Press, New York.

25 Available for download at no charge under Creative Commons license. At www.fordham.edu/images/undergraduate/communications/caseagainstmediaconsolidation.pdf, accessed July 16, 2008.

26 Caves, R. E. (2000) *Creative Industries: Contracts Between Art and Commerce*, Harvard University Press, Cambridge.

27 Mosco, V. (1996) *Political Economy of Communication: Rethinking and Renewal*. Sage, London.

28 Ibid., 25.

29 Murdock & Golding quote from page 311 in Wasko, J. (2004) The political economy of communications. In Downing, J. (ed.) *Sage Handbook of Media Studies*. Sage, London.

30 See Dorfman, A. and Mattelart, M. (1975) *How to Read Donald Duck: Imperialist Ideology in the Disney Comic*. International General Group, New York; for a thorough deconstruction of cultural imperialism also see Tomlinson, J. (1991) *Cultural Imperialism: A Critical Introduction*. Johns Hopkins University Press, Baltimore; Sinclair, J. (2004) Globalization, supranational institutions, and media. In Downing, J. (ed.) *Sage Handbook of Media Studies*. Sage, London, pp. 65–82.

31 Bagdikian, B. H. (2000) *The New Media Monopoly*. Beacon Press, Boston; Herman E. S. and McChesney, R. W. (1997) *The Global Media: The New Missionaries of Corporate Capitalism*. Cassell, London; McChesney, R. W. (1999) *Rich Media, Poor Democracy: Communication Politics in Dubious Times*. University of

Illinois Press, Urbana; McChesney, R. W. (2004) *The Problem of the Media: US Communication Politics in the Twenty-First Century*. Monthly Review Press, New York; Schiller, H. I. (1976) *Communication and Cultural Domination*. M. E. Sharpe, White Plains; Schiller, H. I. (1992) *Mass Communication and American Empire*, 2nd edn. Westview Press, Boulder.

32 Various critical political economists, including Janet Wasko and Eileen Meehan, have acknowledged the contributions of cultural studies and explored ways to integrate political economic and cultural studies traditions. Janet Wasko, for example, discusses the value of combining these approaches in "The Political Economy of Communication" in *Sage Handbook of Media Studies*; also see Wasko's recent collection, McDonald, P. and Wasko, J. (eds.) (2008) *The Contemporary Hollywood Film Industry*. Wiley-Blackwell, Boston; Meehan, E. R. and Riordon, E. (2001) *Sex and Money: Feminism and Political Economy in the Media*. University of Minnesota Press, Minneapolis. In addition, for a useful recent history of media consolidation from a political economic perspective, see Kunz, W. (2007) *Culture Conglomerates*. Rowman & Littlefield, New York.

33 Paraphrased from Wasko, "The Political Economy of Communication," p. 323.

34 For extended discussion of these issues, see Ferguson, M. and Golding, P. (eds.) (1997) *Cultural Studies in Question*. Sage, London.

35 We are drawing here from Stuart Hall's "encoding/decoding" model; see Hall, S. (1980) Encoding/decoding. In Hall, S., Hobson, D., Lowe, A., and Willis, P. *Culture, Media, Language: Working Papers in Cultural Studies*, 1972–9. Hutchinson, London, pp. 128–38.

36 Hall proposed three main readings: dominant, oppositional, and negotiated in his essay "Encoding/decoding." This approach has been used prominently in television studies. For applications of cultural studies to television studies, see Casey, B., Casey, N., Calvert, B., French. L., and Lewis, J. (2002) *Television Studies: The Key Concepts*. Routledge, New York. An application of cultural studies to film studies can be found in Willis, A. (1995) Cultural studies and popular film. In Hollows, J. and Jancovich, M. (eds.) *Approaches to Popular Film*. Manchester University Press, Manchester, pp. 173–91.

37 See Newcomb, H. and Lotz, A. (2002) The production of media fiction. In Jensen, K. B. (ed.) *A Handbook of Media and Communication Research: Qualitative and Quantitative Methodologies*. Routledge,

London, pp. 62–77; Levine, E. (2001) Toward a paradigm for media production research: behind the scenes at *General Hospital. Critical Studies in Media Communication* **18**, 66–82; Havens, T. (2006) *Global Television Marketplace*. British Film Institute, London; Tinic, S. (2005) *On Location: Canada's Television Industry in a Global Market*. University of Toronto Press, Toronto; Curtin, M. (2007) *Playing to the World's Biggest Audience: The Globalization of Chinese Film and TV*. University of California Press, Berkeley.

38 For example, see Caldwell, J. (2008) *Production Culture*. Duke University Press, Durham. Also see Ohmann, R. (ed.) (1996) *Making and Selling Culture*. University Press of New England, Hanover.

39 D'Acci's original version of this model appeared in *Defining Women, Television and the Case of Cagney and Lacey*. D'Acci, J. (1994) *Defining Women: Television and the Case of Cagney and Lacey*. University of North Carolina Press, Chapel Hill. A more recent version can be found in Spigel, L. and Olsson, J. (eds.) (2004) *Television After TV: Essays on a Medium in Transition*. Duke University Press, Durham, 418–45. D'Acci also draws from Du Gay, P., Hall, S., Janes, L., Mackay, H., and Negus, K. (1997) *Doing Cultural Studies: The Story of the Sony Walkman*. Sage, New York.

40 Block, A. B. (1990) *Outfoxed*. St. Martin's Press, New York; Donaton, S. (2005) *Madison & Vine: Why the Entertainment and Advertising Industries Must Converge to Survive*. McGraw-Hill, New York. Also see Guber, P. and Bart, P. (2002) *Shoot Out: Surviving Game and (Mis)Fortune in Hollywood*. G. P. Putnam, New York; Salamon, J. (1992) *The Devil's Candy: The Bonfire of the Vanities Goes to Hollywood*. Delta, London; Griffin, N. and Masters, K. (1996) *Hit and Run: How Jon Peters and Peter Guber Took Sony for a Ride in Hollywood*. Simon & Schuster, New York; Carter, B. (2006) *Desperate Networks*. Doubleday, New York.

41 For example, see Bach, S. (1985) *Final Cut: Dreams and Disaster in the Making of Heaven's Gate*. W. Morrow, New York; Daniels, S. and Littleton, C. (2007) *Season Finale: The Unexpected Rise and Fall of the WB and UPN*. HarperCollins, New York; Vachon, C. (2006) *A Killer Life: How an Independent Film Producer Survives Deals and Disasters*. Simon & Schuster, New York.

42 Klein, N. (2002) *No Logo: No Space, No Choice, No Jobs*. Macmillan, London; Bollier, D. (2005) *Brand Name Bullies: The Quest to Own and Control Culture*. John Wiley, Indianapolis; Alterman, E. (2003) *What Liberal Media? The Truth About Bias and the News*. Basic Books, New York; Klinenberg, E. (2008) *Fighting for Air: The Battle to Control America's Media*. Henry Holt, New York; Chester, J. (2007) *Digital Destiny: New Media and the Future of Democracy*. W. W. Norton, New York.

43 Prominent examples (all founded by activist journalists and scholars) include Public Knowledge, www.publicknowledge.org; Free Press, www.freepress.net; and the Center for Social Media, www.centerforsocialmedia.org. Accessed March 14, 2008.

44 See Lessig, L. (2002) *The Future of Ideas: The Fate of the Commons in a Connected World*. Vintage Books, New York; Lessig, L. (2004) *Free Culture: The Nature and Future of Creativity*. Penguin, New York; and Vaidhyanathan, S. (2001) *Copyrights and Copywrongs: The Rise of Intellectual Property and How it Threatens Creativity*. New York University Press, New York.

45 Bordwell, D., Staiger, J., and Thompson, K. (1985) *Classical Hollywood Cinema: Film Style and Mode of Production to 1960*. Columbia University Press, New York.

46 Wyatt, J. (1994) *High Concept: Movies and Marketing in Hollywood*. University of Texas Press, Austin.

47 Caldwell, J. T. (1995) *Televisuality: Style, Crisis and Authority in American Television*. Rutgers University Press, New Brunswick.

48 For example, see Balio, T. (1976) *United Artists: The Company Built By the Stars*. University of Wisconsin Press, Madison; Feuer, J., Kerr, P., and Vahimagi, T. (eds.) (1984) *MTM: Quality Television*. British Film Institute, London.

49 Thanks to Miranda Banks for her comments here. Additional background can be found in Schatz, T. (1981) *Hollywood Genres: Formula, Film, and the Studio System*. McGraw-Hill, New York; Altman, R. (1999) *Film/Genre*. British Film Institute, London; Neale, S. (2000) *Genre and Hollywood*. Routledge, New York.

50 Mittell, J. (2004) *Genre and Television: From Cop Shows to Cartoons in American Culture*. Routledge, New York; Murray, S. and Ouellette, L. (eds.) (2004) *Reality TV: Remaking Television* Culture. New York University Press, New York; Timberg, B. M. (2002) *Television Talk: A History of the TV Talk Show*. University of Texas Press, Austin; Miller, T., Creeber, G., and Tulloch, J. (eds.) (2001) *The Television Genre Book*. British Film Institute, London.

51 For example, see Lewis, J. (2000) *Hollywood v. Hard Core: How the Struggle Over Censorship Saved the Modern Film Industry*. New York University Press,

New York; Wasser, F. (2002) *Veni, Vidi, Video: The Hollywood Empire and the VCR*. University of Texas Press, Austin; Mullen, M. (2003) *The Rise of Cable Programming in the United States: Revolution or Evolution?* University of Texas Press, Austin; Mann, D. (2008) *Hollywood Independents: The Postwar Talent Takeover*. University of Minnesota Press, Minneapolis.

52 Allen, R. C. and Gomery, D. (1985) *Film History: Theory and Practice*. Knopf, New York.

53 This debate emerged out of dissatisfaction expressed by some cultural studies scholars with the growing number of studies that seemed to be focused merely on celebrating what audiences could do with texts. John Fiske's *Reading Culture* is often cited as representative of what some cultural studies scholars objected to. Meaghan Morris' essay, "Banality in Cultural Studies," represents some of the dissatisfaction felt by cultural studies scholars at the time. Fiske, J. (1989) *Understanding Popular Culture*. Routledge, London; Morris, M. (1990) Banality in cultural studies. In Mellencamp, P. (ed.) *Logics of Television:*

Essays in Cultural Criticism. Indiana University Press, Indianapolis, pp. 14–43.

54 Examples of those who objected to less critical versions of cultural policy studies include McGuigan, J. (1992) *Cultural Populism*. Routledge, London; Miller, T. (1998) *Technologies of Truth: Cultural Citizenship and the Popular Media*. University of Minnesota Press, Minneapolis.

55 Examples of cultural policy research include Streeter, T. (1996) *Selling the Air: A Critique of the Policy of Commercial Broadcasting in the United States*. University of Chicago Press, Chicago; Lewis, J. and Miller, T. (eds.) (2003) *Critical Cultural Policy Studies: A Reader*. Blackwell, Malden, pp. 134–42; Ouellette, L. (2002) *Viewers Like You: How Public TV Failed the People*. Columbia University Press, New York; Goldsmith, B. and O'Regan, T. (2005) *The Film Studio: Film Production in the Global Economy*. Rowman & Littlefield, Lanham.

56 Miller, T., Govil, N., McMurria, J., Maxwell, R., and Wang, T. (2005) *Global Hollywood 2*, British Film Institute, London.

Part I

History

....

Editors' Introduction

....

The essays in this section serve two main purposes: to present readers with background on the history of different media industries and explore historiographical considerations in relation to their study. While the rest of this book focuses primarily on present-day media and thus conceptualizes these industries as integrated and interrelated, the emphasis in this section is largely on their individual and unique histories. We believe this background is important because historically, they have operated relatively independently of one another in terms of business models, modes of production, constructions of audiences, and narrative strategies. The essays in this section underscore the fact that — despite various points of intersection in the past and convergence in the present — these histories are quite distinct. They also illustrate how industry scholarship has tended to be medium-specific, with a handful of notable exceptions. Providing perspective on contemporary industry discourse, the essays here discuss media separately and historicize their forms, businesses, and industrial traditions. Further, they establish a foundation for future scholarship, while offering provocative ideas and innovative avenues for such endeavors.

Michele Hilmes begins the book by tracing how and why industry histories developed in the manner they did. She identifies prominent ways in which humanities-based scholars have made sense of the expansive subject that is "media industry studies." She discusses how media industries scholarship has tended to be structured partly on the basis of manageability and partly according to categories familiar to scholars coming out of the humanities. This often has meant an emphasis on texts, genres, and authors, despite the fact that the serialized character of many texts and the collaborative nature of industrial production complicate these organizational schemes. Hilmes also indicates three prominent tropes — object, nation, and quality — that are productive arenas for more extensive exploration.

Speaking from her vantage point as director of the Texas Archive of the Moving Image, Caroline Frick argues for the vital yet under-examined role that archivists play in relation to media industry history. In addition to illustrating how archivists are a component of the media industries themselves, she shows how they have had an increasingly prominent role in shaping our understanding of media history. Frick explains that a number of economic, cultural, and organizational factors have led preservationists to emphasize Hollywood's history over other more local or regionally based histories both inside and outside the US. She illustrates how decisions made about preservation or access might factor into the emergence of alternative industry histories in the future. Ultimately, she calls for archivists to more aggressively favor open access policies for the public.

Whereas Frick indicates the alternative media industry histories yet to be written, Thomas Schatz supplies a fresh perspective on the oft-explored topic of Hollywood history. Presenting a model for what he describes as a "film industry studies approach," Schatz offers a way for historians to more fully address the convergences and divergences between film and other media industries at both macro- and micro-industrial levels. Schatz's model addresses concerns that have long been of interest to film studies scholars, including matters of style, authorship, and mode of production. In addition, his survey of Hollywood past and present gives readers direction for how such an approach to media industry studies might be conducted.

Victoria E. Johnson turns our attention to American television with a nuanced discussion of how broadcast and cable have been historicized. She sees the media industries as sites of struggle and encourages readers to think about broadcast and cable history as a series of clashes between national and local interests, varying regulatory frameworks, and divergent notions of the public. In order to assess television's place in a conglomerated media landscape, Johnson argues that scholars must investigate TV as a cultural practice, which she does through an examination of cable and the concept of "niche." Her case study on ESPN and its appropriation of hip hop yields a rich analysis of the simultaneous separation and interdependence of the broadcast and cable industries. Through the lens of television sports, she examines the television industry's valuations of the audience and corporate branding strategies as well as the competing dynamics of broadcasting and narrowcasting at work.

Johnson's discussion of the industry's shift from mass to niche audiences intersects with Cynthia B. Meyers' chronicle of the history of advertising and sponsorship in electronic media. In her essay, Meyers surveys the complex web of relationships between broadcasters, networks, and the advertising industry from early radio through the digital era. Her resistance to conventional categorizations is one of many essays in this book advocating more integrated discussions of media industries. Meyers argues for a historicization of the advertising industry that is both informed by and explored alongside histories of other media. This perspective complicates our understanding of the historical dynamics of culture and commerce at work. Addressing various transitions throughout radio and TV history, Meyers explains just how imbricated advertising is in television's forms. The links she makes between early sponsorship models and present-day television-Internet branding practices reinforce the value of a historically informed perspective in media industry studies.

P. David Marshall picks up where Meyers leaves off in her discussion of new media, asking precisely what is "new" about it. The rise of the Internet and other contemporary digital technologies has affected both the media industries as well as culture at large. Not only are existing business models in transition, but the industry's construction of – and interaction with – audience-users is fundamentally changing as well. Marshall outlines an emerging industry ethos centered on specific modes of interactivity and asks whether these new media forms signal the increased blurring between media (industries) and communication (industries). His essay reflects the challenges facing those trying to place the contemporary moment in historical context. In spite of such challenges, he demonstrates how worthwhile the act of looking at "old" media through the lens of new media can be as a means of questioning our assumptions about the practices and products of media industries.

1

Nailing Mercury
The Problem of Media Industry Historiography

· ·

Michele Hilmes

Terminology is important, but like mercury, it's slippery. The term "media industry" covers a huge slice of territory ranging over print, sound, screen, and digital bits in space, in venues as various as corporate communications, advertising, websites, novels, films, recordings, and music being shared person to person on the Internet. Its academic sites of study are just as various; media industry scholars can be found in departments of journalism, mass communications, film, English, art, theater, business, law, cultural studies, area and ethnic studies, music, anthropology, and many more. But, in the United States, the most extended and well-established body of work examining the function of the media industry in its most popular and widely disseminated forms has arisen around the "sound and screen" media: radio, television, and film, now extending to new digital venues such as the web, DVDs, and digital production.[1] This is a relatively new and indeterminate field marked more by what it excludes (or by what has been excluded) than by grounded inclusions. Typically it refers to those texts and practices that are *not* included in the study of literature, art, music, and drama as they have been structured in the academy over the last hundred years or so: namely, the Johnny-come-lately communicative arts, until recently tainted by an association with both machines and the masses, which by the humanities standards of an earlier time disqualified such pursuits as debased

and anti-individual, fodder for sociologists rather than critics or historians.[2]

Over the last half of the twentieth century, however, the admission of these technologically driven, industrially based, mass-produced expressive forms to the purviews of academic study has called into being a radically different conception of the entire process of creative production and reception. Scholarly study of media industries required a re-theorization of the task of the humanities scholar and a rethinking of the ways that we understand and analyze culture more generally in the postmodern world. A media industries focus points directly to those aspects of cultural production in the twentieth century and beyond that most trouble the humanities-oriented categories of coherence and analysis so central to our understanding of culture itself: the author, the text, the reader. These categories, exploded by Foucault and other postmodern theorists some 30 years ago, linger on in our modes of analysis even as we recognize their extreme fragility in the way that culture is produced and consumed. The media of radio, popular music, television, and film refuse to conform to comfortable analytical paradigms. They refute essentialization, require many components and participants, blur creative lines, stretch the boundaries of expressive forms, transgress aesthetic standards, cross over cultural borders, break down disciplined reception, muddy meanings, pervade public and private spaces, and generally make a mess of our accepted ways of doing scholarship.

For historians – and all analysts are historians in some way or another – the media industries present particular problems. Where do we look for "authors" when authorship is dispersed among a host of productive sites (writers, directors, actors, technicians, marketers, advertisers, ratings companies, networks, studios, regulators, national boards and bodies, etc.) and how do existing (and non-existing) historiographical resources complicate this task? How do we approach "texts," when we are confronted by, to take one extreme example, a program that originated in 1937 on daytime radio and still airs daily on television today, compiling such an incredibly voluminous text that no one person could ever possibly "read" it all in a single lifetime? (I refer, of course, to The Guiding Light, my candidate for the world's oldest continuously running serial drama.) How do we understand "readership" when its permutations are so infinitely various and incalculable?

By taking an industries approach to the critical study of media we are indicating a perspective that is inherently contextual and interrelated. The concept of "industry" implies the coming together of a host of interests and efforts around the production of goods or services; it also indicates commercial purposes, meaning the distribution of goods or services in a marketplace for accumulation of profit, though this is sometimes more figurative than literal. In media studies, to nominate the industry as our focus of study indicates a concern for the creative forces of production behind the range of communicative texts and objects that comprise our field of analysis, a place held in more traditional humanistic studies by the author.

Thus industry study is the translation of authorship into a dispersed site marked by multiple, intersecting agendas and interests, where individual authorship in the traditional sense still most certainly takes place, but within a framework that robs it, to a greater or lesser degree, of its putative autonomy – a deeply disturbing displacement for many, and productive of much of the dystopian rhetoric that the concept of "mass media" has inspired over the course of two centuries. But it is also a vital enrichment of our understanding of cultural production

and a necessary corrective to the narrow categories of traditional scholarship.

In the following pages, I want to survey the field of media industry history, looking at various approaches through a lens that situates them within intellectual traditions forged in humanities scholarship. This will serve to indicate where the study of media production diverges from that comfortable scholarly habitus. I wish to link such approaches with the historiographic challenges they pose, from the location and preservation of sources to the complexity of historical narratives that they engender. In addition, I will examine the organizing frameworks these approaches bump up against and consider some key ways that scholars have organized their thinking on this complex subject: author, text, object, nation, quality. I hope this will provide media industry historians with a useful way of thinking through their task, as well as an overview of a rapidly developing field.

Industrial Production

De Certeau (1988) reminds us that histories always begin at the end: the writing of history cannot take place without a framework forged in and by the present, structuring our path into the past and determining the history that we will produce. In this case, my wish to begin with the most basic and taken-for-granted type of authorship, familiar to all, the humanistic author as individual creative figure – writer, director, producer, performer, designer, composer, etc. – actually represents a late-arriving and highly problematic construction for media studies, particularly television. It reflects the status that media industry studies is moving toward, not the direction from which it has come. Therefore I will leave consideration of the author for last, and begin the way that scholarship in this area itself did – with attempts to understand the arrival of the industrial site of creative production with its diffuse set of practices, "mass-produced" texts, and indeterminate audiences.

The site of production

The tradition of media industry analysis has its roots in the 1930s and 1940s. In film, early works like

Benjamin Hampton's (1931) *A History of the Movies*, Howard T. Lewis' (1933) *The Motion Picture Industry* and Mae Huettig's (1944) *Economic Control of the Motion Picture Industry* led to studies like Michael Conant's (1960) *Antitrust in the Motion Picture Industry* and Gertrude Jobes' (1966) *Motion Picture Empire*. All provided overviews of filmmakers and film studios as they analyzed the circumstances of production and the films thus produced. They laid the groundwork for a new type of scholarly analysis that began to emerge during the last few decades of the twentieth century, positioning itself on the uneasy terrain between economics-based business history and literary/critical analysis, and nominating the productive matrix itself as the site of study: studio, production company, recording label, station, and network.

In film, scholars such as Tino Balio, Janet Wasko, Thomas Schatz, Douglas Gomery, Richard B. Jewell, Anthony Slide, Garth Jowett, Robert Sklar, Richard M. Hurst, David Bordwell, Kristin Thompson, and Janet Staiger combined economic analysis with a focus on the emergence of film as a new expressive medium. The burgeoning field of social, cultural, and aesthetic histories of American film that burst forth in the 1970s and 1980s built on these foundations.

Broadcasting history also depends on highly industry-oriented foundational texts with a production organization focus like Gleason Archer's two books, *A History of Radio to 1926* (1938) and *Big Business and Radio* (1939) and William Peck Banning's (1946) *Commercial Broadcasting Pioneer: The WEAF Experiment*. Herman Hettinger filled in the role of the advertising agency in 1933 with his *A Decade of Radio Advertising* and Robert Landry (1946) gave an early overview in *This Fascinating Radio Business*. All of these studies were written either by authors employed in the broadcasting industry or with the industry's cooperation; they are unapologetically boosterish. They rely heavily on access to records provided or produced by industry corporations themselves.

In the late 1930s and 1940s media industries began to receive a more critical treatment as well. Theodor Adorno and Max Horkheimer, displaced from their German universities by the Nazis and largely appalled by the mass-produced American culture they observed around them, took up a critique of the "cultural industries" that combined an awareness of the power of this new type of cultural production with an intellectual disdain for their products and an anxious concern for their cultural and political effects.[3] Llewellyn White's study *The American Radio*, written for the Committee on Freedom of the Press in 1947, along with the work of Charles A. Siepmann in the 1940s and 1950s (highly influential in the early years of broadcasting's admission into the academy), provide a similarly critical take on industrial history and posit a reform agenda. Historians of the broadcasting industry have made fruitful critical use of these sources and of the corporate archives and trade journals upon which they drew for source material. These early works set the stage for broadcasting scholarship to come: focused firmly on industrial questions, almost to the exclusion of the aesthetic or cultural, in contrast to film; and torn between a perspective that glorified the business of broadcasting and one that regarded it as deficient, backward, and sadly lacking in social and cultural substance.[4]

Our single most substantive history of the US broadcasting industry – and it is primarily an industrial account, though with much to interest the social historian – remains Erik Barnouw's three-volume sequence, *The History of Broadcasting in the United States*. Barnouw's task was formidable. Though a few prescient broadcasters had donated their papers to various archives, and one network, NBC, had begun to send its early papers to the Wisconsin Historical Society,[5] Barnouw's major sources consisted of his contacts within the industry along with the trade press and the oral histories of the Broadcast Pioneers project, to which he added considerably as he proceeded.[6] The major networks provide a fair amount of structure across Barnouw's three volumes, but he also visits the more powerful stations scattered across the country, the meeting rooms of advertising agencies, the halls of regulators, the production lots of Hollywood, the propaganda centers of the USIA, and moves outward, into society at large: its political centers, courtrooms, sporting events, battlefields, living rooms, and every other place where radio and television made their presence felt. His cannot be considered an industry history in the sense of concentrating on structures and economics, but it is a work that includes a backbone of economic, structural, and regulatory considerations. As an account that looks about more broadly, it speaks to the concerns of media industry historians, and indeed still serves as one of our most valuable sources.

Barnouw's history stood nearly alone until the arrival of Christopher Sterling and John M. Kittross' groundbreaking textbook, *Stay Tuned: A Concise History of American Broadcasting* in 1978. Here a policy-centered approach dominates, though the industry is well accounted for and textual development traced as well. The importance of public policy to broadcasting industry historiography – as agent, as subject, and as active producer of source materials – is a factor that frequently distinguishes this area of media analysis from others. This is not to imply that state intervention has not played a role in the development of the media generally: intellectual property law, First Amendment protections, and antitrust statutes all enter centrally into industry concerns across media. Yet the policy perspective is one that has run centrally through broadcast historiography and scholarship, for reasons traced below in the consideration of the structuring paradigm of "nation." Broadcasting – more than any other medium – has been the chosen medium of the nation-state around the world, a fact reflected in academic analysis but rarely foregrounded or theorized.

Aside from these key texts, and though many popular accounts of the radio and TV industries sprang up over the decades of the twentieth century, academic attention to the production matrix remained scattered. Until the early 1990s this was a field dominated by a critical sociological approach, perhaps best exemplified by Todd Gitlin's (1983) oft-cited *Inside Prime Time*. With the appearance of works such as Susan Douglas' (1987) *Inventing American Broadcasting*, William Boddy's (1990) *Fifties Television*, Tino Balio's (1990) edited volume *Hollywood in the Age of Television*, my own *Hollywood and Broadcasting: From Radio to Cable* (1990), and Christopher Anderson's (1994) *Hollywood TV: The Studio System in the Fifties*, non-film media industry studies entered scholarly publishing and teaching.

There are major gaps; though Hollywood studios have dominated television ever since the 1960s, very rarely have they been treated as important sites of creative production specifically for television, as opposed to film. Independent television production companies have been neglected equally; studies on MTM (Feuer et al. 1984), Ziv (Rouse 1976), and Desilu (Schatz 1990) are either essay-length or unpublished.

During the formative decades of American broadcasting, as genres were invented, basic structures set in place, and the industry's cultural role extended throughout the world, the main innovation in programming took place in the offices of advertising agencies. Despite this fact, not a single book-length scholarly work has focused on the role of the advertising agency.[7] Television's historical roots in radio are frequently ignored, though over the last 20 years the study of radio and sound media also has experienced a revival. Though constantly nominated in popular frameworks as central organizing institutions, the major American networks still await the kind of comprehensive account Asa Briggs has given the BBC. Recent work has taken on the important but somewhat less daunting task of limning the operations of newer or shorter-lived networks like DuMont (Weinstein 2004), Fox (Zook 1999; Perren 2004), and the WB and UPN (Cole 2005); I served as editor of a compilation of historical essays on the history of America's first and oldest network, NBC, which takes a step in the direction of a network history but hardly can scratch the surface of such a huge and multifaceted social/industrial institution (Hilmes 2007).

Aside from a flourishing field of biographies and autobiographies of the networks' leading figures, there is much here that begs to be explored by the next generation of media industry historians.[8] Further, there are many ancillary industries that form a part of the media industry productive matrix: ratings and market research companies, the trade press, awards organizations, professional associations, craft unions, Congress, and the multitude of social and political organizations that have made the media part of their operations. These include political parties, parents and teachers groups, lobbyists, athletic associations, and religious organizations, just to name a few, and their operations have been affected by their convergence with the media industries just as much as the media themselves. These convergences and connections require far more attention than they have been given, despite the few excellent groundbreaking texts thankfully available.[9]

Texts and genres

Another route into an examination of the media industries is through a focus on the text. This focus need not be the type of purely aesthetic textual exegesis inherited from literary studies, but rather can place the text within a productive context and analyze the forces – both immediate and distant – that work upon it to produce its genesis, development, specifications, narrative structures and trajectories, audience formations and readings, etc. The text-based approach provides critical and historical advantages similar to those of the individual author, but just as equally marked by problems. It nominates an accepted and understandable category of cultural creativity, implying and building on a unity of form that is capable of holding up even where authorship falls apart. The putative unity of the stand-alone text is reflected in the ways that historical information is categorized and indexed, in sources ranging from the popular and trade press to library catalogs, archive finding aids, and web-based sites. It also reflects a dominant way that audiences experience sound and screen media.

The text-centered approach to media industry study is far better suited to film studies, with the nomination of the theatrical film as its primary object (despite the violence thus done to the many types of material actually produced on film; see the discussion of this strategy below), than to the fields designated as radio, television, and popular music studies. Yet, even for television, no matter how broken up, extended, changed, spun off, and re-venued most texts are, a presumed core remains. This can be seen especially in long-running shows, such as *Law and Order* or *ER*, where a completely different cast may pursue completely different story-lines written and produced by completely different authors as the show ages, and is aired on a different network or seen on DVD. In spite of this, certain key elements – the setting, the basic dramatic situation, familiar themes and motifs – provide continuity and a form of unity. A different set of problems exists for popular music studies, where the distinction between text and performance has always comprised a central concern.

For television and to a lesser extent for film, text-based industry analysis has usually taken place within the framework of genre, by which genre is understood as a site in which industry-shaped expectations and needs intersect with dramatic forms to produce variations on familiar tropes, themes, narratives, and characterizations (see, for instance, Mittell 2004). Genre has sometimes been discussed as a kind of mass-produced shortcut to cultural innovation, allowing slightly differentiated texts to be stamped out on the assembly line of the television series or serial: what Gitlin (1983) refers to as "recombinant" texts that simply combine pre-approved elements into a modified but highly predictable product. The fact that most artistic and cultural creation takes place through a similar process – artists, composers, and writers learning from the traditions and cultural production around them, recombining elements into a novel form – often drops out of sight when the subject at hand is media texts, imposing the anti-popular assumptions of the Frankfurt School critique onto popular television, film, and music composition without considering the unique challenges and creative possibilities that the media industry setting also provides.

Recently some defenses of the new "quality" dramas on television – sparked by the successes of pay cable channels like HBO – have defined some specifically televisual characteristics available to TV texts such as intimacy of characterization, everyday-ness, and narrative depth developed over the *long-durée* that few other media can achieve. Yet the vast bulk of the texts that actually appear on television fit least comfortably of all media within humanities-based generic expectations, encompassing as they do forms not easily associated with traditional literary exegesis: news, advertising, makeover and reality shows, documentary, discussion, performances of various types, and so on. I will discuss the structuring paradigm of "object" further (e.g., filmic object, televisual object) in the last section of this chapter;

the problematics of "object" run through the analysis of both film and broadcasting texts, and indeed frame the distinctions made between them.

The individual author

As noted above, one quality of industrial production is the obscuring of the contributions of the individual behind a scrim of group effort and the patterns of mass production. Authorship becomes dispersed, parceled out, and dependent on a number of factors normally simply excluded from view by traditional humanities approaches (necessitating an ancillary industry of digging them out again: the role of the muse, the wife, the editor, the school, the publisher, the patron, etc.). The "individual author approach" has many advantages, following recognizable and well-worn paths of understanding creative production – still valid and important, even within a wider industries approach – and all of the historiographical conveniences that come with that: a limited field of focus, an automatic periodicity, a bounded narrative, and a congruence with the way that source materials tend to be produced (e.g., collected papers of individuals in archives, search terms in indexes, biographical works, journalistic coverage, etc.).

This approach has been more successful in some areas of media industry study than others; it has been slow to arrive in the field more generally precisely because of the ways that media scholarship cuts against the grain of accepted academic practices and categories. Film scholarship attained a position in the humanities largely through its nomination of the director as cinematic *auteur* in the 1960s, thanks to the efforts of French *nouvelle vague* critics such as André Bazin and François Truffaut, translated into the American context by, most notably, Andrew Sarris, and then put into effect by the first generation of academic film scholars and programs. The body of work that began to appear in the late 1960s and 1970s on "pantheon" directors such as D. W. Griffith, Cecil B. DeMille, John Ford, Alfred Hitchcock, Sergei Eisenstein, Fritz Lang, Frank Capra, Ernst Lubitsch, Orson Welles, and many more helped put film study on the map – even as it ex-nominated much that actually made up the field of film production. Biographies and autobiographies of significant

creative figures, particularly the Hollywood star, add to this body of production. Though the focus might be on the individual artist, inevitably he or she is situated within an industrial structure, either happily complicit or in stormy opposition. However, as noted above, in some ways the nomination of the individual *auteur* figure works against the complexity and interdependence of a media industries approach, and thus efforts to isolate the contributions of a particular figure must always fundamentally distort the realities of media authorship; the best and most useful works foreground that relationship and bring the struggle into productive analysis.[10]

It is telling that for television the move toward *auteur*ship has proven more difficult, since the typical television text has multiple sources of creative input, from networks and production companies to producers, writers, directors, performers, and their agents. Only recently has the writer-producer found some purchase as the putative author in television production; the television director remains, it seems, negligible as a contributor to the form, and only a very few studies exist of the television writer (see Wicking & Vahimagi 1979; Heil 2002). Scholarly analyses of television writer-producers as individual creative artists are few in number; surely more than Fred Coe (Krampner 1997), Fred Allen (Havig 1990), Norman Corwin (Bannerman 1986), and Nat Hiken (Everitt 2000) are key US broadcasting auteurs deserving of book-length studies. A few overviews have appeared; again, they are notable in their scarcity. These include Horace Newcomb and Robert Alley's *The Producer's Medium* in 1983, and a recent corrective to that book, *Women Television Producers, 1948–2000* by Robert Alley and Irby Brown in 2001. David Marc and Robert J. Thompson (1992) joined in with their book *Prime Time, Prime Movers* and Thompson with Gary Burns (1990) in a thought-provoking collection of essays, *Making Television: Authorship and the Production Process*. It could be that only now is television opening up to a new form of writer-producer *auteur*ship that is better known in other countries than in the US, with creative producers able to build and sell programs across a variety of platforms that rely upon their authorial "brand" to distinguish their productions, much as literary authorship has always functioned.[11] David

Chase, Dick Wolf, Aaron Spelling, and Steven Bochco, to name a few, have built careers that have transcended individual programs, production companies, and networks in a way that few producers in previous decades could, but all await in-depth critical analyses of the kind extended to film auteurs routinely. However, it is the sign of a field still in development that some of our most productive and innovative writer-producers have not yet been the subjects of full-length critical studies: Irna Phillips, Arch Oboler, Jack Benny, Carlton Morse, Lucille Ball and Desi Arnaz, Rod Serling, Norman Lear, and Grant Tinker, to name a few.

Structuring Paradigms

Important tensions within this field remain to be explored, and until we think them through, media industry studies will remain a divided and contradictory area of research, unable to cope with the challenges that face it in the twenty-first century. I have referred in the pages above to three such determinate frameworks, which always have worked behind our basic assumptions and understandings of what media are and where we should look to examine them: the structuring paradigms of object, nation, and quality.[12] These terms refer to the problem of, first, defining the object of study in a way that avoids the pitfalls of older paradigms and enables fruitful study in an era of converging media forms and industries; second, acknowledging the important role that media have played in the twentieth-century preoccupation with nation-building and that nation-states have played in the development of media; and third, recognizing the shift from a restricted, elitist, and indeed nationalistic view of quality and cultural value to more open, populist, and globally democratic perspectives. As we move away from the old era of analog media and into the digital age and beyond, the basic organizing paradigms of an earlier time need to be acknowledged and critiqued so that we can proceed.

The object

First, what is the media object? The lines that scholars have drawn between various media have been blurred since the beginning, as industry practices clearly show but academics have ignored or even resisted. Take the field best established in the academy and most clear about its object of study: how can we defend the paradigmatic object of "film" study – the stand-alone theatrical film – when it represents a prominent but small subset of works actually produced on film and seen on screens? Most television programs (to name just one excluded area) have been shot on film since the 1960s, and more films are viewed on television sets than in theaters, via cable, video-on-demand, videocassettes, or DVD. Television, as referenced above, has never been as clearly demarcated in form or technology, yet its boundaries grow ever looser: how do we define the parameters of "television," when an increasing segment of the population receives its "television" programs online and views them on a computer, iPod, or cell phone screen? How do we separate the study of radio broadcasting from the study of recorded music, since that has been its primary content since the 1950s? It is a key characteristic of media studies – and, by extension, media industry studies, that the field has been broken up into segments nominated by technology as separate (film, radio, television, video, recordings, DVDs, etc.) even as texts, production, and reception circumstances inevitably violate all such arbitrary divisions. Convergence is not a new phenomenon; it is the very hallmark of modern media.

Clearly, these objects we have designated as technologically determined separate spheres always have converged, and in fact it is academic paradigms that have kept them separate far longer than any logics of production or industrial framework could justify. Further, the separation of these forms of mediated expression from their counterparts in "non-industrialized" spheres such as literature, drama, performance, and documentary remains arbitrary in the extreme, the product more of hierarchical value structures than any inherent or logical distinction. This has been obvious at the level of industrial production for over half a century, as movie studios became radio and then television producers, expanded into recorded music, vied with television and cable networks in film and music production, and now intersect with the fields of new media and new modes of convergence (Jenkins 2006).[13]

The advent of digital technology just has begun to shake apart the structures and distinctions with which we have become comfortable, requiring a rethinking of our approach to the object of study as well as our historiographic methods. As certain forms of source material swirl past us in abundance on the web, archives are digitized, and access to documents and industry information appears to be greater than ever, preservation of traditional forms of text – memos, letters, reports, scripts – ceases and in fact can become even scarcer in the age of instant duplication and fears of lawsuits. Preserving traces of our digital past is a task that archivists and historians are only now beginning to grapple with, a far more complex topic than can be discussed here. As such, a constant interrogation of our categories of analytical object must be a part of media study in the twenty-first century. In their useful 2002 essay, Anderson and Curtin point to the strangely contradictory nature of television as an object of historical study, combining scarcity with overabundance. Certain kinds of historical evidence remain very scarce, especially those having to do with audiences and reception, less celebrated types of texts, and details of the production process simply unavailable to the outside scholar. Yet, at the same time, television's overabundant production, its endless series, 24-hour schedules, and multiple channels provide a landscape that is simply too large and complicated to be taken in properly, and that resists the type of limiting operation necessary to scholarship: canons, hierarchies, careful archiving and inventorying, etc. This contradiction marks digital media as well, with its overabundance of information available at the end of a Google search about almost anything at all, while everyday crucial documentation disappears, swept into the maw of constant digital renewal and demolition.

The nation

The twentieth century, which saw the development of the sound and screen media, also goes down in history as a century of struggle over the idea of the nation. Hobsbawm (1992) calls the years between 1917 and 1950 "the apogee of nationalism," as colonized nations struggled for independence and two world wars redrew national boundaries; the forces of globalization so prevalent since the 1950s worked to highlight the role of the nation-state in both spreading and resisting globalizing forces. The task of construction and preservation of national cultures and identities became centrally bound up in the work of media, which came under the direct supervision of the nation-state at many crucial junctures, particularly during times of war – hot or cold. Even more than film, broadcasting appealed to governments throughout the world as a natural venue for both state control over a powerful domestic means of communication and an outward agent of information and propaganda. As a result, broadcasting was regulated, supervised, policed, and, in many cases, monopolized by the state to a greater degree than other forms of modern communication. Reaching more powerfully into the private sphere than any other medium, radio and television became command central for the public project of nationalism and national identity formation. In many nations this occurred in response to the seemingly unstoppable flood of cultural products from the United States, particularly Hollywood film; national public service broadcasting became the site of resistance to cultural denationalization in most nations around the world, imposing quotas on foreign programs, providing support for domestic production, regulating and restricting content, and transmitting the symbols, rites, and rituals of national culture both inward and outward. Even in the United States, where private ownership and a looser regulatory structure reigned, broadcasting received a greater degree of state guidance and concern than any other medium, out of very similar concerns over national identity and cultural unity. In film, national cinemas defined themselves around a model of auteur-driven noncommercial "quality" production in contradistinction to the threat of Hollywood.

Another familiar dichotomy emerges: while media industries have consistently seen their markets as both global and national, and while globalization – like convergence – continuously plays a role in the history of media production, scholarship has tended to reflect the agenda of the nation-state and focus unreflectively on the national as the primary sphere of production. The majority of analyses have chosen to concentrate (as has this one), without much in the way of theorization, on activities defined within national boundaries, screening out those traces of transnational activity and influence that are plainly there. This is not to say that the national framework does not deserve attention – obviously, it is key – but that it must be understood not as essential and pre-existing but as constructed within the context of media industry transnationalism that in fact helped to inspire it. Flows of capital, of creative personnel, of program forms, of creative concepts, and of cultural experience, from nation to nation and across the globe, are as much a part of any mediated expression as its national roots, and this factor needs to be recognized and included in historical analyses. Resistance and opposition are strong forms of transnational influence as well.

To give one small example, the soap opera, a culturally denigrated form associated with both a passive/addicted female audience and an over-close relationship with the economic imperatives of US commercial broadcasting, has a history that goes far beyond this simple genealogy. Though serialized dramas produced by and for women may have first emerged on American daytime radio in the early 1930s, by the middle of that decade American scripts were being adapted into other national languages and cultures, performed live over the air in Canada, Australia, Cuba, Mexico, Argentina, Brazil, and many other venues – an early example of "format" production. In Quebec, French-language versions of the soaps heard on the Montreal CBS affiliate found wider audiences on local stations, and developed eventually into the well-established Québécois tradition of the *radio-feuilleton*, the radio serial, with its own native writers and celebrated texts. So popular were the *radio-feuilletons* that the Canadian government used them as World War II broke out as venues for morale-building and propaganda – even as concerns over "Americanization" of culture kept such programs off the English-language CBC and made them anathema at the BBC as well. A Canadian producer, Ernest Bushnell, drew on this example while seconded to the BBC. He suggested a similar propaganda vehicle for the BBC North American Service, thus originating *Front Line Family*, Britain's first serial radio drama. Cuban broadcasters performed

a similar act of translation and adaptation in the 1930s and 1940s, producing Spanish-language *radio-novelas* which were broadcast all over Central and South America and the Caribbean, leading to the thriving telenovela industry of today. In Britain, however, the association of serialized drama with American commercialism remained so strong that, despite the popular success of early radio soaps like *The Archers* (begun in 1949 and still on the air today) and ITV's popular *Coronation Street*, it would take until 1985 for the BBC to embrace the form with *EastEnders* (Hendy 2003). This is a tale of transnational influences and resistances that crucially defined broadcasting in a way that both reflects and defies media's national function.

Quality

As can be seen in the transnational history of the serial, the close relationship between the nation and modern sound and screen media is deeply imbricated in the place assigned them within hierarchies of cultural quality. The association of such media with technologized production and a state-driven or market-based reach toward the uneducated masses, as noted above, placed film, broadcasting, and popular music in a sphere outside the more respectable arts. Yet the project of constructing the modern nation-state mandated direct public intervention in the production of such mass-directed culture, far more than for those media elevated by the requirement for literacy or specialized appreciation into the purview of the educated elite. Therefore considerations of quality became the consistent focus of public policy and debate as successive new media emerged. Among the questions that have occupied intellectuals and regulators over the nation-building decades of the twentieth century are: how can we direct media production in certain ways and discourage it in others? How can we best inculcate national cultural unity and fend off disruptive forces? Concepts of "quality" in national media formed around resistance to the denationalizing and "homogenizing" influence of transnational popular culture, usually from "Hollywood."

Governments formed commissions, instituted regulatory bodies, and imposed rewards and penalties on cultural production in a systematic fashion never before possible, or considered necessary. Modern sound and screen media were perceived as vitally necessary to address and recruit into the national public sphere those audiences and elements that challenged it, particularly the subnational (local and regional identities in tension with the national), the pre-national (those social groups seen as requiring particular assistance in being integrated into the model of national citizenship, such as women, children and youth, the working class, and ethnic, religious, and racial minorities), and the transnational (influences seen as "foreign" and denationalizing).

Yet this "downwards address" also placed media industry production on the degraded level of the popular; its violation of the norms of humanistic authorship and textual unity made it unsuitable for academic analysis and respectability. The "highbrow/lowbrow" split that Levine (1988) traces began as the first mass-produced media emerged – in print and photography, later in film, recorded music, and radio – all of them challenging the distinctions and unities of the newly elevated arts and setting a value on widespread accessibility over educated discernment. Indeed, the elevation of high culture necessitated the debasement of popular forms; the denigration of mass media enabled the elevation of the elite arts by contrast and opposition. Only in

the latest decades of the twentieth century, as globalization began to break down carefully nurtured nationalized categories of quality and hierarchies of value, has the democratization of culture begun to bring media into focus in scholarly analysis, in a broader movement to recontextualize and complicate the study of cultural forms and their relationship to the societies that produce them. In particular, the connection between market forces and cultural production has emerged onto the central stage; as global capital drives cultural recombination, boundaries of object, nation, and quality become destabilized, and new approaches to cultural analysis become imperative.

Thus to propose the serious study of media industries is a bold and iconoclastic task, but a necessary one, calling into question some of the dominant analytical frameworks that have shaped not only media scholarship but notions central to humanistic study generally. Now a second generation of media scholars has crossed that Rubicon; this text and the many recent books appearing in this flourishing field mark its increasing legitimacy. Humanities scholarship of the future should and, I believe, will include media industry analysis at its heart. Mercury is, after all, the messenger, the symbol of human communication; as a substance it is difficult to pin down but very good at escaping from arbitrary restraints.

Notes

1 "Media studies" also tends not to include print media such as newspapers and magazines, which have their own history of marginalized inclusion in higher education. Confined to departments of journalism dating back to the first decades of the last century, they struggle still today with the status of "applied knowledge" or "professional training" that has isolated them from mainstream humanities research.

2 See Strinati (2000) for a discussion of the history of "mass" culture.

3 There is a longer tradition of social science-based media critique going back to the Chicago school of sociology and running through the Payne Fund studies to the work of Paul Lazarsfeld and other influential intellectuals like Rudolph Arnheim and Herta Herzog. See Czitrom (1983) for an account of its effects on media scholarship.

4 It should be noted that the late 1970s and 1980s saw the appearance of a variety of essential textbooks, reference works, and other kinds of factual summaries on the broadcasting industry without which subsequent scholarship would have been severely impoverished. See Compaine (1979); Buxton & Owen (1972); Dunning (1976); and Castleman & Podrazik (1982; 1984).

5 Later, it would donate other materials to the Library of Congress; NBC remains the only major network to preserve its historical records in this way.

6 For more on Barnouw, see Hilmes (2004) and Hilmes & VanCour (2007).

7 Two analyses of the agency role exist in dissertation form (Mashon 1996; Meyers 2005).

8 Though I have nominated popular music as another key media field that cannot be truly separated from

film and television, only recently have media scholars such as myself begun to engage with music history and industry studies, and music historians with media history. Similarly, the print media have been separated from "sound and screen" media far more adamantly in academic study than in real-world conditions. We need far more histories that cross these arbitrary boundaries and focus on the many links and cross-influences between media.

9 See Godfried (1997); Hendershot (1998); Swanson (2000); Hangen (2002); and Meehan (2005).

10 See Bignell and O'Day (2004) for an excellent example of a contextualized analysis of one writer's work and by extension what it means to nominate such a figure as an auteur.

11 Both Palgrave Press and Syracuse University Press have series based on the television author premise.

12 These are by no means the only important structuring frameworks that affect media study; I have not attempted to talk about those surrounding texts and audience reception. I single these out as particularly important in the way that media industry studies have been understood academically with an admitted bias toward the course my own work has taken.

13 It should be noted that dominant academic emphasis has also neglected film, television, and sound productions that fall outside the dominant industry designation: home movies and videos, amateur productions, industrial and educational films and broadcasts, fan productions, etc. A few scholars are now attempting to redress that oversight; see the Orphan Film Festival website, www.sc.edu/filmsymposium, the Prelinger film archive, www.archive.org/details/prelinger, as well as Becker (2007). Websites accessed June 30, 2007.

References

Alley, R. and Brown, I. (2001) *Women Television Producers, 1948–2000: Transformation of the Male Medium*. University of Rochester Press, Rochester.

Anderson, C. (1994) *Hollywood TV: The Studio System in the Fifties*. University of Texas Press, Austin.

Anderson, C. and Curtin, M. (2002) Writing cultural history: the challenge of radio and television. In Brugger, N. and Kolstrup, S. (eds.) *Media History: Theories, Methods, Analysis*. Aarhus University Press, Oxford, pp. 15–32.

Archer, G. L. (1938) *A History of Radio to 1926*. American Historical Society, New York.

Archer, G. L. (1939) *Big Business and Radio*. The American Historical Company, New York.

Balio, T. (1976) *United Artists: The Company Built by the Stars*. University of Wisconsin Press, Madison.

Balio, T. (ed.) (1990) *Hollywood in the Age of Television*. Unwin Hyman, Boston.

Bannerman, L. (1986) *Norman Corwin and Radio: The Golden Years*. University of Alabama Press, Tuscaloosa.

Banning, W. P. (1946) *Commercial Broadcasting Pioneer: The WEAF Experiment, 1922–1926*. Harvard University Press, Cambridge.

Barnouw, E. (1966) *A History of Broadcasting in the United States*. Vol. 1: *A Tower in Babel*. Oxford University Press, New York.

Barnouw, E. (1968) *A History of Broadcasting in the United States*. Vol. 2: *The Golden Web: 1933 to 1953*. Oxford University Press, New York.

Barnouw, E. (1970) *A History of Broadcasting in the United States*. Vol. 3: *The Image Empire*. Oxford University Press, New York.

Becker, S. (2007) See and save: balancing access and preservation for ephemeral moving images. *Spectator* **27**, 21–28.

Bignell, J. and O'Day, A. (2004) *Terry Nation*. Manchester University Press, Manchester.

Boddy, W. (1990) *Fifties Television: The Industry and its Critics*. University of Illinois Press, Urbana.

Buxton, F. and Owen, B. (1972) *The Big Broadcast, 1920–1950*. Viking Press, New York.

Castleman, H. and Podrazik, W. J. (1982) *Watching TV: Four Decades of American Television*. McGraw-Hill, New York.

Castleman, H. and Podrazik, W. J. (1984) *The TV Schedule Book: Four Decades of Network Programming from Sign-On to Sign-Off*. McGraw-Hill, New York.

Cole, K. (2005) From homeboys to girl power: media mergers, emerging networks, and 1990s television. Doctoral dissertation, University of Wisconsin, Madison.

Compaine, B. M. (1979) *Who Owns the Media? Concentration of Ownership in the Mass Communications Industry*. Harmony Books, New York.

Conant, M. (1960) *Antitrust in the Motion Picture Industry*. University of California Press, Berkeley.

Czitrom, D. J. (1983) *Media and the American Mind: From Morse to McLuhan*. University of North Carolina Press, Chapel Hill.

de Certeau, M. (1988) *The Writing of History.* Columbia University Press, New York.

Douglas, S. J. (1987) *Inventing American Broadcasting, 1899 to 1922.* Johns Hopkins University Press, Baltimore.

Dunning, J. (1976) *Tune in Yesterday: The Ultimate Encyclopedia of Old-Time Radio 1925–1976.* Prentice-Hall, Englewood Cliffs.

Everitt, D. (2000) *King of the Half Hour: Nat Hiken and the Golden Age of TV Comedy.* Syracuse University Press, Syracuse.

Feuer, J., Kerr, P., and Vahimagi, T. (eds.) (1984) *MTM: Quality Television.* British Film Institute, London.

Gitlin, T. (1983) *Inside Prime Time.* Pantheon, New York.

Godfried, N. (1997) *WCFL: Chicago's Voice of Labor, 1926–1978.* University of Illinois Press, Urbana.

Hampton, B. B. (1931) *A History of the Movies.* Covici, New York.

Hangen, T. (2002) *Redeeming the Dial: Radio, Religion, and Popular Culture in America.* University of North Carolina Press, Chapel Hill.

Havig, A. R. (1990) *Fred Allen's Radio Comedy.* Temple University Press, Philadelphia.

Heil, D. (2002) *Prime-Time Authorship: Works About and by Three TV Dramatists.* Syracuse University Press, Syracuse.

Hendershot, H. (1998) *Saturday Morning Censors: Television Regulation Before the V-Chip.* Duke University Press, Durham.

Hendy, D. (2003) The origins of the soap opera. In Hilmes, M. (ed.) *The Television History Book.* British Film Institute, London, pp. 8–9.

Hettinger, H. S. (1933) *A Decade of Radio Advertising.* University of Chicago Press, Chicago.

Hilmes, M. (1990) *Hollywood and Broadcasting: From Radio to Cable.* University of Illinois Press, Urbana.

Hilmes, M. (2004) Erik Barnouw. In Newcomb, H. (ed.) *The Encyclopedia of Television*, 2nd edn. Fitzroy Dearborn, Chicago, pp. 10–11.

Hilmes, M. (ed.) (2007) *NBC: America's Network.* University of California Press, Berkeley.

Hilmes, M. and VanCour, S. (2007) Network nation: writing broadcasting history as cultural history. In Hilmes, M. (ed.) *NBC: America's Network.* University of California Press, Berkeley, pp. 308–22.

Hobsbawm, E. J. (1992) *The Invention of Tradition.* Cambridge University Press, Cambridge.

Horkheimer, M. and Adorno, T. W. (2002) *The Dialectic of Enlightenment.* Stanford University Press, Palo Alto.

Huettig, M. D. (1944) *Economic Control of the Motion Picture Industry.* University of Pennsylvania Press, Philadelphia.

Hurst, R. M. (1979) *Republic Studies: Between Poverty Row and the Majors.* Scarecrow Press, Metuchen.

Jenkins, H. (2006) *Convergence Culture: Where Old and New Media Collide.* New York University Press, New York.

Jewell, R. B. (1982) *The RKO Story.* Arlington House, New York.

Jobes, G. (1966) *Motion Picture Empire.* Archon Books, Hamden.

Jowett, G. (1976) *Film: The Democratic Art.* Little Brown, Boston.

Krampner, J. (1997) *The Man in the Shadows: Fred Coe and the Golden Age of Television.* Rutgers University Press, Livingston.

Landry, R. (1946) *This Fascinating Radio Business.* Bobbs-Merrill, Indianapolis.

Levine, L. (1988) *Highbrow/Lowbrow: The Emergence of Cultural Hierarchy in America.* Harvard University Press, Cambridge.

Lewis, H. T. (1933) *The Motion Picture Industry.* Van Nostrand, New York.

Marc, D. and Thompson, R. J. (1992) *Prime Time, Prime Movers: From I Love Lucy to LA Law – America's Greatest TV Shows and the People Who Created Them.* Little Brown, Boston.

Mashon, K. M. (1996) NBC, J. Walter Thompson, and the evolution of prime-time television programming and sponsorship, 1946–1958. Doctoral dissertation, University of Maryland, College Park.

Meehan, E. (2005) *Why TV is Not Our Fault: Television Programming, Viewers, and Who's Really in Control.* Rowman & Littlefield, Lanham.

Meyers, C. (2005) Admen and the shaping of American commercial broadcasting, 1926–1950. Doctoral dissertation, University of Texas, Austin.

Mittell, J. (2004) *Genre and Television: From Cop Shows to Cartoons in American Culture.* Routledge, New York.

Newcomb, H. and Alley, R. S. (1983) *The Producer's Medium: Conversations with Creators of American TV.* Oxford University Press, New York.

Perren, A. H. (2004) Deregulation, integration, and a new era of media conglomerates: the case of Fox, 1985–1995. Doctoral dissertation, University of Texas, Austin.

Rouse, M. G. (1976) A history of the F. W. Ziv radio and television syndication companies, 1930 to 1960. Doctoral dissertation, University of Michigan, Ann Arbor.

Schatz, T. (1990) Desilu, *I Love Lucy*, and the rise of network TV. In Thompson, R. J. and Burns, G. (eds.) *Making Television: Authorship and the Production Process*. Praeger, New York, pp. 117–36.

Siepmann, C. A. (1950) *Radio, Television, and Society*. Oxford University Press, New York.

Sklar, R. (1975) *Movie-Made America: A Cultural History of American Movies*. Vintage Books, New York.

Slide, A. (1980) *The Kindergarten of the Movies: A History of the Fine Arts Company*. Scarecrow Press, Metuchen.

Sterling C. and Kittross, J. (1978) *Stay Tuned*. Wadsworth, Belmont.

Strinati, D. (2000) *An Introduction to Studying Popular Culture*. Routledge, New York.

Swanson, D. C. (2000) *The Story of Viewers for Quality Television: From Grassroots to Prime Time*. Syracuse University Press, Syracuse.

Thompson, R. J. and Burns, G. (eds.) (1990) *Making Television: Authorship and the Production Process*. Praeger, New York.

Weinstein, D. (2004) *The Forgotten Network: DuMont and the Birth of American Television*. Temple University Press, Philadelphia.

White, L. (1947) *The American Radio: A Report on the Broadcasting Industry in the United States*. University of Chicago Press, Chicago.

Wicking, C. and Vahimagi, T. (1979) *The American Vein: Directors and Directions in Television*. Dutton, New York.

Zook, K. B. (1999) *Color by Fox: The Fox Network and the Revolution in Black Television*. Oxford University Press, New York.

2

Manufacturing Heritage
The Moving Image Archive
and Media Industry Studies

· ·

Caroline Frick

What is the toughest thing about making film? Putting in the little holes.
The sprocket holes are the hardest thing to make. Everything else is easy,
but all night you have to sit with that little puncher and make the holes on
the side of the film. You could faint from that work. (Mel Brooks)[1]

Although comedian Mel Brooks clearly intended his mention of sprocket holes for laughs, his reference to actual celluloid remains unique in media industries literature. Processing raw film stock into "the movies" remains the exclusive domain of motion picture laboratories – or, in the case of restoring damaged sprocket holes, the moving image archivist. Yet this small, specialized community of moving image archiving (and its closely linked cousin, the film lab) has received very little academic attention in over one hundred years of cinematic history.

Within media studies, scholars have viewed moving image archives primarily as sites within which to conduct research on film and television texts as well as the industries that produce them. Conflating an eclectic range of archival locations and contexts, from corporate warehouses, university collections, and art museums, to private collectors' attics and staid federal repositories, academia sees the role of "the archive" as the same: to enable scholastic endeavor. Such literature has served – unwittingly or not – to promulgate a simplistic, binary opposition between "for-profit" corporations (such

as Fox or Viacom) and "not-for-profit" organizations (such as the academy or the archive).

Moving image archives, too, have helped perpetuate such distinctions. Carefully worded public relations mechanisms exhort the value of film preservation programs to enable public education and scholarly research, as opposed to popular appreciation or entertainment. Apocryphal accounts of saving discarded film prints from dumpsters and helping convince the industry of its own historical value bolster the field's sense of importance and help further its agenda. Viewing archives as user-driven, purely service-oriented institutions, however, overlooks the archive's substantive role in both industry practice as well as governmental policy.

This essay argues that moving image archives on every level – from the regional collection and university archive, to global stock footage libraries and departments in media conglomerates – constitute a specialized, vital industry, if not an outright component of the media industries themselves. The media archive has played a key role in shaping popular and academic conceptions of film and television texts as well as in validating specific (largely national and international) entities involved in media production. If media industries are defined broadly as those organizations, individuals, and/or stakeholders involved and interested in media production, distribution, and consumption, the moving image archive must be viewed as an increasingly invested institutional player. This perspective encourages scholars to consider media preservation as a vital, if under-examined, component to media industry activities. Within the United States, academic implications for this critical shift include a substantive expansion of what can be construed as "American" media. Such a broadened definition empowers new avenues of inquiry by illuminating increased numbers of local and regional players in media production, distribution, and exhibition.

Over the last century, archivists have striven passionately and actively to convert moving image material from entertaining ephemera to art, from "lost" to "restored," and from corporate product to national heritage. In the first decade of the so-called "information age," however, archivists are reevaluating their core constituency and are even reconsidering their own organizational structures – ones that have been specializing in "information" for centuries. As contemporary popular sentiment, as well as major funding bodies, privilege access over preservation and prioritize moving image content over its material format, new technologies are facilitating an era in which the work of the archive as distributor and/or producer appears increasingly transparent to media industry scholars.

Viewing moving image archives as competitive manufacturers, rather than noble preservers, of media heritage can be seen as a radical reconceptualization of this segment of the preservation field and one that bears significantly upon media industry studies. Issues central to the work of the moving image archive, such as copyright protection, funding mechanisms and increasingly access-oriented goals and objectives, illustrate the underlying tensions of a field inexorably, if at times awkwardly, connected to the larger moving image production communities. The moving image preservation movement, however, continues to cultivate and craft itself as a *profession*, rather than trade or industry, in an attempt to separate the field's participants from amateurs as well as conglomerate labor.

The moving image archiving community's conscious decision to distance itself from its vocational roots over the last several decades is relevant to those studying the media industries in two key areas. First, the field's discursive shift to "profession" further validates its members publicly as media "experts," to be consulted for public policy decisions and to be considered for increasingly important federal and foundation monies. Second, the profession's current emphasis upon so-called "orphan" moving image material reflects a growing scholarly, popular, and federally sanctioned interest in alternative industry sites – sites that remain undervalued within traditional media industry studies. Thus a closer look at the evolutionary nature of "professionalism" serves as a critical component to understanding more comprehensively the moving image archive community's impact and relevancy.

The Rise of a "Profession"

A concept firmly and ideologically ingrained within the United States and in many regions around the globe, professionalism connotes the possession of specialized knowledge and advanced degrees and often alludes to membership in a field that works for the social good. Research into the historical evolution of professions generally, however, notes an alternative definitional model that reveals less benign aspects of this social status. According to Friedson (1994), professionalism also serves as "a method of controlling work – one in which an occupation, rather than individual consumers or an agent or agency mediating between occupation and consumer, exercises control over its work" (3). Although media industry studies regularly critiques issues of monopoly, power and control in relation to global entertainment conglomerates or so-called "independent" creative entities, far fewer analyses exist that investigate similar themes within the not-for-profit sector.

Moving image archivists increasingly represent and view themselves as educated professionals, distinct from purely corporate or industrial concerns. Unlike previous decades where those working in moving image preservation learned via apprenticeships or on-the-job experience, the 1990s witnessed the creation of formal academic programs in the area of film and video preservation with which to train the "next generation" of moving image archivists. In 1995, archivist Ray Edmondson (1995) penned an article specifically devoted to the rise of professionalism within the field. Edmondson argued that although audiovisual archivists most resemble those in the "collecting professions," such as librarians or museologists, analogies could also be made with "doctors of medicine, engineers, scientists, schoolteachers, and journalists – professions that require university level education [and] specialized training" (245).

Constantly referenced by moving image archivists to support and validate their own vocational aspirations, Edmondson's occupational list illustrates how professions are "above all, a phenomenon of labor market organization ... exercising the capacity to create exclusive shelters in the labor market" (Brint 1994, 23). Although the recent emergence of New York University's moving image archiving program and the University of California at Los Angeles' moving image archive studies degree track constitute an important step in the evolution of media archiving as a profession, an interesting culture clash has emerged between those "educated" for a career in the field and those more likely to have "trained" while on-the-job – and for whom film archiving is more of an *occupation*, less a *vocation*.

Indeed, during the nineteenth century, a key issue for the emerging "helping professions" (e.g., teaching, library sciences, and social work, within which archives remain solidly placed) was the middle-class rejection of wealth as the sole or ultimate career goal. Middle-class professionals, instead, reflected the larger cultural context of American reform movements of the period in their pursuit of a higher calling or a career that would carry with it an elevating power, a claim closely echoing the statements of the majority of contemporary moving image archivists. Media archivists have traditionally approached their careers with a passion bordering on what even archivists themselves refer to as "evangelistic fervour ... not daunted in that belief by lack of resources or formal recognition" (Edmondson 1995, 247). Professionals thus are able to distance themselves

further from manual laborers or those working solely for cash wages by working for a greater good or purpose.

In his work, *The Culture of Professionalism: The Middle Class and the Development of Higher Education in America*, Burton Bledstein (1976) offered an example of this shift peculiarly relevant to moving image archivists, who continue to be popularly associated with working with obsolete or "dead" artifacts. Bledstein argued that in the United States, undertakers distanced themselves from woodworking laborers who crafted coffins by beginning to refer to themselves first as "funeral directors" (4–5). As coffins morphed into "caskets," "the sealed repository of a precious object," funeral directors became "morticians."

> In a country where there is no titled class ... the chief distinction which popular sentiment can lay hold of as raising one set of persons above another is the character of their occupation ... Success in the middle class increasingly depended [on] elevating the status of one's occupation by referring to it as a profession. Funeral directors, for instance, seized the word – professional – when they decided not to follow in the wake of broom makers, box and basket-makers. (34)

Increased professionalization serves to distance the field from hobbyists and to align themselves more closely with paper or manuscript archivists. Many such "traditional" archivists, however, remain unconvinced, viewing moving image archiving as a component of media production.

According to Richard Pearce-Moses' (2005) work on archival terminology, archives are "materials created or received by a person, family, or organization, public or private, in the conduct of their affairs" (30). Moving image archives fit awkwardly, if at all, into this strict understanding of archives, as films are themselves commodities. The moving image is the product of commercial industry, rather than, for example, the paper documents or receipts generated by producers or directors while creating a film.[2] The early film archives were created by motion picture collectors, critics, and fans rather than out of corporate interest in protecting their own material assets, whether film, paper, or memorabilia. Media archives have pursued professional status while grappling with a historical legacy in which collectors and cineastes fought to showcase and distribute, not simply preserve, motion pictures.

The Semantic Mausoleum
· ·

Although contemporary moving image archivists champion the *preservation* of media artifacts, the work of earlier generations reveals a range of approaches that often prioritized the screening of material along with, if not over, the film object's physical care. Edmondson (1995) even stated that moving image "archives" are a "semantic accident … *Archive* is simply one of the words appropriated, from the 1930s on, to do that job, maybe because of its popular meaning as a place where old material is kept" (246).

A number of media scholars such as Lynn Spigel (2005) and Derek Kompare (2005) have utilized this familiar conception of an archive in discussing the media industry, specifically broadcasting entities. These authors regard television as embodying an archive in and of itself through reruns or cable's "nostalgia networks." Although contemporary archivists would be discomfited by the authors' conflation of archive, museum, and industry, Spigel and Kompare's perspectives share much in common with many pioneers of the film preservation movement who believed that any "archive" dedicated to the moving image was one that must actively and consistently exhibit films, albeit in a prescribed manner. As film archivist Ernest Lindgren (1948) famously stated, the word archive registered a "deathly sound in the world of the cinema, which is so young, vital, and dynamic."

Moving image *libraries*, however, have been a component of the North American and European media industries since the inception of cinema, even though the libraries have differed in terms of their goals and general practices depending on their particular industrial context. While some film libraries distribute features or documentaries, others serve as "stock footage" collections that license segments of audiovisual material for re-use. Some media libraries, such as those located within broadcasting companies, do not interact with the general public,

but rather act as in-house departments to service ongoing production needs (Harrison 1973).

Media studies scholars frequently conflate contemporary media libraries and archives in their discussion of "the archive," viewing such organizations within the framework of the more familiar university archives model – where preservation, along with facilitating academic research, serves as the core function. A vital component to moving image production and distribution, media libraries serve as an interesting contrast to the nonprofit archival models in their expressed belief that film "should be kept and reshown in order to pay for itself. It must be carefully stored and organized for easy retrieval" (Harrison 1973, 14).

Thus the selection of the term "archive" by organizations around the world indicates a proactive decision, rather than passive "accident." By renaming their film library an "archive," the British Film Institute conveyed a prioritization of preservation over access – a change in emphasis that would mollify interested parties invested in intellectual property rights and copyright infringement. This semantic shift is significant when rethinking the role of the archive in media industry studies. Early film collections, now referred to as "archives" by both scholars and archivists, were most concerned with *acquiring* and *exhibiting* films to audiences in their own communities as well as around the world.

Indeed, two of the most prominent early film "archives" were famous as much for their influential and innovative programming as they were for their eccentric and flamboyant leadership. The Museum of Modern Art (MOMA) Film Library's first film library curator, English film critic Iris Barry, and the Cinémathèque Française's founder, Henri Langlois, embodied two critical impulses of the early film archiving movement that should be familiar to those studying media industries: the strategic acquisition and distribution of key titles.

The MOMA Film Library has received significant scholarly attention over the last decade. Popularly considered the first North American film archive, MOMA's history has been chronicled in numerous journal articles and theses in the US, Canada, and Europe. Haidee Wasson's (2005)

Museum Movies: The Museum of Modern Art and the Birth of Art Cinema focused upon the pre-World War II era of the foundling film department and emphasizes its role in nationwide programming and exhibition. Importantly, Wasson observed that MOMA's justification for the film library's creation in 1935 lay as much in the screening of films "in danger of being forever lost *to the public view*" [emphasis added] as in preserving them as material artifact (1). More simply, Iris Barry and her colleagues passionately loved films and wanted to share this material with the public, not just store 35 mm celluloid in vaults.

In the 1930s, Barry and Langlois collaborated with cineastes around the world to create the International Federation of Film Archives (FIAF), which remains the oldest trade or professional association for the field. For years, FIAF's reputation was that of a true industrial cartel, of which the main benefit of joining was the ability to borrow and circulate members' rare feature film prints. These active distribution and exhibition activities strike a noted contrast to film preservation rhetoric of the late twentieth century in which archives, with the support of major Hollywood directors, celebrated and prioritized the preservation of celluloid, rather than insuring public accessibility to this material.

Sharing MOMA's emphasis on public screenings and exhibition, the Cinémathèque Française in Paris achieved a substantive portion of its fame through the influence of its film programming upon French New Wave auteurs such as André Bazin and François Truffaut (the latter of whom proudly called himself one of the "children of the cinémathèque").[3] Langlois, according to apocryphal accounts, was such a film enthusiast that he went so far as to bury the Cinémathèque's growing film collections literally underground to protect them from the Nazis when the Germans occupied Paris during World War II. Charismatic and eccentric, Langlois has been heralded as one of the film archive's early heroes. But at heart, Langlois was a film collector whose erratic and disorganized behavior eventually antagonized the film archiving community with its increased focus upon preservation efforts.

Film collectors have always been, and indeed remain, a critical component to the work of both corporate and nonprofit moving image archives and libraries. Significant media restoration or remastering projects, including those for major Hollywood DVD releases, necessitate communication with archives from all levels around the world as well as with private collectors. Collectors' skittishness over prosecution, however, often precludes much publicity over such relationships. Although high-profile collectors, such as actors Roddy MacDowell and Rock Hudson have suffered little harm for their hobby, lesser known collectors have fared worse (Rebello 1984).

In 1983, a former "vault-librarian" for Columbia Pictures Television was charged with fencing (i.e., the buying and selling of stolen property) over 2,000 cans of stolen material that included features as well as James Dean outtakes and wardrobe tests for Humphrey Bogart. Perhaps most importantly, a Judy Garland number from *A Star is Born* that had ended up on the cutting room floor was found in this stash and then, unsurprisingly, appeared on the special release DVD years after the film bust (Rebello 1984). Many studio employees and archivists possess contradictory views of collectors, seeing such individuals as "complementary to preserving the cultural artifact of the film" and certainly beneficial in creating unique DVD extras (Rebello 1984).

Media studies scholarship, too, has investigated media collectors. However, such literature primarily focuses upon the psychological dimensions of a collector, the phenomenon's relationship to audience reception and, only rarely, collecting's industrial and/or archival implications. Lynn Spigel (2005) concludes her discussion of television archives and museums commenting that "no matter what archivists or museologists say, [media scholars and archivists] are still just collectors … hoping to convince you that despite the archive's search for reason, the reason things are saved are never as reasonable as they appear" (67–9).

Archivists, however, are acutely aware of their relationship with, if not institutional role as, collectors. This connection certainly serves as one factor in the development of training courses, certification programs and the promotion of a professional identity with which to distance themselves further from amateurs and collectors. Archival scholar Richard Cox (1996) has noted that archivists understand that collecting has been central to archival practice since its inception regardless of "whether we dress it up with terms such as acquisition, appraisal or with some other professional jargon" (497).

A more critical approach to moving image archival practice regarding acquisition policies and access mechanisms – from onsite viewing and screenings to DVD production and online streaming – yields exciting new research and teaching opportunities for media industry studies. Scholars must remember that academic and government archives, too, privilege particular media product. According to the Library of Congress' Brian Taves (1999), moving image archives help perpetuate historical canons of " 'great' films" as they "must typically justify [their] existence by proving that it serves a need, of which the cultural uplift of perpetuating the 'art' of the cinema is often a hallmark" (79). Indeed, within the US context, academics and media archivists alike have historically mirrored industrial rhetoric in the conflation of "Hollywood" product with "American" cinema.

The Archival Industry and its Implications for Media Industry Studies

Seen as one of the pioneering "fathers" of film studies, Jay Leyda (1998) bemoaned the state of motion picture history in a 1937 *Publisher's Weekly* article, noting it "curious that the United States ... should publish only business histories of the American film industry ... as if the making of films were no more than a process of manufacture, and its chief problem a financial one" (450). Seventy years later, media industry studies continues to struggle to define itself outside of a limited economic context.

A contributing factor is the discipline's view of archives as troves of research material rather than as industrious manufacturers branding specific moving image material as national heritage. Another lies in the slow emergence of media-focused repositories on the subnational or regional level – organizations whose collections both complement and contradict the familiar narratives of global media conglomerates. Regionally oriented archives contain important artifacts related to truly "independent" media makers who have worked in communities from Dallas and Kansas City to Bangor and Boise.

Within the United States, scholarly investigations of media outside of Los Angeles and New York focus upon audience reception and exhibition practice, rather than production and distribution. In contrast, the recent proliferation of regional moving image archives in the UK and throughout the Commonwealth has supported significant subnational media study. The development of such regional or state-level media archives within the United States has proceeded more slowly. Although this delay is in large part due to the difference in state financial support, the historical academic and archival emphasis upon (as well as popular predilection for) the output of national networks and motion picture studios in New York, Chicago, and Los Angeles as American moving image heritage has undoubtedly played a role.

The relatively scant attention paid to distribution within media studies, too, has contributed to academia's national emphasis. Recently, several works on the home video "revolution" as well as cable networks specializing in older media have offered varying theories as to the impact and significance of these technological changes on the audience, the industry, media studies – and, for a very few, the archive. In his article, "Publishing Flow: DVD Box Sets and the Reconception of Television," media historian Derek Kompare (2006) theorizes that "media is increasingly experienced not as fleeting moments but as consumer commodities and physical objects in domestic spaces" (353). Kompare's work, however, reflects other literature on the rise of home video in that it neglects to include significant attention to the lucrative and longstanding distribution networks offering Hollywood material in smaller gauge formats.

Although relatively ignored by mainstream media studies, recent investigations into the evolution of the film archiving movement offer an important contribution to understanding the historical role of alternative distribution and exhibition sites to both the archival community and the Hollywood industry at large. Although MOMA's reputation as a cultural and archival center for the study of cinema arts has been discussed extensively, MOMA's active participation in both 16 mm distribution as well as film and television production remains relatively unknown. Indeed, MOMA's film department "became an elaborate exercise in nontheatrical distribution and exhibition" featuring films now canonical in cinema studies (Wasson 2005, 4).

MOMA's Film Library created 16 mm versions of specifically chosen features, notable documentaries and other films considered important to national cinemas around the world. These films were then distributed, for a fee, to a disparate range of organizations including churches, social groups like the YMCA, schools, amateur film clubs, and more. MOMA's close ally, the UK's National Film Archive, maintained a similar program that even included archive-produced films to accompany their titles. Such films foreshadowed today's DVD extras in that they "starred" the curator, who patiently, if somewhat painfully, explained to the viewers those parts of the film to which they should pay close attention.

MOMA's involvement with television well illustrates the blurred divisions between the country's major nonprofit moving image archives/libraries and the national media industries themselves. When television arrived in full force during the 1950s and 1960s, MOMA explored how best to incorporate or feature the new technology institutionally. MOMA hired an "avant-garde filmmaker" who, according to Lynn Spigel's (2005) account of the project, aspired "to build a commercially viable, self-supporting TV production company at MOMA and to produce regular series of what the museum called 'experimental telefilms' that would appeal to television's mass audiences but still warrant a museum label" (74). Furthermore, MOMA carefully calculated the financial benefit from potential stock footage requests in weighing their decision to collect television material. Moreover, as they had with the creation of their film library, they would solicit "active help and guidance of the television industry" (Spigel 2005, 75). Although MOMA eventually curtailed their ambitious ideas for television, their active, even industrious, efforts in film distribution survived for decades, including a minimal circulating program still in place today.

The MOMA Film Library's work with 16 mm distribution provides one high-profile example of the thousands of individuals and organizations around the world who worked in this component of the media industries. Indeed, representatives of the Motion Pictures Producers and Distributors Association of American repeatedly voiced the Hollywood studios' frustration with being kept out of this lucrative aspect of the film business throughout the first half of the twentieth century.

Many motion pictures disseminated through the small gauge circuit, however, remain under-examined within media studies, often hidden in smaller, regional collections across the country. Contemporary media audiences, familiar with a surfeit of food networks, DIY shows, and, of course, YouTube, are less and less surprised to learn that home movies, industrial films, religious shorts, and educational material were as historically popular as they are today. The major film archives in the US, however, have chosen to highlight very little of this material until somewhat recently.

In addition, films produced by the federal government, especially those from the Department of Agriculture, proved popular with early twentieth-century rural audiences. The amount of film material generated by the federal government was so significant that those involved with the growing motion picture collections at the Library of Congress during the post-World War II period attempted to become the sole distributor for such films. Not surprisingly, they received criticism from other agencies concerned with the Library's potential monopoly on this enterprise (Frick 2009). Although a formalized distribution program like that at MOMA was eventually rejected, the Library's film staff had already crafted a film logo and fielded thousands of requests from those involved in the 16 mm circuit across the country.

Although scholars may look at MOMA and the Library of Congress' activities as historical anomalies, media archives in Europe, the US, and the Commonwealth have produced and distributed films and videos during the last several decades and continuing through today. In August 2007, the National Archives and Records Administration (NARA) of the United States announced that it had entered into an agreement with a subsidiary of Amazon.com to distribute on DVD public domain films from the agency's collection, selling them for $20 per disc. Unsurprisingly, NARA revealed that Universal Newsreels would be the first collection to be released as a result of this public–private partnership. Universal Studios had donated the company's newsreels to NARA in 1976, sending what remained of the physical materials to the agency's vaults as well as transferring the copyright to "the American people." The Archivist of the United States, Allen Weinstein, employed familiar archival rhetoric when explicating a pragmatic, and partially financially driven, institutional decision as one with loftier goals: "This new program will make our holdings much more accessible to millions of people who cannot travel to the Washington DC area."[4]

For the purposes of this essay, however, NARA's choice should be viewed through the prism of archive as industry, rather than as passive treasure trove. Further, NARA's collaboration with a leading corporation to proactively *distribute* public domain material reveals the longstanding relationship between national level archives and international business entities. The Library of Congress, MOMA, the George Eastman House in Rochester, New York, as well as the UCLA Film and Television Archive all maintain ongoing and mutually beneficial relationships with Hollywood entertainment conglomerates, including Time Warner, Sony, and the National Broadcasting Corporation.

Instead of discussing the historical tradition of interrelationships or the exceedingly blurred boundaries between for-profit and nonprofit media archives (from regional collections to federal institutions), media studies, as well as the majority of media preservation literature, continues to promote tired binary oppositions, pitting "exploitive" media business practice against the publicly funded "Don Quixotes of Film Preservation" (Gracy 1999, 184). Karen Gracy (1999) has written a number of articles on the film preservation movement of the last several decades that look at cultural value, the historical film artifact, and the impact of copyright extension upon nonprofit heritage institutions. Gracy's expressed concerns revolve around her view that "multinational corporations … own copyright on the vast majority of the output of the United States film industry … [and continue to] assert primary

rights over the preservation and restoration of much of America's film heritage" (189).

In calculating this assessment of the country's "film heritage," however, Gracy herself falls prey to the marketing efforts of the corporate entertainment entities that have striven – in conjunction with the large public archives around the world – to connect Hollywood film product with American cinema history. During the 1990s, particularly during the heated debates of colorizing black and white Hollywood films from the 1930s and 1940s, the large not-for-profit media archives joined forces with major motion picture directors through Martin Scorsese's Film Foundation. The Library of Congress, the Museum of Modern Art, the George Eastman House, the UCLA Film and Television Archive, and the American Film Institute worked with American Movie Classics and the Film Foundation, raising millions of dollars to "save" movies featuring Laurel and Hardy or early Frank Capra material and to champion the preservation of celluloid material. Although so-called "orphan" films benefited from this high-profile work, Hollywood material remained the poster-child for the film preservation movement of the 1980s and 1990s.

In the twenty-first century, however, faced with a virtual explosion of a vast array of moving image material across broadband, television screens, megaplexes, and cell phones, media archives are reevaluating priorities and strategies, and such "alternative" material is taking a more central role. Armed with an understanding of moving image archives as manufacturers of particular kinds of media heritage, media industry scholars have the potential to lead the field of media studies in examining all aspects of American media heritage – from Orson Welles and John Ford to Melton Barker and Shad Graham. Although Barker and Graham remain unknown names to the vast majority of media students across the US, a number of University of Texas at Austin Radio-Television-Film majors have learned about Barker and Graham's role in Texas' regional filmmaking legacy alongside Hollywood's features, home movies, Yiddish language films out of New York, and African American films produced in Dallas. A number of students from one class in fall 2006 commented that watching *It Happened One*

Night and *Casablanca* had really bored or irritated them. Instead, they preferred the locally produced newsreels from nearby San Marcos, Texas that showcased Latino celebrations across the street from a movie theatre that featured Spanish-language films in the 1930s – and they wanted to know more.[5]

The United States moving image industry always has been, and continues to be, an exceedingly more complicated realm than traditional media studies (and media preservation rhetoric) has historically shown. The lack of attention to regional production offers an unparalleled opportunity for those interested in media industry studies. Orphan material illustrates the synergy between all levels of American media industries and works toward a more holistic understanding of the history of a diverse array of media industries throughout the United States. Similarly, opportunities have expanded significantly for students out of moving image preservation programs. As Gregory Lukow (2000), Chief of the Motion Picture Broadcasting and Recorded Sound Division at the Library of Congress, notes:

> Twenty years ago, when one heard a student or young person express the desire to work in a moving image archive, this generally meant the hope for a job working hands-on to preserve golden-age Hollywood movies in one of the handful of well-known not-for-profit film archives in the United States. Today, students looking to enter the preservation job market must confront a widely diverse and often confusing array of national and local archives, specialized collections, museums, historical societies, research institutes, production studios, broadcast companies, stock footage suppliers, laboratories, vault facilities, software developers, and other service providers. (138)

In the same way that young moving image archivists must be encouraged to see the multiplicity of options available for those with their interest and skills, media industry scholars and students must be encouraged to see opportunities in heretofore archival absences.

Conclusion

Within the burgeoning field of media industry studies, scholars often cite "the industry's" protective measures and confidentiality as key frustrations in conducting research. For example, Janet Wasko's introduction to her 1982 book, *Movies and Money*, bemoaned the "obstructions of corporate secrecy … [particularly troublesome as her research investigated] the traditionally secretive banking industry and the compulsively skittish film industry" (xxiii). Recurring complaints over the dearth of archival data pertaining to the Hollywood or US entertainment industry appear almost ironic in that one of the key areas rarely, if ever, studied by media industry scholars is that of the archival community itself.

While the majority of film and broadcasting industry scholars have mirrored larger historical trends by focusing upon the national level of media enterprise, the last three decades have witnessed a proliferation of regional or subnational moving image archival collections that actually complicate further contemporary and historical understandings of how the media industries work and function. Within the United States context specifically, greater critique of the historical role of the archive validates substantive new avenues of research. A closer look at the wide range of media archives as proactive industry, rather than barricaded vaults of specialized treasure, illustrates that boundaries between the government, the corporation, and the archive have always been blurred and can offer a glimpse into the future – not just the past.

Over the last several years, digital convergence has exacerbated the moving image archivists' perpetual crises of identity. In virtually every conference panel at the 2006 AMIA conference in Anchorage, archivists debated the impact of Google and YouTube, articulating palpable fears of being subsumed into larger programs or worse yet, becoming irrelevant. Much like the media industries themselves, media archives increasingly feature a work environment where "the blue-collar ranks … are shrinking, giving way to so-called 'super techies' who can cooperate a range of sophisticated computerized equipment … and, moreover, the ability to keep up with and master the newer computerized products and systems that continue to come" (Brown 1996, 74).

In a sense, such fears help fuel the impulse to retrench and further adhere to nineteenth-century modes of preservation in which the material artifact supersedes the value of its content. Media archivists often criticize new technologies' encouragement of "mining the intellectual property of films and [relegating] interest in the material nature of that property ... secondary" (Gracy 1999, 184). At the dawn of the twenty-first century, media archivists face a potent choice: to embrace the highly competitive landscape of digital access or to mimic the work of those earlier funeral directors who distanced themselves from cabinet makers and other laborers by initiating discursive changes, further delineating a specialized and elite profession of "mortuary science" versus trade.

In his article on archival access in the twenty-first century, Richard Cox (1998) connected, yet again, archives and cemeteries, somber locations for rotting relics of the past. Cox, however, utilized his reference to energize and rally his archival peers, imploring, "We ... need to remember that the cemetery ultimately emerged as a centre of social life ... the place for strolling, socializing, and merrymaking" (36–7). For a brief time, Cox argued, the cemetery seemed the setting for the exchange of ideas, information, and culture. In an age where the Internet has become that cultural epicenter, archivists must seize a unique opportunity (Gracy 1999).

For today's media archiving professionals, imbued with the quasi-missionary purpose and vision of the importance of their work "for future generations," viewing themselves as media laborers and equal players in the ever-changing industrial landscape is a painful exercise in redefining both themselves and the overarching profession. What will happen remains uncertain. As some components of the moving image archival community retrench and retreat, implementing stricter access policies to material, others appear to be exploring new modes of practice. Rick Prelinger (2007), co-founder of the Internet Archive and moving image preservation visionary, accurately articulated the profession's contemporary conundrum – and one particularly relevant to media industry scholars:

> Above all, [the moving image archive] needs to recognize that it is a cultural producer playing a primary role in the dissemination and exchange of images and sounds, not simply a wholesale repository relying on presenters, producers, and scholars to expose its treasures. Absent an aggressive and enthusiastic populism, the archives risk irrelevancy and increased marginalization. (118)

Or, as Mel Brooks would say, "The rest is easy ... but the sprockets will tear your heart out."[6]

Notes

1 In Squire (1983), p. 37.
2 See Slide (1992) for more elaboration upon this distinction.
3 Roud (1983), p. viii.
4 See www.archives.gov/press/press-releases/2007/nr07-122.html, accessed August 15, 2007.
5 Author conversations with RTF 345 "American Cinema: Hollywood and Beyond" students, December 2006.
6 Squire (1983), p. 37.

References

Bledstein, B. J. (1976) *The Culture of Professionalism: The Middle Class and the Development of Higher Education in America*. W. W. Norton, New York.

Brint, S. (1994) *In an Age of Experts: The Changing Role of Professionals in Politics and Public Life*. Princeton University Press, Princeton.

Brown, L. (1996) Technology transforms. In Gray, L. S. and Seeber, R. L. (eds.) *Under the Stars: Essays on Labor Relations in Arts and Entertainment*. Cornell University Press, Ithaca, pp. 50–85.

Cox, R. J. (1996) The archivist and collecting: a review essay. *American Archivist* **59**, 496–512.

Cox, R. J. (1998) Access in the digital information age and the archival mission: the United States. *Journal of the Society of Archivists* **19**, 25–40.

Edmondson, R. (1995) Is film archiving a profession? *Film History* **7**, 245–55.

Frick, C. (2009) *Saving Cinema: Moving Image Archives and "American" Film Heritage*. Oxford University Press, Oxford, forthcoming.

Friedson, E. (1994) *Professionalism Reborn: Theory, Prophecy, and Policy*. Polity Press, Cambridge.

Gracy, K. (1999) Coming again to a theater near you: the lucrative business of recycling American film heritage. *Stanford Humanities Review: Inside the Film Archive: Practice, Theory, and Canon* **7**, 180–91.

Harrison, H. (1973) *Film Library Techniques*. Focal Press, London.

Kompare, D. (2005) *Rerun Nation: How Repeats Invented American Television*. Routledge, New York.

Kompare, D. (2006) Publishing flow: DVD box sets and the reconception of television. *Television and New Media* **7**, 335–60.

Leyda, J. (1998) Have you any books about the movies? *Film History* **10**, 448–52.

Lindgren, E. (1948) The importance of film archives. *Penguin Film Review* **5**, 50–1.

Lukow, G. (2000) Beyond "on-the-job": the education of moving image archivists – a history in progress. *Film History* **12**, 134–47.

Pearce-Moses, R. (2005) *A Glossary of Archival and Records Terminology*. Society of American Archivists, Chicago.

Prelinger, R. (2007) Archives and access in the 21st century. *Cinema Journal* **46**, 114–18.

Rebello, S. (1984) State of siege. *American Film*, May, pp. 41–5.

Roud, R. (1983) *A Passion for Films*. Viking Press, New York.

Slide, A. (1992) *Nitrate Won't Wait: A History of Film Preservation in the United States*. McFarland, Jefferson.

Spigel, L. (2005) Our TV heritage: television, the archive, and the reasons for preservation. In Wasko, J. (ed.) *A Companion to Television*. Blackwell, Oxford, pp. 67–99.

Squire, J. E. (1983) *The Movie Business Book*. Prentice-Hall, Englewood Cliffs.

Taves, B. (1999) Marginal films and the mission of the archive. *Stanford Humanities Review: Inside the Film Archive: Practice, Theory, and Canon* **7**, 79–87.

Wasko, J. (1982) *Movies and Money: Financing the American Film Industry*. Ablex, Norwood.

Wasson, H. (2005) *Museum Movies: The Museum of Modern Art and the Birth of Art Cinema*. University of California Press, Berkeley.

3

Film Industry Studies and Hollywood History

....

Thomas Schatz

The purpose of this essay is twofold. One objective, which coincides with the larger aims of this collection, is to delineate the basic characteristics of a media industry studies approach as it applies to Hollywood cinema, thus staking out a *film industry studies* approach within the larger field of media industry analysis. A second, related objective is to trace the general development of the film industry and to assess its current configuration, indicating how and why an industry studies approach is both fundamental and necessary to the analysis of American films and filmmaking – more so now than ever, perhaps, considering the role of Hollywood-produced movies in today's global entertainment arena, as well as the growing rift between the studios' blockbuster output and the robust independent film movement. Both of these objectives center on a distinction between "media" and "film," which is a key concern regarding the New Hollywood due to the increasing convergence between film and other media industries and the related trend toward media conglomeration.

Conglomerate control is in fact the clearest manifestation of this film/media dichotomy. Since the 1980s, all of the major Hollywood studios have been subsumed by a cartel of global media conglomerates: Time Warner (which owns Warner Bros.), Viacom (Paramount), News Corp (20th Century Fox), Sony (Columbia), and GE (Universal). The only major studio to avoid acquisition by a conglomerate, Disney, has in fact become one, expanding its media and entertainment operations worldwide and swallowing up a number of significant media firms including ABC, ESPN, Miramax, and Pixar. At present, these "Big Six" media conglomerates own not only the Hollywood film studios but also all four of the US broadcast television networks and the vast majority of the major cable networks.[1] Their holdings in other media-related industries are extensive but varied, including music and print publishing, video games, consumer electronics, theme parks, toy manufacturing, cable and satellite systems, and online media. In terms of filmmaking, conglomeration has intensified the studios' blockbuster mentality while fostering the strategic expansion of established movie "brands" into worldwide entertainment franchises that benefit any number of the parent company's other divisions. From *Star Wars* to *Pirates of the Caribbean*, the movie-driven entertainment franchise has become the holy grail of the media conglomerates, and has fundamentally transformed studio filmmaking in the process.

Media conglomeration and franchise filmmaking have coincided, paradoxically enough, with a surge in independent filmmaking. The emergent "indie film movement" was scarcely an economic threat to the studios, but it quickly became an important source of "specialty" and niche-market films, a proving ground for new talent, and an arena in which experimentation and innovation are not only welcome but essential for commercial success. Predictably enough, as the indie movement caught on, the studios (and their parent conglomerates) took notice, buying up successful independents and launching "indie divisions" of their own. But despite these efforts, genuinely independent films – that is, commercial features produced and released outside of conglomerate or studio control – consistently comprise over half of the feature films released in the US per year.[2]

Thus the contemporary American film industry is characterized by three distinct classes of producer – the major studios, the conglomerate-owned indie divisions, and the genuine independents – that turn out very different kinds of films. These differences are most effectively addressed in terms of *film style, authorship*, and *mode of production*, which are the key concerns of a film industry studies approach. Film style encompasses the narrative, technical, and formal-aesthetic norms that prevail at any given moment (or period) in industry history, the ways in which those norms are evident in specific films, and what constitutes stylistic innovation. Authorship and mode of production are related aspects of the overall filmmaking process, with authorship best understood in terms of the creation of individual films while mode of production considers the "machinery" of the film industry from top to bottom, so to speak – from a macro-industrial level involving the structure and operations of the film industry as a whole, to a micro-industrial level involving the production and marketing strategies of individual firms and of distinct market sectors. Authorship, style, and mode of production are always and inevitably *in process*, co-existing in a state of constant change due to myriad external and internal industry forces. Hollywood did enjoy a period of stability during the classical era, when the mode of production was controlled by the studios. But the postwar era has seen continual turmoil as a range of larger social, economic, and media industry forces have steadily transformed Hollywood films and filmmaking, and thus our logical starting point is at the macro-industrial level.

Mode of Production

The macro-industrial level

Assessing the structure and operations of the American film industry as a whole demands that we recognize the "movie business" as precisely that: a commercial enterprise requiring enormous capital investment, in which the major corporate powers strive to optimize efficiency and minimize risk. Although the structure of the industry has changed considerably over time, its development has been consistently shaped by three macro-industrial tendencies: *oligopoly, integration*, and *distribution control*. The penchant for oligopoly involves the concentration of power within relatively few firms to ensure their collective control of the industry. From its earliest years through the studio era and to the eventual hegemony of the Big Six media conglomerates, the movie business has been ruled by successive corporate cartels.[3]

Integration involves the effort by the major powers to consolidate control of multiple industry sectors, amalgamating them into an efficient, internally coherent system. The classical era saw the studios' *vertical integration* of production, distribution, and exhibition, giving the eight major producer-distributors (MGM, Paramount, 20th Century Fox, Warner Bros., RKO, Columbia, Universal, and United Artists) a lock on the movie business that was undone by the courts in a series of antitrust rulings in the late 1940s. Decades later, new technologies and the easing of antitrust restrictions resulted in the return to vertical integration and the rapid development of *horizontal integration* as well, whereby individual firms – in this case the media conglomerates – own multiple media "content suppliers" (film studios, TV and cable networks, and so on) and also multiple "pipelines" to media consumers (theater chains, TV stations, cable systems, home video, online delivery, etc.). This relates directly to the third tendency, distribution control, which involves the flow of product through the marketplace. This was vital to studio hegemony during the classical era and to their postwar survival as well, when antitrust rulings and the rise of television impelled the studios to rely even more heavily on distribution.

The twin drives for integration and distribution control generated the current oligopoly structure, although the ascendance of the media conglomerates could not have occurred without key changes in another crucial macro-industry area, *government policy and regulation*. The federal government effectively sanctioned the studio's market controls during the Depression, but then a series of antitrust rulings dismantled the studio system in the late 1940s. Meanwhile the Federal Communications Commission (FCC) forced the movie studios to maintain an arms-length relationship with the nascent television industry – an enforced separation that prevailed until the 1980s, when the Reagan administration's push for media deregulation and free-market economic policies reversed decades of media constraint. This culminated in the Telecommunications Act of 1996 (signed by Democratic president Bill Clinton), which put the final stamp of governmental approval on the cross-ownership and media integration that now characterize the industry.[4]

The film–television dynamic raises key macro-industrial concerns regarding *adjacent industries* and *new media technologies* that have intensified throughout the postwar era. During the classical era, Hollywood was basically a self-contained culture industry despite its dynamic interaction with radio, the recording industry, publishing, and other media. This changed dramatically with Hollywood's postwar decline and the rise of television, and by the late 1950s the movie and TV industries were actively engaged – albeit with the studios in a subordinate role as television "content suppliers." Deregulation and conglomeration brought these adjacent industries into the same corporate realm while steadily integrating other media industries as well, notably cable and home video. Home video underwent a wholesale transformation in the late 1990s with the introduction of DVD, a new media delivery technology that was not only vastly superior to its predecessor (videotape and the VCR), but also brought two other adjacent industries – consumer electronics and personal computers – into the increasingly lucrative "home entertainment" sector.[5]

Another important macro-industrial dimension is the film industry's *self-regulation* via labor and trade organizations. Hollywood's labor unions and talent guilds were formed during the Depression and by the postwar era they exercised significant power – particularly the Screen Actors Guild (SAG) because of the enormous leverage of top stars in the packaging and financing of films.[6] Meanwhile most of the "below-the-line" artists and craft workers joined forces in the postwar era as a single massive union, the International Association of Theatrical Stage Employees (IATSE).[7] All Hollywood's guilds and unions maintain contracts with the AMPTP, the Alliance of Motion Picture and Television Producers (i.e., the film studios and television networks) and are renegotiated on a recurring basis – often contentiously, given the surging economic stakes involved.

Hollywood's principal trade organization, the Motion Picture Association (MPA), has represented "the studios" in various incarnations since the 1920s – initially as the Motion Picture Producers and Distributors of America (MPPDA), which advanced the interests of the eight major studios throughout the classical era. This included the regulation of movie content via the Production Code Administration, Hollywood's self-censorship agency, which was phased out in the 1960s and replaced by the current ratings system administered by the Motion Picture Association of America. More recently, conglomeration and globalization have vastly complicated the MPA's role vis-à-vis the film industry, given major studios' direct affiliation (through their parent companies) with television, cable, satellite, and other media firms on a worldwide basis. The MPA tracks the economic performance of the conglomerates and their film-related divisions, which take in roughly 95 percent of film revenues annually in the US, by far the richest media market in the world, and which dominate the global marketplace as well.[8]

Industry *economics* is another vital macro-industrial dimension, of course, and one that might best be treated here via a brief summary of recent economic developments and trends. First, the film industry finally pulled out of its postwar slump in the mid-1970s, embarking on an economic recovery that continues today.[9] Second, the driving commercial force in that recovery has been the studio-produced blockbuster film, which has dominated not only the US box office but Hollywood's expanding overseas and "ancillary" markets as well. Third, the ancillary (or secondary) markets of television, pay-cable, and home video have in fact surpassed the box office as a source of industry revenues. According to a recent MPA report, all revenues from studio-produced filmed entertainment (inflation-adjusted to 2003 dollars) climbed from $8.2 billion in 1980 to $41.1 billion in 2003. During that period, theatrical revenues fell from 54 percent of the total to just 18 percent, while all TV (broadcast and cable) fell from 44 percent to 36 percent, and home video rose from virtually non-existent in 1980 (.024 percent) to 46 percent of industry revenues in 2003.[10]

A fourth key development involves the transformation of home video by DVD in the late 1990s due to widespread consumer demand for the new technology and also, crucially, the success of a sell-through (versus rental) strategy that returns far more to the studio-distributor.[11] A fifth trend is the explosive worldwide growth of television, leading to record studio revenues in the licensing (syndication) of movies and TV series. Profit margins are enormous here because the production and marketing costs generally are absorbed during initial theatrical or network television release.[12] A sixth and directly related trend is the studios' tendency to regard the theatrical release of movies (as well as network TV series) as loss leaders, products whose manufacturing and marketing costs generally are not recovered on initial release, but whose profitability is virtually assured in subsequent markets.[13] A final point involves independent films, which comprise over half of the features released per annum but are not systematically tracked by the MPA or any other reliable data-gathering agency. The data that are available indicate that independent releases account for less than 5 percent of box-office revenues, and that hundreds of feature films are produced but not released each year.[14]

The micro-industrial level

Here our focus shifts from the film industry at large to individual production companies and to distinct market sectors and "classes" of producers (studios,

indie divisions, genuine independents). Our primary concerns involve the *authority* over production rather than the filmmaking process per se, which is addressed below. Here, too, the industry has changed considerably, although certain key characteristics of classical Hollywood persist – including the central role of the traditional major studios, whose very survival speaks to their remarkable adaptability. During the classical era, the studios all produced feature films but occupied distinct classes depending on whether they had their own distribution and exhibition operations. The postwar collapse of the studio system and general industry decline forced the studios to cede filmmaking authority to the growing ranks of independent producers and to top talent, especially stars, although the studios' control of financing and distribution ensured decision-making ("green-light") authority over their releases.[15] The film studios yielded even this authority to the television networks when they began producing telefilm series in the mid-1950s – a difficult but reasonable forfeiture, since TV production secured their long-term survival.[16] The later movie industry resurgence enabled the studios to reassert their authority over feature filmmaking, although their direct control of "physical production" has remained virtually nil – even for films shot on the lot, which generally are supervised by the studios' producing partners.

During the 1980s and 1990s, deregulation and conglomeration had an enormous impact on the operations of individual companies and the development of distinct market sectors. One of the governing paradoxes of contemporary Hollywood, in fact, is that the concentration of ownership control has been accompanied by increased fragmentation and stratification. All of the conglomerates now include both movie and television series production under "filmed entertainment," with motion picture production subdivided into multiple divisions and sectors. The name-brand movie studios – Viacom's Paramount Pictures, News Corp's 20th Century Fox, and so on – specialize in market-driven, mega-budget films designed for global release and supported by massive ad campaigns. Primarily effects-laden franchise films and star-driven spectacles, these films tend to cost anywhere from $50 million to $200 million to actually produce, with another $20 million to $50 million spent on marketing.[17] Studio executives approve and monitor these productions, although their authority is often shared with (if not subordinate to) executives in the marketing and "home entertainment" divisions.

The conglomerates' indie divisions – Sony Pictures Classics, Fox Searchlight, and others – produce or simply distribute (releasing "pickups" from independent producers) more modest films in the $25–35 million cost range with another $15 million spent on marketing.[18] These films have solid production values and are assured of a theatrical marketing and release campaign, which clearly separates them from genuine independent films. Yet they are far less reliant on effects, spectacle, star power, and franchise status than their big-budget studio counterparts. As the indie film movement has evolved, the conglomerates' indie divisions have themselves become more multifaceted and hierarchical. At the high end are companies like New Line and Miramax, which occasionally broach the blockbuster realm with films like *The Lord of the Rings* (2001) and *Gangs of New York* (2002) but generally concentrate on quality indie fare – New Line's *The Notebook* (2004) and *The New World* (2005), for instance, or Miramax's *Cinderella Man* (2005) and *No Country for Old Men* (2007). Further down the indie hierarchy are producers of lower-cost product for more specialized markets. These range from "genre" outfits like Sony's Screen Gems and Rogue Pictures (a subdivision of Universal's Focus Features) that concentrate on horror and action films, to "specialty" subdivisions like Viacom's MTV Films and Time Warner's HBO Films, which produce features for theatrical, cable, and direct-to-DVD release.

Bona fide independents are another breed altogether, whose ranks have been depleted since the 1990s due to the media conglomerates' aggressive acquisition of successful indie producer-distributors. There are three primary reasons for this acquisition strategy: first, to absorb (if not eliminate) serious competition; second, to acquire the film libraries of successful indies; and third, to recruit executives who know the landscape and the filmmaking talent. The only major independent company to steadfastly resist acquisition has been Lionsgate (formerly Lions Gate); otherwise the indie film sector is comprised of a vast number of widely scattered, under-resourced, economically distressed companies, most of which are in business long enough to produce only one or two features.[19] Commercial success is exceedingly rare, and in fact simply finding distribution is a significant accomplishment at this level. Independent films are produced on such small budgets, ranging from low seven-figures to under $100,000, that a reasonable distribution deal often covers production costs.[20] But despite the daunting financial odds and increasing conglomerate control of the indie film sector, independent production persists due to the lower costs of production (thanks to digital technologies), the high visibility of rare indie breakthroughs like *Clerks* (1995), *The Blair Witch Project* (1999), and *My Big Fat Greek Wedding* (2002), and an expanding film festival "circuit" that has become a market unto itself and a means for filmmakers to expose their work to would-be buyers and prospective financiers of future projects.[21]

Authorship

Operating "below" the macro- and micro-industrial levels and significantly shaped by those larger contexts is the authorial process, the actual production of feature films. The dominant critical paradigm regarding film authorship is of course the auteur theory, which posits the director as a film's principal (if not sole) author. This approach was developed in the 1950s by a group of young French critics to assess classical Hollywood directors like John Ford, Howard Hawks, Vincente Minnelli, and Alfred Hitchcock, whose body of work manifested a distinctive personal style – that is, consistent patterns of narrative, thematic, and formal-aesthetic expression – despite the constraints and commercial requirements of the system. Although auteur analysis severely oversimplified the production process, it gained currency among scholars and critics due to its essential insight into the nature of cinematic expression and due also, crucially, to postwar industry developments that enhanced the director's role and thus reinforced an auteur approach. The postwar shift to independent production gave Hollywood directors far more creative authority than they wielded under the studio system, while a burgeoning international art-cinema market was sparked by writer-directors Federico Fellini, Ingmar Bergman, Akira Kurosawa, and others – including auteur critics Claude Chabrol, François Truffaut, and Jean-Luc Godard, who spearheaded the French New Wave.[22]

This art-cinema movement had enormous influence on Hollywood – and on the embryonic "film school" phenomenon in US higher education – and in the late 1960s the American cinema was swept up by a new wave of its own, propelled by innovative directors like Arthur Penn, Mike Nichols, Sam Peckinpah, Stanley Kubrick, Robert Altman, Francis Ford Coppola, and Martin Scorsese. But this unlikely renaissance proved short-lived, undone in the late 1970s by a new breed of blockbusters (*Jaws, Star Wars, Grease, Superman*, et al.) and a succession of costly, self-indulgent, director-driven debacles like William Friedkin's *Sorcerer* and Michael Cimino's *Heaven's Gate*.[23] The studios reasserted control in the 1980s but the auteurist ethos persisted as directors like Scorsese, Kubrick, and Woody Allen continued to make films on their own terms – and on their own turf, far from the Hollywood studios that financed and distributed their work. Meanwhile a new generation of writer-directors including John Sayles, Jim Jarmusch, Joel and Ethan Coen, and Spike Lee kept the independent impulse alive in the 1980s, laying the groundwork for Steven Soderbergh, Gus Van Sant, Michael Moore, Richard Linklater, Quentin Tarantino, and the other architects of the indie film movement of the 1990s.[24]

As a fundamentally director-driven movement that challenged the studios' intensifying control and blatant commercialism, the independent American cinema is particularly amenable to an auteur approach. But we should beware the pitfalls that have plagued dogmatic auteurism since its formulation. These include the failure to recognize the industrial context for its enabling as well as its constraining factors; the failure to adequately acknowledge the collaborative nature of feature filmmaking; and the failure to consider the complex "work flow" in which certain individuals other than the director are vital creative contributors to successive stages of the filmmaking process. But it is ultimately the director who, as the primary authority during

principal photography, realizes the screenplay and integrates the full gamut of creative contributions – writing, production design, costumes, makeup, performances, sound, camera work, lighting, and so on – into a coherent narrative. The director's role is clearly central to the filmmaking process, although it warrants authorial designation only if the director is actively involved in the writing stage and presides over pre- and post-production as well, thus maintaining creative control of the entire enterprise.

This degree of creative control is exceedingly rare in major studio productions, while it is altogether common – if not taken for granted – in independent filmmaking. In this sense the indie realm is the province of the auteur, particularly those hyphenate writer-directors who now dominate the conglomerate-owned indie divisions as well as the off-Hollywood arena of genuine independents. In fact, by the early 2000s the indie divisions – Sony Classics, Focus Features, Fox Searchlight, and others – had developed into a "director's cinema" *par excellence* for writer-directors like Spike Lee, the Coens, Ang Lee, and Wes Anderson, due to the degree of creative freedom they were allowed and the assurance of adequate production and distribution resources. These resources include name stars, although independent films tend to be far less star-driven than major studio productions. Moreover, a separate class of indie film stars has emerged – Harvey Keitel, Uma Thurman, Samuel L. Jackson, Paul Giamatti, and others – who have talent and name recognition but do not command huge salaries or first-dollar participation deals, and are willing to share top billing with the director. These and other factors keep production costs relatively low, enabling established indie auteurs to avoid the commercial pressures that are endemic to major studio productions.[25]

These pressures tend to weigh so heavily on studio films that directors have little if any opportunity to exercise creative control or to impose their distinctive style. On the contrary, directors in this realm tend to succeed precisely because of their willingness to relinquish creative control and to submit their directorial personality to the material at hand – including a story whose style and structure are fundamentally set prior to the director's arrival. A few top directors like Steven Spielberg, James

Cameron, and Robert Zemeckis are able, on the basis of previous success, to create distinctive mega-budget films on what seem to be their own terms, as long as they deliver audience-friendly blockbusters that are visually spectacular, narratively straightforward, stylistically innocuous, and compatible with the parent conglomerate's global marketing and franchising strategies. The same applies to brand-name producers like Jerry Bruckheimer and Joel Silver, whose authorial stature generally outweighs that of the director on their signature blockbusters. But authorship at this level is exercised by the studio itself through its production, marketing, and home entertainment executives, with the director relegated to the role of narrative craftsman and creative coordinator, whose innovation and vision are welcome only if they enhance a pre-narrativized story and overall market strategy.

One interesting development and possible counter-trend here has been the assignment of indie auteurs (or would-be auteurs) to big-budget, franchise-scale productions. This trend emerged with the Wachowski brothers' high-profile success on *The Matrix* in 1999, and then coalesced in 2000–1 when New Line assigned Peter Jackson to its *Lord of the Rings* trilogy and Sony handed Sam Raimi its *Spider-Man* franchise. The practice soon became commonplace – notably on Warner Bros.' later Harry Potter installments (with Alfonso Cuaron, David Yates, and Mike Newell) and its revitalized Superman and Batman franchises (with directors Bryan Singer and Christopher Nolan, respectively). These filmmakers bring a certain flair to their otherwise formulaic projects while broadening the market appeal, but their authorial role is obviously compromised by corporate and commercial constraints that become more pronounced as the trend develops. The Wachowskis and Jackson were writer-directors on their respective trilogies and exercised considerable authority over production, while these subsequent franchise directors, whatever their writer-director status in the indie realm, are basically directors-for-hire who are more valuable for their name recognition than their creative input. Moreover, the relatively limited filmmaking experience for most of these directors raises questions about their capacity to take decisive command or to challenge the

authority of a studio executive (or producer) when conflicts inevitably arise. One notable exception here is Steven Soderbergh, a seasoned indie auteur who, in the wake of his consecutive hits *Traffic* (2000), *Erin Brockovich* (2000), and *Ocean's Eleven* (2001), has moved rather effortlessly between the independent and the major studio realms, veering from his blatantly commercial *Ocean's* series to more personal, innovative projects while promoting the careers of other independent filmmakers as well.[26]

Film Style

An industry studies approach necessarily starts and ends with actual films and, more specifically, with *film style*, the array of narrative, thematic, and formal-aesthetic characteristics that distinguish films as individual works and also as representative of larger bodies of work – genres, story cycles, period styles, and so on. The experience of "watching movies" leads to observations and questions about patterns of expression, about narrative conventions and techniques, and about what passes for innovation in such a highly standardized medium. These in turn lead to questions about the filmmaking process, encouraging us to investigate what David Bordwell terms the "historical poetics" of cinema, which examines the finished film as the result of a process of construction, assessing the principles and procedures involved in that process and how the process has changed over time.[27]

Film style is evident in three predominant ways. On the most basic level, style refers to the norms and conventions that identify (and effectively define) a "Hollywood movie" as such. A second, more nuanced notion of film style involves the trends and product cycles of a particular period – the very elements, in fact, that encourage us to identify periods in the first place. A third aspect involves the characteristics of individual works, which is a highly complex proposition due to the fundamental tension between the standardization and differentiation of product in the movie industry – a tension that prevails in all culture industries, of course, although the standardization of Hollywood films has been remarkably persistent and acute. Indeed, one quality of the medium that screenwriting gurus like Robert McKee and Syd Field repeatedly note is the durability of the classical Hollywood narrative – that is, the story structure and storytelling techniques that have typified the well-made Hollywood film since the classical era.[28]

Simply stated, the classical Hollywood film centers on an active, goal-oriented protagonist who confronts various obstacles in a quest to attain certain objectives. That quest follows a three-act structure that dates back to Greek tragedy (see Aristotle's *Poetics*), from a first-act setup that establishes the principal characters and governing conflicts, through a second-act intensification of those conflicts to a point of decisive confrontation, culminating in a third-act climax propelled by the protagonist's actions that resolves the conflicts – usually favorably, in the case of Hollywood movies. The principal characters' actions and desires drive the story forward through a sequential cause–effect chain, and their viewpoints are conveyed through standard camera work and editing techniques – framing, close-ups, point-of-view shots, and so on – that literally and figuratively center these characters within the narrative. Hollywood films present a "realistic" narrative universe in spatial and temporal terms, although the emotions and psychology of the principal characters tend to be equally important to our sense of a film's reality. Moreover, the complex interdependence of character and viewer psychology is the basis for the "invisible narration" and seemingly effortless viewer engagement that are so essential to the classical Hollywood style.[29]

The classical Hollywood narrative was scarcely invented by the studios; in fact one could argue much the opposite, that only after this narrative model coalesced could industrialists develop the means to systematically reproduce it. Nonetheless, the studios became remarkably adept at mass-producing films in the classical style, and also at managing innovation – that is, ensuring a degree of product differentiation on the one hand, while maintaining certain standards and production efficiencies on the other. Thus one crucial characteristic and central paradox of Hollywood studio filmmaking was that it codified the standards for quality filmmaking while producing very few truly innovative works. The studios were also adept at assimilating outside challenges and innovations, including technological advances (sound, color, widescreen) and stylistic trends from other national cinemas (German expressionism, Soviet montage). Product differentiation during the classical era was primarily a function of the "house styles" and star-genre formulas developed by the studios, as well as the period styles that often were associated with particular genres – the expressionist style of 1930s horror films, for instance, or the noir stylistics of hardboiled thrillers in the 1940s. A very few Hollywood directors like Alfred Hitchcock and Orson Welles brought a distinctive and innovative style to their films, but the vast majority – including most canonized auteurs – were self-effacing artists whose narration rarely if ever called attention to itself or openly challenged (let alone violated) the conventions of Hollywood storytelling.

The classical narrative survived the postwar collapse of the studio system, but its hegemony over American cinema did not. Challenges and alternatives arose on several fronts, notably exploitation films and the burgeoning avant-garde movement in the US, as well as the international "art films" amidst the growing tide of postwar imports. By 1959–60 American theaters routinely screened breakthrough foreign films like Truffaut's *The 400 Blows*, Bergman's *Wild Strawberries*, and Antonioni's *L'Avventura*, and some – like Fellini's *La Dolce Vita* – were commercial as well as critical hits. Aggressively anticlassical in terms of both narrative structure and cinematic technique, these films featured aimless or inscrutable protagonists, elliptical or incoherent plots, ambiguous or non-existent conflicts, hyperrealistic or excessively formalistic cinematic technique, and above all a penchant for self-conscious rather than self-effacing narration.[30] This art-cinema aesthetic spurred the director-driven Hollywood renaissance mentioned earlier, bringing a distinctly "modernist" edge to the tradition of genres as well as the entrenched classical style. Subversive, unorthodox films from *Bonnie and Clyde* (1967) to *Taxi Driver* (1976) were among the definitive films of the era, challenging Hollywood classicism and signaling the emergence of a "youth market" of cine-literate, politically astute moviegoers. The demise of the Hollywood Production Code in 1967 and eventual emergence of the MPAA rating system also meant that even films made in the classical style often were more "open" in their treatment of sex and violence – a trend that was pushed to the limit in the 1970s rush of "blaxploitation" and "sexploitation" films. Hollywood scarcely abandoned classical narration, of course, but these various factors and developments did signal a deepening crisis in terms of both the accessibility of movies to mainstream audiences and, consequently, the financial health of the industry.

Hollywood recovered its bearings in the late 1970s thanks to a run of blockbuster hits – *Jaws, Star Wars*, and the rest – that were bellwethers of a resurgent classicism. In fact, the emergence of the New Hollywood was directly related to the reassertion of both the studios' authority over the filmmaking process and the classical tenor of the films themselves. And as Hollywood's resurgence reached global proportions in the 1980s and 1990s, this resurgent classicism effectively reversed and overwhelmed the art-cinema dynamic of the earlier era. As Bordwell (2006) asserts in his recent study of New Hollywood narrative, "Classical filmmaking constitutes not just one stylistic school … The classical tradition has become a default framework for international cinematic expression, a point of departure for nearly every filmmaker" (12).[31]

Although classicism did reclaim the mainstream, we should note two important countertrends. One involves independent production, which has provided a nurturing ground for alternative films and filmmaking throughout the New Hollywood era – and with the indie film movement of the 1990s emerged as a forceful challenge to the industry's resurgent classicism. Charles Ramírez Berg (2006) assesses this "surging trend in unconventional narrative" in an in-depth assessment of what he dubs the "Tarantino effect" due to the massive influence of *Reservoir Dogs* (1992) and *Pulp Fiction* (1994), which "emboldened a host of filmmakers to experiment [with] unorthodox film narration" (5). Berg identifies a dozen "nonclassical" approaches to story structure and character, all of which are firmly ensconced in the indie film realm. He does note the migration of alternative narrative techniques into the mainstream – the "existential

plotting" during the excruciating Omaha Beach landing that opens *Saving Private Ryan* (1998), for instance, or the "branched-plot" maneuver at the climax of *Harry Potter and the Prisoner of Azkaban* (2004) – but these occur in isolation and scarcely diminish the predominant classicism of the films themselves or of studio mainstream filmmaking.

A second countertrend, paradoxically, involves franchise filmmaking. The blockbuster film itself tends to be decisively classical in terms of straightforward narrative technique in the service of linear, coherent stories whose characters are essentially plot functions and whose positive, upbeat outcome is assured from the opening credits. But the film's position within an expanding intertextual system complicates matters considerably – and particularly for high-end, high-stakes studio films due to the combined impact of convergence, synergy, digital technologies, and the worldwide entertainment marketplace. As Henry Jenkins (2006) argues in *Convergence Culture*, the "transmedia storytelling" that emerged with *Star Wars* and *Batman* went into another register with *The Matrix* (1999), which introduced "a whole new vision of synergy" in terms of its preconceived and carefully engineered strategy to involve multiple authorial collaborators, to engage a core fan base in unprecedented ways (as spectators, readers, gamers, bloggers, etc.), and to create an internally coherent but eminently adaptable narrative universe. In "transmedia franchises," notes Jenkins, "the art of storytelling has become the art of world-building, as artists create compelling environments that cannot be fully explored or exhausted within a single work or even a single medium" (104, 114).

Conclusion

The prospect of transmedia franchising returns us to our initial film/media dichotomy and to the mode-of-production issues discussed earlier. The macro-level issues involve adjacent industries, new technologies, and conglomeration, as digitization and convergence integrate various "old" media into the same corporate and cultural arena – and into a single product line. The digital era's increasingly active online and interactive environments are key micro-industrial factors, as new entertainment sectors (computer and digital video games, online social networks, etc.) and new corporate players (such as Google, Microsoft, Electronic Arts) operate either in cooperation or in direct competition with Hollywood. The authorial level also is at issue, especially as licensees are allowed or even encouraged to contribute to the strategic expansion of a particular franchise. And these larger industrial factors affect the formal and narrative qualities of individual franchise films, of course, underscoring yet again the complex interplay of film style and mode of production.

This applies to Hollywood throughout its history, as we have seen, although the contemporary film industry represents a particularly complex stage due to the range of films and filmmaking practices as well as the transformative forces at work. The year of *The Matrix*, for instance, also saw the release of *The Blair Witch Project, Being John Malkovich, Run Lola Run, Boys Don't Cry, American Beauty*, and *The Sixth Sense* – films that ran the gamut in terms of unorthodox stylistics, alternative modes of production, and independent distribution, and that dynamically countered the run of predictable studio blockbusters including *Star Wars Episode 1, Toy Story 2, The Mummy*, and *Tarzan*. The year 1999 also saw Apple launch Final Cut Pro, an affordable nonlinear editing system that would transform post-production at all levels; the coining of the term "blogger" (from "web log") and launch of Blogger, the pioneering Internet "publishing" tool; and the final beta tests on the search engine for Google, a 1998 startup whose market value would surpass that of the top two media companies (Time Warner and Disney) combined.[32]

While 1999 was indeed remarkable, the fact is that every year from the late 1990s onward has produced impressive inventories of films and new media breakthroughs – indicators of the relative stability and productivity of the three dominant film industry sectors on the one hand, and of the inexorable process of media convergence on the other. Whether this process destabilizes or radically reconfigures the film industry remains to be seen, but there is no doubt that the film and media landscape is being transformed, and is changing in ways that affect not only film style and storytelling but the very nature of the film experience. Hollywood's younger audience – as ever, its primary demographic – has grown up in a digital age in which they don't simply use or consume media but they actually "do" media via blogs and online social networks, digital video production, self-produced music and films, and so on. Thus media production and consumption are converging, at least for this constituency, along with the media industries themselves. This convergence of production and consumption has significant implications for media industries both old and new, and for those of us doing media industry studies as well. Heretofore, media institutions and media industry scholars have treated the audience as an abstract entity, a veritable construction, a "necessary fiction" constituted out of sales figures and market research. With new media, especially in the ubiquitous online arena, these abstract consumers are becoming active players in various phases of production and distribution, and in ways that may well transform our study of media industries as they transform the industries themselves.

Notes

1   See E. J. Epstein (2005a). See also Columbia Journalism Review's *Who Owns What* Internet site, online at www.cjr.org/tools/owners, accessed January 10, 2008.

2   The Motion Picture Association of America website, (*US Entertainment Industry Market Statistics*, www.mpaa.org/researchStatistics.asp, accessed January 10, 2008), indicates that the studios averaged about 150 releases per annum during the 1980s; about 250 per year in the 1990s; and about 200 per year in the early 2000s. Independent releases, meanwhile, averaged about 270 per year in the 1980s; then after 1990 ran just above the studio output until 2003, when independent releases began a steady surge (from 229 in 2003 to 396 in 2006).

3   On the Edison Trust (aka the Motion Picture Patents Company), see Gomery (1986); Schatz (1989); and Bowser (1990). On the conglomerate era, see Schatz (2008).

4   Holt (2001).

5 See Wasser (2002); Taylor (2000); and Sebok (2007).

6 See Prindle (1988).

7 The terms "above-the-line" and "below-the-line" relate to a longstanding tradition in motion picture budgeting wherein so-called top talent (director, writer, stars, producer) are separated quite literally by a line in the budget from all other production personnel.

8 According to the Nash Information Services (at www.the-numbers.com/market, accessed January 10, 2008), 372 different companies released films in the US from 1995 to 2007. Eleven companies had at least a 1 percent market share, and only 34 had 0.1 percent. Of those 34 companies, 22 were owned by the Big Six media giants; their total market share was 94.82 percent. Globally, the US market alone generates roughly five times the box-office revenues of the next "tier" of countries (UK, Japan, and France).

9 The US box-office earnings (in non-inflation-adjusted dollars) climbed from $2.75 billion in 1980, to $5.02 billion in 1990, to $7.66 billion in 2000. Revenues surged to $9.5 billion in 2002 (a 24 percent climb in just two years), the first year in which international revenues surpassed domestic revenues (see www.mpaa.org/researchStatistics.asp, accessed January 10, 2008). From 2002 to 2006, US box office remained fairly steady at just over $9 billion while foreign revenues climbed from $10.2 billion to $16.33 billion. As of January 2008 (according to Box-Office MoJo, www.boxofficemojo.com, accessed January 10, 2008, and Nash Information Services), all of the top 200 worldwide hits grossed at least $250 million; all were released by Hollywood studios.

10 See Epstein (2005a) p. 20, which includes confidential data (for MPA member companies only) from the *2003 MPA All Media Revenue Report*.

11 Sebok (2007); Taylor (2000), and Wasser (2002).

12 See Epstein (2005b).

13 See Balio (1998) and Epstein (2005a).

14 The MPAA's *2006 Market Statistics* report (at www.mpaa.org/researchStatistics.asp, accessed January 10, 2008) records that the number of feature films rated but not released from 1996 to 2006 ranged from a low of 152 in 1998, to a high of 467 in 2003. The yearly average for the period was just over 275 films.

15 See Staiger (1983).

16 On the major studios' conversion to telefilm production, see Anderson (1994) and Hilmes (1999).

17 *MPAA US Entertainment Industry: 2006 Market Statistics* available online at www.mpaa.org/research-Statistics.asp, accessed January 10, 2008, pp. 15–18.

18 Ibid., p. 16.

19 Perhaps the most important independent distributor at present is Magnolia Pictures, owned and operated by Mark Cuban and Todd Wagner, whose holdings also include 2929 Film, HDNet Films, HDNet (cable TV network), and Landmark Theaters (the nation's premier indie film chain).

20 For an excellent assessment of independent filmmaking from 1985 to 1995, see Pierson (1995).

21 See Biskind (2005).

22 On film authorship and the auteur theory, see Wexman (2003). On international art-cinema, see Bordwell (1985) and Lev (1993).

23 See Biskind (1998) and Kolker (2000).

24 See Pierson (1995) and Levy (1999).

25 On "indie blockbusters," see Perren (2001; 2004).

26 Soderbergh is credited as producer or executive producer on over two dozen films.

27 Bordwell (1989) pp. 369–98.

28 See Field (1984) and McKee (1997).

29 On the classical Hollywood style, see Bordwell et al. (1985).

30 See Lev (1993).

31 Bordwell (2006), p.12.

32 As of January 14, 2008, Forbes pegged Google's market value at $205 billion, Time Warner's at $59 billion, and Disney's at $60 billion (see www.forbes.com/lists/2007/18/biz_07forbes2000_The-Global-2000_Rank_3.html, accessed January 14, 2008).

References

Anderson, C. (1994) *Hollywood TV: The Studio System in the Fifties*. University of Texas Press, Austin.

Balio, T. (1998) A major presence in all of the world's important markets: the globalization of Hollywood in the 1990s. In Neale, S. and Smith, M. (eds.) *Contemporary Hollywood Cinema*. Routledge, New York, pp. 58–73.

Berg, C. R. (2006) A taxonomy of alternative plots in recent films: classifying the "Tarantino Effect." *Film Criticism* 31, 5–61.

Biskind, P. (1998) *Easy Riders, Raging Bulls: How the Sex-Drugs-and-Rock 'n' Roll Generation Saved Hollywood*. Simon & Schuster, New York.

Biskind, P. (2005) *Down and Dirty Pictures: Miramax, Sundance, and the Rise of the Independent Film.* Simon & Schuster, New York.

Bordwell, D. (1985) *Narration in the Fiction Film.* University of Wisconsin Press, Madison.

Bordwell, D. (1989) Historical poetics of cinema. In Palmer, R. B. (ed.) *The Cinematic Text: Methods and Approaches.* AMS Press, New York, pp. 369–98.

Bordwell, D. (2006) *The Way Hollywood Tells It: Story and Style in Modern Movies.* University of California Press, Berkeley.

Bordwell, D., Staiger, J., and Thompson, K. (1985) *The Classical Hollywood Cinema: Film Style and Mode of Production to 1960.* Columbia University Press, New York.

Bowser, E. (1990) *The Transformation of Cinema: 1907–1915.* Charles Scribner, New York.

Epstein, E. J. (2005a) *The Big Picture: The New Logic of Money and Power in Hollywood.* Random House, New York.

Epstein, E. J. (2005b) Hollywood's profits, demystified: the real El Dorado is TV. *Slate* [Online]. At www.slate.com/id/2124078, accessed July 3, 2008.

Field, S. (1984) *Screenplay: The Foundations of Screenwriting*, rev. edn. Dell, New York.

Gomery, D. (1986) *The Hollywood Studio System.* St. Martin's Press, New York.

Hilmes, M. (1999) *Hollywood and Broadcasting: From Radio to Cable.* University of Illinois Press, Urbana.

Holt, J. (2001) In deregulation we trust: the synergy of politics and industry in Reagan-era Hollywood. *Film Quarterly* **55**, 22–9.

Jenkins, H. (2006) *Convergence Culture: Where Old and New Media Collide.* New York University Press, New York.

Kolker, R. (2000) *A Cinema of Loneliness: Penn, Stone, Kubrick, Scorsese, Spielberg, Altman*, 3rd edn. Oxford University Press, New York.

Lev, P. (1993) *The Euro-American Cinema.* University of Texas Press, Austin.

Levy, E. (1999) *Cinema of Outsiders: The Rise of American Independent Film.* New York University Press, New York.

McKee, R. (1997) *Story: Substance, Structure, Style, and the Principles of Screenwriting* Harper Entertainment, New York.

Perren, A. (2001) Sex, lies, and marketing: Miramax and the development of the "quality indie" blockbuster. *Film Quarterly* **55**, 30–9.

Perren, A. (2004) A big fat indie success story? Press discourses surrounding the making and marketing of a "Hollywood" movie. *Journal of Film and Video* **56**, 18–31.

Pierson, J. (1995) *Spike, Mike, Slackers, and Dykes: A Guided Tour across a Decade of American Independent Cinema.* Hyperion, New York

Prindle, D. F. (1988) *The Politics of Glamour: Ideology and Democracy in the Screen Actors Guild.* University of Wisconsin Press, Madison.

Schatz, T. (1989) *The Genius of the System: Hollywood Filmmaking in the Studio Era.* Pantheon, New York.

Schatz, T. (2008) The studio system and conglomerate Hollywood. In McDonald, P. and Wasko, J. (eds.) *The Contemporary Hollywood Film Industry.* Wiley-Blackwell, Boston, pp. 13–42.

Sebok, B. (2007) Convergent Hollywood, DVD, and the transformation of the home entertainment industries. Doctoral dissertation, University of Texas, Austin.

Staiger, J. (1983) Individualism versus collectivism. *Screen* **24**, 68–79.

Taylor, J. (2000) *DVD Demystified*, 2nd edn. McGraw-Hill, New York.

Wasser, F. (2002) *Veni, Vidi, Video: The Hollywood Empire and the VCR.* University of Texas Press, Austin.

Wexman, V. W. (ed.) (2003) *Film and Authorship.* Rutgers University Press, Brunswick.

4

Historicizing TV Networking
Broadcasting, Cable, and the Case of ESPN

....

Victoria E. Johnson

The history of the broadcast and cable television industries in the United States typically has been told either through macro-political analysis (focusing on top-down development in technical, physical, infrastructural and economic terms, including histories of "great" individuals and their achievements), *or* through the study of micro-political struggles with these media (focusing, for example, on content analysis, aesthetic and aural address, and textual representation; on viewing conditions, fan activism and productivity, or on group or community resistance to particular programming). This chapter instead argues that to understand television from a media industry studies perspective requires the necessary interrelation of macro-political and micro-political analyses. Specifically, we can understand the broadcast and cable industries as "a web of relations that exist at the local, regional, and global levels, as well as at the national level" (Curtin 2004, 272).[1] This web is the intersection where the institutions, practices, and "texts" of "the Industry" are met by everyday engagements of audiences (Caldwell 2006). These intersections are the sites at which questions of media access and representation are provoked, energized, struggled over, and translated into real social power.

We can best understand the history of US broadcast and cable when we think of television as a *practice*. "Television is something people do," in particular

historical contexts (Streeter 1996, 3; 5). Thinking about television this way encourages us to overcome the tendency "to compartmentalize power and industry and audience and text into entirely different registers and public spheres" (Caldwell 2006, 101). Such awareness acknowledges that the "industry" is not a top-down monolith, removed from history, but instead is made up of a variety of competing and intersecting interests. These interests both inform *and* are responsive to "the play of cultural and social power in the United States" as a critical element "in the geography lessons and critical spatial practices of industrial culture" (Caldwell 2006, 101). Thinking of television as something people do – from the Chairman's office at CBS to the student taking a study-break with *I Love the 80s* – underscores Lynn Spigel's recent point, as well, that "stories, images, and audience interpretation are never strictly ruled by the logic of the market ... issues of culture and meaning-making are 'messy,' unpredictable, and in no way understood through market analysis alone" (Spigel 2004, 19).[2]

When we understand broadcast and cable television as historic sites of struggle engaging questions of space (the networked web of interconnectedness between local, regional, national, and global), access (literal wired and wireless connection), representation, and cultural power, we are also well-positioned to think about "new" media applications as sites of convergence between "old" *and* new, underscoring television's continued presence and significance in everyday life. Rather than a "post-TV" era, the present moment suggests a "neo-TV" future – one that is significantly built on structures and practices dating from the early 1900s. Historicizing the broadcasting and cable industries as *networked* spatial logics encourages us to think critically about who and what "count" within the media landscape's "distribution architectures" (Parks 2007, 103).

Broadcasting and Cable: The Networked Nation and the Niche Market?

We often think of broadcasting and cable as opposed entities in the historical "progression" of the television industry. While there is certainly a history of contention and struggle between competing broadcast and cable interests, and while broadcast prominence clearly has declined precipitously since the 1990s, it remains crucial to acknowledge the historic and ongoing interdependence of the broadcasting and cable industries (Hilmes 1990; Anderson 1994). This interdependence has escalated with regulatory shifts in the last decade that have encouraged increased media conglomeration, merger and convergence.[3] This is a new context in which cable is, increasingly, "the driver of broadcast fortunes" (James 2007, C7).[4] Thomas Streeter and others thus encourage us to think of history as a series of struggles and shifts, reflecting "not a roller coaster of high hopes and disappointments, but a process of gradual, if occasionally halting, growth and integration … into the American corporate system of electronic media and communications technology" (Streeter 1997, 240). He underscores the overarching significance of *networking* to both broadcasting and cable, asking, "Why draw so much attention to the different ways that individual television sets were linked to the broadcasting system … when in both cases, the links to the individual television sets were themselves connected to another set of links, the network web?" (226–7).

Networking describes the transmission of programs from a single distribution point to multiple points of reception. Both broadcast networks (as of this writing, in the US, ABC, CBS, NBC, FOX, CW, iON) and cable networks (e.g., ESPN, CNN, LIF, MSNBC, et al.) are primarily distributors of programs across interconnected systems of broadcast affiliates or via cable systems operators. As a technological, infrastructural method of market organization and content distribution, broadcast networking emerged in the United States coincident with and integral to the final solidification of cross-continental settlement, the emergence of the mass consumer market, and the conceptualization of a conjoined, national audience in the 1920s.

"Broadcasting" refers to the ability to transmit or to "cast" a signal "broadly" from a central transmission point to multiple points of reception. Broadcasting, in this technical sense, simply refers to a method of distributing sounds and images over the air. In the early 1920s, the first attempts to define broadcasting utilized legal precedents of transportation and interstate commerce through which to conceptualize radio's relationship to region and nation. The Radio Act of 1927, for example, correlated wireless transmission of radio signals to transportation of goods or services to the market. This Act also proscribed that broadcasters must serve in "the public interest, convenience, and necessity." The Communications Act of 1934 reinforced and extended these principles to telegraph and telephone services and created the Federal Communications Commission as broadcast and telecommunications' oversight body (these extensions later allowed the Act's provisions to be adopted for the cable industry).

In 1946 the FCC issued a report that specified the need for individual stations, whether network affiliates or independent, to be responsive to *local* interests. According to this report (known as the Blue Book, for the color of its binding), station license renewal would be premised on two factors: the station's use of local talent wherever possible, and the station's responsiveness to the specific interests of the public it served. Examples outlined in the report pointed to specific, presumed differences in regional identity: while opera might be of interest in urban areas with a diverse public such as New York, for example, folk music was suggested as a more responsible choice for programmers in Missouri (as well as, ostensibly, a more "logical" outlet for local talent). The defining document of public service in broadcasting thus explicitly divided the "mass" postwar American audience into localized markets in terms of presumed geographic affinities or "tastes." In conceptualization, policy, and business practice, then, US broadcasting has been characterized by struggles between differentiated local investments and broader, presumptively shared national interests (Anderson & Curtin 1999; Williams 1999; Johnson 2008). The definition of broadcasting and its regulatory logics remained fundamentally unchanged from the passage of the Communications Act of 1934 until the Telecommunications Act of 1996.[5]

Cable emerged simultaneously with the expansion of television into American homes in the immediate post-World War II era. Originally, cable was used to enhance access to existing broadcast signals (e.g., extending signals to those remote areas that could not capture over-air broadcasts reliably, due to distance from origination or geographic barriers, such as mountains; or conversely, to provide signals that otherwise would bounce and be interfered with, due to signal chaos in more densely populated cities). In its earliest years, then, most cable providers were perhaps the best allies broadcasters could have, as they enabled viewers out of broadcast reach to become enamored with television's offerings.

Soon, however, cable providers offered selections of "certain broadcast signals based on their popularity with subscribers," and developed original, "programming types and programming strategies" (Mullen 2003, 35; 10). As Megan Mullen's history of cable points out, "Between 1948 and 1995, cable television in the United States grew from a form of basic antenna service … into a nationwide entertainment and information medium, capable of providing hundreds of diverse channels of programming" (Mullen 2003, ix). In the 1970s, cable was increasingly hailed as a democratizing and even revolutionary "new media" force – a technology that could be responsive to particularized and previously underserved audiences in ways that broadcast media could or would not be. According to a 1967 report by Eugene Rostow's Task Force on Telecommunications Policy, cable could "reform" broadcast television by providing "an abundance of channels at a relatively low cost per channel … adapted to selective distribution to particular audiences" (Mullen 2003, 71).

The language of the Rostow report points to both the promise and hope for cable and subsequent new media while also suggesting their threat to broadcasters and their potential for critique. While broadcast media were hailed as innately national with programming shared simultaneously by a *mass* audience in exchange for the price of a receiver, cable was trumpeted as an explicitly "narrowcast" medium, responsive to niche audiences in exchange for a subscription fee. Broadcasters thus rhetorically battled the increased competitive threat of cable by claiming to serve a broad public "producing culture for everyone" in an era of otherwise waning social cohesion and public debate (Baughman 1997, 1). The cable industry alternately critiqued broadcasters' claims by arguing that the "mass" logic of broadcasting diluted its content. Producing "culture for everyone," it was charged, would seem to produce merely the "least objectionable" programming for anyone.

These competing tensions and claims regarding public service, democratic access, and shared or niched culture continue to frame popular debates about broadcasting, cable, and cultural identity. For example, critics disparage broadcast media's "homogeneity" and "mass" consciousness, appalled that more Americans voted for their favored *American Idol* (Fox, 2002–present) than for US President. Simultaneously, however, we regularly hear claims that viewers ensconced in their favorite cable "neighborhoods" increasingly inhabit atomized, "à la carte" cultural worlds that encourage interaction only with those with whom they already agree. Grounding both of these recurrent claims is a critique of the perceived increasing commodification of culture along with judgments of that culture's citizens for presumably prioritizing consumption over civic responsibilities. "Broadcast culture" here is portrayed as an indiscriminate mass market populated with discounted goods, while "cable culture" is portrayed as a collection of "boutique" shops, exemplified by TV that is not even TV (as is the claim of HBO).[6]

Such rhetoric stems largely from the mid-1980s, which marked a turning point in the history of broadcast media and in the increased significance of cable. Deregulation policies from the early 1980s through the 1990s helped to relax many of the remaining restrictions on ownership within the broader telecommunications industry and had the effect of encouraging a reinvigorated era of conglomeration. In this era, companies were capable of pursuing elaborate strategies in which company-owned products could be packaged, sold, and promoted across a full range of media platforms. From the 1980s to the present, broadcasters and cable operators increasingly have become siblings with shared interests, within the same large conglomerate family. ESPN, for example, was launched in 1979 (as the "Entertainment and Sports Programming Network") but by the early 1980s Capital Cities/ABC was in negotiation for its purchase. By 1984, Capital Cities/ABC was a majority owner of ESPN with the Hearst Corporation. So ESPN has, historically, been in the same "family" as one of the key Big Three broadcast networks, ABC. The Walt Disney Company purchased Capital Cities/ABC in 1995.

While we think of the conglomerate era of convergence as the hallmark of present-day media industries, such shared, multi-mediated interests are not historically novel. This is apparent in looking more closely at the case of ESPN, for example: The Walt Disney Company began producing films in the late 1920s and became a public corporation in 1940; in the early 1950s, Disney's distribution arm, Buena Vista Distribution Company, partnered with ABC-TV to help provide the network with studio-produced, filmed television series. ABC, in return, offered a platform for Disney to promote its non-TV-related films and tourist attractions, with Disneyland opening in 1955. In the 1980s, Disney expanded its theme park holdings internationally, with the opening of Tokyo Disneyland (and subsequent parks in France and Hong Kong). In 1995 Disney expanded its holdings in media and, particularly, television production and distribution, with its purchase of Capital Cities/ABC. At this point in history, Disney's purchase represented the largest media merger ever (Wasko 2001; Levine 2005). Currently, Disney's other US television interests include ten owned and operated ABC broadcast affiliate stations. Disney also owns several cable

outlets, including ABC Family, Disney Channel, Toon Disney, and SOAPnet, and has partial ownership of E!, Lifetime, and A&E. Beyond its television investments, Disney maintains six different film production and distribution corporations, a multitude of ABC Radio affiliates, several publishing divisions and magazine titles (including *ESPN The Magazine*, which is distributed by Hearst Publications), music production companies (for both stage productions and CD production/distribution), its tourist destination parks, resorts, cruise-line, "brick-and-mortar" retail stores, merchandising interests, and online services.

Considering this conglomerated, multi-mediated present and, looking into the future, we might ask if broadcasting even really exists anymore. This is where it is productive to return to the notion that television is a practice, or something people *do*; that the practice of TV is cultural and social as well as economic and quantifiable; and that networks are sites of differential power in terms of media access and the symbolic economy. Culturally, it has been argued that "broadcasting's provision of a more or less shared cultural menu is still a highly important element in people's construction of their social identities, their sense of selfhood, and their experience of community" (Gripsrud 2004, 213) – as the above example of *American Idol* or the "shared" national frenzy over Janet Jackson's "wardrobe malfunction" at the 2004 Super Bowl XXXVIII might attest. And, as Chris Lucas (2004) has noted, "The cumulative audience for the NBC television network, for example was 81 percent of US television households ... By contrast, one of the highest-rated cable networks, TBS ... could be seen in only 43 percent of US households that year" (343).

Indeed, the question of broadcasting's reach versus cable's "niche" has come to the forefront in debates about the potential unevenness of infrastructural resources and technological access across media platforms. As Beretta Smith-Shomade (2004) asks, "Who benefits from the new technologies and what will others watch who cannot afford it? Phrased another way, 'Who will be interested in the audiences that can't access cable?'" (71). As she noted, "Cable access has not been uniformly available. Nearly 70 percent of US homes are wired, yet the greater percentage of those left without are concentrated in African American neighborhoods" (71). In an era characterized by "the cooperation between multiple media industries, and the migratory behavior of media audiences who will go almost anywhere in search of the kinds of entertainment experiences they want," this is also a context in which "not all participants are created equal" (Jenkins 2006, 3). Arguably, narrowcasting "appears in many aspects, a way to keep the marginal marginal. It encourages a center – a space where the really important demographics reside" (Smith-Shomade 2004, 78). Notably, televised sport represents a field of programming that is still primarily available via "traditional" network broadcasters and basic cable outlets to a broadly "democratic" demographic audience, appealing across race, class, gender, generational, and geographic lines (Johnson 2006).

TV and Sport: From Broadcasting to Cable and Back Again

To a significant degree, modern sport and broadcasting are analogs. Both rest "upon a foundation of individual stations," athletes or teams "that give voice to local communities, promoting the values of citizenship and the unique character of local cultures" (Anderson & Curtin 1999, 289). Both are also integral to "post-World War II ideologies of the 'national' that [each] coincided with and contributed to" (Williams 1999, 222), as seen, for example, in the massive audiences conjoined for the annual, symbolic "cultural forum" that is the Super Bowl (Newcomb & Hirsch 1987). The ability to broadcast and view sporting events was a key promotional appeal from radio's and television's inception. According to the Pro Football Hall of Fame, for example, the first professional football game to be televised was shown to viewers at the 1939 New York World's Fair's RCA Pavilion, where TV was publicly introduced.[7] Sporting events and sport-oriented series were a nightly feature in radio broadcasting that migrated easily into television schedules. Each of the "Big Three" broadcasters featured sports such as wrestling, boxing, and roller derby in 1940s

prime time. In the 1950s and 1960s "highlight" shows such as *Gillette Cavalcade of Sports* (NBC, 1951–60) and *ABC Wide World of Sports* (ABC, 1961–97) became weekly staples (McNeil 1996).

Today, sport is a key field upon which the continued relevance of broadcast networking has been staked. In 1999, CBS brokered, historically, one of the largest telecast rights deals in order to keep the National Collegiate Athletic Association's Men's basketball tournament on its network through 2010. At the 2006 upfronts, Les Moonves reiterated that CBS was the "most stable" network in TV, particularly as evidenced by the broad audience attracted to the NCAA tournament and to National Football League coverage. Significantly here, CBS is currently both the number one network in the top-25 designated market areas[8] *and* it also skews highest for viewership in smaller markets (Mandese 2004, 10). Sport coverage allows the Big Three "classic" broadcast TV networks to cannily position themselves, in Patricia Aufderheide's (1999) words, as "the video medium of the poor, the immigrant, the uncabled" (48), while simultaneously cultivating new fan bases (and cross-conglomerate streams) of consumers who are among the most tech-savvy and well-niched of all media users.[9] All contemporary media industries strive to balance their portfolio of interests in order to engage *both* a broad(cast) audience and increasingly narrower niches within that audience.

ESPN, and ESPN Original Entertainment Programming's Hip-Hop Moment

In what follows, the historic interrelation of broadcasting and cable and their shared interests but different approaches to who counts in the contemporary multi-mediated context, are exemplified through a case study of ESPN's Original Entertainment Programming division from 2001 to 2004. In these years, the division's programming and marketing were designed to attract "African American and Hispanic scene-makers and other 12- to 24-year-old male urban hipsters" (Chunovic 2003, quoting ESPN/ABC Sports Customer Marketing and Sales

Department, 18). Analysis of the inception of ESPN Original Entertainment Programming in 2001 to its restructuring and reconceptualization by 2005 reveals structural, textual/aesthetic, market/economic, and cultural struggles over the meanings of youth, urban culture, race, masculinity, and the *value* of each "as this was played out on" television at the beginning of the twenty-first century (D'Acci 1992, 170). The demise of ESPN's programming specifically to this audience shares historic precedent with broadcast strategies to develop "buzz" and market presence while building a larger audience for a new brand (Gray 1995). Prior examples of such practices include, for example: Fox Broadcasting's early 1990s appeal to urban black youth through programs such as *The Arsenio Hall Show* (1989–94) and *In Living Color* (1990–4), prior to its "mainstream" or, more white, suburban "mass" broadcast audience appeal with *Beverly Hills 90210* (1990–2000), *The X-Files* (1993–2002; or UPN's early 2000s appeal to an African American professional audience with *Girlfriends* (2000–6; CW, 2006–8), prior to its absorption into CW where priority has been given to promotion of "broader"-appeal series such as *Aliens in America* (2007–present).

Within the larger history of ESPN's emergence as a cable network (beginning with one channel, transmitting from Bristol, Connecticut in 1979), and in light of ESPN's contemporary status as a multimedia universe,[10] Original Entertainment Programming's distinct identity from 2001 to 2004 represents an "overt and explicit institutional performance of context" by and through which "TV's industrial discourses can also be viewed as plays of cultural competence and critical-theoretical engagement" (Caldwell 2006, 105). According to ESPN president George Bodenheimer,[11] from 2005 to the present, ESPN explicitly restructured its business focus and its corresponding target audience away from "young, urban hipsters" to presumptively more affluent and more suburban high-tech early adopters (Bodenheimer 2005).

ESPN was launched as a basic cable network in 1979. Originally owned primarily by Getty Oil interests, ESPN was gradually purchased by ABC and is now fully a subsidiary of Disney. ESPN began diversifying its identity and expanding its network in the early 1990s. ESPN's first expansions were into radio broadcasting (ESPN Radio, 1992–present), international networks (begun in 1989 with ESPN International and proliferating at present with multiple outlets specifically engineered for local markets, including ESPN Australia, ESPN Star Sports, et al.), and ESPN Enterprises (1992–present), the merchandising and "lifestyle experience" arm of ESPN (offering, for example, golf schools and racing schools). ESPN's US cable networks have grown exponentially since the 1993 launch of ESPN2. At the time of this writing, ESPN had nine domestic cable outlets, with the most recent launch being ESPN HD2 (2005–present). In 2006, "ESPN on ABC" subsumed the former ABC Sports. ESPN's other divisions include: ESPN Online (since 1995) including ESPN Interactive (2005–present); ESPN Wireless (2005–present); *ESPN The Magazine* (1998–present); ESPN Popular Music, Recording and Distribution (2003–present); and ESPN Sports Zone restaurants and shops (1998–present). ESPN created the X-Games (1995–present) and its spin-off, the Winter X-Games (1997–present) as well as the World Series of Poker (1988–present). ESPN is also a partner in sports league ownership (with Russell Athletics, to underwrite the Arena Football League), and is a partner with Washington Mutual Bank in underwriting the ESPN VISA card.

How can we begin to make sense of such a multimedia universe? Studying a *particular* moment within ESPN's history – one that self-consciously conjoined corporate appeals to diversity, the affective power of network branding, and audience receptivity to the multi-mediated integration and cross-promotion of TV series, video gaming, music, film, fashion, and sport through the language and aesthetic of hip hop – connects historically embedded media industry practices with *social* struggles over representation and questions of cultural power.

Recently it has been argued that hip hop anticipated the conglomerate organization of emerging global digital culture, considering the way it "collapsed art, commerce and interactive technology into one mutant animal from its inception" (Tate 2003, 7). John Caldwell (1995) notes that television has *always* actively used alternative aesthetic forms such as hip hop to "turn the aura" of perceived cultural "threat" of such expression "into practical behaviors and commodities that 'you too could own'" (70). Caldwell argues that such commodification makes the potentially "threatening" safe for mainstream consumption and literally domesticates "alternative" culture into a "product related to family, home and lifestyle" (70). Through the 1990s, hip hop became central to a broader "industrial reconfiguration of the audience" *from* the home and family *to* the niche demographic – a reconfiguration that helped create "the need for cultural- and ethnic-specific styles and looks ... in the name of cultural diversification" (Caldwell 1995, 9). That is, as the 1990s gave way to the 2000s, hip hop increasingly became the key "style and look" in addressing a developing audience – an address that served the interest of corporate diversification.

While clearly hip hop is now a mainstream aesthetic, it retains the power to provoke imagined alternative possibilities to a "mainstream" life. The "alternative" hip hop represents remains its broadly understood affiliation with urban African American culture *as* a "black aesthetic" and, further, as a masculine black aesthetic. While this imagination of hip hop's "essential" cultural "place," practice, and meaning is short-sighted, its consistency with the limited national imagination of sport and sporting achievement as "acceptable" public domain of Black masculine agency has made it an effective branding logic for ESPN. From 2001 to 2004, ESPN branded its new Original Entertainment Programming division (subsequently referred to as EOE) as a field of racialized desire, imagining African American life and culture in ways that intersected with dominant cultural assumptions regarding black masculinity, hip hop, and the life of the city, while *simultaneously* suggesting that corporate culture, in the form of the "team," was the "appropriate" (white, male, professional) place for masculine reward and achievement.

EOE existed as an autonomous programming division at ESPN during this period, engineered to be expressly identified with hip hop in order to attract two groups: heavy viewers of an emerging, dedicated demographic ESPN research and sales identified as "superfans" – African American and Hispanic youth "who describe themselves as 10s on a 1-to-10 scale of fan avidity" (Chunovic 2003, 18);

and viewers that ESPN/ABC's Sports Customer Marketing and Sales Department identified as "light consumers of ESPN" or those "new to the network" who would be attracted by the featured mix of "athletes and celebrities in hip hop, sports, and entertainment." According to president of ESPN/ABC Sports Customer Marketing and Sales, Ed Erhardt, EOE programs were "getting us in to talk to advertisers who may or may not be traditional sports advertisers" including record labels and what he calls "hip hop fashion guys" (Hiestand 2001, 2C).

In its 2001–4 hip-hop incarnation, EOE promised to deliver emerging "superfans" to advertisers across all of its "platforms": from Original Programs, ESPN "sells through" to ESPN's multiple networks, to ESPN.com on the web, to *ESPN The Magazine* in print, to ABC-Urban Advantage Radio Networks and ESPN Radio (with its over 300 affiliated stations), as well as to ESPN's popular music/recording and distribution divisions (which have produced and released almost a dozen hip-hop CDs and launched summer music tours), to ESPN Interactive (including wireless updates, podcasts, and v-cast services, through multiple providers including Verizon), to ESPN Gaming (with an exclusive licensing agreement with EA-Sports), and into ESPN's built-environment destinations (ESPN Sports Zone themed restaurants/stores), as well as to the X-Games, and Arena Football.

From 2001 to 2004 ESPN2's *Friday Night Block Party* of programming offered up a coherent appeal to "young, urban hipsters" – a clear site of "willed affinity" (Caldwell 2004) across ESPN's family of interests, branding ESPN as a destination through distinctive hip-hop aesthetics that one trade industry journalist recently reminisced about as "boisterous" brash and "unescapable"[sic] (Hibberd 2006, 4). Scheduled with all new programming during summers from 2001 to 2004, followed by heavy reruns across ESPN's family of networks throughout the remainder of those years, *The Block Party* included *Friday Night Fights* boxing, the AND-1 sponsored reality program about the Mixtape Tour Streetball league, *Streetball*, as well as alternating screenings of *The Life* and *The Season*, both of which were documentary series that depicted a day-in-the-life of a professional athlete or amateur team, respectively.

During the summer of 2003, hip-hop artist and actor Mos Def was brought in to host *The Block*. As an example of *The Block*'s programming, *The Life* was produced by ESPN with Sprite and in conjunction with *ESPN The Magazine*. The series featured TV's equivalent of sampling – using footage compiled from a variety of "classic" sources such as NFL Films, intercut with hand-held and steadi-cam behind-the-scenes action. Aspect-ratio alternated between wide-screen, filmic address and a televisual, full-screen orientation. Each episode was scored by hip-hop musicians and labels. In episodes of *The Life*, hip hop is allied with pro-social consciousness, literally underscoring the power that an individual's success can have for a larger community. Explicitly addressing a youth audience, each segment of the series emphasizes the proactivity of its selected celebrities – their "bootstrap" rise, within the framework of a team, to the pinnacle of their sport and their resulting power to be charitable and to educate.

EOE's hip-hop aesthetic also characterized its acclaimed but short-lived and controversial series *Playmakers*. Primarily underwritten by Under Armor sportswear, *Playmakers* was cancelled after only one season due to difficulties the program caused between ESPN and the NFL League office (purportedly due to its unvarnished portrayal of drug use, domestic violence, and business relations behind-the-scenes in a thinly disguised, fictionalized NFL). However, *Playmakers* was tremendously popular with ESPN's target audience of urban males aged 12–24. It was also actively embraced by and aligned with the hip-hop community, featuring cameo appearances by stars such as Snoop Dogg. In the logic of both *Playmakers* and *The Life*, hip hop is the presumed language of young, urban-identified fans – fans understood to be inherently multicultural and multi-mediated in their awareness and engagement with the contemporary landscape. Indeed, EOE programs of this period each posit that hip hop and sport both break down racial, ethnic, class, geographic, and educational barriers that are otherwise common in the world outside of ESPN.

And yet, in identifying EOE and related divisions with the imagined social values of "authentic," urban, black, masculine individuality through hip hop, the network's audience simultaneously participates in a racially charged mobility. The "appropriate" athlete featured across ESPN's platforms is portrayed as such because he is allied with corporate culture through communal affiliation with a team or through affiliation with a sponsor (as expressly opposed to the "controversial" individuated "problem" player such as Terrell Owens or Michael Vick). I use the term "he" purposefully here, as ESPN Original Entertainment is consciously designed with a male audience and male subjects in mind. While sporting achievement and hip hop depend upon outstanding individual contributions, there are limits to the *social* acceptability of such exceptionalism within a racialized culture. In this sense, EOE invoked the individualism associated with sporting achievement and hip hop to simultaneously encourage and reward an investment in the status quo and corporate ideals – by idealizing the team and corporate sponsorship as commonsense structures of achievement and reward within contemporary US culture and, as the ideal representative of that culture, globally.

TV and the Multi-Mediated Future

As of this writing, EOE still includes original dramatic programming and reality series that are produced to run on each of the networks' multiple outlets (though, upon inception, the primary home for these programs was the then-fledgling ESPN2). But in 2005 the department was absorbed into a new "Content" division at ESPN, also responsible for all news, online, publication, and mobile "texts" at the network. ESPN's emphasis has since shifted to cultivating a "higher-end," older, primarily white, suburban professional and more broadly *global* audience of high-tech "early adopters." This demographic extends to ESPN Radio and to ESPN.com, which promotes itself as the daily web destination of "young, educated, affluent males," 86 percent of whom have high-speed Internet access at home, whose average age is 30, and whose average household income is $77,000 (Bodenheimer 2005). ESPN's programming, marketing, audience cultivation, and lifestyle branding transition, post-2005 – its revaluing of one kind of "lifestyle" and "niche" market over another – must be understood, therefore, as a business practice that is also significantly textual and social (Caldwell 2006). ESPN now finds it more effective to court "technologically savvy multitaskers" for whom hand-held media devices "have become similar to clothing, jewelry, and other external communicators of the self," rather than to cultivate young urban hipsters via domestic TV screens (Sultan & Rohm 2005, 83). ESPN *now* appeals to the young, urban demographic through its gaming division, rather than, primarily, through "traditional" TV programs with broader appeal.

Such business rationales are also social and cultural choices, reflecting presumptions about who "counts" and what public(s) should be served by "convergent" media strategies. Now iconic of "old" media, "traditional" TV remains the primary information and entertainment medium across racial, geographic, economic, generational, and educational lines within the United States. Indeed, for a significant portion of the US audience – characterized by marketers as "lower-tech," not "early adopters" or "risk takers," "relatively immobile," and at home in "the 26-plus markets" (Johnson 2005, 14) – high-speed Internet access (and, often, reliable cell phone reception) is, notably, *not* a given. Yet, among the estimated 69 percent of the US population *not* defined as "part of the technological elite," over 98 percent have more than one television set within the home (Pew Internet and American Life 2007; Television Bureau of Advertising 2007).[12]

Television study within the academic humanities was founded, in large part, on the revaluing of culturally "disdained" genres and audiences (e.g., Fiske 1987; Allen 1992; Spigel 1992). Thus in addition to interrogating "niche" markets and investments as they are energized and then revalued (or devalued) in particular historical context, the present moment also challenges us to examine that audience which appears "niche-resistant," economically, technologically, and in racial, generational, and geographic terms. While changes in business practices and the competitive media environment have undeniably altered the nature of television's cultural significance from the zenith of the three-network era, continued engagement with TV by the broad US public (across racial, class, gender, generational, geographic, and educational lines) points to its past, present, and future significance as a shared site of cultural production and to the apparent, lingering need for television in these terms.

Notes

1 I consider these network webs to include interests spanning broadcasting and cable media industries as regards: technological invention (struggles over patents, standards, etc.); policy, law, and legislation; public interests (e.g., interest groups and activism); nonprofit interests (e.g., Ford Foundation, Carnegie Commission); organizational relations (e.g., between networks and affiliates, MSOs and cable networks, local franchise boards, etc.); lobbying interests and professional organizations (e.g., NAB, NATPE, NCTA, CTAM, SBCA); academic/professional societies (e.g., NATAS, ATAS, BEA, SCMS, ICA, NCA); trade union organizations (e.g., WGA, IATSE); sales markets (e.g., sites of internal promotion as well as syndication sales, NATPE, Upfronts); research and marketing firms (e.g., Knowledge Networks/SRI, Yankee Group, Mindshare); sponsor relations/advertisers; audience; texts (e.g., per Caldwell (2006), including "programming events, network branding practices, station IDs, making-ofs, video press kits, promo tapes, and ancillary digital media"); relations between and across TV and other media. Each of these sites can be productively studied in isolation or in dialogue and tension with one another.

2 The recent triumph of fans of the CBS series, *Jericho*, to return it to the fall 2007 schedule, following its announced cancellation, is an excellent example of this point. See also, key examples of this methodology – television as something people "do," in historical context, exposing the interrelation and tension between "macro" and "micro" interests and forces – in: Brunsdon & Morley (1978); Bodroghkozy (1992); D'Acci (1994); Miller (2000); Classen (2004); Jenkins (2006); Parks (2007); Johnson (2008).

3 Including, particularly, the elimination of the Financial Interest and Syndication Rules (McAllister 2004; Herskovitz 2007), the abolishment of the Fairness Doctrine (Aufderheide 1999), and the passage of the

Telecommunications Act of 1996 and subsequent deregulatory actions (Aufderheide 1999; Messere 2004).

4 An observation made on the occasion of NBC Universal's fall 2007 purchase of Oxygen network. Oxygen joined NBC's cable network line-up of USA, CNBC, SciFi, Bravo, and MSNBC. According to James' (2007) report, cable outlets account for "50 percent of the company's profit" (C7).

5 However, as recently as 2004 the Federal Communications Commission reiterated the local interest standard in a Notice of Inquiry that asserted, "even as the Commission deregulated many behavioral rules for broadcasters ... it did not deviate from the notion that they must serve their local communities," but that the Commission presumed market forces would accomplish this goal, negating the need for rules that might assure public service needs were otherwise met (Federal Communications Commission 2004).

6 Though, of course, venues like SpikeTV and E! are also routinely called out as crass and "low." But, unlike critiques of broadcasting, cable niches like Spike and E! tend to be dismissed for their programming's understood address to youth, who, it is assumed, will "grow out" of these channels' appeals and move into the more "refined" "neighborhoods" represented, for example, by TNT or Style, respectively.

7 NBC's experimental station W2XBS telecast the game between the Philadelphia Eagles and the Brooklyn Dodgers. See www.profootballhallof.com/history/decades/1930s/first-televised-game.jsp, accessed July 30, 2007.

8 "DMAs" are the metropolitan regions or "market areas" as defined by ratings and conceived as markets (e.g., the top-25 markets) by the television industry. See www.tvb.org/nav/build_frameset.asp, accessed July 30, 2007.

9 Additionally, cable outlets such as ESPN are, arguably, making everything new *old* again by specializing in live television coverage of major events, and, increasingly, partnering with single sponsor "presenting associates" to co-brand programming (as discussed here in the example of ESPN's *The Life* "brought to you by Sprite"). As Cossar (2006) has recently suggested, ESPN's most "excessive" programming strategy – the "Full Circle" coverage of single sporting events – also allows for glitches and low-res disorientation, due to the lack of mediation connecting the different streams. Additionally, ESPN's ratings remain highest for live, "traditional sports coverage" (Hibberd 2006).

10 ESPN can be considered a multimedia universe all its own with: eight differentiated US cable channels and "ESPN on ABC's" broadcast outlet; multiple international cable outlets; regional television distribution and pay-per-view services; and separate divisions for online entertainment, merchandising, wireless technology, magazine and book publishing, popular music recording and dist, brick-and-mortar "destination" entertainment centers, sports league ownership, finance capital partnerships, advertising partnerships, and corporate partnerships through parent company, Disney.

11 As of this writing, Bodenheimer's full title was ABC Sports president and co-chairman of Disney Media Networks.

12 Pew Internet and American Life 2007 Survey available online at www.pewinternet.org; Television Bureau of Advertising available online at www.tvb.org. Websites accessed July 30, 2007.

References

Allen, R. (ed.) (1992) *Channels of Discourse, Reassembled: Television and Contemporary Criticism*, 2nd edn. University of North Carolina Press, Chapel Hill.

Anderson, C. (1994) *Hollywood TV: The Studio System in the Fifties*. University of Texas Press, Austin.

Anderson, C. and Curtin, M. (1999) Mapping the ethereal city: Chicago television, the FCC, and the politics of place. *Quarterly Review of Film and Video* **16**, 289–305.

Aufderheide, P. (1999) *Communications Policy and the Public Interest: The Telecommunications Act of 1996*. Guilford Press, New York.

Baughman, J. L. (1997) *The Republic of Mass Culture: Journalism, Filmmaking, and Broadcasting in America since 1941*, 2nd edn. Johns Hopkins University Press, Baltimore.

Bodenheimer, G. (2005) Keynote Speech: Walt Disney at UBS 33rd Annual Media Conference, New York, 5 December.

Bodroghkozy, A. (1992) "Is this what you mean by color TV?" Race, gender, and contested meanings in NBC's *Julia*. In Spigel, L. and Mann, D. (eds.) *Private Screenings: Television and the Female Consumer*.

University of Minnesota Press, Minneapolis, pp. 142–67.

Brunsdon, C. and Morley, D. (1978) *Everyday Television: Nationwide*. British Film Institute, London.

Caldwell, J. T. (1995) *Televisuality: Style, Crisis, and Authority in American Television*. Rutgers University Press, New Brunswick, NJ.

Caldwell, J. T. (2004) Convergence television: aggregating form and repurposing content in the culture of conglomeration. In Spigel, L. and Olsson, J. (eds.) *Television After TV: Essays on a Medium in Transition*. Duke University Press, Durham, pp. 41–74.

Caldwell, J. T. (2006) Critical industrial practice: branding, repurposing, and the migratory power of industrial texts. *Television & New Media* **7**, 99–134.

Chunovic, L. (2003) ESPN2 gets its Friday night "block party" on. *Television Week*, 5 May, p. 18.

Classen, S. D. (2004) *Watching Jim Crow: The Struggles Over Mississippi TV, 1955–1969*. Duke University Press, Durham.

Cossar, H. (2006) ESPN's "Full Circle" and media convergence. *Flow TV*, 1 December. At http://flowtv.org/?p=88, accessed July 30, 2007.

Curtin, M. (2004) Media capitals: cultural geographies of global TV. In Spigel, L. and Olsson, J. (eds.) *Television After TV: Essays on a Medium in Transition*. Duke University Press, Durham, pp. 270–302.

D'Acci, J. (1992) Defining women: the case of *Cagney and Lacey*. In Spigel, L. and Mann, D. (eds.) *Private Screenings*. University of Minnesota Press, Minneapolis, pp. 143–68.

D'Acci, J. (1994) *Defining Women: Television and the Case of Cagney and Lacey*. University of North Carolina Press, Chapel Hill.

Federal Communications Commission (2004) *Notice of Inquiry in the Matter of Broadcast Localism, Federal Communications Commission MB Docket No. 04–233*. Government Printing Office, Washington DC, 1 July, pp. 1–26.

Fiske, J. (1987) *Television Culture*. Routledge, New York.

Gray, H. (1995) *Watching Race: Television and the Struggle for "Blackness"*. University of Minnesota Press, Minneapolis.

Gripsrud, J. (2004) Broadcast television: the chances of its survival in a digital age. In Spigel, L. and Olsson, J. (eds.) *Television After TV: Essays on a Medium in Transition*. Duke University Press, Durham, pp. 210–23.

Herskovitz, M. (2007) Are the corporate suits ruining TV? *Los Angeles Times*, 7 November. At www.latimes.com/news/printedition/asection/ la-oe-herskovitz7nov07, 1, 6072340.story, accessed November 10, 2007.

Hibberd, J. (2006) ESPN's skipper sails rough seas: role of sports network's original series division changes under new chief. *Television Week*, 29 May, pp. 4, 44.

Hiestand, M. (2001) ESPN is going far beyond the "SportsCenter" universe. *USA Today*, 14 November, p. 2C.

Hilmes, M. (1990) *Hollywood and Broadcasting: From Radio to Cable*. University of Illinois Press, Urbana.

James, M. (2007) NBC adds a gal pal to its TV holdings. *Los Angeles Times*, 10 October, p. C7.

Jenkins, H. (2006) *Convergence Culture: Where Old and New Media Collide*. New York University Press, New York.

Johnson, B. (2005) Money Mapped. *Television Week*, 11 April, p. 14.

Johnson, V. E. (2006) Sporting Community? TV as cultural center and "level" playing field? At www.flowconference.org/rt22johnson.doc, accessed July 30, 2007.

Johnson, V. E. (2008) *Heartland TV: Prime Time Television and the Struggle for US Identity*. New York University Press, New York.

Levine, E. (2005) Fractured fairy tales and fragmented markets: Disney's *Weddings of a Lifetime* and the cultural politics of media conglomeration. *Television & New Media* **6**, 71–88.

Lucas, C. (2004) Broadcasting. In Newcomb, H. (ed.) *Encyclopedia of Television*, 2nd edn. Fitzroy Dearborn, New York, pp. 343–6.

McAllister, M. (2004) Financial interest and syndication rules. In Newcomb, H. (ed.) *Encyclopedia of Television*, 2nd edn. Fitzroy Dearborn, New York, pp. 875–7.

McNeil, A. (1996) *Total Television: A Comprehensive Guide to Programming from 1948 to the Present*, 4th edn. Penguin Books, New York.

Mandese, J. (2004) Beyond the top-25 markets. *Television Week*, 29 January, p. 10.

Messere, F. (2004) Telecommunications Act of 1996. In Newcomb, H. (ed.) *Encyclopedia of Television*, 2nd edn. Fitzroy Dearborn, New York, pp. 2285–8.

Miller, T. (2000) Hullo television studies, bye-bye television? *Television & New Media* **1**, 3–8.

Mullen, M. (2003) *The Rise of Cable Programming in the United States: Revolution or Evolution?* University of Texas Press, Austin.

Newcomb, H. and Hirsch, P. M. (1987) Television as a cultural forum. In Newcomb, H. (ed.) *Television: The Critical View*, 4th edn. Oxford University Press, New York, pp. 455–70.

Parks, L. (2007) Where the cable ends: television beyond
    fringe areas. In Banet-Weiser, S., Chris, C., and
    Freitas, A. (eds.) *Cable Visions: Television Beyond
    Broadcasting*. New York University Press,
    New York, pp. 103–26.

Smith-Shomade, B. E. (2004) Narrowcasting in the new
    world information order: a space for the audience?
    Television & New Media **5**, 69–81.

Spigel, L. (1992) *Make Room for TV: Television and the
    Family Ideal in Postwar America*. University of
    Chicago Press, Chicago.

Spigel, L. (2004) Introduction. In Spigel, L. and Olsson, J.
    (eds.) *Television After TV: Essays on a Medium in
    Transition*. Duke University Press, Durham, pp. 1–40.

Streeter, T. (1996) *Selling the Air: A Critique of the Policy
    of Commercial Broadcasting in the United States*.
    University of Chicago Press, Chicago.

Streeter, T. (1997) Blue skies and strange bedfellows:
    the discourse of cable television. In Spigel, L. and
    Curtin, M. (eds.) *The Revolution Wasn't Televised:
    Sixties Television and Social Conflict*. Routledge,
    New York, pp. 221–42.

Sultan, F. and Rohm, A. (2005) The coming era of
    "brand in the hand" marketing. *MIT Sloan
    Management Review* **47**, 83–90.

Tate, G. (ed.) (2003) *Everything But the Burden: What
    White People are Taking from Black Culture*. Harlem
    Moon, New York.

Wasko, J. (2001) The magical-market world of Disney.
    Monthly Review **52**, 56–71.

Williams, M. (1999) Issue introduction: US regional and
    non-network television history.
Quarterly Review of Film and Video **16**, 221–8.

5

From Sponsorship to Spots
Advertising and the Development
of Electronic Media

....

Cynthia B. Meyers

Advertising has been analyzed as an ideological vehicle for hegemonic values (Ewen 1976; Williamson 1978), a mediating text (Browne 1987), an economic function of a free press (Potter 1954), a discourse intersecting with myriad cultural discourses (Wicke 1988; Lears 1994), a mirror of American culture (Marchand 1985), and a social force (Leiss et al. 2005). Advertising can be considered all of these, and more. What might be a media industry studies approach to advertising? To begin with, we should resist conventional categories, since media industries are inevitably interrelated, interactive, and interdependent. Broadcasting in particular cannot be understood separately from the advertising industry which, throughout most of its history, has provided all its revenue.

The interrelation of television and advertising is complex and reciprocal; we must avoid the temptation either to reduce the texts of programming and advertisements to economic determinants, or to infer the industry only from textual evidence. Furthermore, the media institutions themselves are not unified, singular mechanisms but complex, conflicted, dynamic, and changing formations with active agents working inside and outside constraining structures. To understand these institutions we must therefore examine internal conflicts and intra-institutional debates about strategy, practice, and business models (Gledhill 1988). By sifting differences

among individuals, agencies, institutions, and fields, we will come to recognize the historical contingency of industry practice, avoiding simple teleological conclusions. For example, for the past hundred years in advertising, strategists have debated the efficacy of the "hard sell," the direct, hard-hitting, repetitive, product-centered approach, versus the "soft sell," the indirect, subtle, humorous, user-centered approach. These debates have had specific and lasting impact not only on advertising texts but on radio and television program genre development, sponsorship forms, and relationships between program and advertising texts.

My first aim in this chapter is to survey key developments in advertising and sponsorship on radio and television from the 1920s to the present, analyzing the inter-institutional relations among broadcasters, networks, advertisers, and agencies. Such a project involves integrating previously discrete categories of media studies while differentiating among the conflicting agents. Although the importance of media integration today is well known – conglomerates own film, television, and publishing companies – the participation of the advertising industry in most of those media over the past century is not nearly as well known as it should be. Through this brief survey I hope to demonstrate how deeply integrated the advertising industry is in the structures and practices of other media.

My second aim in this chapter is to challenge simplistic models of the relations among economic and cultural spheres. Advertising, driven by the profit motive, also produces cultural meanings and cultural artifacts; while its economic imperative may be its structuring force, effective advertising must also articulate contemporary cultural tensions in order to communicate with its audiences. As anthropologist Marshall Sahlins (1976) notes, advertisers must "be sensitive to the latent correspondences in the cultural order … whose conjunction in a product-symbol may spell mercantile success" (117). By considering how and why advertisers have used electronic media, I hope to improve our understanding of the dynamic relationship between the cultural and commercial.

The Rise and Fall of Radio as a National Advertising Medium, 1920s–1940s

Long before there was television, there was radio. Although scholars have debated the point at which radio was permanently established as a commercial medium (Barnouw 1978; Douglas 1987; McChesney 1993; Smulyan 1994), Michele Hilmes (1995) argues persuasively that there was no one single moment of decline into commercialism: radio was commercial from its "very earliest moments" (2). Although the earliest commercial radio stations were founded for publicity purposes, businesses such as department stores found operating their own stations too expensive, and some began to wonder how else radio might be used commercially. In 1921 AT&T, anxious to have a hand in radio in case it replaced telephones, took an important step by developing "toll broadcasting." Like a telephone booth of the air, AT&T's radio station WEAF sold time to businesses to present promotional "selling talks," but unable to attract many listeners to these, advertisers stayed away (Banning 1946, 152). Because it viewed toll broadcasting as a type of public service, in 1923 AT&T prohibited "direct advertising," or the mention of specific product and price information, and "confined" advertising to the mention of the

advertiser's name and product (Banning 1946, 90). Instead, AT&T encouraged "indirect advertising," which was designed to generate "good will" and to "bring about a feeling of gratitude and pleasant obligation" toward the advertiser (Arnold 1927). To accomplish this, AT&T began to allow advertisers to provide entertainment to attract listeners. Program sponsors would therefore promote themselves through the program title and a brief message. For example, *The Gold Dust Twins* featured two performers, Goldy and Dusty, based on the brand's trademark image of two young African Americans, who incorporated Gold Dust cleaning powder into their act; the slogan, "Let the Gold Dust Twins do your work," was also the program concept (NBC 1926).

The growing popularity of broadcast entertainment led some advertisers to link stations together by telephone line in "chains" for simultaneous broadcasts of programs. For example, Clicquot Club ginger ale distributed *The Clicquot Club Eskimos*, featuring a band of banjo players dressed in furry Eskimo outfits and named after the fictional Eskimo boy who served as the brand trademark, to multiple linked stations in New York, Providence, Philadelphia, and others by 1925 (Banning 1946, 264). The prospect of sharing program costs gave individual stations a strong incentive to join regional networks (Smulyan 1994) and eventually the national networks, NBC and CBS, founded in 1926 and 1927. These networks, touting radio as the "fourth dimension of advertising" (Arnold 1927), solicited large advertisers seeking national audiences. Radio, they claimed, might reach a national audience simultaneously through regularly scheduled weekly or daily broadcasts, with an impact impossible in print media.

Fears that direct advertising would alienate audiences began to fade during the Great Depression, when economic exigencies pressured advertisers into "hard sell" strategies (Angus 1931) and broadcasters, reluctant to bear the costs of programming, turned to advertisers to cover more programming costs through sponsorship. Thus, despite an overall drop in advertising spending, radio advertising spending grew from $18 million in 1929 to $165 million in 1937 (Dygert 1939, 7). For advertisers, one significant difference between radio and other advertising media was its reliance on entertainment as the advertising vehicle; the task, as explained by one advertising executive, was to bring "the show world to the world of commerce" (Young 1949, 93). Just as Hollywood had discovered the power of named stars, radio sponsors recruited seasoned entertainers from the worlds of theater, vaudeville, and popular music to attract listeners (Angus 1932).

Sponsors, however, as manufacturers of soap or cereal or automobiles, tended to have little entertainment experience, and so sought help from their advertising agencies, whom they trusted to keep advertising goals at the forefront of any sponsored programs. Hence, during the "golden age" of radio, the 1930s and 1940s, advertising agencies became the de facto producers of most national network programming (Meyers 2005). For example, Benton & Bowles produced comedian Fred Allen's *Town Hall Tonight*; J. Walter Thompson produced the *Kraft Music Hall* hosted by Bing Crosby; Blackett-Sample-Hummert produced dozens of soap operas, including *Stella Dallas* and *Ma Perkins*; and Young & Rubicam produced *The Jack Benny Program*. Radio presented serious challenges to ad agencies accustomed to print media, including, as explained by one frustrated advertising executive, its "1. Lack of visual aids. 2. Fleeting impression. 3. The human voice in place of type as medium. 4. Censorship barriers. 5. Need for showmanship" (J. Walter Thompson 1930). Agencies approached these problems in various ways. Blackett-Sample-Hummert devised for advertisers such as Procter & Gamble serial dramas whose open-ended narratives could guarantee a high rate of audience return and whose plots mirrored the problem/solution paradigm employed in their hard sell advertising strategy. The term "soap opera" derives from the products of most radio serial sponsors. Young & Rubicam, proponents of soft sell advertising, focused on humor and gentle self-reflexivity in order to disarm audiences, as in comedian Jack Benny's product integrating line, "Jello again. This is Jack Benny."

During the radio era, the networks' main business was to sell air time to an advertiser, who bought it in a block of 15, 30, or 60 minutes, which became its "time franchise" to program as it and its advertising

agency saw fit. A program was designed to support that advertiser's goals, and entertainment strategies were integrated with advertising strategies. The product's or advertiser's name was made part of the program title, as in *The Chase & Sanborn Hour, Palmolive Hour*, and *Lux Radio Theatre*. Often the product was named as sponsor, as in this introduction to a 1930 broadcast of the *Coca-Cola Top Notchers*: "Good evening, ladies and gentlemen of the radio audience ... We bring you a period of delightful entertainment sponsored by Coca-Cola, the pure drink of natural flavors, served nine million times a day." Sometimes the product was integrated directly into the program by its characters, as when Captain Henry, main character of the variety show *Show Boat*, asked Tiny Ruffner, the well-known radio announcer, about the "full value" of Maxwell House Coffee (Varencove 1935). Crooner Rudy Vallee pretended to eavesdrop on conversations in a nightclub to overhear a patron admit that "the secret of his success" was the use of Fleischmann's Yeast (J. Walter Thompson 1929). A 1946 episode of *Lux Radio Theatre*, which presented radio plays based on current films, included a description of how the stars of the film *To Have and Have Not*, Humphrey Bogart and Lauren Bacall, used Lux Soap in their new home.

Each of these integration strategies was predicated on listener "gratitude" and "sponsor identification" with the entertainment. But advertisers and their agents worried about how well audiences associated programs with sponsors. In cases where star talent changed sponsors, the problem of identification was acute. Most notoriously, vaudeville and radio star Eddie Cantor performed in a number of programs including *The Chase & Sanborn Hour* and *The Eddie Cantor Radio Show*, with a variety of sponsors, including Old Gold cigarettes, Sunkist, Chase & Sanborn coffee, Camel cigarettes, and Texaco (Hughes 1939). Would audiences become confused and not know with which product Cantor should be associated? Would the Cantor fan smoke Old Golds or Camels? Was the association of a star entertainer effective for selling a product? By the 1940s, when most network programming had shifted to Hollywood and sponsors competed for film stars, programming costs surged, raising doubts about the strategy.

One advertising executive warned against advertisers' reliance on expensive entertainment and stars:

> A $20,000 all-star program on a coast-to-coast network may get fine press notices and win the sympathetic applause of those self-appointed advertising critics who are working for high cultural standards – but it's a dead loss to the advertiser if it's all showmanship and no salesmanship. (Brown 1932)

The advertisers' desire for a reasonable return against their investment in programming was in potential conflict with the audiences' desire for high-quality entertainment. Maneuvering between these desires was tricky. As Hubbell Robinson, then a Young & Rubicam executive and later a chief of CBS TV programming, noted in 1932, "On the horns of this dilemma the radio advertising men balance themselves as best they can" (48).

Radio reached its peak financial success in 1948. Network radio advertising revenues totaled $210 million and 94 percent of American households owned radios. After 1948, the dominance of network radio as a national advertising medium eroded rapidly. Its percentage of advertising revenues slid from 46 percent of all radio advertising revenues in 1945 to 25 percent in 1952 (Sterling & Kittross 1978). By the end of the 1950s, most radio stations had disaffiliated with networks, shifted to cheaper programming, primarily recorded music, and turned to local advertising. Radio, then, was transformed from a national to a local advertising medium, and its centrality in American popular culture was rapidly eclipsed by television, the rise of which resulted in radio's role as the foundational electronic medium being "thoroughly forgotten" (Hilmes 1997, xiv). Our consideration of television, then, as Hilmes argues, should begin with the understanding that it "grew directly out of three decades of radio broadcasting" (xiv).

The Transition to Television in the 1950s

The transition to television was complex, fraught, and risky for the radio and advertising industries. The radio business model suffered from weaknesses:

no centralized editorial authority presided over programming decisions; advertiser "time franchises" prevented networks from building an effective broadcast schedule; program production was dispersed among dozens of agencies, beholden only to clients; and program innovation was constrained by the reliance on advertisers, whose aims are product sales. By the end of the 1950s, many of the institutional practices of the radio era – including single sponsorship, advertiser ownership of programming and control of a time franchise, and advertising agency program production – were being replaced by new practices: participating sponsorship, advertisements separable from programs, network program ownership, and network scheduling control.

Television, a visual medium, required elements unnecessary for radio production: sets, cameras, lights, blocking rehearsals, makeup, and costumes. A different actor had to be hired for each part. Advertisers had enjoyed a much lower cost per audience member on radio than in print media because of its lower production costs and more certain national reach. Television, on the other hand, had tenfold higher production costs and, in the early 1950s, no proven national reach (Mashon 1996, 84). Television's future success was not then obvious to advertisers or broadcasters. Some advertising executives dismissed television altogether, such as the JWT radio writer who assumed that "television will never be the world force radio is, because television will leave little or nothing to the imagination, and it is imagination that gives radio its power" (Carroll 1944). Michael Mashon (1996) argues that broadcasters, advertisers, and their agencies were all internally conflicted over the shift to television. Broadcasters sought greater programming control, yet still looked to sponsorship for financing; meanwhile, even as advertisers and their agencies expected to continue program control, they were reluctant to finance the greater expense. The commissions that agencies charged sponsors on talent and time costs could not cover television programming costs; according to one agency man, "When we get into television, we lose our shirt" (Harrington 1949).

Reluctant to lower costs by producing television programs on the cheap and thus alienating audiences, some advertisers tried alternating weekly with others. Nonetheless, sponsors worried that alternate sponsorship would confuse viewers. A third sponsorship model, "participating" sponsorship, in which no advertiser owned the program but bought slots of time within it for advertising, offered an even more radical solution. Notably, this model eventually prevailed. Participating sponsorship's earlier success on a number of daytime radio programs (e.g., *Breakfast Club, The Marjorie Mills Hour*) reassured many advertisers that audiences could distinguish among different advertised products and that a program and a product did not require tight association for the advertising strategy to be successful.

One of the most vocal proponents of participating sponsorship was Sylvester "Pat" Weaver, NBC Television president from 1949 to 1956, who played an important role developing the *Today* and *Tonight* shows. Weaver argued that television could not follow the radio "pattern" because "[t]here is not enough money to put on full programs for a single product (as generally the case in radio)" (Weaver 1949). His experiences in advertising at Young & Rubicam, where he produced Fred Allen's *Town Hall Tonight* (1935–8), had already convinced him that sponsor control was detrimental. Networks could take a "broader" view of programming, unlike an individual advertiser, "whose chief aim was to sell his commodity" (Weaver 1994, 164). Furthermore, advertiser ownership of programs left networks vulnerable to losing the program to another network if the advertiser chose; thus networks were motivated to take ownership stakes in programs themselves (N. W. Ayer ca. 1956). Weaver used the term "magazine plan" to suggest that participating sponsorship was like buying interstitial "pages" of time within a program and leaving the editorial content, or program, to the network, an idea that had floated around the advertising industry for years (*Advertising & Selling* 1931). Eventually sponsors and their agencies were forced to concede: "One sacred cow that we all believed in was ground to hamburger. That was 'sponsor identification'" (Brower 1974, 213).

Networks sought to impose more control over the broadcast schedule by removing lower-rated programs from their time franchise. *Voice of Firestone*, on the air since 1927, was moved by NBC to a less

desirable time slot in 1954 over Firestone's protests (Baughman 2007, 270). Like other sponsors such as US Steel, Alcoa, and DuPont, Firestone practiced "institutional" or corporate image advertising; their broadcasting strategy was to provide culturally uplifting programs, such as *Theatre Guild of the Air, Cavalcade of America, US Steel Hour,* and *Alcoa-Goodyear Playhouse.* While these anthology dramas – with their different weekly stories often emphasizing social issues or historical figures – might succeed in increasing the prestige of their sponsors, they could not build consistent viewership in the manner of episodic series with continuing characters, plot lines, and situations. So the networks, in their eagerness to attract the largest audiences possible and thereby raise their time prices, turned instead to the series format, sponsored by the makers of toiletries and food, to whom unit sales were more important than corporate prestige, and who often spent more on advertising than manufacturing.

By 1956, toiletry and food advertisers accounted for about half of all television advertising (Baughman 2007, 217). Procter & Gamble sought large and loyal audiences; by the mid-1950s, their television investment included 13 daytime soap operas, including the former radio soap *Guiding Light*, programs whose open-ended narratives almost guaranteed repeated viewership. Hard sell strategies dominated commercials, such as the Listerine commercial featuring Marge, whose prospects for marriage improve after using Listerine because "[i]n actual scientific tests, Listerine antiseptic stopped bad breath four times better than toothpaste."[1]

To meet the relatively high costs of television programming, the networks reorganized the sites of production. Rather than sponsors and agencies, they turned to in-house producers or specialized program packagers, which could reap economies of scale by producing several programs in the same genre (e.g., quiz shows). By the end of the 1950s, the film studios had become key program suppliers, especially of filmed episodic series (Anderson 1994). To enforce network program control, networks demanded that program producers license programs to them rather than to sponsors. In 1957, a third of programs were licensed to sponsors; by 1964, the proportion had dropped to 8 percent (Boddy 1990, 171).

Additionally, live programming was gradually replaced by film and, after 1956, videotape. The networks, which demanded profit participation from producers in exchange for scheduling their programs, had found that recorded programs could be rerun, syndicated, and sold overseas, opening more opportunities for profit; by 1960 networks enjoyed profit participation in about two-thirds of programs (Boddy 1990, 181).

By separating program and advertisement, networks had more flexibility to develop programming strategies that would attract the largest possible audiences. These audiences, in turn, enabled networks to sell interstitial minutes at the highest possible prices to advertisers seeking access to audiences aggregated around programs. Once advertisements were unlinked from programs, advertisers no longer had to look for a *program* to fit the commercial message; advertisers and their agencies looked for *audiences* and were now free to follow them to whichever program they viewed. No longer closely tied to a program or star, advertisers could benefit from the mobility of their commercials and lower the risk of disastrous associations, such as with politically suspect performers or writers. The fear that such associations would cause audience alienation drove the blacklisting phenomenon in the early television era. Furthermore, advertisers grew less likely to impose self-serving constraints on programming, such as the time when writer Rod Serling was asked by a tobacco manufacturer to change the word "American" to "United States" so that competitor American Tobacco would not be inadvertently promoted (Fox 1984, 212). Separable and mobile commercials put an end to most such practices.

The single sponsorship model was finally finished off by the quiz show scandals of 1958–9, during which producers of programs such as Geritol's *Twenty-One* admitted rigging contests for dramatic crowd-pleasing effects. But already single sponsorship had fallen victim to the cumulative effects of high production costs, the increasing need for advertising mobility, the full entry of the Hollywood film studios into series production, and the networks' realization of the advantages of central editorial control over content and scheduling. The shift to the network television business model was beneficial to

advertisers and broadcasters alike, as evidenced by the increase in television advertising spending from $454 million in 1952 to $1.6 billion in 1960 (Sterling & Kittross 1978). The shift to network control in the late 1950s is usually represented by scholars as a triumph over advertisers. The advertisers who may have felt harmed ceding their prerogatives as programmers to networks were likely the corporate image advertisers – the sponsors of anthology dramas – for whom product sales were a secondary consideration. However, most advertisers saw the advantage in being relieved of the burden and expense of programming in return for a more effective advertising medium.

The Tripartite Network Oligopoly, 1960s–1970s

During the 1960s and 1970s, three networks, NBC, CBS, and ABC, consolidated bottleneck control over programming and advertiser access to audiences (Litman 1990). While radio at its peak in 1948 accounted for 12 percent of all advertising spending, by 1976 television accounted for 20 percent of all advertising spending, becoming the single most important national advertising medium. Advertisers, once able to create or destroy programs at will, could only either buy in or cancel out of a program determined entirely by the network; as one advertising executive lamented, "An advertiser's power to control or affect programming is reaction rather than action" (Shanks 1979, 96). The limited inventory of air time, enforced through a trade association code that capped the number of minutes available during prime time, helped propel air time prices upward, from an average of $30,000 per minute in the early 1960s to over $100,000 in the late 1970s (Sterling & Kittross 1978).

Assuming a captive audience (roughly 90 percent of viewers) with few options, and seeking only to maintain a marginal advantage against its two competitors, each network tended toward "least objectionable programming." *The Beverly Hillbillies* (1962–71), *The Andy Griffith Show* (1960–8), and *Green Acres* (1965–71) continued in their folksy, inoffensive way, unconscious of the social and cultural upheavals around them, whether racial politics or protests against the Vietnam War. As one television executive explained, networks sought programs "that will attract mass audiences without unduly offending these audiences or too deeply moving them emotionally. Such ruffling, it is thought, will interfere with their ability to receive, recall, and respond to commercial messages" (Shanks 1979, 94). The advertisers no longer needed the programming to reflect their corporate image, only to package their commercials. As one adman philosophized, making the best of it, "Bad television is better than no television" (Shanks 1979, 97). Former adman and NBC TV president Pat Weaver had believed that dislodging sponsor control would allow television to develop into a high-quality culturally uplifting medium (Weaver thought television's future lay in live "spectaculars"), but Weaver did not anticipate that the networks, facing enormous pressure to increase ratings and retain large audiences, would seek the lowest common denominator rather than cultural uplift (Baughman 2007, 301).

The 60-second commercial spot rapidly evolved into a significant cultural form in its own right, as advertisers and their agencies shifted their resources into capturing audience attention in this brief moment. As Jonathan Price (1978) notes, commercials adapted a variety of cultural forms: "In an hour of TV we are likely to see all these aftertraces from several generations of myths – the primitive, the print, the modern film, and the postmodern scene, all jumbled up. Commercials move in fast; tightly edited, quickly paced, their style fits TV better … than the programs" (165). Rising costs led to an eventual shift to 30-second spots by the end of the 1960s. However, some advertisers and agencies first resisted the briefer format not only because it allowed them less time for their sales message, but also because they worried about "clutter," or viewers distracted by competing commercials (Brown 1971, 67). Doubling the number of commercial slots meant more advertisers competed for viewers' attention, which affected advertisers' commercial and narrative strategies as they each sought to break through the "clutter" (Arlen 1980).

During the radio era advertisers bought air time; after the network era began, however, they bought

audience attention. Naturally, advertisers have demanded to know how much of it they get for their money. Networks and advertisers require metrics they can agree on; the Nielsen Company ultimately persuaded the industry to make it the sole supplier of viewing data, drawn from a tiny sample (of about .001 percent) of the national audience designed to be demographically representative by age and sex. The Nielsen ratings, acknowledged by buyers and sellers to be imperfect, only provide a starting point for price negotiation. During the "upfront" period, the spring before a new fall season, advertisers and networks negotiate prices for future broadcasts and their ratings points. If that broadcast does not deliver the ratings points promised for it, a network often "makes good" by providing the advertiser with enough free time to make up the difference in numbers of viewers reached. Advertisers buy gross ratings points (GRPs), each point representing a number of people undifferentiated by age or sex, or targeted ratings points (TRPs), each point representing audiences defined by age and sex, such as women aged 18–35. Advertisers bid prices up or down depending on competition and the elusiveness and desirability of the targeted demographic. Although particular advertiser targets vary, broadcast networks target adults aged 18–49 and schedule programming to attract them. In the late 1960s, ABC, long the third-ranked network, convinced advertisers that its programs attracted a predominantly younger audience, a demographic that advertisers should value more highly due to their putative willingness to experiment with new brands (Brown 1971, 285). Thus despite CBS's higher gross ratings, ABC charged a higher cost per thousand (CPM) viewers; although CBS countered that older viewers had more spending power, by 1971 CBS drastically shifted its programming strategies in an effort to attract those younger viewers with controversial programs such as *All in the Family*.

The 1970s shift away from "least objectionable programming" and toward programming that addressed contemporary social tensions, such as *All in the Family* (1971–9), *Maude* (1972–8), *The Jeffersons* (1975–85), *Sanford & Son* (1972–7), *M*A*S*H* (1972–83), and others, came well after the advertising industry had shifted strategies to address changing social conditions.[2] While the 1950s were characterized by treating consumers as an undifferentiated mass, by the 1960s advertisers realized that multiple product brand extensions marketed to different consumer "segments" would improve sales. So, for example, Procter & Gamble's toothpastes included Crest, for those fighting cavities; Gleem, for those seeking white teeth; and Denquel, for those with sensitive teeth. Furthermore, after decades of spelling it out and saying it twice, as hard sell strategy dictated, in the 1960s advertising agencies shifted decisively toward a soft sell approach to reach those segmented markets. This shift, called the "Creative Revolution" within the industry, was evident in high concept, user-centered campaigns that often used humor to disarm audiences (Fox 1984). Well-known television advertising agency Wells Rich Greene devised Alka-Seltzer campaigns ("I can't believe I ate the whole thing" and "Try it – you'll like it") and Benson & Hedges cigarette commercials, featuring the perils of their extra-long cigarettes (lighting a beard on fire, exploding a balloon, getting caught in a door), which were admired within the industry for addressing realistic situations with light humor (Fox 1984, 269). Advertising agencies outdid each other in their efforts to tap into the cultural zeitgeist, adopting countercultural dress and engaging in behaviors such as using marijuana, taking LSD, and having encounter group therapy. With these strategies, advertising executives hoped to generate advertising that communicated more effectively with their audiences (Meyers 2000).

Cable Television and the Fragmenting of the Audience, 1980s–2000s

The three networks' success reached its peak during the 1970s. CPMs for network television more than doubled from an average of $1.81 in 1971 to an average of $4.12 in 1981 (TVB 2008). But network success bred anxiety in advertisers that clutter undermined their commercials' effectiveness. One study claimed that viewer recall of specific commercials declined from 18 percent in 1965 to only 7 percent

in 1981 (Schudson 1984). However, a greater threat was the rise of alternative program services delivered by cable operators. Regulatory policies had for decades protected broadcasters from competition from wired and "pay" television services, but regulators' increasing concerns about network hegemony at last led them to curb network power. When cable operators were allowed to import distant signals after 1977, they could finally provide competition for broadcast network programming. Cable "penetration" into households rose from about 10 percent in 1973 to 34 percent in 1983, to about 70 percent in 2000 (TVB 2008).

Early cable audiences paid subscription fees to the cable operator, which selected cable networks and paid a portion of those subscription fees, ranging from a few cents to several dollars per subscriber, to each network in exchange for commercial-free programming. Advertisers worried that these audiences would forsake broadcast television for commercial-free paid services (Turow 1997). However, most cable networks soon began selling advertising time, establishing a "dual revenue stream" of both advertising and subscription fees that enabled them to offer specialized, niche programming designed for specific demographics. Theme networks offering nonstop programming in one area, such as news, music, children's programming, or sports, could make do with transient audiences tuning in briefly because the greater proportion of their revenues, up to 80 percent, came from subscribers, who paid a flat fee whether they watched the network or not (Vogel 2001). Cable networks, then, were not compelled to attract and retain large audiences in order to be profitable; they simply had to keep programming costs low while bringing in specific audiences attractive to cable operators seeking new subscribers, and to particular advertisers seeking more defined audiences at a lower price.

The three broadcast networks began to lose their share of the national audience; from a peak of about 90 percent in the 1970s, broadcast viewership gradually dropped to 40 percent of prime-time viewing in the 2000s. As cable networking expanded dramatically, viewer options increased to hundreds of cable networks. Broadcasters and advertisers worried about "audience fragmentation," the term for the splintering of the mass audience that once gathered around three networks but now was spread across a multitude of cable and broadcast networks. By 1993, Coca-Cola chief Donald Keough noted, "We can no longer buy tonnage ... audiences are being carved up into smaller channels of communication ... You start asking yourself: What is media?" (*Advertising Age* 1993). Viewer mobility presented serious challenges to advertisers used to the ease of accessing national mass audiences with one air time buy at a network, as well as to the broadcasters who could no longer offer such access.

Unable to beat the cable system, broadcasters responded by joining it. The broadcast networks, freed from regulatory constraints, merged with film studios, cable networks, satellite operators, and cable operators. By the mid-1990s, each major broadcast network was part of a large media conglomerate heavily invested in cable programming.[3] In 2002, for example, CBS with its sister broadcast network UPN captured only 18 percent of viewers; however, when combined with its sister cable networks, MTV, BET, VH1, Nickelodeon, Comedy Central, and others owned by its then-corporate parent Viacom, they collectively captured nearly 26 percent of the viewing audience (*Broadcasting & Cable* 2002). Since gathering mass audiences around one network or on one medium was no longer viable, aggregating demographically specific audiences (such as youth at MTV) across a group of networks would allow Viacom to attract advertisers interested in "one-stop shopping" for audiences.[4] Other media conglomerates, such as Time Warner, have organized their divisions by how heavily they rely on advertising revenue (magazines, television networks, websites) or on unit sales or subscriptions (films, books, cable service).

Despite the relative affluence of early cable's audiences, advertisers paid lower prices for cable time, a price gap that continued through the early 2000s. In 2001, while broadcast networks charged about $15 per thousand viewers during prime time, cable networks charged between $6 and $10 (Higgins & Romano 2002). An oversupply of cable time, exacerbated by the increasing number of cable networks, helped keep prices down. More important, broadcast networks provided larger single audiences,

averaging 5 to 10 million households, whereas the top cable networks averaged 1 million. Advertisers seeking "reach" were willing to pay the premium. Paradoxically, then, audience fragmentation has made broadcast network audiences even more valuable to advertisers. As individual program ratings decline, advertisers find themselves bidding up the price in competition with each other because they each must purchase more time in order to reach the same number of viewers as before. By 2007 the average broadcast network CPMs were nearly $23, the highest ever, despite falling audience shares (TVB 2008).

Television and New Media

Clearly television is no longer an appliance watched by the entire family in the living room. Viewers "placeshift" when viewing programs on mobile devices – laptops, cell phones, game consoles, iPods – and "timeshift" by using digital video recorders and online streaming. Younger viewers especially are becoming accustomed to watching "what I want, when I want, where I want" (Palmer 2007), a habit that threatens existing distribution channels, audience measurement systems, and scheduling strategies. The digitization and networking of digital media over the Internet "disintermediates" the relationships between broadcast networks and local station affiliates, between cable operators and cable networks, and undermines traditional business models, as viewers sidestep subscription fees by online file sharing and avoid advertising by timeshifting on digital video recorders.

Consequently, television networks and advertisers are returning to some of the strategies of the radio era, such as product placement and single sponsorship, which integrate program and advertisement. For example, NBC's *Heroes* features its sponsor Nissan's automobiles; Fox's *24* features Ford automobiles; and CBS's *Survivor* includes products such as Doritos and Mountain Dew. Advertising agencies have raced to serve their clients accordingly; J. Walter Thompson plans to "migrate entertainment to the core of our thinking" in an effort to solve "this equation of marrying the advertiser and their enterprise and interfacing efficiently with what Hollywood does on a daily basis" (Goldsmith 2005). However, integrating products into entertainment reintroduces the problems evident in the radio era: advertisers risk negative associations (say, if a star misbehaves) and they lose the mobility of advertising that is separable from the program. Furthermore, product integration may be effective only for some products, such as automobiles and packaged goods; for other advertisers it may not solve the problem of how to reach increasingly mobile audiences.

As television networks and advertisers scramble to reorganize the way they reach, measure, value, buy, and sell audiences, they face an even greater challenge than audiences' increased mobility. Media industries have been built on revenue from advertisers purchasing access to time and space adjacent to exclusive content in which they enjoyed guaranteed access to that content's audience. In a digital networked environment, not only are audiences more mobile, but so is *content*. Just as audiences are no longer captive, content is no longer exclusive. Digital copies are instant, perfect, and easy to transmit on computer networks. Controlling content in order to organize and buy and sell audiences is thus becoming more difficult.

Meanwhile, Google has become one of the single largest advertising companies, bringing in $16 billion in revenues in 2007 (Google 2008), not by controlling advertiser access to audiences or audience access to programming, but by directing users *away* from its site toward content they seek. Through its YouTube subsidiary, Google applies search principles to short video clips; in one month of 2007, YouTube claimed 71 million viewers scattered across millions of videos varying from homemade "user-generated content" to professionally produced programming (Donohue 2007). If search and other yet undeveloped Internet applications prove more effective than traditional advertising media, advertisers will need to reevaluate not only the way they find audiences but the way they conceive the very practice of advertising. As one observer notes, "Marketers are in a slow, denial-laden shift from buying content-attached audiences, like those of television shows, to buying intent-attached audiences, like those of search engines and personal video recorders" (Battelle 2003, 68).

This brief survey of electronic media from early radio to online media should suggest how deeply advertisers and the advertising industry have been involved not only in its financial underpinnings but in its key cultural forms. But involvement does not imply identity; I am not suggesting that we should collapse all distinctions between advertising and the electronic media it enables. Instead, I have tried to show more clearly how conflicting agendas, goals, and strategies play out across different institutions, such as networks, advertisers, and agencies, shifting the balance of power among and within those institutions and changing their very structure. These shifts and changes have complex causes — economic, technological, regulatory, and cultural — but too often the role of advertisers in these changes has been oversimplified. Both advertisers and the advertising industry are diverse; different advertisers and agencies may pursue competing ideas, strategies, and goals. As scholars consider the current drastic changes in media industries, they cannot afford to ignore past eras of technological and cultural transition. As programming control, financial models, and cultural forms evolve in new media, the best analyses of these changes must incorporate discussion of the complex, conflicted, variable, and changing field of advertising.

Notes

1 For more on 1950s television commercials, see Samuel (2001).

2 The Financial Interest and Syndication Rules (1971–95), preventing networks from owning or participating in the syndication profits of programs, and the Prime Time Access Rules (1971–95), which effectively forced the networks to give up an hour of prime time to local stations, also affected network programming strategies.

3 In 2008, the Disney conglomerate includes broadcast network ABC; cable networks ESPN, Disney, ABC Family; film studios Disney and Pixar. General Electric

owns NBC; Universal Studios; Bravo, CNBC, Sci-Fi; and Telemundo. News Corp owns Fox; FX, Fox News, Fox Sports; and 20th Century Fox.

4 Unfortunately for Viacom, most advertisers resisted the "one-stop" concept, preferring to retain flexibility.

Owner Sumner Redstone spun off CBS in late 2005 to ensure that its predicted decline would not jeopardize the cable networks' continued success.

References

Advertising Age (1993) Coca-Cola will look anywhere for creativity. 12 April.

Advertising & Selling (1931) When will radio quit selling its "editorial pages"? 22 July.

Anderson, C. (1994) *Hollywood TV: The Studio System in the Fifties*. University of Texas Press, Austin.

Angus, H. (1931) Preparation of commercial copy is hardest task of radio advertiser. *Broadcast Advertising*, December.

Angus, H. (1932) The importance of stars in your radio program. *Broadcast Advertising*, February.

Arlen, M. (1980) *Thirty Seconds*. Penguin Books, New York.

Arnold, F. (1927) *Commercial Broadcasting: The Fourth Dimension of Advertising*. NBC, New York.

Banning, W. (1946) *Commercial Broadcast Pioneer*. Harvard University Press, Cambridge.

Barnouw, E. (1978) *The Sponsor*. Oxford University Press, New York.

Battelle, J. (2003) Gone in 30 seconds. *Business 2.0*, November.

Baughman, J. (2007) *Same Time, Same Station*. Johns Hopkins University Press, Baltimore.

Boddy, W. (1990) *Fifties Television*. University of Illinois Press, Urbana.

Broadcasting & Cable (2002) The corporate scoreboards. 2 December.

Brower, C. (1974) *Me, and Other Advertising Geniuses*. Doubleday, Garden City.

Brown, L. A. (1932) Radio broadcasting as an advertising medium. In O'Neill, N. (ed.) *The Advertising Agency Looks at Radio*. Appleton, New York, pp. 1–11.

Brown, L. (1971) *Television: The Business behind the Box*. Harcourt Brace Jovanovich, New York.

Browne, N. (1987) The political economy of the television (super)text. In Newcomb, H. (ed.) *Television: The Critical View*. Oxford University Press, New York, pp. 585–99.

Carroll, C. (1944) Memo, 28 April. JWT Files, Duke University.

Donohue, S. (2007) YouTube dominates internet video. *Multichannel News*, 30 November.

Douglas, S. (1987) *Inventing American Broadcasting, 1899–1922*. Johns Hopkins University Press, Baltimore.

Dygert, W. (1939) *Radio as an Advertising Medium*. McGraw-Hill, New York.

Ewen, S. (1976) *Captains of Consciousness*. McGraw-Hill, New York.

Fox, S. (1984) *The Mirror Makers*. Vintage, New York.

Gledhill, C. (1988) Pleasurable negotiations. In Pribram, E. D. (ed.) *Female Spectators*. Verso, New York, pp. 64–89.

Goldsmith, J. (2005) Media ad-ventures. *Daily Variety*, 20 January.

Google (2008) Investor relations. At http://investor.google.com/releases/2007Q4.html, accessed February 24, 2008.

Harrington, T. (1949) Can an advertising agency handle television at a profit? *The Advertising Agency*, May.

Higgins, J. and Romano, A. (2002) Cheaper by the thousand. *Broadcasting & Cable*, 4 February.

Hilmes, M. (1995). Beating the networks at their own game. Presentation, Society for Cinema Studies, Pittsburgh.

Hilmes, M. (1997) *Radio Voices*. University of Minnesota Press, Minneapolis.

Hughes, L. (1939) Should you hitch your business to a star? *Sales Management*, 1 March.

J. Walter Thompson (1929) Staff Meeting Minutes, 6 August. JWT Files, Duke University.

J. Walter Thompson (1930) Staff Meeting Minutes, 12 August. JWT Files, Duke University.

Lears, J. (1994) *Fables of Abundance*. Basic Books, New York.

Leiss, W., Kline, S., Jhally, S., and Botterill, J. (2005) *Social Communication in Advertising*, 3rd edn. Routledge, New York.

Litman, B. (1990) Network oligopoly power: an economic analysis. In Balio, T. (ed.) *Hollywood in the Age of Television*. Unwin Hyman, Cambridge, pp. 115–44.

McChesney, R. W. (1993) *Telecommunications, Mass Media, and Democracy*. Oxford University Press, New York.

Marchand, R. (1985) *Advertising the American Dream*. University of California Press, Berkeley.

Mashon, K. M. (1996) NBC, J. Walter Thompson, and the evolution of prime-time television programming and sponsorship, 1946–1958. Doctoral dissertation, University of Maryland, College Park.

Meyers, C. (2000) Psychedelics and the advertising man. *Columbia Journal of American Studies* **4**, 114–27.

Meyers, C. (2005) Admen and the shaping of American commercial broadcasting, 1926–1950. Doctoral dissertation, University of Texas, Austin.

NBC (1926) Pamphlet. James Papers, State Historical Society of Wisconsin, Madison.

N. W. Ayer (nd. [ca. 1956]) The development of the packager. N. W. Ayer Archives, New York.

Palmer, S. (2007) Broadcasters: creating and monetizing content. Paper presented at the Digital TV: Beyond HD & DTV Conference, Columbia University, 2 November.

Price, J. (1978) *The Best Thing on TV: Commercials*. Penguin Books, New York.

Robinson, H. (1932) What the radio audience wants. In O'Neill, N. (ed.) *The Advertising Agency Looks at Radio*, Appleton, New York, pp. 42–54.

Sahlins, M. (1976) *Culture and Practical Reason*. University of Chicago Press, Chicago.

Samuel, L. (2001) *Brought to You By*. University of Texas Press, Austin.

Schudson, M. (1984) *Advertising, the Uneasy Persuasion*. Basic Books, New York.

Shanks, B. (1979) Network television: advertising agencies and sponsors. In Wright, J. (ed.) *The Commercial Connection*. Dell, New York, pp. 94–107.

Smulyan, S. (1994) *Selling Radio*. Smithsonian, Washington DC.

Sterling, C. and Kittross, J. (1978) *Stay Tuned*. Wadsworth, Belmont.

Television Bureau of Advertising/TVB Online (2008). Research Track. At http://tvb.org/nav/build_frameset.asp?url=/rcentral/index.asp, accessed February 24, 2008.

Turow, J. (1997) *Breaking up America*. University of Chicago Press, Chicago.

Varencove, M. (1935) The peeled ear. *Advertising & Selling*, 11 April.

Vogel, H. (2001) *Entertainment Industry Economics*, 5th edn. Cambridge University Press, New York.

Weaver, P. (1949) Memo, 26 September. NBC Records, State Historical Society of Wisconsin, Madison.

Weaver, P. (1994) *The Best Seat in the House*. Knopf, New York.

Wicke, J. (1988) *Advertising Fictions*. Columbia University Press, New York.

Williamson, J. (1978) *Decoding Advertisements*. Marion Boyars, London.

Young, J. (1949) *Adventures in Advertising*. Harper, New York.

6

New Media as Transformed Media Industry

P. David Marshall

Over the last century, a common technique in advertising has been to describe something as "new" in order to regenerate the sales of an older product. Delineating the newness of new media should stimulate a similar skepticism: is new media significantly different from its predecessors, or is "new" media just another form of technological hype that drives consumer culture to satisfy its old wants and desires?

This chapter is an exploration of the emergence of what industry, academics, and popular culture have commonly described as new media and how it is transforming the media industries. What is meant by "new media" varies somewhat, but generally it includes the Internet, video and computer games, and mobile devices including iPods, PDAs, and telephones. In its wider scope, new media is sometimes broadly defined as the digitalization of our culture; its effects and repercussions flow back into the production of older media such as film and television through new production techniques. Moreover, new media expresses a shifted relation of an audience to media use: what we are seeing is a media industry that is as much about media production, exhibition, and distribution as it is about facilitating communication among its audience. This chapter works to explore this shifted focus of the "new" in the media industries.

What's in a Name?

There are many possible entry points into making sense of the "new" of new media and linking them to the historical emergence of the media industries. One of the most effective ways is to begin with some of the principal names of Internet and web-related companies and contrast these with earlier twentieth-century media brands. The company names of media-related entities provide a fascinating history of how entities imagine their role in the social world and how they constitute themselves. And it is very clear from this study of names that something transformed from the era of broadcast companies into Internet companies. In the United States, for instance, the corporate names of the major network broadcasters expressed both a seriousness and a sense of national self-importance. Thus emerging from RCA, the Radio Corporation of America, was the *National* Broadcasting Company or NBC. Its arch-rival was the Columbia Broadcasting System or CBS, which perfected the affiliate structure of networks. Splintering from the red and blue networks of NBC was the *American* Broadcasting Company or ABC (Couzens 2004, 1634–9). These expressions of national interest are even more strongly indicated in the publicly run networks in much of the rest of the world. In Canada, there was the CBC or Canadian

Broadcasting Corporation; in Australia, the ABC: both of these, along with a host of others, were modeled on the mother of public broadcasters, the BBC. Indeed, by the 1970s a regional Canadian network launched with the name of *Global* Television Network. Although this list is far from complete, invoking the nation or perhaps something larger with the advent of satellite television was elemental in naming any major broadcasting entity in the mid-to-late twentieth century (see Collins 1990). If these national-like brands were not used, then stations were generally known in the United States in terms of their call letters, which evoked a technocratic symphony of station identification for most of the twentieth century. Smaller networks relied on family names to define their regional interests. In some national markets, stations became known purely by their signal: in Australia, the three major national commercial networks were known as Seven, Nine, and eventually Ten, and traded commercially under such names. In Britain, radio and television networks took on a numerical moniker for their simplicity but also for the pervasive centrality of the network signal.

The early commercialization of the Internet had similar patterns but their names were indexical of a shift in power and use of the new media forms. For instance, one of the major players in Internet service was CompuServe. CompuServe emerged as a company that worked to share computer time on a mainframe computer. It charged by the minute for access to the processing power of its PDP-10. The system worked under dial-up access and over time expanded as the Internet spread to service the home and business use of the Internet. At one time, it was one of the dominant companies in providing Internet service for the millions not connected to university networks. In its name, CompuServe, one can identify a clear change in the relationship to use, a change that is fundamentally different from the uses made of television: Internet company names were connected to service. Possibly because their first access to the domestic market (and the business market for that matter) was via telephone lines, there was an effort to construct the Internet's range of early companies as services replicating telephone companies (CompuServe 2007).

Successors and rivals to CompuServe played within this same realm of universal service that had been established through the ubiquity of phone service. America Online, or AOL, developed a structured Intranet that provided an organized "Internet" of content for its dial-up customers beginning in late 1991. AOL was designed for the neophyte home user of the Internet, and it was very successful at producing a comfort zone of service and information as well as connected worlds for email and "chat." Thus the first commercial generation around the Internet was the proliferation of Internet Service Providers. Once it was possible for smaller and local companies to provide access to the Internet through a bank of servers connected directly to the Internet and a bank of phone hook-ups for clients to dial-up their access, a flood of companies became service providers. Because of their originally close connection to telephony, their names invoked notions of service as opposed to any other broader claim to content or values. This was the first stage of the commercialization of the Internet: it was organized around time and perhaps a monthly fee of access. And its clients used the service and even thought of the service in a manner very similar to telephones. The key difference was that once online, the user had a different relationship to his experience and in that difference we are able to discern the second generation of both the commercialization and industrialization of the Internet.

Subscription and timed use, which represent the core profitability of the early Internet, replicated the business models of not only telephone companies but also those of cable companies. In the broader development of the industry, these kinds of business models allowed for the key companies in telephone and cable delivery to become the dominant players in successive generations of Internet delivery. Since 2000, broadband connection expanded dramatically despite the dotcom bubble economy bursting. Broadband company growth countered the collapse of many other Internet-related companies. Although dial-up Internet service providers have continued to operate in the new millennium, Internet service was increasingly concentrated with telephone and cable companies.

While there was a consolidation of ownership of Internet service providers, a fundamentally different model of industry was emerging on the Internet itself. If the service quality of names such as AOL and CompuServe expressed a different relationship to the new media form of the Internet and highlighted the quality and power of transmission, the World Wide Web has led to a very interesting group of companies that actually played with the idea that the Internet was free. The freeness of the Internet has to be thought of in two ways. First, the idea of "free" was related to the delivery of content that in the past would have cost something to receive. The Internet's origins – and the World Wide Web for that matter – were deeply connected to university culture. The original designers of Mosaic, the web browser that was the direct precursor to the commercial launch of Netscape, were graduate students from the University of Illinois. The ready expansion of use of the Internet is also related to its proliferation through the university nodes of the network of networks. Although there was nothing free in the production of the network, its ethereal quality, its connection to university and university life, and its capacity to instantly connect people from far-flung places by email exchanges at the very least embodied a sense of free exchange. In other writing, I have identified the Internet's origins as closely related to the gift economy, where the idea of sharing information or producing elaborate websites was for the benefit of others (Burnett & Marshall 2003). The persistent organizational model that connects to this history of freeness is the shareware movement, and ultimately other major computer businesses have recognized and catered to this portion of the new media economy and industry (Moore 2007).

Second, the Internet's freeness was a form of liberation from past media forms and previous techniques and structures involved with the movement of information. This notion of freeness is expressed in a kind of libertarianism that has enveloped the Internet. Beacons that have celebrated this freedom from the past and championed the openness of the Internet's possible forms of production have emerged from the Freedom Forum and John Perry Barlow (1993). Extrapolations of this form of expression have continued in the challenges to intellectual property that Lawrence Lessig among others has written and spoken about extensively (Vaidhyanathan 2001;

Lessig 2002; Lessig 2004). Quite different from the organization of broadcasting and its various levels of regulation that were generated by the fear of the power of the media, the Internet as the key element of the new media industries has attempted to herald the value of deregulation.

These two conceptions of freedom – an idea of something for nothing, and the idea of liberation from the past hierarchies – led to a kind of frivolity that rarely is part of business culture. Some of the early success stories of the Internet and the World Wide Web are the antithesis of the serious kinds of corporations that dominated mid- and late-twentieth-century media. Once again, the names reveal a great deal. Yahoo!, the original organizer of hierarchical categories of what was available on the web, is emblematic of this relationship to breaking the mold of what kind of world and industry the Internet was. Its story of formation further highlights the giddiness of the Internet, a relationship to fun as much as a relationship to information. The various search engines to emerge in this second generation of the Internet were also not clearly linked to serious missions. Ask Jeeves constructed an avatar of a butler to represent the search engine. Inktomi and Lycos, some of the largest early players, were not names where one could readily discern their purposes but were oblique references that celebrated a kind of nerd-like obscurantism. Even Amazon, the first large-scale online retailer, did not clearly identify a spatial orientation that made much sense nor did it attempt to explain its choice of retail name. Out of this cauldron of sophomoric origins emerged the company name that defined this second generation of Internet experience as a media industry – Google. Onomatopoeically, Google as a name blended the giggle with the connection to schoolboy fascination with mathematical infinity. As its connection to online use expanded, the search engine name became a recognized verb of more than one language: by 2004, the brand name Google defined the online search and became part of the popular vernacular.

Much like the scatological or ironic band names of popular music – such as the Police, U2, Anthrax, or Arctic Monkeys – which somehow lose their connotative link to shock the better known they become, Internet company names also become incorporated into everydayness and there is a collective loss of understanding of the rationale for their original choices as markers of identity. In many ways, this second generation of the Internet finally apotheosized with the rise of Google inverting the organization of culture provided by television. Television's serious exterior – epitomized by its corporate name culture – was the exact opposite of its superficial content. Certainly some programs contained the seriousness of the company and this was articulated by news-related programs, but American television was primarily the home of series such as *Gunsmoke, Leave it to Beaver, Bewitched*, and *Hogan's Heroes*. With the Internet, the corporate name expressed the fun of the very functionalist quality of Boolean searches for content.

Audience-Subject to User-Subject
· ·

Because new media forms like the Internet are elastic in their capacity to absorb other forms and practices, it is easy to lose the insight that a different industrial model has been emerging (Burnett & Marshall 2003). With television, there is a linearity in its organization that is best understood in terms of programming and is clearly laid out in forming and reforming of the audience through slightly reconfigured tastes from each half-hour and hour, and from channel to channel (see Williams 1974; Feuer 1983). The ratings system works to concretize this continuous production of the audience and form the economic and capitalization structure of the industry. The industrial model of the Internet and new media more generally is defined not by its programming, but by its ethos.

As developed above, there is some sense of exploration in new media where the experience of engagement with the form is not fully defined. As an amorphous media form, the Internet (unlike television) is not connected to a public but defines itself more centrally through a private experience. Whereas television has been designed for an open display of its content – after all, its predominant location has been the most public rooms of the house – the Internet's conveyance has been through the much more individualized experience of the computer. In that individualized and private realm, the sense of exploration and discovery has elements that are similar to the privatized experience of reading. It is a way that differentiates the individual from what others are doing – it is antisocial at least in the sense of how it connects to the flows of life around it. The ethos of new media that organizes it as an industry goes beyond this privatized reception; nonetheless, it is the private reception of the Internet that has allowed it to dominate pornography and its means of delivery. Indeed, while other industries that have used the Internet may have suffered setbacks, online pornography has been and continues to be a clear success (Burnett & Marshall 2003). The illicit and hidden structure of the industry matched well with the private, individualized delivery of content that the Internet permits and celebrates. In a similar vein, the expansion in the use of cell phones personalizes the telephone as a technology: where a landline is organized to a particular address and anyone at that address may answer the phone, the cell phone guarantees that if the call is successful the *intended individual* will answer and no one else.

To go further into the new media ethos that has helped define its success, it is necessary to work out the distinctive subjectivity that is cultivated through this industry. If we can characterize broadcast media as continually producing an "audience-subjectivity," that is, an experience that can be collectively organized and sold as a coherent commodity, new media forms such as the Internet produce what I would call a "user-subjectivity" (Marshall 2006). The user-subject hails the individual to see themselves *producing* their cultural activity. Bruns (2005) captures this activity through his term "produser," where the individual through their online activities is implicated in producing as much as consuming. Placing this production of cultural activity into an economic model identifies some of the most successful variations of new media. Thus we find the user-subject is hailed to personalize their cell phone: not only is the communication itself a form of production that connects the cell phone user to others in time and space more and more accurately, it is also "sold" as a technology that allows the user to personalize it both through ringtones and the collection of images and videos. Industrially, the selling of music through ringtones, which has expanded to become a major determinant for the selling of popular music in Japan and a major source of revenue in North America and Europe (May & Hearn 2005, 197), is an example of a successful economic model embracing the idea of the user-subject. Similarly, the success of both online and stand-alone video games is related to their capacity to produce the sense of self-production (Marshall 2006). In the context of the game, the user-as-player invents their actions – albeit within the structure of a virtual world, a virtual sporting event, or a virtual fighting arena.

User-subjectivity forms the basis of the most successful new media entities. Enabling users to fabricate their own stories, their own connections, and their own social networks provides an interesting adaptation of how phone companies facilitated connection and use of the phone through simply laying the cables and wires. In the various online services that have emerged in the latest generation of the Internet, what is highlighted is the ease of use for personal expression, exhibition, and distribution. The rapid proliferation of weblogs or blogs from the early part of this century to 2006 was tied to simplifying the requirement of knowledge of html for setting up a web page. Augmenting this with software structures that allowed others to post and thread discussions created the ubiquitous Internet subject position of the "blogger." Similarly, the successful expansion of E-Bay, the online auctioneer, was very much related to its ease of use: uploading and downloading images, simplicity in the presentation of any product, and ultimately the capacity of any user to quickly and effortlessly participate in an auction all made E-Bay a successful Internet company.

Interactivity: Enabling the User

From the perspective of producing this quality of user-subjectivity, the idea of interactivity can be thought of quite differently in terms of how it is deployed to expand the new media industrial model. Interactivity is involved in producing relationships that move between screen and individual divide or interface. Economically, as a new media form, interactivity is an enabler or facilitator that allows for

greater self-production/expression. To make sense of this process of enablement and how it fits into the emerging industry ethos, interactivity can be understood in three related ways.

First, interactivity is very much about cybernetics and producing systems where individual users are included in that system. Thus a successful new media business model is one that attempts to encompass an activity that is deemed valuable by users. Interactivity then is a structure of feedback loops that make the experience containable within a given system. The best way to imagine this is the structuring of virtual worlds such as Second Life or Everquest (Castronova 2005; Taylor 2006). The virtual world sets up a space that in its vastness of place and geography, in its construction of possibility, and in its perpetual potential in meeting others and constructing new scenarios and new exchanges, the player/user is happy to inhabit and play.

Second, interactivity is a deployment of "smartness" and in this way anticipates a user's desires and caters to them. On the simplest level, smart technology may streamline and demystify the production of an html weblog or Facebook site; it may structure its order and categorization into patterns that make sense to the user and further enable productive expression. Similarly, interactivity as smart technology may facilitate the uploading and downloading of images taken on a cell phone to simplify their exchange into several other formats, including structuring something into the now ever-present "slideshow." Embodying all of the deployments of smart interactive features into various digital media is very much about democratizing the technology. Providing an intuitive connection to the user's desires makes the interactive quality of smartness a channel for the expression of the self that reverses the democratic desires that underpinned older media forms of simple access. In essence, interactivity as smart technology is designed to expand *productive* capacity of the individual user.

Third, and perhaps most importantly, interactivity is designed to facilitate the expansion of expression with others and develop the engagement with new social networks. The interactive in this sense is less concerned with a technology/user interface and more about the facilitation of human-to-human communication. Email, in its capacity of providing connection between people, has formed the base of expanding systems that draw the user into a particular use pattern. For instance, Yahoo's success is at least partly attributable to the way people use its service to access their email regularly. Yahoo's free email intersects with its other information services and advertising structures. The expansion of hotmail is often mythologized in terms of the way that its growth moved from one user to another – virally – in an expanding friendship network. Internet relay chat programs that worked in real-time dimensions of exchanges were another version of this kind of inter-activity that has been privileged in new media. Chat programs that populate online games allow for a further investment in new media at an interpersonal exchange level. Text-messaging via cell phones replicates these models and extends the interactivity both spatially and temporally. Services such as Skype, which provide Internet voice and video connection along with chat programs, try to integrate the possible forms of interpersonal communication – voice, video, and written – among users chosen by the individual. They add to this model of interpersonal connection services, which are much like the old country party lines where individuals join a conversation on a particular issue. Essential to all these services is their facilitation of social networks. Their form of interactivity is to produce what White (1996) has described as transactional spaces, spaces of exchange that allow for other services and perhaps other products to be inserted. So, paralleling the interactive quality of new media is the commercial message that attempts to twin with the human-to-human forms of communication.

In these elaborate structures of interactivity, one finds the economic models of new media forms that are often in contradistinction to the broadcast models of television and radio. New media forms interweave the interpersonal to construct new spaces for the generation of economic activity. The industrial component of this model is very sophisticated in its production of traffic. Pre-existing social networks become fundamental to the sustenance of new media. As opposed to early theories of the anonymous self being at the center of Internet activity (Turkle 1995), one has to understand that knowing someone builds the network outward. Strong social bonds more or less establish the significance of a communication form such as a cell phone. Similarly, strong social bonds generally determine the range of users one is connected to via services such as Skype. These close connections form the nodes of activity and use in new media. The expansion into wider use is accomplished in two ways: channeling and then spreading.

Channeling in this new media industry sense is working to get some form of social activity filtered through its electronic gateways. In some senses, it is the transformation of one kind of task or social moment that is now *mediated* by an electronic layer of exchange. It is worthwhile to list these moments of channeling that have worked with some success in contemporary culture. As noted above, email channels the range of correspondences into a given electronic and network structure in its at least partial replacement of mail, private correspondence and memoranda if nothing else. The free email services of hotmail, gmail, and yahoo thus produce an easy-to-use space to channel traffic through specific sites. Electronic organizers, BlackBerries, cell phones, and online calendars work to channel our organization in their replacement of paper versions of how we plan our everyday lives. E-vite, a company that works to channel our practices of invitation to a variety of social functions, has successfully colonized the interpersonal dimension of party organization (Marshall 2004). E-vite then becomes a channel through which the simplest and perhaps the most personal get-togethers are planned. Birthday parties, holiday drinks, and book launches are now partially channeled through E-vite's sophisticated organization of call and rsvp through email. E-Bay channels the physicality of an auction and the logistics of organizing such a face-to-face structure through its online system of presenting, displaying, and distributing goods. Skype, in its latest version, transforms any phone number listed into a hyper-link that successfully dials the number via Skype's system. There is a cumulative effect of all these moments and uses: greater portions of our everyday lives become mediated through these information and communication technologies. For instance, the computer becomes a ubiquitous channel for both work and home life and works to integrate our working self with our private self.

Spreading identifies the expansion of existing social networks and is provisioned by the new media technology. If channeling represents the colonizing of experience for its relocation in some electronic reincarnation, spreading refers to the capacity of new media technologies to interconnect and make new, larger networks. There may be weaker social bonds in the way new media spreads the network, but the capacity to extend to larger and larger groups is intensified because the techniques are forms of interpersonal communication or, at the very least, resemble interpersonal forms of connection. The most obvious examples of spreading as a primary new media business are Facebook, MySpace, and Friendster. Within these social network platforms, there are structured systems to build personal networks through invitations. These invitations are differently structured than the E-vite system in their invocation of acknowledged friendship. Facebook, for instance, produces personal websites/presences that are defined between their public and accessible locations and those designated for acknowledged friends. Each person's Facebook site is thus an exclusive club for a network of friends; as well in its outer ring public presentation it is a form of promotion of the self and a clear point to expand the friendship network. The number of friends defines the popularity of a particular person and their Facebook site. The proliferating numbers also point to the new systems of value that new media produce through these techniques of spreading. For corporate owners of these sites – News Corp purchased MySpace in 2005, while Microsoft took an ownership stake in Facebook in 2007 – the key value generated is traffic. The number of people in aggregate involved in exchanges via social networks is in the tens of millions and this connection can be spread to an array of interested companies and corporations for connection. A secondary value for the corporations is the generation of information and content so that commercial messages can be better targeted toward the most likely consumers. For the individuals involved, the key value is making connections and then sustaining and building on those connections. Because of the extent of the network, the social

network offers the possibility for fame or infamy in its viral capacity to intersect with more and more people. Established entertainment and political personalities use their social network site as a place both to establish their relationship with a fan base and to maintain some kind of continuous connection.

The new media economic model of channeling and spreading must be understood as a comprehensive challenge to the way in which we should study the media industry and develop media industry studies. In other words, new media is invasive as an economic model for the entire industry. It is quite evident that the television industry has invested heavily in innovating new relationships to their programs through developing websites, blogs, and full or partial content of their programs. The objective is to establish a more social networked connection with their audience. And certainly the generation of programs and films detailed in Jenkins' (2006) work in *Convergence Culture* underlines the intensive efforts to create cult followings as well as deepened participatory moments for new reality programs and intricate drama programs.

Understanding the New Media Industry: The Case of YouTube

To comprehend this tectonic shift in how the media industry operates, it is worthwhile pulling together what we have developed here in a brief study of YouTube. The name, YouTube, sets up once again a different relationship to the idea of media and media use and replicates the insouciant yet service orientation that envelops new media companies. YouTube, in its rapid rise from first appearing in late 2005, has managed to develop a unique site for the presentation of videos of less than 10 minutes in length. The content has not been overly determined by existing networks and distributors, but rather is either the production of users or the cutting and pasting of passages from the mainstream flow of media for its iteration online. To add to this user construction is the flattening of content: although there are various techniques in place to identify popular videos, there is no differentiation between commercially produced content and home videos that have been uploaded to the site. Critical to the success of YouTube is its connection to further distribution via email networks and links on social network sites. Thus YouTube's site is not the end point, but rather the starting point for a kind of viral movement of video content from friend to friend, email post to Facebook site.

There are further efforts on YouTube to create followings and patterns in how it is used. On a basic level, the user searches for interesting content using key words. The user might remember a singer and want to hear what that singer has produced of late; but just as likely is the random access of the unknown by interesting titles. What we are witnessing via YouTube is a different configuration of what is popular and successful in contemporary culture. The popularity of a particular video emerges out of a complex web of interpersonal exchanges and interchanges that ultimately lead to a heavily viewed video on the YouTube site. YouTube also has developed sites described as "channels" where those interested in specific content can congregate or where an individual source of programming can be grouped and constructed into something resembling a serial. The successful 2006–7 video diary of *Lonelygirl15* – which ultimately turned out to be fictional – established an audience base for periodic new "episodes" about a home-schooled teen who lived with strict evangelical Christian parents and made video confessionals about her life. Micro-niche groups – for instance, lovers of Brazilian women's feet – have a channel devoted to their particular fetish. What makes these sites more interactive and enabling for the user is the possibility of providing a written commentary that can be accessed by anyone viewing a particular video. The effect of this add-on "chat program" feature to any exhibited video is to further develop a social network around any particular video content.

There are many other dimensions of YouTube that are deserving of a much longer study; but what can be concluded from this brief discussion is that YouTube intersects well with the new media economic model of spreading and channeling. It effectively ensures that its content is both networked outward through other techniques of interpersonal communication and it produces the capacity to

build niche groups of users closely attached in a cult-like way to particular content. Its very indeterminacy allows the users to construct its meaning: thus YouTube's success is that it works to service the productive capacities of its various users and to allow that produced content to lead to social connection. YouTube has blended the open content structure of telephones – where the conversation is contingent but ultimately valuable to its users – with an engaged spectatorship that shifts video culture dramatically toward its access via the Internet and virally at least away from its former source on television.

New media forms such as YouTube, social networks, games, and mobile media allow us to rethink the way in which we need to comprehend media industry studies. The media industry is now a much more complex entity than its previous incarnations with print, popular music, radio, television, and film. As we have detailed, the media industry has both in an elaborate and sometimes uncertain way integrated an understanding of its audience as users. Likewise, the industry has realized the new undulating and opaque divides between the realm of the public and the private and, in that understanding, has learned to play in the now-connected dimensions of mass communication and interpersonal communication. As an industry that now straddles in a different way the public and the private, the media industry has an increased sensibility with the way new media technologies dramatically transform the divisions between work and leisure.

Perhaps the best way to express this new complexity is to understand the media industry as a convergence of media *and* communication where the communicative dimensions of the media industry have invaded, informed, and mutated the media elements. This form of convergence is not so much technologically inspired; rather, media–communication convergence implies that the "product" or cultural artifact is less fixed and stable and is subject to its transformation through communication channels/discussions and through forms of exhibition and expression by its users. Media industry studies needs to be adept at understanding the economic and cultural patterns and implications of this media–communication nexus.

References

Barlow, J. P. (1993) Putting old wine into new bottles: the economy of ideas. *Wired* [Online] **2**.

Bruns, A. (2005) *Gatewatching: Collaborative Online News Production*. Peter Lang, New York.

Burnett, R. and Marshall, P. D. (2003) *Web Theory: An Introduction*. Routledge, London.

Castronova, E. (2005) *Synthetic Worlds: The Business and Culture of Online Games*. University of Chicago Press, Chicago.

Collins, R. (1990) *Culture, Communication, and National Identity: The Case of Canadian Television*. University of Toronto Press, Toronto.

CompuServe. (2007) *Wikipedia: CompuServe*. At http://en.wikipedia.org/wiki/Compuserve, accessed February 8, 2008.

Couzens, M. (2004) Networks: United States. In Newcomb, H. (ed.) *Encyclopedia of Television*, 2nd edn. Fitzroy Dearborn, New York, pp. 1634–9.

Feuer, J. (1983) The concept of live television: ontology as ideology. In Kaplan, E. A. (ed.) *Regarding Television: Critical Approaches: An Anthology*. University Publications of America, Frederick, pp. 12–22.

Jenkins, H. (2006) *Convergence Culture: Where Old and New Media Collide*. New York University Press, New York.

Lessig, L. (2002) *The Future of Ideas: The Fate of the Commons in a Connected World*. Vintage Books, New York.

Lessig, L. (2004) *Free Culture: How Big Media Uses Technology and the Law to Lock Down Culture*. Penguin, New York.

Marshall, P. D. (2004) *New Media Cultures*. Hodder Arnold, London.

Marshall, P. D. (2006) New media – new self: the changing power of the celebrity. In Marshall, P. D. (ed.) *The Celebrity Culture Reader*. Routledge, London, pp. 634–44.

May, H. and Hearn, G. (2005) Mobile phone as media. *International Journal of Cultural Studies* **8**, 195–211.

Moore, C. L. (2007) Don't panic!: An unhurried critique of copyright and the potential for alternatives. Doctoral dissertation, University of Wollongong, Wollongong NSW.

Taylor, T. L. (2006) *Play Between Worlds: Exploring Online Game Culture*. MIT Press, Cambridge.

Turkle, S. (1995) *Life on the Screen: Identity in the Age of the Internet*. Simon & Schuster, New York.

Vaidhyanathan, S. (2001) *Copyrights and Copywrongs: The Rise of Intellectual Property and How it Threatens Creativity*. New York University Press, New York.

White, P. B. (1996) Online services: the emerging battle for transactional space. *Media International Australia* **79**, 4–11.

Williams, R. (1974) *Television: Technology and Cultural Form*. Wesleyan University Press, Hanover.

Part II

Theory

·····································

Editors' Introduction

....

In theorizing media industry studies, the authors in this section have given us five visions with which to structure our thinking and interventions in this field. The models they propose are all effective means of organizing analyses of media in relation to constructs of industry. All of the arguments are meant to be applicable across media forms, technologies, spaces, and places. These essays work to position global media convergence within a larger perspective while presenting, as Michael Curtin writes, concepts that allow scholars to take into account "both the general and the particular, both the forest and the trees." These authors also help us to think more proactively about the many directions we can take in this field.

Douglas Kellner employs a theoretical framework for analyzing media industries drawn largely from the Frankfurt School and British cultural studies. His essay outlines a critical media/cultural studies model that engages production, political economy, textual analysis, and audience analysis as a means of supporting social change, media literacy, and media activism. Kellner lays out a detailed road map of key dynamics in political economic study, emphasizing the role of ideology and power and their impact on critical studies of media culture and industries. He rejects the notion that political economy and cultural studies are at odds with one another and calls on media industry scholars to rise above what he labels as an artificial divide "rooted in an arbitrary academic division of labor." Arguing that it is imperative to put the economic and political into dialogue with the cultural, technological, and social, Kellner does just that by "unpacking the implosions between news and entertainment" and linking his larger critique of media industries to an activist politics.

Michael Curtin helps us understand what it means to be "thinking globally" when studying media industries. Articulating a theoretical model that moves beyond Anglo-American media, he identifies principles and tendencies shaping media dynamics worldwide. His essay re-envisions how we view media "centers" by speaking of "nodes in the transnational flow of culture, talent, and resources" instead. Curtin's construct of media capital also complicates previous models of analyzing global media. In particular, he calls attention to the movement of creative labor, the fluidity of geographical boundaries, and the variability of cultural politics around the world. Integrating traditions in media studies with cultural geography, he discusses markets, texts, audiences, and the state to illuminate the many variables shaping the contexts of media production and consumption worldwide.

In her essay on regional media, Cristina Venegas theorizes transnational and local media flows in relation to Latin American cinema. Her case study looks at trade relations, economic alliances, cultural policies, industrial histories, and political realities to present the regional as a valuable theoretical tool for media industries researchers. She defines the idea of region and alerts the reader to its many constitutive elements. Along with putting the regional in dialogue with the global, the international, the national, and the local, her essay indicates how ideas of unity and difference function in relation to a regional approach. Venegas examines shifts in government support, market behavior, industry initiatives, and production throughout Latin America via the lens of region, ultimately theorizing this trope as a set of dynamic and potentially political forces inspiring community activism, trade, distinctive artistic practices, and cultural identity and exchange.

After these considerations of media industries at the global and regional level, Nitin Govil examines how the national functions. Govil offers a complex discussion of how "thinking nationally" actually creates avenues for thinking globally and locally as well. Looking at how media industries "think" nationally via considerations of scale (piracy), subsidies (location shooting), and subjectivity (diasporic media and cultural citizenship), Govil examines the opportunities afforded by media globalization in relation to the nation. In mapping and imagining the trajectory of the national, he surveys a range of media industries – Chinese, Canadian, American, South African, and British – and views the national as a framework through which local and global capabilities are exploited. He makes ideological, economic, and cultural connections between these paradigms, highlighting why there remain powerful incentives for media industries to continue to think nationally even in the global age of convergence.

In the final essay of this section, Mark Deuze picks up the idea of convergence explored in several previous essays and theorizes it specifically in relation to media work. Deuze defines convergence as "blurring the lines between economics (work) and culture (meaning), between production and consumption, between making and using media, and between active or passive spectatorship of mediated culture." This definition suggests that a key challenge in theorizing media industries lies in adequately addressing the "process, content, and consequences of consumption and production" when current media practice includes all of them at the same time. He examines several modes of convergence, including place (sites of production), identity and experience, labor, workspace, markets, and regulatory contexts. All are seen as constructs that exceed simple technologically based definitions of convergence and create their own cultural logics. For scholars of media industries, Deuze brings a holistic view of the new media ecosystem – a view that sees the media landscape in terms of "webs" of diffuse power structures, transnational connections, and citizen-consumers in a fluid media marketplace.

7

Media Industries, Political Economy, and Media/Cultural Studies
An Articulation

....

Douglas Kellner

The media industries today stand at the center of our economy, politics, culture, and everyday life.[1] Radio, television, film, digital media, and the other products of media culture provide materials out of which individuals in contemporary media and consumer societies forge their very identities, including sense of self, notion of what it means to be male or female, and conception of class, ethnicity and race, nationality, and sexuality. Media culture helps shape both an individual's and a society's view of the world, defining good or evil, their positive ideals and sense of who they are, as well as who and what are seen as threats and enemies, creating, in some cases, sharp divisions between "us" and "them." Media stories provide the symbols, myths, and resources through which individuals constitute a common culture and through their appropriation become part of the culture and society. Media spectacles demonstrate who has power and who is powerless, who is allowed to exercise force and violence, and who is not. They dramatize and legitimate the powers that be and show the powerless that they must stay in their places or be oppressed.

The media industries are powerful forces in contemporary societies, and it is essential to comprehend how they work in order to understand, act in, and transform the environment in which we live our lives. The media industries produce entertainment, news, and information; they are commercial enterprises and thrive on advertising, thus helping to reproduce a consumer society. The media industries are an essential economic force, helping manage and promote consumer demand, constructing needs and fantasies through advertising and entertainment. Further, the media are key instruments of political power, constituting a terrain upon which political battles are fought and providing instruments for political manipulation and domination.

In this essay, I discuss the potential contributions of a critical media/cultural studies perspective to theorizing media industries. First I show the importance of the Frankfurt School and their theory of the culture industry for conceptualizing the media industries. This is followed by discussions of how a model developed by the Frankfurt School and British cultural studies that engages production and political economy, textual analysis, and audience reception study can provide comprehensive perspectives to engage media industries and their production, texts, audiences, and impacts.[2] I then offer a proposed model of a critical media/cultural studies to engage media industries. One of my goals is to stress the importance of critical analysis of both news and entertainment, and the need to combine history, social theory, political economy, and media/cultural studies in order to properly contextualize, analyze, interpret, and criticize products of the media industries. The project thus requires inter- or supra-disciplinary perspectives to engage the full range of the import of media industries.

The Frankfurt School and the Culture Industry
● ●

The Frankfurt School inaugurated critical communications studies in the 1930s and combined political economy of the media, cultural analysis of texts, and audience reception studies of the social and ideological effects of mass culture and communications.[3] Organized around the German Institute for Social Research in Frankfurt in the 1930s, their core members were Jewish radicals who later went into exile to the US after Hitler's rise to power. Establishing themselves in a small institute in New York affiliated with Columbia University, the Institute for Social Research, they developed analyses of the culture industry that had emerged as a key institution of social hegemony in the era that they called state-monopoly capitalism (Kellner 1989). Max Horkheimer, Theodor W. Adorno, Herbert Marcuse, and Walter Benjamin (the latter of whom was loosely affiliated with the Institute) analyzed the new forms of corporate and state power during a time in which giant corporations ruled the capitalist economies and the might of the state grew significantly under the guise of fascism, Russian communism, and the state capitalism of Roosevelt's New Deal, which required a sustained government response to the crisis of the economic Depression in the 1930s. In this conjuncture, ideology played an increasingly important role in inducing consent to a diverse spectrum of social systems.

Frankfurt School theorists argued that the media were controlled by groups who employed them to further their own interests and power.[4] They were the first social theorists to see the importance of what they called the "culture industry" in the reproduction of contemporary societies, in which so-called mass culture and communications stand in the center of leisure activity, are important agents of socialization and mediators of political reality, and should be seen as primary institutions of contemporary societies with a variety of economic, political, cultural, and social effects.

They coined the term "culture industry" to signify the process of the industrialization of mass-produced culture and the commercial imperatives that drove the system. The critical theorists analyzed all mass-mediated cultural artifacts within the context of industrial production, in which the commodities of the culture industries exhibited the same features as other products of mass production: commodification, standardization, and massification. The products of the culture industry had the specific function, however, of providing ideological legitimation of the existing capitalist societies and of integrating individuals into the framework of mass culture and society.

Furthermore, the critical theorists investigated the culture industry in a political context as a form of the integration of the working class into capitalist societies. The Frankfurt School were one of the first neo-Marxian groups to examine the effects of mass culture and the rise of the consumer society on the working classes, which were to be vehicles of revolution in the classical Marxian scenario. They analyzed the ways that the culture industries were stabilizing contemporary capitalism, and accordingly they sought new strategies for political change, agencies of social transformation, and models for human emancipation that could serve as norms of social critique and goals for political struggle. Their approach suggests that to properly understand any specific form of media culture, one must understand how it is produced and distributed in a given society and how it is situated in relation to the dominant social structure. The Frankfurt School thought, for the most part, that media culture simply reproduced the existing society and manipulated mass audiences into obedience.

Despite their many virtues, there are serious flaws in the original program of critical theory that requires a radical reconstruction of the classical model of the culture industries. Overcoming the limitations of the classical model would include more concrete and empirical analyses of the political economy of the media and the processes of the production of culture; the construction of media industries and their interaction with other social institutions throughout history; and of audience reception and media effects. A reconstructed critical theory would also involve the incorporation of emergent theories of culture, the media, and society into the project, just as the classical critical theorists, and more recently Habermas, have engaged and incorporated the insights of novel theories of the day into their work. Cumulatively, such a reconstruction of the classical Frankfurt School project would update the critical theory of society and its activity of cultural criticism by incorporating contemporary developments in social and cultural theory.

In addition, the Frankfurt School dichotomy between high culture and low culture is problematical and should be superseded for a more unified model that takes culture as a spectrum and applies similar critical methods to all cultural artifacts ranging from opera to popular music, from modernist literature to soap operas. In particular, the Frankfurt School model of a monolithic mass culture contrasted with an ideal of "authentic art," which limits critical, subversive, and emancipatory moments to certain privileged artifacts of high culture, is highly problematic. The Frankfurt School position that all mass culture is ideological and debased, having the effects of duping a passive mass of consumers, is also objectionable. Instead, one should see critical and ideological moments in the full range of culture, and not limit critical moments to high culture and identify all of low culture as ideological.[5] One should also allow for the possibility that critical and subversive moments could be found in the artifacts of the cultural industries, as well as the canonized classics of high modernist culture that the Frankfurt School seemed to privilege as the site of artistic opposition and emancipation. It is also important to distinguish between the encoding and decoding of media artifacts, and to recognize that an active audience often produces its own meanings and uses for products of the cultural industries, points that I will expand upon below.

In spite of these limitations, the critical focus on media culture from the perspectives of commodification, industrialization, reification, ideology, and domination provides an optic useful as a corrective to more populist and uncritical approaches to media culture that surrender critique. Against approaches that displace concepts of ideology and domination by emphasis on audience pleasure and the construction

of meaning, the Frankfurt School is valuable for inaugurating systematic and sustained critiques of ideology and domination within the culture industry, indicating that it is not innocent and a "creative industry," as certain contemporary idiom would have it. The notion promoted by Hartley (2003) and other proponents of the "creative industries" model provides an ideological gloss of positivity on media industries. Such perspectives suggest media are inherently bastions of enlightenment, creativity, and abundance and one might prefer the Horkheimer and Adorno notion of "culture industry" that is more critical and less ideological.[6]

Moreover, on the level of metatheory, the Frankfurt School work preceded the bifurcation of the field of media and communication studies into specialized subareas with competing models and methods. This bifurcation is documented in the 1983 *Journal of Communications (JoC)* issue *Ferment in the Field* (vol. 33, no. 3). Some of the participants in this discussion of the state-of-the-art of media and communication studies noted a division in the field between a humanities-based culturalist approach that focuses primarily on texts and more empirical social science-based approaches in the study of mass-mediated communications. The culturalist approach at the time was largely textual, centered on the analysis and criticism of texts as cultural artifacts, using methods primarily derived from the humanities. The methods of communications research, by contrast, employed more empirical methodologies, ranging from straight quantitative research to interviews, participant observation, or more broadly historical research. Topics in this area included analysis of the political economy of the media, audience reception and study of media effects, media history, and the interaction of media institutions with other domains of society.

Some contributors to the 1983 *JoC* symposium suggested a liberal tolerance of different approaches, or ways in which the various approaches complemented each other or could be integrated. Yet I would suggest that the Frankfurt School approach is valuable because it provides an integral model to overcome contemporary divisions in the study of media, culture, and communications. Their studies dissected the interconnection of culture and communication in artifacts that reproduced the existing society, idealizing social norms and practices, and legitimating the dominant organization of society.

For the Frankfurt School, the study of communication and culture was integrated within critical social theory and became an important part of a theory of contemporary society, in which culture and communication were playing ever more significant roles. Certain theorists in the tradition of British cultural studies continue this project in a later conjuncture and overcome some of its limitations, as well as updating the project of analyzing the products and effects of the media industries.

British Cultural Studies and the Circuits of Culture

Over the past decades, British cultural studies has emerged as a globally influential set of approaches to the study of culture and society that has had wide international influence. The project was inaugurated by the University of Birmingham Centre for Contemporary Cultural Studies, which developed a variety of critical methods for the analysis, interpretation, and criticism of cultural artifacts. Through a set of internal debates, and responding to social struggles and movements of the 1960s and the 1970s, the Birmingham group came to focus on the interplay of representations and ideologies of class, gender, race, ethnicity, and nationality in cultural texts, including media culture. They were among the first to study the effects of newspapers, radio, television, film, and other popular cultural forms on audiences. They also focused on how various audiences interpreted and used media culture differently, analyzing the factors that made different audiences respond in contrasting ways to various media texts.

Under its director Richard Hoggart, who led the Centre from its opening in 1964 to 1968, and his successor Stuart Hall, who directed the Centre from 1968 to 1979, the Birmingham groups developed a variety of critical perspectives for the analysis, interpretation, and criticism of cultural artifacts, combining sociological theory and contextualization with literary analysis of cultural texts. The now classical period of British cultural studies from the early 1960s to the early 1980s adopted a Marxian approach to the study of culture, one especially influenced by Althusser and Gramsci.

From the beginning, British cultural studies systematically rejected high/low culture distinctions and took seriously the artifacts of media culture, while criticizing what it claimed to be the elitism of dominant literary approaches to culture. Likewise, British cultural studies overcame the limitations of the Frankfurt School notion of a passive audience in their conceptions of the popular and of an active audience that creates meanings. Reproducing the activism of oppositional groups in the 1960s and 1970s, the Birmingham school was engaged in a project aimed at a comprehensive criticism of the present configuration of culture and society, attempting to link theory and practice to orient cultural studies toward fundamental social transformation. British cultural studies situated culture within a theory of social production and reproduction, specifying the ways that cultural forms served either to further social control, or to enable people to resist. It analyzed society as a hierarchical and antagonistic set of social relations characterized by the oppression of subordinate class, gender, race, ethnic, and national strata. Employing Gramsci's model of hegemony and counterhegemony, British cultural studies sought to analyze "hegemonic," or ruling, social and cultural forces of domination and to locate "counterhegemonic" forces of resistance and contestation.

British cultural studies aimed at a political goal of social transformation in which location of forces of domination and resistance would aid the process of political transformation. From the beginning, the Birmingham group was oriented toward the crucial political problems of their age and milieu. Their early spotlight on class and ideology derived from an acute sense of the oppressive and systemic effects of class in British society and the movements of the 1960s against these inequalities. The work of the late 1950s and early 1960s Williams/Hoggart/Hall stage of cultural studies emphasized the potential of working-class cultures. In the 1960s and 1970s, the Birmingham group began appraising the potential of youth subcultures to resist the hegemonic forms of capitalist domination (see Hebdige 1979 and 1988). Unlike the classical Frankfurt School (but similar to Herbert Marcuse), British cultural studies looked to youth cultures as providing potentially fresh forms of opposition and social change.

As it developed into the 1970s and 1980s, British cultural studies successively appropriated emerging analyses of gender, race, sexuality, and a wide range of critical theories. They developed ways to examine and critique how the established society and culture promoted sexism, racism, homophobia, and additional forms of oppression – or helped to generate resistance and struggle against domination and injustice. This approach implicitly contained political critique of all cultural forms that promoted oppression, while positively affirming texts and representations that produced a potentially more just and egalitarian social order.

Developments within British cultural studies have been in part responses to contestation by a multiplicity of social movements and distinct groups that have produced new methods and voices within cultural studies, such as a variety of feminisms, gay and lesbian studies, many multiculturalisms, critical pedagogies, and projects of critical media literacy. Hence, the field of British cultural studies at any given moment was determined by the struggles in the present political conjuncture, and their major work was conceived as political interventions. Their studies of ideology and the politics of culture directed the Birmingham group toward analyzing cultural artifacts, practices, and institutions within existing networks of power. In this context, they attempted to show how culture both provided tools and forces of domination and resources for resistance and opposition. This political optic provided an extremely productive focus on audiences and reception, topics that had been neglected in most previous text-based or industry-based methods.

British cultural studies, in retrospect, emerges in a later era of capital following the stage of state and monopoly capitalism analyzed by the Frankfurt School into a more variegated, globalized, and conflicted cultural formation. The forms of culture described by the earliest phase of British cultural studies in the 1950s and early 1960s articulated conditions in an era in which there were still significant

tensions in England and much of Europe between an older working-class-based culture and the newer mass-produced culture whose models and exemplars were the products of American culture industries. The subsequent work of Stuart Hall and his colleagues in the 1960s and 1970s was more influenced by the New Left, youth culture, and emerging social movements organized around race, gender, and sexualities, while the post-1980s work inspired by British cultural studies became global in impact and responded to the new cultural and political conditions described in postmodern theory.[7]

The tradition of British cultural studies is valuable because it provides tools that enable one to read and interpret culture critically. It also subverts distinctions between "high" and "low" culture by considering a wide continuum of cultural artifacts and by refusing to erect any specific cultural hierarchies or canons. Previous approaches to culture tended to be primarily literary and elitist, dismissing media culture as banal, trashy, and not worthy of serious attention. The project of cultural studies, by contrast, avoids cutting the field of culture into high and low, or popular against elite. Such distinctions are difficult to maintain and generally serve as a front for normative aesthetic valuations and, often, a political program.

Frankfurt School and British cultural studies approaches open the way toward more differentiated political valuations of cultural artifacts in which one attempts to distinguish critical and oppositional from conformist and conservative moments. For instance, studies of Hollywood film show how key 1960s films promoted the views of radicals and the counterculture and how film in the 1970s was a battleground between liberal and conservative positions; late 1970s films, however, tended toward conservative positions that anticipated a right turn in US society, which helped elect Ronald Reagan as president (see Kellner & Ryan 1988).[8]

There is an intrinsically critical and political dimension to the initial project of British cultural studies that distinguishes it from objectivist and apolitical academic approaches to the study of culture and society. British cultural studies, for example, analyzed culture politically and historically in the context of its societal origins and effects. It situated culture within a theory of social production and reproduction, specifying the ways that cultural forms, practices, and institutions served either to further social domination or to enable people to resist and struggle against domination. It analyzed society as a hierarchical and antagonistic set of social relations characterized by the oppression of subordinate class, gender, race, ethnic, and national strata.

A common critique of cultural studies in recent years has been that it overemphasizes reception and textual analysis, while underemphasizing the production of culture and its political economy. While the Birmingham groups regularly focused attention on media institutions and practices, and on the relations between media forms and broader social forms and ideologies, this emphasis has waned in recent years, to the detriment of current work in cultural studies. For instance, in his classical programmatic article, "Encoding/Decoding," Stuart Hall (1980b) began his analysis by using Marx's *Grundrisse* as a model to trace the articulations of "a continuous circuit," encompassing "production-distribution-consumption-production" (128ff.). He concretizes this model by focusing on how media institutions produce messages, how they circulate, and how audiences use or decode the messages to produce meaning. Hall (1980a) claimed that:

> The abstraction of texts from the social practices which produced them and the institutional sites where they were elaborated was a fetishization ... This obscured how a particular ordering of culture came to be produced and sustained: the circumstances and conditions of cultural reproduction which the operations of the "selective tradition" rendered natural, "taken for granted." But the process of ordering (arrangement, regulation) is always the result of concrete sets of practices and relations. (27)

Against the erasure of the system of cultural production, distribution, and reception, Hall (1980a) called for problematizing culture and "making visible" the processes through which certain forms of culture became dominant.[9] Meanwhile, Raymond Williams (1981), another of the formative influences on British cultural studies, called for a "cultural materialism ... the analysis of all forms of signification ... within the actual means and conditions of

their production" (64–5), focusing attention on the need to situate cultural analysis within its socio-economic relations. Moreover, in a 1983 lecture published in 1986/87, Richard Johnson provided a model of cultural studies, similar to Hall's earlier model. This "circuit of culture" model was based on a diagram of the circuits of production, textuality, and reception. This analysis is parallel to the circuits of capital stressed by Marx, and places particular emphasis on the processes of production and distribution. Although Johnson highlighted the importance of production in cultural studies and criticized the British film journal *Screen* for abandoning this perspective in favor of more idealist and textualist approaches (63ff.), much work in cultural studies has replicated this neglect.

Indeed, in the mid–1980s a populist and postmodern turn became evident in cultural studies that has continued for decades (see McGuigan 1992; Kellner 1995). Hence, there is a danger that media/cultural studies in various parts of the world might lose the critical and political edge of earlier forms of British cultural studies. Cultural studies could easily degenerate into a sort of eclectic populism of the sort evident in the Popular Culture Association that is largely celebratory and uncritical of the textual artifacts it deals with. Neglecting political economy, celebrating the audience and the pleasures of the popular, ignoring or downplaying social class and ideology, and failing to analyze or criticize the politics of cultural texts will make cultural studies merely another academic subdivision, harmless and ultimately of benefit primarily to the culture industries themselves. Avoiding such a conservative development of cultural studies, I submit, requires a variety of disciplinary and critical perspectives and linking cultural studies, ultimately, to critical social theory and radical democratic politics.

Political Economy and the Media Industries

At their strongest, both the Frankfurt School and British cultural studies contain a threefold project of analyzing the production and political economy of culture, cultural texts, and the audience reception of those texts and their effects. This comprehensive approach avoids too narrowly focusing on one dimension of the project to the exclusion of others.[10]

Since political economy has been neglected in many modes of recent media and cultural studies, it is essential to stress the importance of analyzing the products of media industries' texts within their system of production and distribution, often referred to as "political economy." The term *political economy* calls attention to the fact that the production, distribution, and reception of culture take place within a specific economic and political system, constituted by relations between the state, the economy, social institutions and practices, culture, and organizations such as the media. For instance, in the US a capitalist economy dictates that media production is governed by laws of the market, but the democratic imperatives of the system mean that there is some regulation of media culture by the state. There are often tensions within a given society concerning how many and what activities should be governed by the imperatives of the market, or economics, alone, and how much state regulation or intervention is desirable. For some, the democratic imperative of media industries requires efforts to assure a wider diversity and sources of broadcast programming, or the promotion of "net neutrality" that would guarantee the right to fast wireless Internet access to all (McChesney 2007), as well as the prohibition in network broadcasting of phenomena agreed to be harmful, such as cigarette advertising or pornography. Media politics is thus a contested terrain as some would preclude all state "interference" in broadcasting media under the banner of neoliberalism. In countries with state-supported and managed media like the UK or France, the public interest and democratic imperative in state broadcasting media might be to promote national British or French culture.

A political economy approach highlights that capitalist societies are organized according to a dominant mode of production that structures institutions and practices according to the logic of commodification and capital accumulation. Cultural production and distribution is accordingly profit- and market-oriented in such a system. Forces of production (such as media technologies and creative practice) are shaped according to dominant relations of production (such as the profit imperative, the maintenance of hierarchical control, and relations of domination). As suggested below, the system of production and the relations between the economy and state sector are important in determining what sort of cultural artifacts are produced and how they are consumed. Hence "political economy" does not merely pertain solely to economics, but to the relations between the economic, political, technological, and cultural dimensions of the social context in which media industries function. The structure of political economy links culture to its political and economic context and opens up cultural studies to history and politics. It refers to a field of contestation and antagonism and not an inert structure as caricatured by some of its opponents.

Political economy should also discern and analyze the role of technology in media industry production and distribution, seeing, as in Innis (1951) and McLuhan (1964), how technology and forms of media help structure economic, social, and cultural practices and forms of life. In our era, the proliferation of new technologies and multimedia – ranging from Blu-Ray to iPods and satellite radio – calls attention to the intersection of technology and economics in everyday life. In a time of technological revolution, political economy must thus engage the dominant forms of technology, new forms of culture being produced, and new audience practices, as well as developments and changes in the media industries.

Media industry studies should thus engage both old and new media, see the convergences and divergences, and track the changes. There is a dramatic transformation going on in media industries with the explosion of new digital technologies that is affecting business and political economy, production and distribution, the forms of texts, and audience reception. Obviously, a critical media industry studies must follow these developments, which also highlight the importance of political economy, as well as technology, to doing critical media/cultural studies.[11]

In the present stage of capitalist hegemony, political economy grounds its approach within empirical analysis of the actual system of media industry production, investigating the constraints and structuring influence of the dominant capitalist economic system and a commercialized cultural system dominated by powerful corporations. Inserting texts into the system of culture within which they are produced and distributed can help elucidate features and effects that textual analysis alone might miss or downplay. Rather than being antithetical approaches to culture, political economy can contribute to textual analysis and critique. The system of production often determines what type of artifacts will be produced, what structural limits there will be as to what can and cannot be said and shown, and what kind of audience effects cultural artifacts may generate.

Because of their control by giant corporations oriented primarily toward profit, film and television production in the US, and increasingly in global media, is dominated by specific genres such as reality shows, talk and game shows, soap operas, situation comedies, action/adventure series, and so on. These economic factors help explain why there are cycles of certain genres and subgenres, sequelmania in the film industry, crossovers of popular films into television series, and homogeneity in products constituted within systems of production marked by rigid generic codes and formulaic conventions.

Further, political economy analyses can help determine the limits and range of political and ideological discourses and effects. My study of television in the US, for instance, revealed that takeover of the television networks by major transnational corporations and communications conglomerates was part of a "right turn" within US society in the 1980s whereby powerful corporate groups won control of the state and the mainstream media (Kellner 1990).

In spite of its strengths, one must recognize the limitations of political economy approaches. Some political economy analyses reduce the meanings and effects of texts to rather circumscribed and reductive ideological functions, arguing that media culture merely reflects the ideology of the ruling economic elite that controls the culture industries and is nothing more than a vehicle for the dominant ideology. It is true that media culture overwhelmingly supports capitalist values, but it is also a site of intense conflict between different races, classes, genders, and social groups. Thus in order to fully grasp the nature and effects of media culture, one should see contemporary society and culture as contested terrains and media and cultural forms as spaces in which particular battles over gender, race, sexuality, political ideology, and values are fought.

The conception of political economy proposed here goes beyond traditional, sometimes excessively economistic approaches that limit their focus to issues such as ownership, gatekeeping, and the production and distribution of culture. Instead, political economy in its broadest concept involves relations between the economy and polity, culture and people, as well as the interconnection between production and consumption, distribution and use, texts and audiences. Although some conceptions of political economy are reductive, focusing solely on the economic dimension, far richer notions are possible.

Moreover, in the present configuration of the global economy, a critical cultural/media studies needs to grasp the international, national, and local systems of media production and distribution. In the 1960s, critics of the global capitalist system described the domination of the world economy by transnational – mostly American and European – corporations as "imperialism" or "neo-imperialism," while its supporters celebrated their roles in "modernization." Today, the term "globalization" is the standard concept used to describe the new world economy and culture. One of the features of globalization is the proliferation of new voices and perspectives on culture and society and the politicization and contestation of forms of culture previously taken for granted. In a global culture, the valorization of difference and the emergence of new actors are part of the landscape and the question of representation becomes intensely politicized and contested (Canclini 1995; Flew 2007). Within the global communication system, the media industries have become increasingly important and influential, and so it is necessary to develop comprehensive theoretical perspectives and models to study their political economy, products, audiences, and effects.

Overcoming the Divides: Toward a Critical Media Industry Studies

In "Overcoming the Divide: Cultural Studies and Political Economy" (Kellner 1997b), I argued against splitting the field of media/cultural studies into competing camps such as a text- and theory-based cultural studies versus an empiricist and social science-based communication studies. Now I would again propose that the emerging field of media industry studies overcome the divide between media-communication studies and cultural studies. In addition, I would suggest that it explore and engage both entertainment and news and information. As I argue below, divisions between the two are imploding in an era of tabloid journalism and politicized entertainment, and media industry studies should follow their trajectories and interaction.

For a critical media/cultural studies approach to the media industries, both political economy and more sociologically and culturally oriented approaches to the study of media culture should be combined, as should text- and theory-based humanities approaches with critical social science approaches. For some decades now, however, advocates of media and cultural studies based in textual or audience analysis have been at war with those who advocate a political economy optic. The hostility between political economy and cultural studies reproduces a great divide within the fields of communication and cultural studies between different methodologies, objects of study, and, by now, bodies of texts that represent the two opposing schools.

The hostility between political economy and cultural studies replicates a bifurcation within the fields of communications and culture between competing paradigms. In my view, the divide is an artificial one, rooted in an arbitrary academic division of labor. These conflicting approaches point to a splintering of the field of media and communications studies into specialized subareas with competing models and methods, and, ironically, to a lack of communication in the field of communications. The distinction between "culture" and "communications" is arbitrary and rigid, and should be deconstructed. Whether one takes "culture" as the artifacts of high culture, the ways in which people live their lives, or the context of human behavior, it is intimately bound up with communication. All culture, to become social, and thus properly "culture," is both a mediator of and mediated by communication, and is thus communicational by nature. Yet

"communication," in turn, is mediated by culture; it is a mode through which culture is disseminated and rendered actual and effective. There is no communication without culture and no culture without communication, so drawing a rigid distinction between them, and claiming that one side is a legitimate object of a disciplinary study, while the other term is relegated to a different discipline, is an excellent example of the myopia and futility of arbitrary academic divisions of labor.

A critical media/cultural studies approach theorizes the interconnections between culture and communication, and explores how they constitute each other. The cultural studies tradition attacked the positivistic transmission model of communication dominant in the communication sciences in North America and offered a very different model of communication. In James Carey's (1997) useful summary (1ff.), which I am reconstructing here, communication was denaturalized, removed from nature and put into culture and society so that its ritualistic, symbolic, and contextual features could better be taken into account. The process of communication was seen as taking place in a space and time continuum and thus mediated by geography, history, and politics. Technology was conceived as part of the process of shaping social relations and experience and was not seen as a mere neutral instrument of transmission, as it was in the positivist tradition. Communication thus constituted experience and was at the center of social and cultural life.

The split between culture and communication reproduces an academic division of labor that – beginning early in the century and intensifying since the end of World War II – followed the trend toward specialization and differentiation symptomatic of the capitalist economy. The university has followed a broader trend that some theorists equate with the dynamics of modernity itself, interpreted as a process of ever-greater differentiation in all fields from business to education. This trend toward specialization has undermined the power and scope of cultural and media studies and should be replaced by a more transdisciplinary position.

Today divisions within media and communication studies continue to be severe, as are divisions between cultural studies and media-communication studies. The academic fields that study media, culture, and communication are clearly contested terrains. Not only is there a division between text- and theory-based cultural studies contrasted to social science-based media-communication studies, but there are divisions and fragmentation within these fields, with some arguing for the primacy of political economy, some focusing largely on text or audience, and others specializing in topics in isolation from contextualization in the broader field of culture and society.

Further, there is a division within media/culture and communication studies between emphases on entertainment contrasted to news and journalism, as well as differences between methodologies, theories, and what issues count as important. In my view, both the spheres of entertainment and information/journalism are immensely important and my own work over the past several decades has attempted to embrace both. For some, hard news and journalism are the lifeblood of a democratic society (McChesney 2007), while many within media/cultural studies argue that it is entertainment that is a dominant form of pedagogy, a major source of political ideology and indoctrination, and the battleground upon which major struggles of class, race, gender, sexuality, and other politics are fought.

I would argue, however, that the division between news and entertainment is no longer even remotely justified in an era of convergence of media, communication technologies, and media industries. Since at least the 1980s, there has been a severe crisis in journalism that is part of a crisis of democracy. The media industries have been taken over by corporate conglomerates that have severely reduced news and journalism divisions, as pointed out above. Accordingly, corporate broadcast networks have cut news budgets, focused on further developing them as profit centers, and cut back on foreign bureaus, to the extent that certain forms of news have practically disappeared in contemporary US corporate television (McChesney 2007). Likewise, newspapers are in crisis with corporate conglomerates taking over once locally and family-owned newspapers, making them profit centers and cutting back. The takeover of major broadcasting, print publications, and emergent Internet culture by corporate

conglomerates has thus severely undermined journalism, news, and information in the US, producing a crisis of democracy that continues to accelerate (Kellner 1990; 2005).

Furthermore, within the production of news and information in the broadcasting industry in particular, there has been the incursion of values from entertainment and tabloid journalism. The result is what has broadly been described as "infotainment," which represents an implosion between news and entertainment. Tabloidized journalism was all too apparent in the 1990s with the media spectacle of the O. J. Simpson trials dominating the news for years on end, succeeded by the Clinton sex and impeachment scandals (Kellner 2003). With the growth of 24/7 cable channels in the US there has been increased focus on human interest stories and "breaking news" stories orchestrated as media spectacles. These involve the latest natural disasters and weather coverage of hurricanes, political scandals, or human tragedies.

Examples of how media spectacle has become a major focus of media industries abound. Such spectacles have supplanted traditional journalism and substituted a form of mass entertainment for news and information. In an arena of intense competition with 24/7 cable TV networks, talk radio, and blogs – along with the proliferation of emergent media sites like Facebook, MySpace, and YouTube – competition for attention is ever more intense. This has contributed toward the mainstream media going to sensationalistic tabloidized stories, which they construct in the forms of media spectacles that attempt to attract maximum audiences for as much time as possible.

Analyzing and criticizing the increasing role of tabloid entertainment in the news arena and the processing of political events as media spectacle requires a media/cultural studies approach that incorporates political economy of media industries, textual analysis of specific media artifacts and spectacles, and reflections on their impact on audiences. We must consider, for example, the ways that political events like the Iraq war, the scandals of the Bush–Cheney administration, and the 2008 presidential election are processed as media spectacle, occurring in an increasingly contested terrain over which the battles of the present and future are fought. In this matrix, news, information, and key political events are presented as narrative, spectacle, and entertainment, with image and framing as important as the actual discourses and video footage of events. Unpacking the implosions between news and entertainment requires the comprehensive tripartite approach to the media industries that I have suggested here.

This type of critical perspective enables individuals to dissect the meanings, messages, and effects of dominant and oppositional cultural forms. Textual analysis should utilize a multiplicity of perspectives and critical methods, and reception studies should delineate the wide range of subject positions through which audiences appropriate culture. This requires an insurgent multicultural approach that sees the importance of analyzing the dimensions of class, race and ethnicity, and gender and sexual preference within the politics of representation of texts of media culture, while also studying their impact on how audiences read, interpret, and use the products of media industries and emergent technologies.

A critical media/cultural studies attacks sexism, racism, or bias against specific social groups (i.e., gays, intellectuals, youth, seniors, and so on), and criticizes texts that promote discrimination or oppression. Articulating media culture discourses and representations with social movements, it illuminates how media artifacts advance or oppose specific political movements and positions in the contemporary moment. A critical media/cultural studies should be linked to a critical media pedagogy that enables individuals to resist media manipulation and to increase their freedom and individuality. It is deeply important to teach individuals how media function within contemporary societies and to critically read, interpret, and decode media representations, as well as to produce media themselves. A critical media industry studies can help individuals become aware of the connection between media and forces of domination and resistance, and can help make audiences more critical and informed consumers and producers of their culture.[12] It can empower people to gain sovereignty over their culture and to be able to struggle for alternative cultures and political change. The blending of key components of media and cultural studies approaches into the emerging field of media industry studies is thus not just another academic fad, but can be part of a struggle for a better society and a better life.

Notes

1 In this paper, I draw on Kellner (1995; 2003) and Durham and Kellner (2006) to elaborate critical perspectives on media/cultural studies that could contribute to the emerging field of media industry studies. Thanks to Jennifer Holt for inviting me to contribute, discussing possible contributions, providing comments that helped with revision and development of my perspectives, and skillful editing.

2 I develop this tripartite model of media/cultural studies that I find in both figures of the Frankfurt School and British cultural studies in Kellner (1995) and dissect the "missed articulation" between the Frankfurt School and British cultural studies in Kellner (1997a).

3 On the Frankfurt School theory of the culture industry, see Horkheimer and Adorno (1972) and the discussion of the Frankfurt School approach in Kellner (1989).

4 On earlier traditions of cultural studies in the US, see Aronowitz (1993) and Carey (1997), and for the UK, see Davies (1995). There are many different versions of media/cultural studies and many individuals and groups contributed to the tradition, but I am focusing on the Frankfurt School and British cultural studies, as they have developed some of the most articulated and useful models for studying media industries.

5 For an argument that popular artifacts of media culture have utopian elements that appeal to audiences wishes, fantasies, and hopes, as well as ideological components, see Jameson (1979) and the development of this argument in Kellner (1995).

6 For a critique of Hartley's model of cultural studies and cultural populism, see Hammer and Kellner (2006). For critique of Hartley's and others' celebration of the "creative industries," see McRobbie (1998; 1999).

7 For critical takes on the postmodern turn in British cultural studies, see Kellner (1995) and McGuigan (1992) and for a positive appropriation of a critical and political postmodernism, see McRobbie (1994). For defense of poststructuralist and other recent theoretical discourses within "new cultural studies" see Hall and Birchall (2006).

8 While I am here valorizing the political-economic-ideological readings emphasized by the Frankfurt School and certain phases of British cultural studies, I would also support in many interpretive contexts more philosophical, ethical, and aesthetic versions of cultural studies since media texts are polysemic, with multiple dimensions of meaning, and multiple uses.

9 Yet in another article from the same period, Hall (1986) rejected the political economy paradigm as reductionist and abstract (46–7). But note that he is rejecting the most economistic base/superstructure "logic of capital" model and not the importance of political economy per se ("This approach, too, has insights which are well worth following through"). Yet from the late 1970s through the present, the dimension of political economy has receded in importance throughout the field of cultural studies

and some have been arguing for reinserting its importance in a reconstructed approach that overcomes the reductionism of some versions of Marxism and political economy; see McGuigan (1992), Kellner (1995), and Grossberg (1997).

10 This model was implicit in the Frankfurt School culture industry model and adumbrated in Hall (1980a) and Johnson (1986/87) and guided much of the early Birmingham work. Around the mid-1980s, however, some associated with British cultural studies began to increasingly neglect the production and political economy of culture (some believe that this was always a problem with their work) and some culture studies became more academic, cut off from political struggle.

11 On convergence, see Jenkins (2006), who notes a broad spectrum of technological, economic, and cultural convergences and highlights contradictory trends between increased concentration and power of corporate ownership contrasted with new opportunities for the masses and grassroots groups to use new technologies to democratize society.

12 For more on media literacy see Kellner (1998), Kellner and Share (2007) and Kahn and Kellner (2006).

References

Aronowitz, S. (1993) *Roll Over Beethoven*. University Press of New England, Hanover.

Canclini, N. G. (1995) *Hybrid Cultures: Strategies for Entering and Leaving Modernity*. University of Minnesota Press, Minneapolis.

Carey, J. (1997) Reflections on the project of (American) cultural studies. In Ferguson, M. and Golding, P. (eds.) *Cultural Studies in Question*. Sage, London, pp. 1–24.

Davies, I. (1995) *Cultural Studies, and After: Beyond Fragments of Empire*. Routledge, London.

Durham, M. and Kellner, D. (eds.) (2006) *Media and Cultural Studies: Keyworks*, 2nd edn. Blackwell, Boston.

Flew, T. (2007) *Understanding Global Media*. Palgrave, London.

Grossberg, L. (1997) *Bringing It All Back Home: Essays on Cultural Studies*. Duke University Press, Durham.

Hall, S. (1980a) Cultural studies and the centre: some problematics and problems. In Hall, S., Hobson, D., Lowe, A., and Willis, P. (eds.) *Culture, Media,*

Language: Working Papers in Cultural Studies, 1972–9. Hutchinson, London, pp. 15–47.

Hall, S. (1980b) Encoding/decoding. In Hall, S., Hobson, D., Lowe, A., and Willis, P. (eds.) *Culture, Media, Language: Working Papers in Cultural Studies, 1972–9.* Hutchinson, London, pp. 128–38.

Hall, S. (1986) On postmodernism and articulation: an interview. *Journal of Communication Inquiry* **10**, 45–60.

Hall, G. and Birchall, C. (2006) *New Cultural Studies: Adventures in Theory*. Edinburgh University Press, Edinburgh.

Hammer, R. and Kellner, D. (2006) Book review. *A Short History of Cultural Studies. Communication and Critical/Cultural Studies* **2**, 77–82.

Hartley, J. (2003) *A Short History of Cultural Studies*. Sage, London.

Hebdige, D. (1979) *Subculture: The Meaning of Style*. Methuen, London.

Hebdige, D. (1988) *Hiding in the Light*. Routledge, London.

Horkheimer, M. and Adorno, T. W. (1972) *Dialectic of Enlightenment*. Herder & Herder, New York.

Innis, H. A. (1951) *The Bias of Communication*. University of Toronto Press, Toronto. (Reprinted edition published 1991.)

Jameson, F. (1979) Reification and utopia in mass culture. *Social Text* 1, 130–48.

Jenkins, H. (2006) *Convergence Culture: Where Old and New Media Collide*. New York University Press, New York.

Johnson, R. (1986/87) What is cultural studies anyway? *Social Text* **16**, 38–80.

Kahn, R. and Kellner, D. (2006) Reconstructing technoliteracy: a multiple literacies approach. In Dakers, J. R. (ed.) *Defining Technological Literacy*. Palgrave Macmillan, New York, pp. 253–74.

Kellner, D. (1989) *Critical Theory, Marxism, and Modernity*. Polity Press, Cambridge; Johns Hopkins University Press, Baltimore.

Kellner, D. (1990) *Television and the Crisis of Democracy*. Westview Press, Boulder.

Kellner, D. (1995) *Media Culture: Cultural Studies, Identity, and Politics Between the Modern and the Postmodern*. Routledge, London.

Kellner, D. (1997a) Critical theory and British cultural studies: the missed articulation. In McGuigan, J. (ed.) *Cultural Methodologies*. Sage, London, pp. 12–41.

Kellner, D. (1997b) Overcoming the divide: cultural studies and political economy. In Ferguson, M. and Golding, P. (eds.) *Cultural Studies in Question*. Sage, London, pp. 102–20.

Kellner, D. (1998) Multiple literacies and critical pedagogy in a multicultural society. *Educational Theory* **48**, 103–22.

Kellner, D. (2003) *Media Spectacle*. Routledge, London.

Kellner, D. (2005) *Media Spectacle and the Crisis of Democracy*. Paradigm Press, Boulder.

Kellner, D. and Ryan, M. (1988) *Camera Politica: The Politics and Ideology of Contemporary Hollywood Film*. Indiana University Press, Bloomington.

Kellner, D. and Share, J. (2007) Critical media literacy, democracy, and the reconstruction of education. In Macedo, D. and Steinberg, S. R. (eds.) *Media Literacy: A Reader*. Peter Lang, New York, pp. 3–23.

McChesney, R. W. (2007) *Communication Revolution: Critical Junctures and the Future of Media*. New Press, New York.

McGuigan, J. (1992) *Cultural Populism*. Routledge, London.

McLuhan, M. (1964) *Understanding Media: The Extensions of Man*. McGraw-Hill, New York.

McRobbie, A. (1994) *Postmodernism and Popular Culture*. Routledge, London.

McRobbie, A. (1998) *British Fashion Design: Rag Trade or Image Industry*. Routledge, London.

McRobbie, A. (1999) *In the Culture Society: Art, Fashion, and Popular Music*. Routledge, London.

Williams, R. (1981) *Culture*. Fontana, London.

8

Thinking Globally
From Media Imperialism to Media Capital

· ·

Michael Curtin

It is difficult to think globally about media industry studies simply because most research focuses on media industries in the United States. This bias is no doubt due to our fascination with the power and influence of these media, but it also stems from the fact that American media produce a tremendous amount of information about themselves. Critical scholars in the US (who are well-funded compared to their peers abroad) then mine this data and publish their studies with presses that prefer subjects that attract wealthy English-language audiences. Canada, Australia, and the UK have received some attention for similar reasons, but research on these media industries is often motivated by concern about the negative impact of Hollywood on their national cultures. Outside of this Anglo orbit of scholars, the pickings have been slim. It was not until 1999 that the first major study of media industries in Latin America was published. No comparable volume exists for African or Eastern European media. Arabic, Indian, and Chinese media began to generate more attention during the 1990s, but it is only recently that we are beginning to see systematic and comprehensive studies of these industries.[1] As a result, it is difficult to think globally about media industries when so much of what we know is derived from American contexts.

It is also difficult to think globally because research keeps circling back to national policy and aesthetics. The conventional frame for studying cinema around the world is the national cinemas approach. Television is likewise examined as discrete national systems and much of the debate revolves around national policy issues. Media industries themselves tend to function as self-consciously national institutions as well. To the extent that they operate internationally, the business of film and television is conducted country-by-country under regulation and licensing arrangements that conspicuously observe national borders. Consequently, national frameworks and biases prevail in media industry studies and operations, and yet, as we know, the world is changing. Media imagery today flows across borders far more fluidly than ever before and popular artists embrace opportunities that allow them to reach broader and more diverse audiences. Likewise, the most successful media enterprises today attempt to extend their influence abroad. This not only includes Time Warner and Sony but also Globo, Media Asia, and Zee TV as well. So although the residual influence of national frameworks remains strong, the media industries are changing and media studies must change with them.

What then would it mean to think globally about media industries? Certainly it would mean that we should extend our perspective beyond Anglo-American media and it would encourage us to consider the world as a whole. But how can we do this without seeing global media as the sum of their parts, as simply a collection of discrete units? Or conversely, how can we do this without seeing media institutions around the world as pale reflections of the dominant American media system? That is, how can we shift our perspective so that we take into account both the general and the particular, both the forest and the trees? How can we escape an Anglo-American bias? Which principles shape the development and interactions of media enterprises worldwide? Which tendencies present themselves regardless of the many contexts in which media operate? And how do the production, circulation, and consumption of media help to engender spatial relations and patterns that shape our lives?

These are not entirely new questions. Indeed, they can be traced back to the pioneering work of Harold Innis (1950; 1951). Yet it was not until the late 1960s that lively debates began to emerge about international media relations, and it was not until the 1990s that we began to discuss media industries with respect to globalization. In the first section of this chapter, I provide a brief overview of international media industries research. I then follow with a discussion of the recent literature on globalization, which provides a context for explaining key principles that help us to think globally about media industries today.

From Imperialism to Globalization

In the late 1960s, Thomas Guback (1969) and Herbert Schiller (1969) published pioneering studies of American media influence around the world. Both describe self-conscious collaboration between industry executives and government officials seeking cultural, commercial, and strategic influence abroad. Kaarle Nordenstreng and Tapio Varis (1974) soon followed with potent empirical evidence of US domination in the international TV market, showing that exports from America comprised a substantial portion of television imports in many countries around the world. Throughout the 1970s and 1980s the *media imperialism* thesis flourished, asserting that the US and its European allies controlled the international flow of images and information, imposing

media texts and industrial practices on unwilling nations and susceptible audiences around the world. According to this view, western media hegemony diminishes indigenous production capacity and undermines the expressive potential of national cultures, imposing foreign values and contributing to cultural homogenization worldwide.

The basic unit of analysis for media imperialism researchers was the modern nation-state, which meant that domination was usually figured as a relationship between countries, with powerful states imposing their will on subordinate ones, especially in news reporting, cinematic entertainment, and television programming. Based initially on data gathered in the 1960s and 1970s, when American media had few international competitors, media imperialism's founding scholars anticipated enduring relations of domination, presuming that the US would be able to perpetuate its structural advantages. So influential was this critique that it helped to inspire an energetic reform movement among less developed nations that called for a New World Information and Communication Order (NWICO). This campaign crested in the 1980s with a set of United Nations reform proposals that would have sailed through the General Assembly if not for the fierce opposition of the Reagan and Thatcher governments, both champions of "free flow" of information over the reformers' demands for "fair and balanced flow" (MacBride 1980). This Anglo-American alliance thoroughly undermined the momentum behind NWICO; furthermore it led to a counteroffensive aimed at promoting the commercialization of media institutions around the world.

While these political struggles were raging, researchers began to critically reexamine some of the essential tenets of the media imperialism thesis. One of the first and most telling critiques was posed by Chin-Chuan Lee (1979), a young scholar from Taiwan who interrogated the theoretical consistency and empirical validity of the media imperialism hypothesis by considering case studies of media in Canada, Taiwan, and the People's Republic of China. Lee argued that foundational assumptions, such as a correspondence between economic domination and media domination, did not hold up under close scrutiny. Canada, a wealthy developed nation, was thoroughly saturated by Hollywood media, while Taiwan, an economically dependent and less developed nation, had established a relatively independent media system that nevertheless failed to nurture "authentic" local culture, preferring instead commercial, hybrid forms of mass culture. The PRC, although the least developed of the three, was even more removed from Hollywood domination but thoroughly authoritarian, making it the most elitist and least popular media system at the time. Supporting neither the free flow doctrine nor the media imperialism critique, Lee argued for middle-range theory and regulatory policies that would be sensitive to the complexities of specific local circumstances.

Scholars in cultural studies and postcolonial studies also began to question media imperialism, especially the presumption that commercial media have clear and uniform effects on audiences. Might audiences read Hollywood's dominant texts "against the grain," they wondered? Might they be more strongly influenced by family, education, and peer groups than by foreign media? Critics also challenged the presumption that all foreign values have deleterious effects, noting that the emphasis on aspiration and agency found in many Hollywood narratives might actually have positive effects among audiences living in social systems burdened by oppressive forms of hierarchy and/or patriarchy (Fejes 1981; Liebes & Katz 1990; Ang 1991; Lull 1991). Moreover, critics pointed to the media imperialism school's troubling assumption that *national* values were generally positive and relatively uncontested, arguing for example that during the twentieth century Indian national media tended to cater to Hindu elites at the expense of populations from diverse cultural and linguistic backgrounds, such as Tamil and Telegu (Chakravarty 1993; Mitra 1993). Finally, they pointed out that cultures are rarely pure, autonomous entities, since most societies throughout history have interacted with other societies, creating hybrid cultural forms that often reenergize a society by encouraging dynamic adaptations (Appadurai 1996; Clifford 1997). According to these critics, media imperialism's notion of a singular, enduring, and authentic national culture simply overlooks the many divisions within modern nation-states, especially in

countries whose borders were imposed by colonial masters, such as Indonesia and Nigeria. Overall, cultural studies scholars pointed out that media imperialism's privileging of "indigenous culture," tends to obscure the complex dynamics of cultural interaction and exchange.

Empirical research data also began to suggest that western media dominance might be diminishing. As television industries around the world matured, audiences increasingly showed a preference for national and regional productions, especially in news, talk, and variety formats but also in drama and comedy. In Latin America, for example, Peruvian TV audiences tend to prefer Mexican or Venezuelan telenovelas as opposed to Hollywood soap operas (Tracey 1988; Straubhaar 1991; Reeves 1993; Sinclair et al. 1996; Sinclair 1999). New media technologies further complicated consumption patterns, as VCRs and satellites began to expand the range and quantity of available films and television programming in the 1980s, a trend that was amplified by digital media in the 1990s. As the range of viewer choice expanded, researchers found that US media comprised a relatively small part of overall media consumption in many parts of the world. Researchers also suggested that the revolution in communication technologies seemed to be facilitating a wave of cultural and political transformations, such as the fall of the Berlin Wall and demonstrations at Tiananmen (Lull 1991; O'Neill 1993; Wark 1994). Coupling these communication trends with dramatic changes in shipping and transportation, as well as the continuing march of neoliberal free-trade policies, popular and scholarly critics began to contemplate a seismic shift from the existing state-based international system to a nascent global order, one that was more open, more hybrid, and more thoroughly interconnected than its predecessor.

Within this context, media industries have undergone significant changes since the 1980s, as the number of media producers, distributors, and consumers has grown dramatically, first in Europe and then in Asia, with China and India adding almost two billion new viewers during this period. Although powerful global media conglomerates were active contributors to these trends, local, national, and regional media firms expanded rapidly as well. For example, Rupert Murdoch's News Corporation entered Asia with hopes of transmitting satellite TV programs to audiences across the continent on its Star TV platform. Using films and television programs from his Fox studios, Murdoch programmed Star for a pan-Asian, English-speaking, elite audience and used the technology of satellite delivery to gain entry to markets that previously had been protected by national broadcasting regulations. At first Star succeeded, drawing the attention of middle-class viewers and forcing governments to liberalize their media regulations. Yet liberalization cut both ways. Star gained access to new markets, but so too did dozens of new services organized by Asian companies, most of them telecasting in local languages. Star helped to pry open national media markets, but it soon found that it had to adapt its services to conditions within those markets. Instead of transmitting four channels across the continent, Star now delivers more than 60 television services, each of them targeted at specific geographical regions of Asia and each fashioned for the distinctive cultures, languages, and markets in which they operate (Curtin 1999; Kumar 2005; Curtin 2007; McMillin 2007).

Such developments challenged media imperialism's structural notions of center and periphery, as it became clear that even the world's most powerful media corporations were having a difficult time imposing their agendas in many parts of the world. Instead, companies like Star TV were avidly localizing their programming and institutional practices, so as to adapt to competitive forces in places like India, Indonesia, and Taiwan. Though Star's original intention was to penetrate and dominate Asian markets with western technology and Hollywood programming, it soon found itself pulled into lively competition with new creative enterprises in diverse locales. Conversely, as Star localized its operations, Asian media institutions became more globalized in their perspectives and practices, adapting many of the creative and marketing strategies of their foreign competitors. Rather than exhibiting concrete patterns of domination and subordination, Asian media institutions at a variety of levels seemed to be responding to the push–pull of globalization, as increasing connectivity inspired significant changes in textual and institutional practices at a variety of levels.

Globalization of media therefore should not be understood reductively as cultural homogenization or western hegemony. Instead it is part of a larger set of processes that operate translocally, interactively, and dynamically at a variety of levels: economic, institutional, technological, and ideological. As John Tomlinson (1991) observes, globalization "happens as the result of economic and cultural practices which do not, of themselves, aim at global integration, but which nonetheless produce it. More importantly, the effects of globalization are to weaken the cultural coherence of all nation-states, including the economically powerful ones – the 'imperialist powers' of a previous era" (75). In other words, unlike theories of media imperialism that emphasize the self-conscious extension of centralized power, globalization theories suggest that the world's increasingly interconnected media environment is the outcome of messy and complicated interactions across space. The challenge for media industry studies is to come up with theories and approaches that identify the most significant forces driving these interactions and to explain why some places become centers of cultural production and therefore tend to be more influential in shaping the emerging global system.

Although US media are no longer perceived as a singular cultural force worldwide, issues of power and influence are nevertheless matters of ongoing concern, only now the emphasis has shifted from nations to cities. Increasingly we find that cities such as Beirut, Mumbai, and Miami function less as centers of national media than as central nodes in the transnational flow of culture, talent, and resources. Rather than asking about relations among and between nations, we should explore the ways in which media industries based in particular cities are participating in the restructuring of spatial and cultural relations worldwide. In an effort to clarify the spatial dynamics of media industries in the global era, this essay examines three principles of *media capital* that have shaped film and broadcasting throughout their histories. It shows that despite the many changes that have taken place over the past few decades, media industries are fundamentally driven by 1) a logic of accumulation, 2) trajectories of creative migration, and 3) forces of sociocultural variation. The character and balance among these principles has undergone a dramatic transition since the 1980s, but the principles themselves remain the same and therefore provide a firm foundation for thinking about practices and performance of media industries. For example, they encourage us to think about capitalism as a social process that shapes the spatial contours of media, bearing only contingent or "not necessary" relation to the nation-state. These principles also direct our attention to the fundamental role that creative labor plays in the spatial deployment of media resources. And they invite us to reflect on the particularities of culture and politics both as boundary markers and as creative resources. In all, the principles of media capital encourage us to develop spatially complex and historically specific accounts of media globalization.

The Logic of Accumulation

The logic of accumulation is not unique to media industries, since all capitalist enterprises exhibit innately dynamic and expansionist tendencies. As David Harvey (2001) points out, most firms seek efficiencies through the concentration of productive resources and through the extension of markets in hopes of realizing the greatest possible return on investment in the shortest amount of time. For example, companies reorganize the spatial layout of their factories to increase productive efficiency or they use new modes of transportation to expand their market reach. These *centripetal* tendencies in the sphere of production and *centrifugal* tendencies in distribution were observed by Karl Marx (1973) more than a century ago when he trenchantly explained that capital must "annihilate space with time" if it is to overcome barriers to accumulation (539).

As applied to contemporary media, this insight suggests that even though a film or TV company may be founded with the aim of serving a particular national culture or a local market, over time it must redeploy its creative resources and reshape its terrain of operations if it is to survive competition and enhance profitability. Implicit in this logic of accumulation is the contributing influence of the "managerial revolution" that accompanied the rise

of industrial capitalism (Chandler 1977). For over a century, modern managers have sought to apply scientific techniques and technologies of surveillance to the refinement of corporate operations. During the twentieth century capitalism became more than a mode of accumulation, it also became a disposition toward surveillance and adaptation, as it continually reorganized and integrated manufacturing and marketing processes.

The history of the American cinema – the world's most commercial and most intensively studied media industry – provides an instructive example of these core tendencies. During the first decade of the twentieth century, US movie exhibitors depended on small, collaborative filmmaking crews to service demand for filmed entertainment. Yet as theater chains emerged, as distribution grew more sophisticated, and as competition intensified, movie companies began to centralize creative labor in large factory-like studios with an eye toward improving quality, reducing costs, and increasing output. By refiguring the spatial relations of production, managers concentrated the creative labor force in a single location where it could be deployed among a diverse menu of projects under the guidance of each studio's central production office. The major film companies furthermore separated the domains of planning and execution, creating a blueprint (or script) for each film that guided the work of specialized craftspeople in lighting, makeup, and dozens of other departments deployed across the studio lot. As American cinema entered this factory phase during the 1910s, the intensification of production accelerated output and yielded cost efficiencies, providing theater operators around the country with a dependable flow of quality products (Bordwell et al. 1985; Bowser 1990; Scott 2005).

Similar patterns emerged in the Indian commercial film industry with major studios emerging in Bombay and Calcutta by the 1930s. Although the studio system would fall by the wayside for a number of reasons, the concentration of productive resources would intensify, allowing Bombay to emerge as the center of a South Asian film industry that would distribute movies across the subcontinent (Prasad 1998; Pendakur 2003; Rajadhyaksha 2003). In Chinese cinema, transnational theater circuits were firmly in place by the 1930s, but the mode of production was initially more dispersed for a variety of reasons. During the post–World War II era as prosperity returned to the industry, both Cathay and Shaw Brothers established integrated production operations in Hong Kong that rivaled the scope and productivity of their American counterparts (Bordwell 2000; Fu 2003; Curtin 2007; Fu 2007). The capital-intensive factory model prevailed with major movie companies around the world. Nevertheless it is important to note that unlike the auto or steel industries, film-making employees were creating distinctive *prototypes* rather than redundant batches of products with inter-changeable parts. Each commodity was relatively unique, even if production routines grew increasingly standardized and even if the films were intended for mass audiences (Bordwell et al. 1985).

Not only was film production distinctive from other forms of industrialized manufacturing but so too was film distribution, since movies are what economists refer to as public goods (Kepley 1990; Hesmondhalgh 2002). That is, each feature film is a commodity that can be consumed without diminishing its availability to other customers. And given the relatively low cost of reproducing and circulating a film print when compared to the cost of creating the prototype, it behooves the manufacturer to circulate each artifact as widely as possible. Unlike other cultural institutions that needed to be close to live audiences or patrons (e.g., vaudeville and opera), and unlike industrial manufacturers that incurred substantial shipping costs for their finished products (e.g., automobiles and washing machines), movie studios could dispatch their feature films expansively and economically. The key aim of the distribution apparatus was therefore to stimulate audience demand and ensure access to theaters in far-flung locales. They achieved the latter by establishing theater chains or by collaboration with major exhibitors, both nationally and internationally (Thompson 1985; Gomery 1986; Balio 1993; Pendakur 2003; Curtin 2007).

Trajectories of Creative Migration

The second principle of media capital emphasizes trajectories of creative migration, since audiovisual

industries are especially reliant on creativity as a core resource. Recurring demand for new prototypes requires a workforce that is self-consciously motivated by aesthetic innovation as well as market considerations. Indeed, attracting and managing talent is one of the most difficult challenges that screen producers confront. At the level of the firm this involves offering attractive compensation and favorable working conditions, but at a broader level it also requires maintaining access to reservoirs of specialized labor that replenish themselves on a regular basis. This is one of the main reasons why media companies tend to cluster in particular cities.[2]

Nevertheless as a longer historical perspective would seem to indicate, it is rare for such centers of creativity to emerge strictly as a response to market forces. During the pre-modern era, for example, artists and craftspeople congregated at sites where sovereigns and clergy erected grand edifices or regularly commissioned devotional works of art. Patronage drew artists to specific locales and often kept them in place for much of their working lives, and they in turn passed their skills along to succeeding generations and to newly arrived migrants. Rather than market forces, one might imagine that spiritual inspiration and feudal relations of patronage significantly influenced trajectories of creative migration during this period, but it is also important to acknowledge the tendency of artists to seek out others of their kind. Artists are drawn to co-locate with their peers due to the mutual learning effects engendered by such proximity. That is, artists improved their skills and enhanced their vision through their ongoing association with other artists.

As the bourgeoisie rose to prominence in the early modern era, commercial cities became new centers of artistic production and exhibition, even though pre-existing centers retained residual prestige among the cognoscenti (DiMaggio 1986). Industrialists built performance venues, established galleries, and subsidized educational institutions, all of which attracted fresh talent to cities such as Berlin, New York, and Shanghai. Popular culture was layered over this topography of creative labor flows in the fine arts. Outside the major cultural institutions, popular artists and performers found it difficult to subsist in any one locale since they lacked access to the wealth of powerful patrons. Instead, they established circuits of recurring migration, playing to crowds in diverse towns and villages. These circuits were formalized in the nineteenth century by booking agents who rationalized the scheduling of talent across regional chains of performance venues. By concentrating creative laborers into performance troupes and then circulating them around a circuit, vaudeville made it possible for performers to earn a living and to learn new techniques from their fellow artists (Gilbert 1940; McLean 1965; Allen 1980). As vaudeville flourished, it attracted fresh talent from among enthusiastic audiences in diverse locales, bringing them into the circuit of production. Film industries would draw from the talent reservoirs of popular theater and they would cultivate new talent of their own. However, they would also anchor creative talent to particular locations where the capital-intensive studios were located. Despite their success, reversals in the American (1950s), Indian (1940s), and Chinese (1970s) film industries brought an end to the studio system of production. Artists and laborers consequently found themselves shifting from the security of long-term employment to the uncertainties of casual labor at a growing number of independent production houses.

Why then did Hollywood, Bombay, and Hong Kong continue to act as magnets for cultural labor? One might suggest that like prior transitions, the residual aura of these cities helped to sustain their status as centers of creative endeavor, but geographers Michael Storper and Susan Christopherson (1987) contend that more importantly, a disintegrated (or flexible or post-Fordist) mode of production in the movie industry actually encourages and sustains the agglomeration of creative labor due to the fact that constant changes in product output require frequent transactions between contractors, subcontractors, and creative talent. Their study of Hollywood shows that the number of inter-firm transactions in the movie business has grown dramatically over the past 50 years. At the same time, the scale of transactions has diminished, indicating that many small subcontractors now provide the studios with crucial services, such as wardrobe, set construction, and lighting, as well as key talent. Storper and Christopherson argue that although the

production system went through a period of disintegration, the spatial concentration of labor persisted. That is, film producers today subcontract hundreds of tasks, but most contracts go to *local* companies because it is easier to oversee their work and suggest changes as the project progresses. As for the workers, they cluster around Hollywood where studios and subcontracting firms are based, since it helps them "offset the instability of short-term contractual work by remaining close to the largest pool of employment opportunities."[3]

Geographer Allen J. Scott extends this principle of talent agglomeration to industries as diverse as jewelry, furniture, and fashion apparel, arguing that manufacturers of *cultural* goods tend to locate where subcontractors and skilled laborers form dense transactional networks. Besides apparent managerial and cost efficiencies, Scott points to the mutual learning effects that stem from a clustering of interrelated producers. Whether through informal learning — such as sharing ideas and techniques while collaborating on a particular project — or via more formal transfers of knowledge — craft schools, trade associations, and awards ceremonies — clustering enhances product quality and fuels innovation. "Place-based communities such as these are not just foci of cultural labor in the narrow sense," observes Scott (2000), "but also are active hubs of social reproduction in which crucial cultural competencies are maintained and circulated" (33).

The centripetal agglomeration of labor encourages path-dependent evolution such that small chance events or innovations may spark the appearance of a culture industry in a particular location, but clustering engenders a growth spiral, as creative labor migrates to the region in search of work, further enhancing its attraction to other talent. Locales that fail to make an early start in such industries are subject to "lock-out," since it is difficult to lure talent away from an existing media capital, even with massive government subsidies. Scott suggests that the only way a new cluster might arise is if its producers offer an appreciably distinctive product line.

In general, we can conclude that cultural production is especially reliant upon mutual learning effects and trajectories of creative migration, and that particular locations inevitably emerge as centers of creativity. These principles have operated throughout history under various regimes of accumulation, but the modern era is distinctive because the centripetal logic of capitalist production has been married to the centripetal trajectories of creative migration, engendering the rise of powerful transnational media production centers. One might imagine that in today's world of increasing commercial flows and diminishing trade barriers we might be approaching a time when one city would become a dominant global center attracting talent from around the world and producing a majority of the world's popular screen narratives. Yet the complexities of distribution undermine such pretensions to singular dominance, especially when media products rub up against counterparts in distant cultural domains often served, even if minimally, by competing media capitals that are centers of creative migration in their own right. Such complexities therefore direct our attention to the third principle of media capital.

Forces of Sociocultural Variation

Cities such as Hollywood, Mumbai, and Hong Kong lie across significant cultural divides from each other, which helps to explain why producers in these cities have been able to sustain distinctive product lines and survive the onslaught of distant competitors. These media capitals are furthermore supported by intervening factors that modify and complicate the spatial tendencies outlined above. Consequently, the forces of sociocultural variation direct our attention to the fact that national and local institutions have been and remain significant actors despite the centripetal biases of production and creativity, and the centrifugal bias of distribution. Indeed, the early years of cinema were exceptional in large part because the logic of media capital unfolded relatively unimpeded by national regulation, but as the popularity of Hollywood narratives increased, many countries established cultural policies to address the growing influence of this new commodity form.

Motion pictures presented governments with a unique policy challenge since they were distributed even more widely than newspapers, magazines, or books, the circulation of which was limited to literate consumers within shared linguistic spheres. By comparison, silent era cinema overcame these barriers and challenged class, gender, and racial boundaries as well. Hollywood movies circulated widely, swelling the size of audiences dramatically and fueling the growth of large-scale enterprises. According to Thompson (1985), US movie companies became dominant exporters by the mid-1910s, a trend that contributed to a further concentration of resources and talent in the Los Angeles area. By the 1920s, however, opinion leaders and politicians abroad grew wary and cultural critics began to clamor for regulation. Many countries imposed import quotas and content regulations on Hollywood films and some set up national film boards to subsidize cinema productions with national themes and talent (Higson 1989; Jarvie 1992; Crofts 1993; O'Regan 2002).

Most importantly, however, national governments embraced the new technology of radio broadcasting, which in almost every country outside the western hemisphere was established as a public service system intended as a bulwark against cultural invasion from Hollywood. Britain, which would serve as a model to others, explicitly charged the British Broadcasting Corporation with responsibility to clear a space for the circulation of British values, culture, and information (Scannell & Cardiff 1991; Hilmes 2003). Radio seemed an especially appropriate medium for intervention, since many of its characteristics helped to insulate national systems from foreign competition. Technologically, radio signals traveled only 30 to 60 miles from any given transmitter. As in Britain, one could interconnect a chain of transmitters that would blanket the countryside, but the only way for foreign competitors to reach one's domestic audiences was via shortwave radio, a temperamental technology that was comparatively inaccessible to the masses. Such insulation was furthermore ensured by an international regulatory regime that allocated radio frequencies on a national basis, minimizing technical as well as cultural interference between countries. Language provided another bulwark, since radio relied on aural competence in the state's official language, helping to distinguish national radio productions that played in one's parlor from Hollywood "talkies" that played at the cinema. Finally, public service radio systems were bolstered by indigenous cultural resources, since literary and theatrical works were commonly appropriated to the new medium, as were folk tales and music. State ceremonies and eventually sporting events also filled the airwaves, as the medium participated in self-conscious efforts to foster a common national culture.

Radio also promoted a shared temporality among audiences. Its predecessor, the nineteenth-century newspaper, pioneered this transformation by directing readers to stories that the editors considered significant and by encouraging them to absorb these stories at a synchronous daily pace (Anderson 1983). Radio extended the daily ritual of newspaper consumption to nonliterate groups, which expanded the horizon of synchronization, such that program schedules began to shape daily household routines and create a national calendar of social and cultural events. Radio insinuated itself into the household, interlacing public and private spheres, and situating national culture in the everyday world of its listeners (Scannell & Cardiff 1991; Hilmes 1997; Morley 2000). Even though radio systems were founded under the guiding hand of politicians, educators, and cultural bureaucrats, radio would over time open itself up to audience participation, employing yet another distinctive cultural resource as part of its programming repertoire: the voice of the people. In each of these ways public service radio accentuated national contours of difference in opposition to media capital's desire to operate on a smooth plane of market relations worldwide.

Although the BBC served as a template for public service radio, national radio systems were diverse and their success varied. All India Radio was exceptionally elitist and therefore relatively unpopular. It was not until the incursions of foreign satellite competitors that Indian radio and television were forced to compete for the favor of audiences (Jeffrey 2006). India was not the only country to experience the negative effects of state monopoly. Nigerian broadcasting was rife with political favoritism and censorship until it found itself competing in the 1990s with popular Nigerian video films (Haynes & Okome 1998; Adesanya 2000; Haynes 2000; Larkin 2004; McCall 2004). Despite such problems, regulation

of the airwaves provided an effective way for governments to refigure the centripetal and centrifugal tendencies of media capital. It allowed them to staunch the flow of culture from abroad and to cultivate domestic talent and resources. Regulation provided a defensive response to the spatially expansive tendencies of commercial media industries.

Regulation also has acted as an influential enabler of commercial media industries. Intellectual property laws are especially compelling examples in this regard, as are media licensing regimes.[4] The commercial development of broadcasting in the US was facilitated by regulations that in effect made it possible to "sell the airwaves" to corporate operators. In so doing, the government created a market-driven system out of an intangible public resource, enabling a national program distribution system that stimulated the growth of national advertising and concentrated creative resources in a handful of urban centers (Streeter 1996). Just as the British system became a model for public service systems around the world, the commercial licensing regime of American broadcasting became the standard for satellite regulation, which in turn pressured governments around the world to adapt to commercial models during the 1990s.

As we can see, the boundaries and contours of markets are subject to political interventions that enable, shape, and attenuate the dynamics of media industries. Concepts such as "free flow" and "market forces" are in fact meaningless without self-conscious state interventions to fashion a terrain for commercial operations. Markets are made, not given. And the logic of accumulation must therefore be interrogated in relation to specific and complex mixtures of sociocultural forces.

Finally, it should also be pointed out that self-conscious state policies are not the only actors that organize and exploit the forces of sociocultural variation. Media industries in Mumbai, Cairo, and Hong Kong have themselves taken advantage of social and cultural differences in their production and distribution practices. Operating across cultural divides from Hollywood and from other powerful exporters, they have employed creative talent and cultural forms that resonate distinctively with their audiences. These industries have furthermore made use of social networks and insider information to secure market advantages, and they invoke cultural and national pride in their promotional campaigns. Forces of sociocultural variation can therefore provide resources for carving out market niches that are beyond the reach of foreign competitors.

Conclusion

Media capital is a concept that at once acknowledges the *spatial* logics of capital, creativity, culture, and polity without privileging one among them. Just as the logic of capital provides a fundamental structuring influence, so too do trajectories of creative migration and forces of sociocultural variation shape the diverse contexts in which media are made and consumed. The concept of media capital encourages us to provide dynamic and historicized accounts that delineate the operations of capital and the migrations of talent, while at the same time directing our attention to forces and contingencies that give shape to spheres of cultural exchange. Media capital invites us to think in terms of global Chinese media, not simply PRC, Taiwanese, or Singaporean media. It encourages us to consider the dramatic growth of Indian film audiences and satellite

subscribers in Europe and North America. And it prompts us to wonder at the complex and expansive channels of Nigerian video film distribution in sub-Saharan Africa and even worldwide.

The principles of media capital help us clarify our understanding of culture industries during the global era. They also encourage us to acknowledge the continuing importance of media policy. Market dynamics and talent migrations increasingly privilege a small number of global media capitals. Therefore policymakers must be willing to intervene where the market comes up short. In many cases, governments will need to prioritize and even subsidize media institutions because they provide vital resources for local, national, and alternative cultures. Like public parks and libraries, media play a vital role in making particular places worth living in. They foster identity, enhance social cohesion, serve local businesses, enhance property values, and provide spaces for public discourse. Some of these functions will be supported by the market, but others will not. The principles of media capital suggest that the only way to attenuate or redirect the spatial tendencies of media industries is through exertions of public will. As we have seen, media policies can establish barriers but just as importantly they can act as enablers, helping to nurture and sustain spaces for local voices in a global era.

Notes

1 An exception is Jarvie's (1977) exemplary study of the Chinese movie industry.
2 Although it does not address media industries specifically, an extensive literature discusses the impact of human capital on the clustering of business firms in particular locations (Jacobs 1984; Porter 1998; Florida 2005).
3 Despite the development of new communication technologies that allow creative collaborations across vast expanses, creative labor still needs to congregate so as to build relationships of trust and familiarity that can enable and sustain long-distance collaborations. Giddens' (1990) discussion of facework and Bourdieu's (1986) notion of social capital both point to the importance of physical proximity.

4 In the US, court rulings during the 1910s provided movie studios with intellectual property rights so that they – rather than their employees – might claim protection for the films they "authored." Although copyright laws originally aimed to foster creative endeavor by *individuals*, the courts allowed movie factories to claim artistic inspiration as well. Interestingly, they furthermore ruled that waged and salaried laborers at the major studios were neither creators nor authors but were rather "work for hire." In this way, the American legal system profoundly transformed copyright law, facilitating the industrialization of cinematic production and providing expansive legal protection for movie distributors (Bordwell et al. 1985).

References

Adesanya, A. (2000) From film to video. In Haynes, J. (ed.) *Nigerian Video Films.* Ohio University Press, Athens, pp. 37–50.

Allen, R. C. (1980) *Vaudeville and Film: 1895–1915: A Study in Media Interaction.* Arno Press, New York.

Anderson, B. (1983) *Imagined Communities: Reflections on the Origin and Spread of Nationalism.* Verso, New York.

Ang, I. (1991) *Desperately Seeking the Audience.* Routledge, New York.

Appadurai, A. (1996) *Modernity at Large: Cultural Dimensions of Globalization.* University of Minnesota Press, Minneapolis.

Balio, T. (1993) *Grand Design: Hollywood as a Modern Business Enterprise, 1930–1939.* Charles Scribner, New York.

Bordwell, D. (2000) *Planet Hong Kong: Popular Cinema and the Art of Entertainment.* Harvard University Press, Cambridge.

Bordwell, D., Staiger, J., and Thompson, K. (1985) *The Classical Hollywood Cinema: Film Style and Mode of Production to 1960.* Columbia University Press, New York.

Bourdieu, P. (1986) The forms of capital. In Richardson, J. G. (ed.) *Handbook for Theory and Research for the Sociology of Education.* Greenwood, New York, pp. 241–58.

Bowser, E. (1990) *The Transformation of Cinema: 1907–1915.* Charles Scribner, New York.

Chakravarty, S. S. (1993) *National Identity in Indian Popular Cinema, 1947–1987.* University of Texas Press, Austin.

Chandler, A. D. (1977) *The Visible Hand: The Managerial Revolution in American Business.* Harvard University Press, Cambridge.

Clifford, J. (1997) *Routes: Travel and Translation in the Late Twentieth Century.* Harvard University Press, Cambridge.

Crofts, S. (1993) Reconceptualizing national cinema/s. *Quarterly Review of Film & Video* **14**, 49–67.

Curtin, M. (1999) Feminine desire in the age of satellite television. *Journal of Communication* **49**, 55–70.

Curtin, M. (2007) *Playing to the World's Biggest Audience: The Globalization of Chinese Film and TV.* University of California Press, Berkeley.

DiMaggio, P. (1986) *Non-Profit Enterprise in the Arts: Studies in Mission and Constraint.* Oxford University Press, New York.

Fejes, F. (1981) Media imperialism: an assessment. *Media, Culture & Society* **3**, 281–9.

Florida, R. (2005) *Cities and the Creative Class.* Routledge, New York.

Fu, P. (2003) *Between Shanghai and Hong Kong: The Politics of Chinese Cinemas.* Stanford University Press, Stanford.

Fu, P. (2007) Modernity, diasporic capital, and 1950s Hong Kong Mandarin cinema. *Jump Cut* **49**. At http://ejumpcut.org/archive/jc49.2007/Poshek/index.htm, accessed July 5, 2008.

Giddens, A. (1990) *The Consequences of Modernity.* Stanford University Press, Stanford.

Gilbert, D. (1940) *American Vaudeville: Its Life and Times.* McGraw-Hill, New York.

Gomery, D. (1986) *The Hollywood Studio System.* St. Martin's Press, New York.

Guback, T. H. (1969) *The International Film Industry: Western Europe and America since 1945.* Indiana University Press, Bloomington.

Harvey, D. (2001) *Spaces of Capital: Towards a Critical Geography.* Routledge, New York.

Haynes, J. (ed.) (2000) *Nigerian Video Films*, rev. edn. Ohio University Center for International Studies, Athens.

Haynes, J. and Okome, O. (1998) Evolving popular media: Nigerian video films. *Research in African Literatures* **29**, 106–28.

Hesmondhalgh, D. (2002) *The Cultural Industries.* Sage, London.

Higson, A. (1989) The concept of national cinema. *Screen* **30**, 36–46.

Hilmes, M. (1997) *Radio Voices: American Broadcasting, 1922–1952.* University of Minnesota Press, Minneapolis.

Hilmes, M. (2003) Who we are, who we are not: the battle of global paradigms. In Parks, L. and Kumar, S. (eds.) *Planet TV: A Global Television Reader.* New York University Press, New York, pp. 53–73.

Innis, H. (1950) *Empire and Communications.* Clarendon Press, Oxford.

Innis, H. (1951) *The Bias of Communication.* University of Toronto Press, Toronto.

Jacobs, J. (1984) *Cities and the Wealth of Nations.* Random House, New York.

Jarvie, I. C. (1977) *Window on Hong Kong: A Sociological Study of the Hong Kong Film Industry and Its Audience.* University of Hong Kong, Hong Kong.

Jarvie, I. C. (1992) *Hollywood's Overseas Campaign: The North Atlantic Movie Trade, 1920–1950.* Cambridge University Press, Cambridge.

Jeffrey, R. (2006) The mahatma didn't like the movies and why it matters. *Global Media and Communication* **2**, 204–24.

Kepley, V. (1990) From "frontal lobes" to the "Bob-and-Bob" show: NBC management and programming strategies, 1949–65. In Balio, T. (ed.) *Hollywood in the Age of Television*. Unwin Hyman, Boston, pp. 41–62.

Kumar, S. (2005) *Gandhi Meets Primetime: Globalization and Nationalism in Indian Television*. University of Illinois Press, Urbana.

Larkin, B. (2004) Degraded images, distorted sounds: Nigerian video and the infrastructure of piracy. *Public Culture* **16**, 289–314.

Lee, C. (1979) *Media Imperialism Reconsidered: The Homogenizing of Television Culture*. Sage, Beverly Hills.

Liebes, T. and Katz, E. (1990) *The Export of Meaning: Cross-Cultural Readings of Dallas*. Oxford University Press, New York.

Lull, J. (1991) *China Turned On: Television, Reform, and Resistance*. Routledge, New York.

MacBride, S. (ed.) (1980) *Many Voices, One World: Communication and Society, Today and Tomorrow: Towards a New More Just and More Efficient World Information and Communication Order*. Report by the International Commission for the Study of Communication Problems. UNESCO, Paris. At http://unesdoc.unesco.org/images/0004/000400/040066eb.pdf, accessed August 19, 2008.

McCall, J. C. (2004) Juju and justice at the movies: vigilantes in Nigerian popular videos. *African Studies Review* **47**, 51–67.

McLean, A. F. (1965) *American Vaudeville as Ritual*. University of Kentucky Press, Lexington.

McMillin, D. C. (2007) *International Media Studies*. Blackwell, Malden.

Marx, K. (1973) *Grundrisse: Foundations of the Critique of Political Economy*. Vintage, New York.

Mitra, A. (1993) *Television and Popular Culture in India: A Study of the Mahabharata*. Sage, Thousand Oaks.

Morley, D. (2000) *Home Territories: Media, Mobility, and Identity*. Routledge, New York.

Nordenstreng, K. and Varis, T. (1974) *Television Traffic: A One-Way Street? A Survey and Analysis of the International Flow of Television Programme Material*. UNESCO, Paris.

O'Neill, M. (1993) *The Roar of the Crowd: How Television and People Power are Changing the World*. Times Books, New York.

O'Regan, T. (2002) A national cinema. In Turner, G. (ed.) *The Film Cultures Reader*. Routledge, New York, pp. 139–64.

Pendakur, M. (2003) *Indian Popular Cinema: Industry, Ideology, and Consciousness*. Hampton Press, Cresskill.

Porter, M. E. (1998) Clusters and the new economics of competition. *Harvard Business Review* **76**, 77–90.

Prasad, M. (1998) *Ideology of the Hindi Film: A Historical Construction*. Oxford University Press, New York.

Rajadhyaksha, A. (2003) The "Bollywoodization" of the Indian cinema: cultural nationalism in a global arena. *Inter-Asia Cultural Studies* **4**, 25–39.

Reeves, G. (1993) *Communication and the "Third World"*. Routledge, London.

Scannell, P. and Cardiff, D. (1991) *A Social History of British Broadcasting*, vol. 1. Blackwell, London.

Schiller, H. I. (1969) *Mass Communication and American Empire*. Westview Press, Boulder. (Second edition published 1992.)

Scott, A. J. (2000) *The Cultural Economy of Cities*. Sage, Thousand Oaks.

Scott, A. J. (2005) *On Hollywood: The Place, The Industry*. Princeton University Press, Princeton.

Sinclair, J. (1999) *Latin American Television: A Global View*. Oxford University Press, New York.

Sinclair, J., Jacka, E., and Cunningham, S. (eds.) (1996) *New Patterns in Global Television: Peripheral Television*. Oxford University Press, New York.

Storper, M. and Christopherson, S. (1987) Flexible specialization and regional industrial agglomerations: the case of the US motion picture industry. *Annals of the Association of American Geographers* **77**, 104–17.

Straubhaar, J. D. (1991) Beyond media imperialism: asymmetrical interdependence and cultural proximity. *Critical Studies in Mass Communication* **8**, 39–59.

Streeter, T. (1996) *Selling the Air: A Critique of the Policy of Commercial Broadcasting in the United States*. University of Chicago Press, Chicago.

Thompson, K. (1985) *Exporting Entertainment: America in the World Film Market, 1907–34*. British Film Institute, London.

Tomlinson, J. (1991) *Cultural Imperialism: A Critical Introduction*. Johns Hopkins University Press, Baltimore.

Tracey, M. (1988) Popular culture and the economics of global television. *Intermedia* **16**, 9–25.

Wark, M. (1994) *Virtual Geography: Living with Global Media Events*. Indiana University Press, Bloomington.

9

Thinking Regionally
Singular in Diversity and Diverse in Unity

· ·

Cristina Venegas

> *Throughout this [twentieth] century, Latin American cinema, audiovisual arts, and television have been financed by people, technicians, and talent from Latin America ... If we lose sight of this, we give up our cinematic history. Filmmakers must ... appeal to their people and look within, which means not only to the national context, but also the regional – Latin American or Ibero American. If this is accomplished, it's not as if they were inventing gunpowder, but rather filmmakers would be repeating the history of the best of world cinema. (Getino 2004, 149)*

Changing national production models, technological transformations, and rising circulation of media products come into focus from a regional view of Latin American film industries in the twenty-first century. As the industries of the region respond to both local economic conditions and global markets, they do so in ways that are far from new. Film education, training, and production are on the increase, filmmakers work (temporarily or permanently) outside of their countries, and governments and investors pursue national and transnational markets.

The cross-border economic and cultural exchanges characterizing present changes have occurred since the arrival of the cinema in Brazil in 1896. But today, the multiplication of delivery systems seen with globalization produces a much increased flow of media products. This movement forces a move away from narrow, mainly nationally based analyses to more comprehensive readings of media industries. In order to identify the fundamental mechanisms that

drive media industries, scholarship has become increasingly attentive to transnational and local interactions as they occur within regional landscapes. The variety and depth of sustained exchanges arising in the Latin American film industries exemplify the richness, scope, and complexity of what is studied under the heading of "regional." As a case study, Latin American cinema provides an opportunity to examine the characteristics of the broad regional approach.

What is "Regional"?
· ·

"Regional" as used here is defined as territorial geographies of political, economic, and cultural interactions that shape the spatial and ideological contours of media industries. Multi-nation trade agreements or common languages, for instance, go beyond the national, constituting regional markets.

For example, the circulation of actors, television shows, and DVDs frequently occurs in territories demarcated by both national and regional regulatory mechanisms. The societal interactions involved create the space of a "region."

Regional assemblages do not follow a single form (Farrell et al. 2005, 1), and economic regionalism is a reality (Drucker 1993, 149). Regions can fall inside or outside political borders to embrace cultural diasporas. To think of region is to be attentive to migration patterns and their causes, and to the variety of linguistic and cultural zones created by dispersal and displacement. Regional groupings are not limited to territorial constraints, and the increasing movement of peoples demands consideration of new ways of accounting for the resulting cultural landscape. The variety of possible regional arrangements occurs in response to the sets of "different processes of globalization" and the "different and contradictory globalizations" noted by Boaventura de Sousa Santos (2006). In the case of Latin America, the regional can refer to the integration of multinational, multilingual, and multiethnic groupings across diverse territories of North, Central, and South America, and the Caribbean. It also describes subregional economic arrangements (e.g., regional television, such as Telesur), counterhegemonic projects including micro-regional ethnic groupings (often labeled as "marginal," e.g., the Ukamau group) or language networks (e.g., Spanish, Portuguese, or Guaraní), individual geographic zones (e.g., South or Central America), and economic blocs (e.g., MERCOSUR).

The intensification of globalization and its attendant local consequences have renewed interest in the concept of the regional. In other words, regionalization can be seen as part of both the process and the results of globalization (Sousa Santos 2006, 396). For example, once globalized, media technologies call for decisions about appropriation that consider local and regional economic conditions, competition, labor practices, and markets. As the recent adoption by Brazil of Japan's high definition television standard shows, a decision by a single nation has to take into account the position and power of players within regional as well as national markets. Correct determination of subregional or regional industry alliances thus increases national advantage in global markets.

Examination of the relations that make up the regional on any scale necessarily leads to an inquiry into regional ideologies, practices, and contestations. According to Marsha Kinder (1993), such investigation is indispensable in apprehending the regional/national/global interface. In her study of Spanish cinema, Kinder finds that because "regionality is an ideological construct … 'regional film' and 'regional television' are relativistic concepts" (388). The concept of the region shifts in relation to a perceived center. A study of how this occurs in media industries reveals their potential to unsettle hegemonic ideologies and political structures.

Related past approaches

Transnational approaches to film history and film industry scholarship examine myriad interconnections that both inform and are part of a framework of regional analysis.[1] Investigating the New Latin American Cinema Movement (NLCM) from a transnational focus reveals how an ideological project can create unifying factors that produce the infrastructure of a cinema movement. The "united, but distinct" conjunction addresses the potential to idealize "unity" as an unproblematic goal by maintaining that local characteristics were always potentially disruptive and productive for the overall project.

Encompassing the period from the mid-1960s to the mid-1980s, the NLCM was a pan-national cultural and ideological cinema project that drew strength from political events in order to promote "decolonized" Latin American cinema industries. Films like *Memorias del Subdesarrollo* (Tomás G. Alea, 1969) and *La Batalla de Chile* (Patricio Gúzman, 1972–9) expressed the range and complexity of aesthetic trends. Humanistic ideals lent coherence to this artistic movement, which in turn produced enduring relationships, institutions, and films. What's more, the NLCM shows how a shared identity, rather than homogenizing national practices, relies on differences (Daicich 2004, 244). Both of these transnational strands, of unity and difference, are necessary to regional thinking.[2]

For film scholar Ana M. López (2000b), transnational approaches must emphasize the value of historical placement. Dominant narratives of 1970s English-language research presented the NLCM "ahistorically" failing to provide a chronology of the evolution of the NLCM, thus separating the complexity of the factors behind the movement from larger film histories. López (2000a) filled in a missing historical link by exploring how early twentieth-century modernity affected the early practices of the region's cinema. In this sense, modernity involved "complex negotiations between local histories and globality through differential and overlapping chronologies" (150). Identified as fundamental to a transnational framework, a historical perspective pays attention to the local conjunctures as they influence the circuits of diffusion and production. Regional media analysis thus requires a novel methodology that does not break with the past but instead expands the understanding of new media formations and constellations of meaning (Sarkar 2008).

In contrast to integrated transnational perspectives, area studies proposed a globe divided into discrete units as subjects of study. Originating in the post-World War II era, area studies research sought to study, collect, and compile information about areas of vital interest to perceived enemies of the US (Misrepassi 2002; Miyoshi & Harootunian, 2002; Farred 2003). As such, it failed the "Who does it serve?" test, putting political and economic interest ahead of social realities. Unlike multi-layered regional approaches of the present moment, the Cold War model of area studies produced universalizing narratives, neglecting to address the transnational interests of individuals, groups, and institutions and their relevance to national visions, agendas, and policies. Recent changes to area studies provide a much needed "focus on location, place, and situation [that] calls attention to how thoroughly scholarship and teaching in the humanities and social sciences have abandoned universal models of truth in favor of analyses rooted in the theoretical, the contingent, the provisional, and the pragmatic" (Jay 2006, 176).

Despite past emphasis on theories of the national and the global, the regional has nevertheless existed as a useful subfield of both transnational and area studies scholarship in the study of media industries. Findings from both can still inform a broader approach and guide important future work that encompasses the complexity of the present media age.

A Framework for Thinking Regionally

Argentine filmmaker Fernando Birri poetically described the NLCM of the mid-twentieth century as "singular in diversity and diverse in unity" (Daicich 2004, 17). This insight lies behind the way regional analysis of media industries accounts for the multiple levels of interaction across varying cultural territories. Birri's observation provides focus for the regional lens, suggesting the value of a search for and identification of disparate elements arranged in dynamic composition. A regional approach involves teasing out insistent (if limited) national identity that simultaneously finds reciprocal support in a larger identity. From investigation of earlier transnational operations like the NLCM, five key strands of a regional analysis emerge: 1) identification of the existence of a unifying drive that attempts to represent an area as a coherent set of production practices, ideas, and histories; 2) enquiry into the way media industries construct regionality out of an assortment of sociopolitical circumstances and economic conditions; 3) examination of the way the "unity" of a region responds to changing circumstances (a regional analysis would, for example, look for the key features signaling the decline of the utopian unity of the NLCM once the Cold War ended); 4) investigation of the nature of the relationships among different media industries in a region (e.g., film and television); and 5) enquiry into what the regional dynamics of media industries reveal about the processes of globalization.

Incorporation of all five aspects helps ensure that attention to cultural, linguistic, and historical differences does not preclude the emergence of regional genealogies that are neither bound to nor seeking a unified project. In-depth analysis avoids generalizing the characteristics of a region (e.g., South America as Spanish-speaking). Regional analysis can account for exclusion from, resistances, and limits to any given unifying project. It weighs trans-border exchanges, whether among ethnic groups or caused by migration, war, or technology. It renders visible the assumptions behind the invention of a region, and identifies the forces leading to changes in regional formations.

Regional analysis of media industries helps to show how a multiplicity of factors creates the flexible, permeable boundaries of audiovisual landscapes. Useful examination starts from investigation of the label of a region, to the origin of its classification, and on to its operation as a whole.

What's in a name?

Who names a region and for what purpose? Answering this question reveals how regions come about in response to political and economic changes. Naming a region identifies an ideological space, one that accommodates and claims certain fluid socio-economic and political elements. The label "Latin America" – in place since the nineteenth century – serves as illustration. It refers to land masses that extend from Mexico to the Straits of Magellan and north to the Caribbean islands, territories named "America" when encountered in European (Spanish, Portuguese, British, French, Dutch) expansionist voyages. In *The Idea of Latin America*, Walter Mignolo (2005) seeks to locate the "imperial/colonial foundation of the 'idea' of Latin America [to] unravel the geo-politics of knowledge from the perspective of coloniality, the untold and unrecognized historical counterpart of modernity" (xi). Indeed, for Mignolo the naming of all geographical continental divisions, as well as ideas of East and West, North and South, hides the imperial constructs behind them. In this way, the name of a region occludes the historical process that imposed a cultural knowledge system over indigenous forms.

Mignolo explores the significance of the "Latin" American label, tracing its reappropriation as a form of defiance of its Eurocentric origins. Marxist views expressed in the 1920s under nationalist ideologies led to a self-conscious use of the idea of "Latin" America as a means of decolonizing knowledge and culture. Mignolo maintains that:

In the 1950s, intellectuals in South America and the Caribbean began to express … a subcontinental concern about national as well as subcontinental identities. They introduced the "invention of America" theory … and began to question the imperial foundation of "Latinidad." For lack of a better term, "Latin" America continued to be used, not only as an entity described by European scholars and area studies specialists, but as a *critical self-consciousness of decolonization*. (44)

The NLCM became a major expression of the self-defined impulse for independence from the existing neocolonial relationship with US and European cultures. The movement articulated a cinematic reflection on Latin American identity. Filmmaker manifestos projected both national and pan-national identities, defining the project in terms of decolonization, nationalism, and plurality. The ideology of the movement formed part of a larger constellation of theoretical and political proposals focused on anti-imperialist and anti-colonial claims. The name "Latin America" associated with artistic experimentation became a cultural and political movement proposed as regional in scope, intention, politics, production, and institutional framework. Cultural events and film festivals like the International Film Festival of Viña del Mar (Chile, 1967) contributed to the dissemination of the pan-national consciousness of the NLCM.

The Viña del Mar International Film Festival was instrumental in founding regional associations such as the *Comité de Cineastas Latinoamericanos* (Committee of Latin American Filmmakers, 1974) in Caracas, Venezuela. The associations enacted the inclusive-ness of the movement, bringing together national counterparts in an infrastructure that reflected the unity and diversity of the project of Latin America that it supported.[3] The Foundation for the New Latin American Cinema (FNCL) further institu-tionalized cross-national legislative support, co-operation, training, and research.[4] As the case of Latin American cinema and the NLCM shows, the mature ideological project generates practical mech-anisms to sustain it. Fomenting national film indus-tries is thereby a function of a larger regional concept imbued with sociopolitical transformative aims.

In referring only to geopolitical limits, a name obscures the existence of displaced populations, lessening their power and influence. Recognizing the importance of the "Latin" diaspora in pan-national claims, the NLCM included US Latino/a practitioners and audiences in order to expand the meaning of the label "Latin America" and contest US hegemony in cultural terms. Chicano film-makers in the US conversely identified the early ide-ology of their cinematic movement with the NLCM. Any truly regional study of Latin American cinema needs to consider changes in audiences as a result of migration, and the work of Mexican filmmaker Alfonso Arau in the US, as much as it automatically covers that of Emilio Fernandez in Mexico. Expanding the breadth of analysis of a regional media industry to include the work of displaced populations entails investigating the way a regional name evolves and is defined by the constant friction between ideologies and challenges to them, real or perceived.

Naming a region is invested in the formation of knowledge as expressed through geography, eco-nomics, policies, culture, and technology. Which aspect becomes a dominant shaping force within an established region at any given time is determined by the historical events and conditions. A regional perspective of media industries illuminates both generative and normalizing aspects. No single strand exerts an isolated influence. Formed by exchanges arising among these characteristics, audiovisual industries at all scales respond to markets and the push and pull of regional geopolitics increasingly driven – rather than diminished or obliterated by – globalization. In the latter part of the twentieth cen-tury, Latin American cinema found new value on world cinema screens and the name became associ-ated once again with renewal and transnational trends in filmmaking.

Economics and the Regional

Distribution as key

The domestic, regional, and global economic factors that help to determine the characteristics of a region also drive the film, television, and music industries of a region. In Latin America, national distinctive-

ness – market size, subregional grouping, cultural affinities, etc. – informs the scope of interaction, competition, and market compatibilities among these separate audiovisual industry sectors. Studies dedi-cated to regional overviews can select from a pan-orama of economic and regulatory indices as a base for industry comparisons (Cocq & Levy 2006). For example, the UNESCO 2006 study *Trends in Audiovisual Markets: Regional Perspectives from the South* reports on the slow economic growth and influence of global trade on national policy decisions in Colombia, Peru, and Venezuela as a subregion (Rey 2006). Since surveys of this type are produced from a variety of institutional, national, and political per-spectives, evaluation must also consider how histo-ries and practices define the scope and purpose of the regions under review. Reporting on media indus-tries needs to address the institutional philosophy and intentions of the reporting agency.

Generally, film industries are divided into the three core sectors: production, distribution, and exhibition. As Albert Moran (1996) notes, "distribution is the key to the film industry" since it provides the economic support for the entire industrial process (1–2). Lack of distribution opportunities – domestic or interna-tional – has been a major obstacle to the growth of the cinemas of Latin America. In general, producers rely on a return from domestic distribution in order to recoup some of their original investment. Yet the scale of the domestic markets in Latin America has been too small to make such recoupment possible. Uruguay, for instance, has a population of 3.4 million and as cinematographer Cesar Challone explains, "no matter how low the budget it is very difficult to cover a film's cost" (Sardon 2007). The reasons are com-plex, and include the sizable place occupied by foreign film companies in Latin American territories. As a result, in most Latin American countries, the state joins with the private sector in efforts to move film industries beyond domestic arenas into regional and international markets.

Historical trade relations and distribution

Historical work has shown that at its inception, cinema in Latin America was a foreign import. This con-ditioned its unequal dissemination and appropriation throughout the territory of the Americas (López 2000a, 48). The arrival of the Edison and Lumière *cinématographe* operators in 1896 created a market dynamic that Paulo Antonio Paranaguá (2003) describes as a "triangular" configuration of motion picture competition in the region. European and US distributors established a foothold in Latin America, defining commercial territories as well as the way technology would be appropriated, and the development of audiences over time. The triangular relationship also defined Latin American interests against the larger, better-funded producers of Europe and the US. Essentially, the early competition over international territories between French and US distributors in particular established patterns of operation in Latin America that have proven to be resilient and in favor of foreign companies.

The problem of film distribution still remains so striking in the "Latin" Americas that filmmakers and students of the region often complain about their lack of access to the films of neighboring countries even given Spanish as a common language. Argentine director of *Hijo de la Novia* (Son of the Bride) Juan José Campanella wryly observes that "there is a total lack of communication between Latin American countries" (Daicich 2004, 163), and that domestic audiences lack interest in Argentine films. To be distributed beyond national territories, Latin American films have to be picked up by foreign companies for theatrical, satellite television, or consumer DVD release. Distribution could translate into economic success if it led to lasting structural – institutional, distribution, and exhibition – changes to support a solid regional film industry. Miriam Haddu's case study of the failed international distribution of *La Otra Conquista* (Salvador Carrasco, 1998) reveals that even great domestic box-office business is not enough to override conflicts that arise over the commercial viability of indigenous images (Haddu 2007).

Foreign distributors continue to maintain a strategic relationship to domestic industries as they attempt to expand the market for their own products. US companies are overwhelmingly dominant. Parties on both sides of this issue take a protectionist approach. Motion Picture Association of America (MPA) companies vehemently defend their corporate territories in Latin America, while Latin American states attempt to create economic and exhibition space for national culture. Nationally, the MPA "promote[s] regulatory frameworks that foster the expansion of film industry activities and co-production of national films."[5] It operates a regional office that "protects and defends the interests of its member companies in each distribution sector – theatrical, television, pay TV, home entertainment, digital and new technologies – through activities aimed at the improvement of market access and the protection of intellectual property rights."[6] By providing high levels of funding, the MPA also prioritizes anti-piracy efforts through a variety of channels and regulatory enforcement.

Since the 1990s, as regional trade pacts have restructured the flow of cultural production and its profits, MPA film companies have increasingly co-produced and distributed Latin American films. Buena Vista International for example, has distributed domestically and internationally Fabian Bielinsky's *Nine Queens* (Argentina, 2000) and Columbia and Sony Pictures Hector Babenco's *Carandiru* (2003) to very successful box-office revenues (Alvaray 2008). In Mexico, the state's Instituto Mexicano de Cinematografía (IMCINE) and independent producers turn to MPA companies such as 20th Century Fox and Warner Bros for both regional and international distribution, although not always with success. Of course, the MPA grip on distribution extends far beyond its hold on the Latin American regional film industry. Looking at the experience of national cinemas across the globe, Albert Moran (1996) points out that "Hollywood is no longer out there, beyond the national borders, but is instead very much a component of their own national cinema" (7). Focus on distribution practices and their history in a regional media industry casts light on international currents of commercialization and political economy.

The Construction of Regions

Economic and institutional alliances

A variety of sociopolitical and economic conditions and motivations lead to regional alliances among media industries. Objectives for an alliance range from the expansion of markets to the improvement of production capability and the promotion of national industries. National cultural policies in turn contribute and respond to these goals. Economic partnerships – among producers, distributors, and exhibitors – and their effect on markets and policies define the degree to which media industries extend beyond their national base and contribute to the creation of identifiable regional entities.

In the case of Latin America, multinational co-operative agreements vested in the long view, such as Programa Ibermedia, fund not only projects and prizes, but also industry development. Marcelo Piñeyro's *Plata Quemada* (2000) and Lucrecia Martel's *La Cienaga* (2001) both received support in 1999 from the nascent Ibermedia. To establish a regional theatrical and television market for its films, for example, Ibermedia has signed distribution agreements with some film festivals, and distributed films to specialized sites such as New York's Museum of Modern Art. This approach to film funding creates a niche market within a highly competitive marketplace. Where Ibermedia generates an Ibero-American shared cultural space and market, joint action by regional and subregional funding agencies, like the multi-nation Central America group Cinergía, creates effective synergies aimed at fruitful fragmentation of the regional marketplace. Under the support of Cinergía, the output of the smallest industries in Latin America and the Caribbean (Costa Rica, Guatemala, El Salvador, Belize, etc.) is integrated into the larger market of Latin America and beyond. Regionalism as expressed through these mechanisms of integration provides ways of "facing up to Hollywood" (López 2000b). These types of alliances incorporate production aesthetics and market strategies within an increasingly global mediascape.

Another trend sees the internationalization of film, TV, and music industries, as "local" media conglomerates create economic partnerships across media to expand their market. Alliances fall into two main classes: those of conglomerates that expand into regional markets; and those that produce regional associations in order to secure their various national stakes and avoid being subsumed by trans-national conglomerates. The regional infrastructure is incidental to expansion by conglomerates into a regional market. It is likely, however, to be deeply rooted in a geopolitical base when in the hands of organizations informed by social and cultural goals that aim to preserve or create a market.

Latin American countries work in alliance to strengthen the market reach of the most recent incarnation of Latin American cinema. Since the declaration of the NLCM in the early 1960s and the subsequent creation of institutions to enable co-operation in the 1970s, there are now new forces centered around and bound by new cultural, political, and industrial sources. Moving away from a political response to media as cultural imperialism, new political motivations push against other ideological forms, and articulate a regionalism now facilitated by different modes of globalization. Brazil's role, for example, can be read as an assertion of political identity, bringing it out from domination under earlier film industry configurations.

The economic and political systems in place lead to the growth or repression of national industries, and also influence the terms of integration. Cuba's film industry, albeit small, is an example of a vertically integrated national industry, as it controls its domestic production, distribution, and exhibition and has done so since the inception of the Instituto Cubano de Arte e Industria Cinematográfica (ICAIC) in 1959. Entirely centralized and owned by the state, the Cuban film industry is unique within Latin America where foreign investment plays an important role in key aspects of distribution and exhibition. Cuba has also long served as a hub for regional activities such as the International Film Festival of New Latin American Cinema.[7] However, reflective of limited national resources, and, again, of regional weakness as a legacy of historical trade embargo, the ICAIC has had to rely increasingly since the 1990s on international co-productions outside the region to finance Cuban film projects. Foreign distribution of ICAIC's films is now handled both internally and through foreign partnerships.

Shared languages, common histories, and cultural similarities form the basis for joint cultural and economic enterprises in search of both a greater share of growing media markets and stronger industry foundations. Sharing resources helps the cinema of a country find support within a larger economic framework, enabling the development and promotion of human and financial resources. The joint arrangements that arise, usually formalized as transnational agreements and institutional alliances, demonstrate the flexibility of the term "regional."

Internal markets

The case of Latin America also illustrates how collaborative or competitive practices – at the level either of industry or of institutions – along with personal relationships forge a territorial media landscape comprising economic interests, transnational audiences, and dominant media centers (Mexico, Brazil, and Argentina) (López 2000c; D'Lugo 2003). Countries with smaller industries such as Colombia respond as much to regional centers as to larger forces such as Hollywood cinema or European imports.

Competition, influence, emergence, unequal levels of economic development and appropriation of technology produce transnational exchanges of people, music, images, and ideas in search of work, funding, audiences, and expertise. Political turmoil has also driven entrepreneurs into neighboring territories to establish new media enterprises, as in the case of Cuban television entrepreneurs in the 1950s (Rivero 2007). In North America, Miami, Florida is an important center for Spanish-language broadcast media production and distribution attracting talent and producers from throughout Latin America (Yúdice 2003, 192–213). These new coordinates for production and distribution benefit Latin film and television stars and distribution companies such as Venevision and Ondamax. Through the evolution of internal markets, the national becomes increasingly embedded in the larger, regional scale, and the geography of media industries expands accordingly.

Cultural Policy

A regional analysis of cultural policy reveals how legislation determines what is defined as national culture, the manner of state or private sector intervention, and the protectionist or economically liberalizing role of foreign interests. To paraphrase Miller and Yúdice (2002), cultural policy arms organizations with institutional mechanisms for the support of creative expression within and outside government (1). Inside the realm of the state, policy guides cultural production, its uses, and dissemination, underpinned by legal frameworks that facilitate the policing of media practices. How culture is defined within the realm of national policy controls the degree to which it becomes protected, supported, produced, and marketed. States that either overtly or indirectly make culture a subject of policy – and therefore of national identity – negotiate international agreements for the protection of national artistic expression. Regional media alliances and cultural policies exert a reciprocal influence where alliances foster changes in international trade, cooperation, and dominant centers of production. These, in turn, prompt revisions to or creation of cultural policies.

In the case of Latin America, the tenor of national film laws has been strongly influenced by the dominance of foreign distributors. Direct government support of national film industries is the rule rather than the exception as governments have sought to defend domestic production and markets against foreign interests (Johnson 1996, 133). A review of changes to protectionist policies over time provides an indication of the value put on culture by a nation as well as the difficulties encountered in implementing such policies. States adjust their strategies in response to technological changes, regional and world trade agreements, increased diversification and convergence of media industries, and the worldwide circulation of cultural goods.

For example, since the 1930s and 1940s, Brazil, Mexico, and Argentina have utilized screen quotas to guarantee the exhibition of national films. But as Jorge A. Schnitman (1984) points out, "the choice and implementation of state protectionist measures for local mass media industries in developing countries is not a simple process of social engineering" (45). Schnitman distinguishes three types of protectionist policies of which screen quotas are one. Difficult to enforce and troublesome to exhibitors in their restrictiveness, such quotas often meet with resistance and failure. Of the two other types of policies, one provides supportive mechanisms, the other a combination of restriction and support (46). Because protectionist laws are produced within intricate economic, political, and social arenas, their implementation is complex. Despite its problematic nature, as the case of Latin America illustrates, some form of state protectionism is necessary as laws have to adapt to international forces as well as private sector developments acting on the production of culture.

The aforementioned UNESCO study reports that, following the collapse of their media industries in the 1990s, Colombia, Peru, and Venezuela updated their national film laws, employing new strategies to generate funds for filmmaking (Rey 2006). Peru, for example, sought to encourage creation and promotion of the cinema by integrating filmmakers into regional co-production efforts. In an attempt to preserve its cinematographic heritage, it has established a national film registry. Similar to legislation in Brazil and Mexico, Colombia's 2003 film law supports the decentralization of culture and the cinema in a way that creates incentives for private industry participation in the national film industry.

By the 1990s, in the shadow of the North American Free Trade Agreement (NAFTA), screen quotas in Mexico were being phased out while new financing incentives (Article 226) increased the number of films in production and the participation of foreign distributors. New institutional backing also came from government initiatives such as Fondo de Inversión y Estímulos al Cine Mexicano (FIDECINE), which has a comprehensive approach to film industry support.[8] One attempt to address the inequality of markets in the region comes from support for international marketing of national films to increase exhibition of Latin American films abroad. National film legislation and intricate support strategies reveal how the national becomes invested in regional networks, leading to co-produced cultural products that address multiple audiences through various platforms. Televisa Cine's theatrical foreign distribution debut in the US was Sergio Arau's *Day Without a Mexican* (2004) an

Altavista, Fidecine co-production that satirizes the growing dependency of the US on undocumented workers.

The complexity of national perspectives has brought about film laws that simultaneously respond to national and regional cultural concerns as well as to the specific economic histories and circumstances of particular national media industries. National film laws stem from and incorporate the many factors that contribute to cultural policies in a region. A study of Latin America shows how a combined examination of the history of economic and creative cooperation among film industries and of related regional and national legislative histories can trace important dimensions of state and private sector involvement not only in the evolution of media industries, but also of culture (Pelayo 2005; Martín Peña 2007).

New Geographies

Regional configurations demand adaptation to a greatly enlarged field of play. In the field of culture, realignment involves reluctant and emboldened actors alike in defensive integration, aggressive moves to secure markets or resources, and community building. International trade arrangements organize an economic regional landscape while establishing a territorial configuration. But an inward shift also occurs when media industries act against global tendencies in order to create a strong national identity.

Regional trade agreements of the 1990s typically implemented neoliberal economic policies with concomitant privatizations of broadcast media, the lifting of protectionist policies, an onslaught of foreign products in the domestic arena, and a loss of control to foreign investors. Latin American policymakers responded by introducing mixed investment programs, which marked a move away from centralized support in several countries. Film industries became more assertive in the market, trying to turn trade agreements to their advantage. In cultural-linguistic markets, local and national producers have had an edge over imported product (Straubhaar 1991). Brazil, for instance, proves the limits to Hollywood's incursion as the majority of images on television screens consumed by domestic audiences are nationally produced.

The cultural linguistic perspective of the region identifies the market advantages of domestic producers, but the implications of trade interactions, like cultural exception, are not always clear on paper. As is evident in the case of NAFTA, whereas Canada entered the trade arrangement with a cultural exception agreement, Mexico did not. As a result, Mexico's cultural products under NAFTA are considered "transborder services," thus placing Mexican culture industries under the control of the treaty, just like agriculture or automobiles. NAFTA interactions however, do not tell the whole picture. Rather, a range of internal factors also contributed to the Mexican industry's problems. These included the continuation of earlier policies of limited and uneven support for film, differences in investment rules and labor costs, and media deregulation that contributed to a global trend of media ownership convergence (Ugalde 2006). All these elements are uncovered by thinking of the region as a set of dynamic forces, in this instance acting in synergistic interplay around the implementation of NAFTA.

Against the backdrop of regional trade pacts – principally NAFTA and Mercado Común del Sur (MERCOSUR) – nations working in partnership lobbied for cultural exception as necessary to integrate and build stronger culture industries (Falicov 2002). The Group of the Common Market, an organ of MERCOSUR, established the *Reunión Especializada de Autoridades Cinematográficas y Audiovisuales del Mercosur* (Specialized Group of Cinematographic Authorities of Mercosur, RECAM), giving regional partnerships greater official and institutional recognition.[9] Also looking globally, RECAM successfully negotiated transregional economic collaboration for MERCOSUR film industries with the European Union. Although cultural exception can establish essential ground for sustainable media industries, it cannot alone guarantee an equitable playing field for members of a regional trade agreement.

The necessity for national film laws has become more salient with the advent of neoliberalism as a driver of trade pacts. As outlined, negotiation of

cultural exception has helped to ensure conditions necessary for adopting policies that value culture as a national resource. Cultural exception facilitates the work of regional alliances and national legislators faced with continuing incursion by foreign distributors.

Grassroots Regionalism

Thinking regionally beyond commercial circuits, alternative networks of cultural integration and survival are often expressed by micro-regions. This form of regionalism is central to indigenous communities like the *Coordinadora Latinoamericana de Cine y Comunicación de los Pueblos Indígenas* (Latin American Film and Communication Coordination of Indigenous Peoples, CLACPI). An international grassroots organization, CLACPI is a network of indigenous media makers in Bolivia, Brazil, Chile, Colombia, Cuba, Guatemala, Mexico, and Peru. In its aims to "increase the production and distribution of indigenous media, and develop viable financing alternatives," CLACPI represents the type of community goal underlying the hundreds of similar audiovisual projects across the region.[10] Focusing on community development, education, and social motivation, networks such as CLACPI function both at the regional and community level. Unlike commercial networks, their use of digital media in particular is geared to assisting the poor, linking communities, and preserving memories – vital cultural and educational functions in a region where populations have endured long periods of economic turmoil, civil and political strife, urban growth, and rural degeneration.

Conclusion

The study of regional interconnections would benefit from much more research on large *and* small national industries, labor practices, cultural policy, institutions and infrastructures, aesthetic traditions, and artistic interactions. Increased attention of this kind would help to prevent inadvertent disregard of significant factors in a region, which can occur with a focus on a particular regional configuration, arrangement, or scale of interaction. This chapter's opening quote from Octavio Getino reiterates a shared history of film in Latin America and re-affirms the constant dialogue between national and regional domains even as the terms of exchange have changed. Relations extend across national bor-ders deliberately forged through cultural institutions or out of the need to expand production paradigms. The example of Latin American cinema industries shows how a regional approach can reveal not only the parameters of an explicit movement but also the overlap between unified projects, structures of col-laboration, market integration, and co-production partnerships. Regional thinking, as it grapples with historical conditions and globalization, can also inform the development of media practices in all scales and scopes of production. In their sense of unity based on ideological perspectives and shared goals for relevance in economic and cultural territo-ries, fresh generations of film, music, television, and new media makers are today shaping both regional and global terrains rich with interactions fundamen-tal to the shape of future media industries every-where.

Notes

1   See for example D'Lugo (2003); Devadas (2006); and Durovicova & Newman (2009).
2   Film scholars Ana M. López, Julianne Burton, Michael Chanan, Michael T. Martin and others have written about the New Latin American Cinema and its pan-American dimension.
3   Initially the committee was made up of 40 filmmakers from around the continent who met annually since 1974 in places such as Mérida, Brasilia, Rio de Janeiro, Quito, Caracas, Cartagena, Mexico, Madrid, and La Habana. The organization was situated in Caracas, Venezuela. The foundational resolution was signed September 11, 1974. Text is available at www.cinelatinoamericano.org/texto.aspx?cod=45, accessed October 22, 2007.
4   Founded in 1985 and located in Havana, Cuba.
5   Quote from MPA website, www.mpaa.org/inter_latin_america.asp, accessed July 6, 2008.
6   Quote from MPA Latin America website, www.mpaal.org.br, accessed July 6, 2008.
7   Founded in 1979 as a further articulation of the NLCM, the International Film Festival of New Latin American Cinema held in Havana, Cuba, con-tinues to be an important venue for gathering and forging regional and international alliances. In 2007 the Festival has received significant funding for prizes through new partnerships with Venezuela.
8   The federal government and the Secretaria de Hacienda y Credito Público established FIDECINE in 2001. The FIDECINE executive committee is made up of representatives from the private and public sectors.
9   Quote from RECAM website, www.recam.org/noticias/union_europea.htm, accessed July 6, 2008.
10 Quote from CLACPI website, www.clacpi.org, accessed June 30, 2008.

References

Alvaray, L. (2008) National, regional and global: new waves of Latin American cinema. *Cinema Journal* **47**, 48–65.

Cocq, E. and Levy, F. (2006) Audiovisual markets in the developing world. In *Trends in Audiovisual Markets: Regional Perspectives from the South*. UNESCO, pp. 21–88. At http://portal.unesco.org/ci/en/ev.php-URL_ID=22361&URL_DO=DO_TOPIC&URL_SECTION=201.html, accessed June 30, 2008.

Daicich, O. (ed.) (2004) *Apuntes Sobre el Nuevo Cine Latinoamericano: Entrevistas a Realizadores Latinoamericanos*. Fundación del Nuevo Cine Latinoamericano, Havana.

Devadas, V. (2006) Rethinking transnational cinema: the case of Tamil cinema. *Senses of Cinema* [Online] **41**. At www.sensesofcinema.com/contents/06/41/transnational-tamil-cinema.html, accessed July 6, 2008.

D'Lugo, M. (2003) Authorship, globalization and the new identity of Latin American cinema: from the

Mexican "ranchera" to Argentinian "exile." In Guneratne, A. R. and Disanayake, W. (eds.) *Rethinking Third Cinema*. Routledge, London, pp. 103–25.

Drucker, P. (1993) *Post-Capitalist Society*. HarperCollins, New York.

Durovicova, N. and Newman, K. E. (eds.) (2009) *World Cinemas, Transnational Perspectives*. Routledge, New York.

Falicov, T. L. (2002) Film policy under MERCOSUR: the case of Uruguay. *Canadian Journal of Communication* **27**, 33–46.

Farred, G. (2003) Crying for Argentina: the branding and unbranding of area studies. *Nepantla: Views from South* **4**, 121–32.

Farrell, M., Hettne, B., and Langenhove, L. (2005) *Global Politics of Regionalism: Theory and Practice*. Pluto Press, London.

Getino, O. (2004) Octavio Getino. In Daicich, O. (ed.) *Apuntes sobre el Nuevo Cine Latinoamericano: Entrevistas a Realizadores Latinoamericanos*. Fundación del Nuevo Cine Latinoamericano, Havana, pp. 133–51.

Haddu, M. (2007) The power of looking: politics and the gaze in Salvador Carrasco's *La Otra Conquista*. In Shaw, D. (ed.) *Contemporary Latin American Cinema: Breaking Into the Global Market*. Rowman & Littlefield, Lanham, pp. 153–72.

Jay, P. (2006) Locating disciplinary change: the afterlives of area and international studies in the age of globalization. *American Literary History* **18**, 175–89.

Johnson, R. (1996) Film policy in Latin America. In Moran, A. (ed.) *Film Policy: International, National, and Regional Perspectives*. Routledge, London, pp. 128–47.

Kinder, M. (1993) *Blood Cinema: The Reconstruction of National Identity in Spain*. University of California Press, Berkeley.

López, A. M. (2000a) Early cinema and modernity in Latin America. *Cinema Journal* **40**, 48–78.

López, A. M. (2000b) Facing up to Hollywood. In Gledhill, C. and Williams, L. (eds.) *Reinventing Film Studies*. Hodder Arnold, London, pp. 419–37.

López, A. M. (2000c) Crossing nations and genres: traveling filmmakers. In Noriega, C. A. (ed.) *Visible Nations: Latin American Cinema and Video*. Minnesota University Press, Minneapolis, pp. 33–50.

Martín Peña, F. (2007) Estudios cinematográficos en Argentina: el problema de las Fuentes. Paper presented at the Latin American Studies Association, Montreal, September 3–5.

Mignolo, W. (2005) *The Idea of Latin America*. Blackwell, Oxford.

Miller, T. and Yúdice, G. (2002). *Cultural Policy*. Sage, London.

Misrepassi, A. (2002) Area studies, globalization, and the nation-state in crisis. *Nepantla: Views from South* **3**, 547–52.

Miyoshi, M. and Harootunian, H. D. (eds.) (2002) *Learning Places: The Afterlives of Area Studies*. Duke University Press, Durham.

Moran, A. (ed.) (1996) *Film Policy: International, National, and Regional Perspectives*. Routledge, London.

Paranaguá, P. A. (2003) *Tradición y Modernidad en el Cine de América Latina*. Fondo de Cultura Economica de España.

Pelayo, A. (2005) El cine mexicano en los años ochenta: la generación de la crisis. Doctoral dissertation, Universidad Nacional Autonoma de México, México, D.F.

Rey, G. (2006) Trends and perspectives of the audio-visual markets in Colombia, Peru, and Venezuela. In *Trends in Audiovisual Markets: Regional Perspectives from the South*. UNESCO, pp. 155–222. At http://portal.unesco.org/ci/en/ev.php-URL_ID=22361&URL_DO=DO_TOPIC&URL_SECTION=201.html, accessed June 30, 2008.

Rivero, Y. M. (2007) Broadcasting modernity: Cuban television 1950–1953. *Cinema Journal* **46**, 3–25.

Sardon, V. (2007) *Latin American Cinema Goes from Strength to Strength*. Monsters and Critics.com. At http://movies.monstersandcritics.com/features/article_1302167.php/Latin_American_cinema_goes_from_strength_to_strength, accessed June 30, 2008.

Sarkar, B. (2008) Postcolonial and transnational perspectives. In Donald, J., Fuery, P., and Renov, M. (eds.) *Handbook of Film Studies*. Sage, Thousand Oaks, pp. 123–44.

Schnitman, J. A. (1984) *Film Industries in Latin America: Dependency and Development*. Ablex, New Jersey.

Sousa Santos, B. de (2006) Globalizations. *Theory, Culture & Society* **23**, 393–9.

Straubhaar, J. (1991) Beyond media imperialism: asymmetrical interdependence and cultural proximity. *Critical Studies in Mass Communication* **8**, 1–11.

Ugalde, V. (2006) Panorama de la producción cinematográfica nacional. Paper presented at Symposium on Mexican Cinema, Los Angeles, March 10–12.

Yúdice, G. (2003) *The Expediency of Culture: Uses of Culture in the Global Era*. Duke University Press, Durham.

10

Thinking Nationally
Domicile, Distinction, and Dysfunction in Global Media Exchange

....

Nitin Govil

> It's not a system – it's a country.
> John McClane (Bruce Willis) in Live Free or Die Hard

Against "mis-underestimation"
. . . .

George W. Bush's summer 2001 proclamation, "Our nation must come together to unite" (Bush 2001), was quickly enshrined in the lexicon of presidential yuk-yuks by his detractors on the US political left. It would soon become clear, however, that there was some method in his malapropism (if not in his madness). After September 11th of the same year, Bush's tautological reasoning would frame the project of a resurgent American self-justification, where the nation served to both *describe* the state of social collectivity and *prescribe* the role of the state in securing its formation around the world. Read against the current geopolitics of military intervention, where effects are manufactured to precede causes, Bush's flaunting of rhetorical convention in order to justify the open jurisdiction of American unilateralism reminds us that the national is a way of looking backwards and forwards as well as staring down at our own feet.

Bush's evocation of the nation as retrospect and prospect devolves with the history of the concept. Associated with forms of belonging derived from early modern political formations, the nation has a much longer history of deployment as a marker of

racial, and later religious, differentiation. In contemporary usage, nations are (more or less) large groups of people affiliated by – or through a combination of – ancestry or descent, language, belief systems, heritage and custom, territorial cohabitation, ethnicity, or sometimes even vocation or disposition. Traditions of social and political theory since the mid-nineteenth century have suggested that nations justify state power by establishing the nature of commonality, the mechanisms of its constitution and assembly, and enacting, through contractual and communal obligation, the forms of identification that establish inter- and intra-subjective coherency and maintain it over time. The terms of this national identification are thought to be discovered through a process of retroactive primordialism, the re-creation of "a sentiment of wholeness and continuity with the past to transcend that alienation or rupture between individual and society that modernity brought about" (Eriksen 1993, 105).

While nations are conventional rather than natural, the articulation of origin in the racial and ethnic chauvinism of "objective" determinations of national character has been inscribed in the brutality of slavery, colonialism, genocide, and state repression committed in the name of nationalism. Yet the "subjective" and liberal traditions of national voluntarism, integration, and the difficult but necessary production of solidarity, attest to the fundamental condition of incompleteness at the heart of individual and social identity (see Calhoun 2007). The oscillation of the national between the recovery of a mythic unity and the material enactment of a modern polity based on voluntarist principles constitutes the "liberal-rationalist dilemma" for western nationalisms. At the same time, as part of a collective struggle for self-determination, first and colonized peoples have deployed the idea of an essential national identity as a bulwark against the violent imposition of foreign particularities masquerading as universals (Chatterjee 1986; 1993).

For better or (often) worse, the national has facilitated the mobilization of the symbolic and material itineraries that characterize modernity as well as its alternatives. Media industries play an important role in assembling the technologies of interconnection associated with the imagination and narration of the national. Indebted to the modern project of collective address and mobilization, media industries have found the national "good to think with" (Douglas & Isherwood 1979, 40), even as nationalism has been implicated in unthinking prejudice and unthinkable violence. The national has given the media industries a way to think both globally and locally: the multilateral agreements that sustain disparate economies of cultural production such as outsourcing and runaway production (see Elmer & Gasher 2005) would be impossible without the site-specific strategies that secure the cultural labor of audiences and workers. Central here is the role of language, with "localization" strategies for multinational media industries defined through dubbing, subtitling, and production in local vernaculars; translation, after all, remains crucial to globalization of moving-image media (see Nornes 2007). For the media industries, the nation has served as a unit of analysis for the investigation of state imperatives and the dynamics of cultural reception. The national has also served as a way of periodizing the historical transformations of media industries, particularly in terms of pre- to post-colonial transitions and planned economy to market formations.

Focusing on the spheres of operation, tension, and conflict between media industries and national configurations, this chapter considers *scale, subsidy*, and *subjectivity* as a series of overlapping – though not necessarily conjunctural – modalities through which the media industries think nationally. *Scale* refers to the mechanisms through which media industries are inscribed across a range of territorial and temporal practices, as well the ways in which these practices are produced, arranged, and articulated in relationship to one another. *Subsidy* refers to the exercise of incentives through which the state preserves distinction in the field of cultural production, as well as the ways in which these distinctions are structured and deployed through various mechanisms of *scale*. Finally, *subjectivity* refers to those experiential processes through which persons and groups align and commit to particular forms of life, the processes that facilitate interaction across space, and the provisions for reconfiguring identities over time.

Focusing on the screen industries, this chapter describes these three modalities of scale, subsidy, and subjectivity in terms of piracy, location shooting, and diasporic media. My basic premise is simple enough. Media globalization provides opportunities for industries to deploy the national as a way to structure accumulation across a variety of contexts: the account of scale and piracy, for instance, describes the ways in which the national serves to position the media industries, taking advantage of territorial opportunities to structure transborder flows; the account of state subsidization of location shooting describes the ways in which authenticity is inscribed in the preservation and protection of media industries as national; and audience engagement of "trans-local" media demonstrates the ways in which the national functions as an elastic form capable of stretching across territorial boundaries to address the repertoire and itineraries of diasporic culture.

These modalities of scale, subsidy, and subjectivity are interwoven, particularly in the ways that media industries characterize communicative competencies, programming preferences, and reception habits as proof of the presence of "national character," a kind of shorthand for rendering legible the complexities of cultural production across local and global contexts. That these presumptions are enabled, legitimated, and challenged by material practices is largely the point of what follows.

Scale: The National as a Means of Position (and Maneuver)

Box-office revenues rise and fall, but counting revenues lost to global film piracy remains a growth industry. During the late 1990s, American film industries claimed that annual losses from media piracy stood at US $3–3.5 billion (MPA 2003). In 2006, loss estimates increased to $6.1 billion, part of a total output loss of $20.5 billion for film-related US media industries, while counterfeiting and piracy cost the US economy up to $250 billon and 750,000 jobs annually (MPA 2006). Tabulated by the very enforcement agencies set to gain from their maximization, these figures inform a statistical imaginary that legitimates criminalization and tighter copyright restrictions (Yar 2005). The enumeration of piracy losses produced through an alignment of state and market interests serves as a crucial "center of calculation" for the media industries (Olds & Thrift 2005). The key to the extrapolation of revenue losses is the presumption that the cost of each seized pirated unit can be measured as an equivalent loss of a unit of "legitimate" revenue.

That the legitimate and the pirate are mirror-opposites is a fiction designed to isolate the domain of legality and define communities by their comparative aspiration toward it. This is why banners hanging over the Xiangyang market in Shanghai read "maintain intellectual property … strive to be a civilized nation" (Lewis 2005). As territorial obligations, intellectual property regimes engage the nation as the horizon of innovation for media industries. In this way, infractions can be diagnosed as flaws in national character (Bond 2005). So, for example, the Chinese are assumed to be "prone" to piracy given Confucianism's prioritization of emulation and compilation over originality and composition, as well as the customary spirit of compromise over litigation as a way of resolving disputes over cultural authenticity (Cornish 2007. For counter-arguments to these "cultural barriers" to intellectual property protection, see Yu 2008). By pushing for changes in state intellectual property regimes, American and European governments have used the national – via bilateral sanctions and boycotts

directed at noncompliant governments – to cordon off those places that do not meet their standards.

In encouraging strong anti-piracy pronouncements by the Chinese government, western media industries have misinterpreted the relationship between national authority and local practices. Pirate commodity manufacture and distribution is critical to small-scale urban and rural economies in China, and local officials – drawn from populations reliant on these economies – are generally loath to enforce national policy objectives, particularly when they negatively impact the local economy. China's gradual shift from planned to market economy has facilitated the autonomy of local jurisdictions and officials as the national government has decentralized (Ting 2007). In the Chinese anti-piracy context, the national actually insulates against the transformation of local practice. At the same time, local pirate production coupled with a dilapidated theatrical exhibition sector has fueled the desire of Chinese film producers to seek international markets.

The interoperability of legitimate and pirate industries demonstrates that architectonic assertions of "layers" or levels of practice characterized as local, regional, national, international, and global, are knowable only in terms of "the connections, mediations, negotiations and the very real existence of power relations among them" (Mattelart 1994, 242). So, while western policy technocrats assume that the national scales down to the local, the Chinese example provides evidence that it often does not. Yet the national does make possible certain local interventions. Until 2006, for example, Canada barely rated a mention in frequent piracy reports commissioned by the US film studios, who cast China as the poster-child for Hollywood's campaign to shut down large pirate distribution networks. After video-recording in a US movie theater was reclassified as a felony in 2005, media pirates took advantage of Canadian laws permitting videotaping in theaters without intent of commercial distribution. Canada has emerged as a central player in pirate film production, responsible for 20 to 50 percent of theater-taped titles that comprise the bulk of newly pirated films distributed over the Internet and in markets around the world (MacDonald 2007;

Puzzanghera 2007). Because of the presence of English and French audio-tracks in Montreal, the city's pirate industries "produce" over 150 films per year, double the "legitimate" Canadian output. It seems that film piracy has not escaped the transformative effects of Canadian runaway production!

Piracy has also created opportunities for the media industries. When the cartel of major film studios represented by the US Motion Picture Association boycotted Russia in the early 1990s to protest piracy, smaller American film companies such as American International Pictures and Ifex International were able to take advantage of the vacuum created by the absence of large-scale US exhibition and establish a foothold in the Russian market even though overall piracy numbers increased (Mickiewicz 2001). More recently, Hollywood companies like Warner Bros. and Disney have started releasing legitimate DVDs priced competitively with pirate DVDs in China. In addition, US-based entertainment companies, having reached domestic saturation, are registering their intellectual properties in "frontier" markets, particularly in Eastern Europe and South Asia (outside India), with relatively weak regulatory regimes, prioritizing the presence of local agents in the exploitation of national markets. As the head of international licensing for DreamWorks animation put it, "You must know the culture and customs of consumers to make the right products" (Schmelzer 2007).

Despite the consistent charges of regulatory inefficiency directed at "developing" markets by western media industries, creating what they charge is a structural barrier to legitimate markets, regulatory differences allow these same industries certain strategic advantages. While structural adjustment policies were setting the agenda for international economic reform, the invention of the "emerging market" by World Bank economists in the 1980s configured the essentially permanent nature of transition in certain national economies, especially Brazil, Russia, India, and China, with built-in volatility and risk but also the possibility of enormous returns on (and for) western investment. When the stubborn persistence of planned economies lag behind the liberal requirements of international investors, these same economies carve out locations enabled by but still outside the domain of the national. These include industrial estates for the production of computer monitors and televisions as well as special economic zones for their eventual "de-manufacture" and dispersal into the local water table (see Parks 2007). For emerging markets, the nation is a conduit for global venture capital movements rather than their final destination, which is why one Delhi-based brand consultant describes India as "the proverbial bus in today's business world ... no one knows where it is going, no one knows whether there is space on it for them – but no one wants to miss that bus" (Timmons 2007).

Given the widespread "institutionalization of uncertainty" (Robertson 1990, 16) created by the rapid movements of investment capital around the world, the national provides a way for media industries – whether they are legitimate, pirate, or a mix of the two – to articulate a nodal point for the exploitation of local and global capabilities. It is clear that risk and volatility are the structural conditions of the new global economic configuration, and the national plays a distinctive role in the ideological work of scaling these conditions in relationship to territorial obligations, shaping the "social and material and cultural commitments [through which] localities or globalities come, tentatively, into being" (Tsing 2000, 348).

Subsidy: Media Policy and the Production of National Authenticity

Modernization theory and other functionalist orthodoxies that formed the dominant intellectual justification for area studies beginning in the 1940s relied on the idea of nations as distinctive organic totalities, where "modern" nations were simply more advanced than "traditional" ones. This was the operating largesse of the new development communications (Lerner 1958), where American foundations like Ford and Rockefeller, alongside state agencies like the National Aeronautics and Space Administration, worked to create national media institutions throughout the Global South. For the newly decolonized countries that formed the backbone of the Non-Aligned Movement after World

War II, the developmental paradigm offered western support for nationalist elites to implement state monopolies in emerging media institutions. However, the combined impact of early postcolonial theory influenced by Fanon (1965), dependency discourse in the late 1960s (Gunder Frank 1967), and the articulation of cultural imperialism (Schiller 1976), helped to crack open the ideological foundations of modernization theory. The MacBride Commission would suggest that the surrender of national sovereignty to international capital could be countervailed by the countries of the Global South achieving "self-reliance in communication capacities and policies" (MacBride 1980, 134), and a number of substitution initiatives were created to combat western media imports in the 1970s. The trajectory of international communications from the close of World War II through to the early 1980s suggests that the national was implicated in a movement away from the extraction of distinction for the purposes of development toward the prioritization of sovereignty as a means of sustainability.

The contemporary multilateral media policy environment, predicated on the harmonization of national legislative and regulatory difference in trading bodies like the World Trade Organization (see Chakravartty & Sarikakis 2006), seems to have dissolved the national into the global. After all, the point of harmonization is to achieve consensus through the enacting of common policy principles that exceed local and regional regulatory idiosyncrasies. Yet, as we saw in the previous section, transnational capital flows still rely on national institutional frameworks to structure and implement the global economy. As one of the most significant ways of investigating and transforming the media industries, critical political economy recognizes the continued importance of national indicators of media ownership, diffusion, export, and import. Furthermore, critical political economy's dominant registers of inequality – monopolization and the division of labor – as well as its central solution – amelioration through economic redistribution – are oriented toward the state and population, where the national has played a traditional enumerative function in the exercise of governmentality. In fact, rather than the erasure of the national, we are now seeing distinctive

"spatio-temporal orderings" that reconstitute the national as an *assemblage* rather than a predetermined set of capabilities constituted by an existing and exclusive territoriality (Sassen 2006, 406–15).

One of the most remarkable spatio-temporal orderings of the national is the emergence of incentives for local and international cinema production. Here, states acquire legitimacy by drawing on the national as a symbolic resource. O'Regan (1996) suggests a number of factors for the alignment of cinema and the national in cultural policy: cinema provides a "common civic culture" for heterogeneous audiences; it provides the possibility for representing certain cultural forms as both essential and exceptional to national self-definition; it can serve as a way to promote the symbolic resources of the nation on the global stage; and the screen industries serve as a mechanism for articulating local practices to national institutional priorities. It is important to note that the national can also be legitimated through a movement external to the geography of state borders. For example, smaller screen industries can be celebrated as "national cinemas" through their transnational circulation (Elsaesser 1989; Hjort 2005); at the same time, distinctions between diverse local and regional screen industries can be erased under the overarching category of the national (Govil 2007; Mazumdar 2007).

While there has been an overall decline in direct state subvention of media arts, the capitalization of cultural production is now seen as even more essential to the overall economic sustainability of a nation. This prioritization might be productively located within the interrelationship of products and services, instantiated by new communication and labor technologies that have narrowed boundaries between software and hardware as distinctive drivers of the information economy. Culture is a key instrument in the materialization of contemporary economic transformation. Yúdice (2003) notes that the "expediency of culture," the transformation of culture into a *resource* that informs the institutionalization of the "new" economy, the "creative" economy, and the "creative industries" in Australia, Britain, and the US, "focuses on the strategies implied in any invocation of culture, any invention of tradition, in relation to some purpose or goal" (38; see also Miller 2004).

Historically, international film producers were drawn to location shooting because unique local geographies provided the authenticity necessary to anchor a film's narrative. Nowadays, producers are also drawn to locations because they fulfill a film's budgetary rationalization, which is why the village scenes for *Borat: Cultural Learnings of America for Make Benefit Glorious Nation of Kazakhstan* were shot in Romania and, as of 2004, 80 percent of the Czech film industry was supported by foreign productions (Hofmann 2005). Lured to location shooting by tax breaks and other production incentives, international screen investment is supposed to galvanize local industries, but this doesn't always happen. Location shooting subsidies invoke what Miller (2003) characterizes as the "commerce–culture dilemma," the struggle between subsidizing a cultural sector that might serve as a catalyst for economy at large and the creation of a cinema that speaks in the vernacular language of the popular. This dilemma is well illustrated by the South African and British cases.

In early 2005, a South African film commission proposed a small "transaction-based moving image tax" on film imports in order to fund a subsidy system designed to quintuple the country's 1 percent share of global screen production. While South Africa remains one of the top destinations for international location shooting, less than 0.1 percent of film management, technical, and service personnel are black, while black audiences, constituting 80 percent of the population, buy just 15 percent of tickets sold annually (Marrs 2005). Here, the national underwrites the pre-eminence of diversity in global recruitment over prevailing gross inequities in local film production and reception. National incentives can also be localized in an attempt to address a lack of global visibility. Founded in 2000, the UK Film Council, backing films such as *Bend it Like Beckham* and supported by a mix of British governmental funds and National Lottery proceeds, funnels £70 million annually toward training programs and film schools, local cinemas and screen agencies, and project development for independent cinema. Yet in 2004, British films accounted for 16 percent of the year's releases, earning just over 5 percent at the box office; American films, including

non-UK co-productions, accounted for 39 percent of 2004 releases in Britain and took over 73 percent of the box office (Beaujeu 2006).

Since subsidies are like loans taken from public coffers, they are subject to intense political scrutiny. In many contexts, production subsidies have served as a way for wealthy citizens to divert their income tax obligations by investing in short-term bundles of film projects, rather than encouraging local production sectors through increased employment and by creating a multiplier for ancillary industries like leisure and tourism. To address these concerns, governments have resorted to tests of authenticity in order to determine whether a film production is worthy of national subvention. Is the production principally shot in the country providing the subsidy? What proportion of the lead cast, crew, and producers are from the country in question? Are the storylines set in the country and does the subject matter reflect or contribute to "national culture"? Consideration for these tests of authenticity led to the British government's decision in 2006 to withdraw tax incentives for films that were not "culturally British" (Coates 2006).

One of the enduring questions in subsidizing national film industries is the issue of spatial and temporal direction. Should subsidies be directed at production, distribution, or exhibition? What mix of these sectors is appropriate in an age of horizontally integrated media industries? Some governments are experimenting with allowing film producers to defer immediate tax credits for greater subsidies down the line, a way of promoting long-term commitments in national industries rather than short-term investments. Shadowing all these developments is the popular perception of Hollywood's free market, sustained by publications like *The Economist*, which asserts that "the world's best films are produced by America's unsubsidized industry" (*The Economist* 2004). Never mind the history of currency and export assistance provided to Hollywood and its contributions to Democratic and Republican election campaigns, or continued US federal support for media conglomeration, or state subsidies for local film production that include wage and income tax rebates, sales tax credits, and refunds on food, hotel stays, and film equipment purchase and repairs (Miller et al. 2005). Might it be that the most powerful "national cinema" on earth operates behind the disavowal of its very existence – and if so, what better way to live out the fantasy of its "universal" appeal?

Subjectivity: Identity, Mobility, and the Itineraries of the National

Finding an "internalism" common to the work of Deutsch (1966), Gellner (1983), and Anderson (1983), where nations are defined as spaces "strongly bounded by their socially communicative structures of interaction," Schlesinger (2000) faults an almost exclusive focus on the national as an interiority constituted by and through geographic boundaries. It is beyond question, however, that mass media have been central to "transforming the political 'idea' of nationhood into the daily experience and feeling of nationhood" (Martín-Barbero 1993, 165). For example, a number of recent studies have examined how right-wing political movements in India were able to use television to empower the fiction of national unity in order to legitimate a majoritarian cultural politics (Rajagopal 2001; Brosius 2005; Kumar 2005). In its generation of an affective proximity across dispersed spaces and the linkage of "individuals to persisting communities whose generations form indissoluble links in the chain of memories and identities" (Smith 1986, 176), media industries operate by combining technologies of contiguity with narratives of continuity.

While the media situate our everyday lives and provide a means for our interrelation, they are also central to our experiences of fluidity. If, as Peters (1999) claims, "movement is one of the central resources for social description," the national has provided both constancy and variability in the definition of identities beyond the territorial borders of the state (18). One reason for the nation's longevity is that it is able to articulate, much like media, an alignment between centripetal, place-based logics of coherency and centrifugal, space-based logics of dispersion. The nation is equally at home with the production of local communities bound to particular

realms in the political and economic discourse of citizenship, and comfortably homeless with the production of global communities tied to collective traditions in the discourse of diaspora. If geographic borders have been central to the circumscription of nations as communicative spaces, the itinerancy of diaspora has framed the articulation of "cultural" citizenship, enabled by migration and characterized by the experiences of minority disenfranchisement and the pressures of assimilation (Miller 2006). When it comes to analyzing media reception practices implicated in movement and migration, however, traditional methods of media analysis have needed some refinement.

For media studies, ethnography's inquiry into reception practices has provided a useful corollary to critical political economy's traditional focus on production contexts. With its focus on participant observation, its attention to the occasions of media reception and the economies of attention that inform them, ethnography has also served to provide a more reflexive alternative to the functionalism implicit in mass communications accounts of media transmission. However, ethnographic analysis has been susceptible, as Seiter (1999) notes, to short-term observation of single media interaction. Given its spatial investment in the localization of interpretive communities, ethnography seems to have certain limitations in the analysis of transnational reception.

To address this limitation, Kraidy and Murphy (2003) advocate "translocal" media ethnography, whose "importance lies more in its capacity to comprehend the articulation of the global with the local than its supposed ability to understand the local in isolation of large-scale structures and processes" (304). An early exemplar of translocal methodology, Gillespie's (1995) study of Punjabi youth in London explores the ways in which ethnic identity is mediated through collective forms of media consumption. Gillespie's multi-sited ethnography articulates the micro-processes of identity construction to the macro-processes of global migration through a kind of "peripatetic, translative mapping" (Marcus 1998, 99). Here, diaspora functions as an "intermediate concept" between the local and the global, transcending the spatial boundaries of the nation but also reinventing English, Indian, Punjabi, Sikh, and youth cultures through shared experiences of dislo-cation. It is important to note, however, that media's role in the dispersion and re-imagination of national identity is not limited to the practices of diasporic reception. The reflexivity associated with the re-articulation of national identities to the movements of migration can also inform new modes of diasporic media production.

Small-scale media industries engaged in pro-ducing for diasporic audiences invoke the national as a way to intervene and reinvent the dominant hier-archies of commercialized media. For example, Naficy's (2001) evocation of the national through "accented" media production by diasporic film-makers, which cut across capitalized, non- and semi-commercial, collective, and artisanal practices, draws differences between *interstitial* and *collective* modes of film production. The interstitial mode refers to complex, multilingual, and low-output filmmaking produced through a set of integrated labor practices that address the fact that diasporic filmmakers find primary employment as technicians across an array of media industries, impacting the multi-generic textuality of their films. Such work, financed with practitioner funding and augmented by additional public and private investment, is pri-marily distributed through festival and academic markets. On the other hand, the collective mode of production refers to collaborative filmmaking, dis-tribution, and exhibition that are often subsidized by organizations with a broad mandate of promot-ing ethnic media culture. This mode of production creates multiple pressures for accented filmmakers, who must contend with hostility from their "home" governments' censorship of politically charged films that might foment criticism and unrest. The pol-itical economy of interstitial and collective film-making, Naficy (2001) suggests, entails the diasporic filmmaker's "horizontal and vertical involvement in all aspects and phases of their work," generating a set of "organizational and textual counter-practices [through which] the filmmakers are transformed from displaced subjects to active agents of their own emplacement" (100).

Naficy convincingly demonstrates how the dia-critics of "minor" media production help to situate small-scale media practices in relation to large commercialized structures, creating the possibility of co-optation, resistance, and disidentification. Small-scale diasporic media producers attend to the needs of their art and their audience by taking advantage of funding networks designed to sup-port the proliferation and investigation of the national beyond certain geographic domains. The fashioning of diasporic media through dynamic reception and production practices deploys the national in a way that demonstrates that the "idea of the territorial nation-state as a transcendent and exclusive ideal form is no longer tenable" (Berry 2006, 154). While these media forms can end up substantiating the majoritarian fiction of national collectivity or recapitulating the "proper" location of minority production within mainstream prac-tices, diasporic media might also designate a pro-cess of permanent deferral, where the identity of the national is oriented toward contingency rather than actuality.

Conclusion: The National as Somewhere, Everywhere, and Nowhere

While I have tended to conflate cinema and televi-sion, two exemplary studies of global media, Chaudhuri's (2006) *Contemporary World Cinema* and Straubhaar's (2007) *World Television*, highlight important differences in the engagement of the national across different screen forms. Chaudhuri's book offers a careful criticism of the traditional "national cinema" approaches that have dominated film studies, advocating a more integrative approach that considers audiovisual media as constituted by the materiality of cultural flows such as film festi-vals, trade regulation, satellite television, and piracy. Nevertheless, *Contemporary World Cinema* is organ-ized around chapters that reference traditional regis-ters of national and regional cinemas, with headings like "European Cinema," "Iranian Cinema," and a chapter on "Indian Cinema" that is separate from another on "South Asian Cinema." Straubhaar's book suggests that television's powerful mobiliza-tion of "cultural proximity" provides a mechanism through which national culture produces affective connections beyond the "origin" points of production and transmission. Yet *World Television* is organized around conceptual chapters that engage national formations largely as they intersect across processes of hybridization, asymmetrical interdependence, market and institutional constraints, and the politics of identity formation. This begs an intriguing question: why do two "world" media texts differ in their evocation of the national as an organizing principle?

One answer lies in our everyday hunches about film and television as supposedly distinctive spatial and temporal practices, differences that are inelegant but operative nonetheless, if only in the realm of common presumption. Primary among these distinctions is the materiality of celluloid versus the immateriality of electronic media: film is about location and *place*, while television is about *space*, which is why it, and not cinema, informs an entire discourse of flow. We continue to presume that, as an object, film needs to be packaged in order to travel; while, as a service, television travels seemingly of its own accord. Consequently, for film studies, the national is traditionally site-specific, describing cultures of production and reception that are indebted to a conception of the studio as the primary location for the exploitation of labor, the cinema hall as a discrete place for public exhibition, the audience as a real rather than imagined community, and distribution as an engagement of uneven territorial development. Television studies has certainly engaged the role of national institutions, particularly given the interrelationships between public and commercial broadcasting, but its focus on transmission and distribution, as well as early inquiries into the semiotics of encoding and decoding, has tended toward disaggregating the territorial assumptions that accompany the national. To be sure, there have been place-based analyses of television (notably McCarthy 2001) and space-based accounts of cinema (e.g., Jameson 1995), but there remains the prevailing assumption that informs the difference between Chaudhuri's approach to the national in "world cinema" and Straubhaar's deliberation of the national in "world television." It is important that we raise what seem to be operative differences between national accounts of media forms, especially since

contemporary horizontally integrated media industries call attention to the fact that distinctions between film and television have been moribund for some time. When read against each other, Straubhaar and Chaudhuri signal the importance of considering the ways in which the national has both enabled and responded to the emergence of convergence in the media industries.

Clearly, the national remains a powerful mode for engaging the spatial and temporal practices that organize the contemporary media industries across varied economies of scale. This chapter has considered the ways in which media industries engage the national across an array of locations, institutions, and modes of expression and address. Supported by the bureaucratic sanction of states and markets, media industries are implicated in national legitimation in the domain of law (through intellectual property, authorship and domicile), propriety in the routines of cultural work (through labor laws and censorship), and exclusivity in the field of cultural policy (through quotas, import restrictions, spectrum allocation, and communications infrastructures). Intersecting these institutional itineraries is the dimension of culture in the experiential sense, where the national delimits an archive of vernacular forms linked by custom, habitation, and language that can transcend territorial limitations and create new forms of collectivity and practice. Taken together, the notional concept of the national as a common frame of reference for cultural belief/action and the notational concept of nation as a marker of attribution and circulation have created a powerful incentive for media industries to continue to "think nationally" even in a globally dispersed field of cultural production.

At the 2006 World Economic Forum in Davos, Switzerland, the Confederation of Indian Industry unveiled a new promotional scheme called "India Everywhere." Given that this campaign was designed to highlight the specific benefits that India might hold for foreign investment, defining the national through a universal spatiality seems a little counterintuitive. However, a slogan that advertises being in *all* places while being embodied by a particular location in *one*, describes exactly the convoluted trajectory of the national that the media industries have mapped, tracked, and attempted to duplicate.

Note

Many thanks to Carl McKinney and Kate Levitt for their research support, and to the editors for their suggestions.

References

Anderson, B. (1983) *Imagined Communities: Reflections on the Origin and Spread of Nationalism.* Verso, New York.

Beaujeu, G. de (2006). Lights, camera, bonanza! *Guardian,* 23 June, p. 7.

Berry, C. (2006) From national cinema to cinema and the national: Chinese-language cinema and Hou Hsiao-hsien's "Taiwan trilogy." In Vitali, V. and Willemen, P. (eds.) *Theorizing National Cinema.* British Film Institute, London, pp. 148–75.

Bond, P. (2005) Chinese do not play by rules. *Hollywood Reporter,* 22 November, p. 3.

Brosius, C. (2005) *Empowering Visions: The Politics of Representation in Hindu Nationalism.* Anthem Press, London.

Bush, G. W. (2001) Remarks by the President in tax relief celebration. At www.whitehouse.gov/news/releases/2001/06/20010605-1.html, accessed November 4, 2007.

Calhoun, C. (2007) *Nations Matter: Culture, History, and the Cosmopolitan Dream.* Routledge, New York.

Chakravartty, P. and Sarikakis, K. (2006) *Media Policy and Globalization.* Edinburgh University Press, Edinburgh.

Chatterjee, P. (1986) *Nationalist Thought and the Colonial World: A Derivative Discourse.* Zed Books, London.

Chatterjee, P. (1993) *The Nation and its Fragments.* Princeton University Press, Princeton.

Chaudhuri, S. (2006) *Contemporary World Cinema: Europe, the Middle East, East Asia and South Asia.* Columbia University Press, New York.

Coates, S. (2006) Films face Britishness test for tax breaks. *The Times,* 11 December, p. 23.

Cornish, J. (2007) Cracks in the Great Wall: why China's copyright law has failed to prevent piracy of American movies within its borders. *Vanderbilt Journal of Entertainment and Technology Law* **9**, 405–38.

Deutsch, K. (1966) *Nationalism and Social Communication: An Inquiry into the Foundations of Nationalism.* MIT Press, Cambridge.

Douglas, M. and Isherwood, B. (1979) *The World of Goods.* Basic Books, New York.

Elmer, G. and Gasher, M. (eds.) (2005) *Contracting Out Hollywood: Runaway Productions and Foreign Location Shooting.* Rowman & Littlefield, Lanham.

Elsaesser, T. (1989) *New German Cinema: A History.* Rutgers University Press, New Brunswick.

Eriksen, T. H. (1993) *Ethnicity and Nationalism: Anthropological Perspectives.* Pluto Press, London.

Fanon, F. (1965) *The Wretched of the Earth.* Grove Press, New York.

Gellner, E. (1983) *Nations and Nationalism.* Blackwell, Oxford.

Gillespie, M. (1995) *Television, Ethnicity and Cultural Change.* Routledge, New York.

Govil, N. (2007) Bollywood and the frictions of global mobility. In Thussu, D. (ed.) *Media on the Move: Global Flow and Contra-flow.* Routledge, New York, pp. 84–98.

Gunder Frank, A. (1967) *Capitalism and Underdevelopment in Latin America.* Monthly Review Press, New York.

Hjort, M. (2005) *Small Nation, Global Cinema: The New Danish Cinema.* University of Minnesota Press, Minneapolis.

Hofmann, K. (2005) European cinema. *Variety,* 6 December, p. 5.

Jameson, F. (1995) *The Geopolitical Aesthetic: Cinema and Space in the World System.* British Film Institute, London.

Kraidy, M. and Murphy, P. (2003) Media ethnography: local, global, or translocal? In Murphy, P. and Kraidy, M. (eds.) *Global Media Studies: Ethnographic Perspectives.* Routledge, New York, pp. 299–307.

Kumar, S. (2005) *Gandhi Meets Primetime: Globalization and Nationalism in Indian Television.* University of Illinois Press, Urbana.

Lerner, D. (1958) *The Passing of Traditional Society: Modernizing the Middle East.* Free Press, Glencoe.

Lewis, J. (2005) Hollywood takes on China in the fight over fakes. *Sunday Business*, 11 September.

MacBride, S. (ed.) (1980) *Many Voices, One World: Communication and Society, Today and Tomorrow: Towards a New More Just and More Efficient World Information and Communication Order.* Report by the International Commission for the Study of Communication Problems. UNESCO, Paris. At http://unesdoc.unesco.org/images/0004/000400/040066eb.pdf, accessed August 19, 2008.

McCarthy, A. (2001) *Ambient Television: Visual Culture and Public Space.* Duke University Press, Durham.

MacDonald, G. (2007) Pirates of the Canadians. *The Globe and Mail*, 13 January, p. R1.

Marcus, G. (1998) Ethnography in/of the world system: the emergence of multi-sited ethnography. In Marcus, G. *Ethnography through Thick and Thin.* Princeton University Press, Princeton, pp. 79–104.

Marrs, D. (2005) Film report moots tax for subsidies. *Business Day*, 31 January, p. 3.

Martín-Barbero, J. (1993) *Communication, Culture and Hegemony: From the Media to Mediation.* Sage, Newbury Park.

Mattelart, A. (1994) *Mapping World Communication: War, Progress, Culture.* University of Minnesota Press, Minneapolis.

Mazumdar, R. (2007) *Bombay Cinema: An Archive of the City.* University of Minnesota Press, Minneapolis.

Mickiewicz, E. (2001) Piracy, policy, and Russia's emerging media market. *Press/Politics* **6**, 30–51.

Miller, T. (2003) The film industry and the government: endless Mr. Beans and Mr. Bonds? In Lewis, J. and Miller, T. (eds.) *Critical Cultural Policy Studies: A Reader.* Blackwell, Malden, pp. 134–42.

Miller, T. (2004) A view from a fossil: the new economy, creativity, and consumption – two or three things I don't believe in. *International Journal of Cultural Studies* **7**, 55–65.

Miller, T. (2006) *Cultural Citizenship: Cosmopolitanism, Consumerism, and Television in a Neoliberal Age.* Temple University Press, Philadelphia.

Miller, T., Govil, N., McMurria, J., Maxwell, R., and Wang, T. (2005) *Global Hollywood 2.* British Film Institute, London.

MPA (2003) MPA commends USTR "special 301" report. At www.mi2n.com/press.php3?ej=md&press_nb=51295, accessed February 8, 2008.

MPA (2006) Worldwide study of losses to the film industry and international economies due to piracy and pirate profiles. At www.mpaa.org/press_releases/2006_05_03leksumm.pdf, accessed February 8, 2008.

Naficy, H. (2001) *An Accented Cinema: Exilic and Diasporic Filmmaking.* Princeton University Press, Princeton.

Nornes, A. M. (2007) *Cinema Babel: Translating Global Cinema.* University of Minnesota Press, Minneapolis.

O'Regan, T. (1996) *Australian National Cinema.* Routledge, New York.

Olds, K. and Thrift, N. (2005) Cultures on the brink: reengineering the soul of capitalism – on a global scale. In Ong, A. and Collier, S. J. (eds.) *Global Assemblages: Technology, Politics, and Ethics as Anthropological Problems.* Blackwell, Malden, pp. 270–90.

Parks, L. (2007) Falling apart: electronics salvaging and the global media economy. In Acland, C. (ed.) *Residual Media.* Duke University Press, Durham, pp. 32–47.

Peters, J. D. (1999) Exile, nomadism, and diaspora the stakes of mobility in the western canon. In Naficy, H. (ed.) *Home, Exile, Homeland: Film, Media, and the Politics of Place.* Routledge, New York, pp. 17–41.

Puzzanghera, J. (2007) Film piracy mushrooming in Canada. *Los Angeles Times*, 9 May, p. C1.

Rajagopal, A. (2001) *Politics After Television: Religious Nationalism and the Reshaping of the Public in India.* Cambridge University Press, Cambridge.

Robertson, R. (1990) Mapping the global condition. *Theory, Culture & Society* **7**, 15–30.

Sassen, S. (2006) *Territory, Authority, Rights: From Medieval to Global Assemblages.* Princeton University Press, Princeton.

Schiller, H. (1976) *Communication and Cultural Domination.* International Arts & Sciences Press, White Plains.

Schlesinger, P. (2000) Sociological scope of "national cinema." In Hjort, M. and MacKenzie, S. (eds.) *Cinema and Nation.* Routledge, New York, pp. 17–28.

Schmelzer, R. (2007) Emerging marts help cure US biz blahs. *Variety*, 19 June, pp. A1, A9.

Seiter, E. (1999) *Television and New Media Audiences.* Oxford University Press, Oxford.

Smith, A. (1986) *The Ethnic Origins of Nations.* Blackwell, Oxford.

Straubhaar, J. (2007) *World Television: From Global to Local.* Sage, Los Angeles.

The Economist (2004) British films and tax relief, 28 February.

Timmons, H. (2007) India, a stirring giant, is the new place to see and be seen. *New York Times*, 13 December, pp. C1, C6.

Ting, O. (2007) Pirates of the Orient: China, film piracy, and Hollywood. *Villanova Sports and Entertainment Law Journal* **14**, 399–444.

Tsing, A. (2000) The global situation. *Cultural Anthropology* **15**, 327–60.

Yar, M. (2005) The global "epidemic" of movie "piracy": crime-wave or social construction? *Media, Culture & Society* **27**, 677–96.

Yu, P. K. (2008) The sweet and sour story of Chinese intellectual property rights. In Dutfield, G. and Suthersanen, U. (eds.) *Technology, Progress and Prosperity: A History of Intellectual Property and Development*. Palgrave Macmillan, New York, forthcoming.

Yúdice, G. (2003) *The Expediency of Culture: Uses of Culture in the Global Era*. Duke University Press, Durham.

11

Convergence Culture and Media Work

·····································

Mark Deuze

Many occupations in the different areas of the media started out quite distinct from each other. However, during the course of the twentieth century, media work has become increasingly similar across the various media industries. Bustamante (2004) analyzes the key trends contributing to the emergence of a singular model for media industries in the digital age as 1) the ongoing international deregulation of formerly protected media markets, 2) increased concentration and conglomeration of media companies, and 3) a global standardization of forms and principles of media management. These trends must be seen as further supercharged by innovations and developments in new information and communication technologies. Consequently, "media work has become more similar and also more similar to office work in general" (Tunstall 2001, 22). Although Bustamante rejects the notion of a move toward a single global model of media, along with Canclini (2001) he does conclude that a global reconstruction of "world culture" and "local creativity" is taking place under the paradigms of technology and the market.

In these opening sentences, several claims are made about the media industries in general and the work of media professionals in particular that refer to the concept of convergence. Convergence refers to a number of things including the gradual bureaucratization of workspaces in media organizations across different fields of cultural production (such as entertainment, news, and advertising), the worldwide integration of markets for media products, the emergence of cross-media or multimedia productions (where content is produced across multiple media channels), and the adaptation of nation-based media regulations to facilitate an increasingly "lawless" transnational media corporate context.

What must be clear, then, is that convergence:

- means many different things in different contexts;
- has been occurring for quite some time now; and
- has been amplified or "supercharged" by new information technologies and digitalization.

Furthermore, many authors in the field of media studies assume that convergence as a generic concept has more or less the same consequences. Specifically, in the coming together of industries, standards, and processes, some of the particularities and diversity of formerly distinct practices gets lost. However, it has become quite difficult to argue that in the media world today diversity is something that is lacking. The range of media on offer is astounding, and the media ecosystem is more complex, chaotic, and omnipresent than ever before. Every year, more media channels and formats (in print, broadcast, and online) appear, and there seems to be no end in sight with the global move of telecommunications operators and, albeit more reluctantly, cable companies into the realm of personalized video channels using Internet Protocol Television (IPTV).

What is particularly fascinating about such media abundance is that the vast majority of these new media offerings are in fact produced outside of traditional media companies and corporations. This does not just mean that many media offerings today are financed, distributed, or otherwise enabled by non-media companies (such as the "Fab Four": Microsoft, Google, Yahoo, and AOL), but also that media production tends to increasingly take place outside of the domain of professional contexts altogether. More precisely, most of the media today – and especially online content – gets produced by audiences. The majority of the top-ten most visited websites on the planet are places where all the content and experiences are produced by users: YouTube, MySpace, Orkut, Wikipedia, Hi5, and Facebook.[1] Our understanding of convergence therefore must also include an appreciation of the role of the consumer in the media production process. In this chapter, the study of media industries is considered in a context of increasingly complex and boundary-breaking relationships between media companies, media technologies, media producers, and consumers – what Henry Jenkins (2006) describes as an emerging "convergence culture."

In the current convergence culture – within which all media industries operate – the key question for theorizing media industries must be how we can adequately explain the process, content, and consequences of consumption and production when people's contemporary media practices seem to include both at the same time. Further, the blurring of real or perceived boundaries between makers and users in an increasingly participatory media culture challenges consensual notions of what it means to work in the media industries (Deuze 2007a). This convergence can be seen as driven by an industry desperate for strong customer relationships, technologies that are increasingly cheap and easy to use, and a media culture that privileges an active audience (Turow 2005).

After considering more or less traditional theories of media industry studies – looking at the political economy of the industry and considering the different roles of audiences – I develop convergence culture as a third perspective. Although this perspective allows for a more mixed, hybrid, and complex understanding of the roles, functions, and work of media industries in society, it is not without problems – particularly regarding the co-optation of all creativity by corporations, and the colonization of consumer/producer agency by markets. After these critical considerations, the chapter concludes with suggestions for further research.

Media Industries and Society

The media industries, in the broadest sense, can be seen as the key drivers and accelerators of a global culturalization of economies. Media are our window to the world, yet also function as its mirror; media reflect and direct at the same time. Theorizing the way the media industries operate means understanding the elements of the human condition in the information age – living in a world that can be considered a "mediapolis": a mediated public space where media underpin and overarch the experiences of everyday life (Silverstone 2006). As such, the convergence of production and consumption of media across companies, channels, genres, and technologies is an expression of the convergence of all aspects of everyday life: work and play, the local and the global, self and social identity (especially in the use of social networking sites). The media as cultural industries act as trend amplifiers by flexibly adapting to a globalizing marketplace for products and generating a global production network for creative labor (Power & Scott 2004).

Beyond the crucial role media industries play in everyday life and the significance of their products and production networks in the global marketplace, another reason for carefully examining the media business and its workers is its influence on the cultural economy of contemporary cities. Cultural and creative industries tend to cluster close to certain urban regions – such as Los Angeles, New York, Vancouver, Milan, Wellington, Munich, and Manchester – and thus catalyze a flurry of economic, cultural, and social activities in those regions, reinvigorating those areas. This, in turn, has led many local and regional governments to invest in public relations campaigns, profiling themselves as "creative" or "media" cities, as in the case, for example, of Dubai (United Arab Emirates), Singapore, Islamabad (Pakistan), Leiden (Netherlands), Lille (France), Tampere (Finland), and Bristol (England). These trends may seem counterintuitive, considering the global proliferation of new information and communication technologies that would facilitate teleworking and other forms of fragmentation (as opposed to locational agglomeration of cultural production). Perhaps one would rather expect a sort of universal deterritorialization of world capitalism facilitated by virtual and networked workspaces (Scott 2000, 24). However, quite the opposite is occurring – especially in industries like cinema, music, advertising, and multimedia. Those industries are attracted to, and attract, investors and generate business for restaurants, clubs, theaters, galleries, and other ingredients of cultural and economic life. Media thus are not only central to an understanding of everyday life in terms of the aesthetic quality and the utility they bring to information, entertainment, and communication. The media are also key to analyzing the converging economic and cultural environment of the world's "postindustrial" urban spaces. Much of the work in the media industries is interconnected on a global scale through international co-production, outsourcing, offshoring, and subcontracting practices. Combined with their role as accelerators of urban regeneration, these interconnected creative clusters contribute to a shift in power away from states and national territories to a globally converging cultural economy and economy of culture (Du Gay & Pryke 2002; Deuze 2007b).

Whatever we do with our media – what we read, watch, listen to, participate in, create, or use – is much more than the tightly corporate-controlled substance offered through cable television, dot-com websites, or frequency modulation (FM) radio. It is also the bewildering array of community and "alternative" media, pirate radio, our use of the office photocopier as "the people's printing press," letters we write, Short Message Service (SMS) texts we send to participate in a TV show or to ask someone

for a date, postings we make to our own or someone else's weblog, pictures taken with the built-in digital camera of our cell phones and uploaded to photosharing social networking sites like Flickr … and so on. Media industries increasingly make use of this "productive" consumer behavior, which means that the role of creative labor and the management of cultural production taking place within such organizations are becoming increasingly complex as well.

In short, when conceptualizing media industries, one is struck by the simultaneous occurrence of many instances of what we could call convergence:

- convergence of *place*, as in the sites of media production;
- convergence of *identity*, as in notions of professional identity versus the "cult of the amateur" (Keen 2007);
- convergence of *experience*, as in the way people interact with, give meaning to, and even actively make their media as a window to the world.

The media industries are thus comprised of far more these days than we might initially think … and, in turn, convergence is far more complex as well. I will interrogate this complexity of convergence culture by articulating it with the experience of work in the global media industries.

Media Industries and Work

The ecosystem of media organizations consists of a combination of (large and small) public service and for-profit companies dealing with the industrial and creative production and circulation of culture. In terms of media work, this culture refers not only to the production of spoken and written words, audio, still or moving images, but also (and increasingly) to providing platforms for people to produce and exchange their own content. In contemporary definitions of what the work within these industries involves, four elements tend to get mixed up, which to some extent makes an adequate assessment of media industries rather difficult: content, connectivity, creativity, and commerce – all of which translate into the production of culture. Media industries produce content, yes, but they also invest in platforms for connectivity – where fans and audiences provide free labor (Terranova 2000). Media work is culture creation, yes, and it tends to take place within a distinctly commercial context.

In the current digital and networked global media ecosystem, the roles played by advertisers, media producers, and content consumers are converging. Marketing communicators, advertising creatives, and public relations officers communicate directly with audiences (by creating their own content, by investing in dialogical online platforms where they can "meet" their clients and consumers) in addition to sponsoring the creation of content by other media industries (such as journalism or motion pictures). Journalists and TV producers interact directly with audiences by inviting them to become part of the production or product innovation process: as "citizen journalists" or as members of brand communities forming around specific stories, characters, and shows. At the same time, the production system of media becomes networked on a "translocal" scale, integrating different locales of cultural production into a global production system. Many industries – such as computer and video game development, motion pictures, and television – offshore, subcontract, and outsource various elements in the production process to save costs and redistribute risks. Examples are securing international co-financing deals for television projects, filming and post-producing a movie at several locations (often in different countries), moving an editorial division or marketing department of a news organization to another part of the world (a practice called "remote control journalism"),[2] mixing music recorded in Los Angeles in a studio outside of London, localizing game titles set in one regional, cultural, or national context in another part of the world, adding local soundtracks and hit songs to generic advertising campaigns generated for global brands, separating out the marketing and distribution of titles, and so on. Such translocal forms of market-based cultural production primarily benefit and in part result from structural trends characterizing the media industries in recent decades: growth, integration, globalization, and concentration of ownership.

In terms of media work, then, convergence relates to:

- the *inclusion* of various stakeholders – professional producers, audiences, sources, and sponsors – in the (co-)creation of media content and experiences;
- the *integration* of various media industries in a global production network;
- the complex *coordination* between distinctly different goals – creativity, commerce, content, and connectivity – in the media production process.

Media Industries and Production

Media companies are both pioneers and benchmarks for what Lash and Urry (1994) call a "reflexive productivity" typical of postindustrial industries. This means, for example, that media work is often not only organized informally in ways that enable instant adaptation to changing consumer demands, but also that the media enterprise must be understood in radically different terms than traditional industrial-era factories. In terms of the management and organization of work, media organizations can indeed be considered as quite special, partly because of the delicate and contested balance between the creative autonomy of culture creators, and partly because of the scientific management of commercial enterprises. This relationship between commerce and culture can be seen as a sibling rivalry, as both management and culture creators not only need each other, but much of the work of managers and of culture creators is cultural and economic at the same time. Indeed, cultural and economic concerns are not necessarily different, but in the context of media work rather must be seen as constituent material practice: the combination of specific technical and organizational arrangements as these influence and are shaped by the generally idiosyncratic habits of individual media practitioners, whether managers or producers, professionals or amateurs (McFall 2004, 14). This rather recent conceptualization of culture and economy accentuates convergence, in that it stresses "complimentaries and interdependencies" (Throsby 2001, 165) between economics and culture. It attributes the products – and experiences – of media industries with cultural as well as economic value, and suggests the same about the production processes within such industries.

Media industries contribute to the culturalization of economic life through a constant remix of commercially viable yet generic work, next to or combined with innovative, flexible, and highly creative production processes. This is a unique blend of the unstable and continuously contested dialectic between linear and liquid differentiations in the creative process of media work (Turner 2003, 138). Examples of linearity in cultural production are predictable iterations of the same franchise (such as the *James Bond* movies, a soap opera like *EastEnders*, or the *Legend of Zelda* video game series). Liquid differentiation occurs in the production of groundbreaking, unconventional new media formulas, hybrid genres, and unexpected or otherwise experimental storytelling formats (consider for example the interlocking storyworld of *The Matrix* as it extends across movies, animation series, comic books, conceptual art, and digital games). It is important to note here that the same companies – or indeed the same professionals – tend to be engaged in both types of production. This converged production process makes the media as an industry uniquely responsible for cookie cutter-style McDonaldization, as such an approach guarantees short-term success and provable returns on investment. Yet at the same time, often within the same companies or at the hands of the same producers, media industries can be considered key agents in introducing social, technological, and economic innovation and change.

It must be clear that in a cultural economy the role of media industries is extremely important, and not just because of the clustering of these industries in certain city regions, or because of the significance of cultural intermediaries (such as journalists, scriptwriters, and advertising creatives) in the manufacturing of ideas, signs, images, and symbols that help human beings to give meaning to their lives. Indeed, the fact that the media above all else deal in ideas, information, and culture has been used to set them apart in studies of their organization and structure. However, as Nicholas Garnham (2000) has argued,

studies of the media tend to fetishize their existence as institutions, content, and audiences. Such an approach all too often limits one to instrumental explanations of media production, focusing on the complicity of media industries in the commoditization and mainstreaming of culture, or on the resistance by increasingly savvy audiences to the inscribed and preferred meanings of media messages. On the one hand, it makes sense to look at media industries strictly in terms of the commercially successful transnational enterprises they are. On the other hand, studies of how people engage their media suggest that a notion of either "passive" or "active" consumption does not do justice to the complex ways in which we consume, produce, and generally give active meaning to whatever we see, hear, read, or click on when multitasking our media. What both of these important views omit, then, is an understanding or respect for the moment of cultural production in an increasingly mixed (new) media ecology, where participation, interactivity, and co-creation have moved to center stage in both the deliberations within industries and the manifestations of what Jay Rosen calls the "people formerly known as the audience."[3]

Convergence Culture

In today's digital culture, media work can be seen as a stomping ground for the forces of increasingly differentiated production and innovation processes, and the complex interaction and integration between work, life, and play, all of which get expressed in, and are facilitated by, the rapid development of new information and communication technologies. This convergence is not just a technological process. Media convergence must also be seen as having a cultural logic of its own, blurring the lines between economics (work) and culture (meaning), between production and consumption, between making and using media, and between active or passive spectatorship of mediated culture.

The ongoing merger of media production and consumption signals the emergence of a global convergence culture, based on an increasingly participatory and interactive engagement between different media forms and industries, between people and their media, as well as between professional and amateur media makers (Jenkins 2006). As Jenkins (2004) notes:

> Convergence is both a top-down corporate-driven process and a bottom-up consumer-driven process. Media companies are learning how to accelerate the flow of media content across delivery channels to expand revenue opportunities, broaden markets and reinforce viewer commitments. Consumers are learning how to use these different media technologies to bring the flow of media more fully under their control and to interact with other users. They are fighting for the right to participate more fully in their culture, to control the flow of media in their lives and to talk back to mass market content. Sometimes, these two forces reinforce each other, creating closer, more rewarding, relations between media producers and consumers. (37)

Indeed, the role of the customer as co-creator of the media message increasingly finds acceptance throughout the cultural industries. Among creatives and brand managers in ad agencies the contemporary focus is on interactive advertising, which can be defined as the paid and unpaid presentation and promotion of sponsored products, services, and ideas involving mutual action between consumers and producers (Leckenby & Li 2000). Marketing communicators brainstorm about the potential of "social," "upstream," or even "spherical" marketing (Svensson 2005), which refers to the strategic process of identifying and fulfilling consumer needs early in product development, up to and including customers and users at various stages in the total production and product innovation cycle. In journalism, editors of news publications actively consider adding what is called "citizen journalism" to their websites, allowing members of the audience to respond, comment, and submit their own news (Outing 2005). In particular, convergence culture has been part of the organization of work in the computer and video game industries. Game publishers often consider their consumers as co-developers (Jeppesen & Molin 2003), where product innovation and development largely depends on online consumer communities. These "mods" are then integrated into new commercial versions of the original computer or video game and can extend the shelf life of such games (Sotamaa 2005).

When combined with ongoing efforts throughout the media industries to develop multimedia formats (either through mergers and integrating different company units, or by the increasingly popular networking of the production process across numerous subcontracted business partners), producer–consumer convergence poses significant challenges to theorizing media industries. Traditional frames of reference interpret these trends from distinctly different perspectives, looking at either the industry or the audience. However, a scholarly appreciation of the various instances of convergence mentioned above perhaps could benefit from an equally convergent approach. In what follows, I dissect and critique the different ways of making sense of the new media ecosystem, and propose a more holistic and complex view.

Industry Perspective

One way that the increasing use of user-generated content in professional media production can be seen is as an example of the global media industries' attempts to secure, harness, and thus win back control over the circulation and consumption of culture. It can thus be viewed as evidence of the increasing rationalization and (thus) homogenization of all forms of public communication (including news and entertainment) in the hands of fewer and fewer multinational companies. However, such a traditional political economy of industry belies three contemporary developments in the media industries: vertical disintegration (partly because of failed synergies), media deconcentration, and outsourcing.

Although most of the major media corporations and production businesses consolidated their holdings into large corporate conglomerations in the 1990s, a parallel development of media deconcentration and corporate dysfunctionalism has been recorded at the same time. Examples include the rapid ascendance and equally fast dismantling of the Vivendi Universal business empire, the failure of the

AOL/Time Warner merger, and the ongoing disintegration of media giant Viacom (Shafer 2005). Research in the fields of news (Deuze 2004), marketing and advertising (Cornelissen 2003), and the motion pictures industries (Blair et al. 2003) consistently suggests that infighting and turf wars, slow centralized decision-making processes, mismanagement, difficulties of building or sustaining a knowledge-sharing work culture, as well as a general lack of cooperation among different media properties within the same corporation or holding firm are among the key reasons why mergers or efforts toward achieving synergies in the cultural industries generally fail or do not deliver the expected results (Chan-Olmsted & Chang 2003).

Partly in response to these failures, but also in an attempt to develop flexible strategies to cope with increasingly unpredictable and complex markets, the trend toward deconcentration is accelerating throughout the media industries. In particular, the largest media corporations continually split off business enterprises, splinter holdings across numerous self-sustaining groups, or altogether sell off parts of the company. Another trend that serves as a warning against arguments about an "all-powerful" or monolithic global media system relates to the production of media using the dominant processes in media work across all fields of cultural production: outsourcing, subcontracting, and offshoring (Deuze 2007b). Whether in the movies, advertising, journalism, or video game development, most of the work in these industries is done by independent contractors, loosely affiliated teams, temporarily hired work groups, or otherwise contingently employed labor, often spread across translocally situated contexts (Hesmondhalgh 2006). Beyond a disintegration of management and deconcentration of ownership lies a complex web of mostly temporary connections, transient links, short-lived joint ventures, and thus diffuse power relationships between individual professionals, media organizations, and public stakeholders (including governments and audiences) in a wide variety of fields. The media industry is becoming increasingly interconnected on a transnational scale, where global production networks consist of multifunctional entertainment corporations as well as networks of thousands of

specialized firms under more or less independent ownership (Coe et al. 2004).

The roles of all those companies, holding firms, networks, and even individuals in the creative process of the media industries converge (and diverge) in countless unpredictable, confusing, and complex ways. My reading of the industry perspective on convergence culture does not assume large corporations control all aspects of the production of news or entertainment. However, neither has the global market completely opened up to hundreds of thousands of small or independent companies. This complex and symbiotic two-tier production system runs throughout the cultural and creative industries, where independent companies can be under long-term contract of corporations, the same multinational companies can completely outsource production or acquire a show or movie after production elsewhere, and ownership of different media properties has a tendency to change quickly.

Not only does this perspective on convergence culture from the view of the industry offer us a more complex, hybrid, and colorful palette for looking at the production of culture, it also opens the door to include the audience, the consumer, and the user into our framework for understanding the collisions and collusions of "old" and "new" in the contemporary media ecology.

Audience View

The extent to which this convergence culture plays a significant role in the entire media ecology, and therefore in the development of a professional identity among media workers, can be illustrated by a November 2005 survey by the Pew Internet and American Life Project among teenagers in the United States. The report concludes:

Some 57% of online teens create content for the internet. That amounts to half of all teens ages 12–17, or about 12 million youth. These Content Creators report having done one or more of the following activities: create a blog; create or work on a personal webpage; create or work on a webpage for school, a friend, or an organization; share original content such as artwork, photos, stories, or videos online; or remix content found online into a new creation.[4]

Studies among teenagers in other countries including Iran, the Netherlands, and New Zealand reveal similar findings, showing how the use of media for the majority of people – and especially for those who grew up with game consoles, cell phones, and the Internet – has become an active act of remixing, bricolage, and media participation (Deuze 2006) as well as "media meshing." According to a 2005 study commissioned by Yahoo among teenagers in Chicago, Mexico City, London, Berlin, Seoul, and Shanghai, media meshing is "a behavioral phenomenon that occurs when people begin an experience in one medium, such as watching television, then shift to another, such as surfing the Internet, and maybe even a third, such as listening to music. The explanation for this behavior is the constant search for complementary information, different perspectives, and even emotional fulfillment."[5] Media meshing is similar to the multitasking behavior researchers find among people of all ages when using media, but includes a distinct element of media co-creation, ranging from the customization of media devices (ringtones, wallpapers, screensavers, channel programming) to the production of fan movies, citizen journalism sites, advertising clips, and computer games. Similar studies, surveys, and reports on the increasingly (co-)creative behavior of media users by the Organization for Economic Co-operation and Development (in April 2007)[6] and market research company Forrester (later that same month)[7] document how the majority of young people (especially those in the 16–24 year range) enthusiastically consume user-generated content, and that a small but growing group (Forrester puts it at approximately one-third of US adult consumers) actively contributes to the creative process online.

It must be clear that contemporary citizen-consumers also demand the right to participate – to be an active part in the production, circulation, and interpretation of their culture and to exert a shaping role over the content of the popular culture that is such a formative influence and vital resource within their lives. Alongside corporate-controlled broadcast or mass media channels (Bagdikian 2000)

and their counterparts in alternative (Atton 2002) or citizen's (Rodriguez 2001) media, there emerge hybrid spaces such as Flickr or YouTube, MySpace or Hi5. Such spaces provide a common environment for grassroots media makers, both individuals and groups, to come together and share what they have created with each other, enabling citizen journalists, viral marketers, ambitious musicians and an army of amateur producers to gain much greater visibility and influence within the culture than ever before. They do this even as companies are trying to figure out how to profit from these media channels. Contemporary media users are not only making their own media in a relatively invisible sphere of production through neighborhood newsletters or low-power radio, but also via the World Wide Web and the widespread diffusion of WYSIWYG ("What You See Is What You Get") production and dissemination technologies. This is not to say that media industries are enthusiastically embracing this participatory media culture. It must be clear that for many companies, opening their products and production process to customer co-creation is deeply problematic. Consider for example the value of original intellectual property in a media culture of collective remixing, or the notion of creative autonomy so central to a media workers' professional identity.

With the gradual development of industrial standards and the growing financial successes of media companies embracing audiences as co-creators of content, a glimpse is offered into the possible outcomes of the suggested convergence between sender and receiver. Considering the corporate enclosure of the information commons, one has to note the triangular tactics of increasingly restrictive regulations of copyright as a form of property, disintermediatory practices of soliciting users' free labor in the creative process, and opaque uses of social media to establish new ways of "taming" or controlling the otherwise unpredictable behavior of consumers. This is not to say that Internet users step blindly into such traps, nor that when they do, companies are necessarily successful in harnessing their creativity. Indeed, the strategic or tactical opposition among certain individuals or groups feeds into the deliberate construction of consumers as "unpredictable masses" by the contemporary mainstream in marketing and corporate communication. Such a view allows companies both to aim at taming the consumer mass into controllable segments, lifestyle groups, or subcultures, as well as to interact with consumers as active agents (Turow 2005).

A traditional audience perspective would focus on the behavior of audiences as either successful consumers, or as active in a strict sense of meaning-making. In a context of convergence culture, one could add a more explicit reference to emerging read/write multimedia literacies (Hartley 2007) with a necessity to articulate legal rights and protections for the producing consumer – what Aoki (1993) has described as audience "recoding" rights. Such approaches seem to be more responsive to the emerging complex relationships between media industries, their producers, and the consumers.

Mixed Media Ecology

The culturally convergent practices of media industries – involving remixing professional content and user-generated content in the creative process – led *The Economist* (20 April 2006) to ask the fundamental question: what is a media company? Traditionally, media companies would be seen as audience aggregators: engaging in the production of content aimed at mass audiences. Considering the social, technological, and economic trends outlined above, such a definition has become problematic. Instead of "audiences," media businesses today talk about "networks," emphasizing media work as a practice that would (or should) generate endless opportunities for people to form communities of interest around content. This creates interesting dysfunctional family effects within large media corporations, where some parts of the firm are actively restructuring to meet the demands of what *The Economist* describes as a race to become "the most liquid media marketplace,"[8] while other sectors of the company are still very much in the process of developing intricate Digital Rights Management (DRM) software intended to prevent all this arguably profitable audience activity from actually taking off (Benkler 2006).

It is important to note that much of this culturally convergent content not only dissolves the distinctions between the producer and consumer of media, but in many cases also blurs the institutional lines drawn between the professional and the amateur. In this context, using British examples, Charles Leadbeater and Paul Miller (2004) map the emergence of the "Pro-Am": people pursuing amateur activities with professional standards, using their leisure time to enthusiastically engage in commercially viable activities in fields as diverse as computer programming, astronomy, technical research, and now, increasingly, cultural production. In 1980, futurist Alvin Toffler predicted the rise of a "prosumer" economy, considering the release of do-it-yourself pregnancy tests in the Netherlands during the late 1970s as the earliest example of such a mixed economy. Prior to that, Marshall McLuhan foresaw in 1964 how increasing computerization and automatization would not just affect the production, but also the consumption of media, arguing that the consumer would become a producer in the automation circuit.

More recently, through surveying numerous online examples such as Wikipedia and OhmyNews, Axel Bruns (2005) introduces the concept of the "produser" as people who, when online, continually combine some kind of using and producing of information. For instance, such people browse and publish websites, read and submit news, and receive and process information in private and for their own ends. The key here is a "not only, but also" perspective on media use – people consume and produce information and communication while connected to many others involved in similar media meshing behaviors. Beyond the quest for compelling media experiences, people seem to be increasingly willing to participate voluntarily in the media-making process to achieve what can be called a "networked reputation." By generating discussion and comments to their voluntary work on websites such as Amazon (book reviews) or YouTube (user-submitted video clips), people are recognized – which at times can lead to a book contract or the chance to work professionally in television. These kinds of reputation-based publication mechanisms can be a benefit to the individual, as small business proprietors, independent cultural entrepreneurs, freelancers, and aspiring writers or moviemakers can quickly gain an audience and build a positive reputation that they hopefully can translate into actual business opportunities.

The Dark Side

This chapter has suggested how convergence culture takes place on both sides of the media spectrum – production and consumption. Within this spectrum, the distinctions between the traditional role-players in the creative process are dissolving. The key to understanding the currently emerging relationships between media consumers and producers, or between media owners and media workers (whether paid or voluntarist), is their complexity. These relationships are constantly reconfigured in a convergence culture, and at times are both reciprocal and antagonistic. Such "liquid" relationships are seldom stable, generally temporary, and at the very least unpredictable. Lev Manovich (2005) calls this a "culture of remix and remixability," where user-generated content exists both within and outside of commercial contexts, and supports as well as subverts corporate control. While this may be true, it is safe to say that professionals – and the companies that employ them – are better protected and more powerful in negotiating terms of service than is the average consumer. The work that citizen-consumers do as part of what Von Hippel (2005) calls "user-innovation communities" (103ff.), operating in a system of what Benkler (2006) describes as "commons-based peer production" (60), is at least in part dependent on, contingent with, and benefiting the market-driven efforts of the multinational media enterprise.

It is possible to see the various end-user licensing agreements and terms of service of the major user-created content sites (including but not limited to game modding platforms, corporate citizen journalism initiatives, and upstream marketing sites) as informal labor contracts controlling and exploiting the voluntary work of user communities. However, it may be a mistake to presume that the collective intelligence of the user community thus is completely harnessed and tamed by corporations (or vice versa). For example, research among professionals

throughout the news and entertainment industries (both in the US and elsewhere), suggests that many if not most of them openly express the fear that they have lost control over their own creative work. They show concern as their products and brands get taken up and deployed by consumers and users in diverse, disorganized, decentralized, but very public ways (Jenkins & Deuze 2008). It must be clear that the notion of an audience member as more or less a potential colleague is not wholeheartedly embraced by all, indeed not by most media professionals (Deuze 2007b). Some evidence suggests that a lot of these technological and cultural innovations in the media industries go hand-in-hand with job losses and flexibilization of creative labor (McKercher 2002; Rossiter 2007).[9] It is therefore not surprising that professionals in these industries are likely to adopt a skeptical, if not prohibitionist attitude toward this new cultural logic of media convergence.

Faced with intense competition, an increasingly critical and unpredictable user, and heightened commercial pressures from a global market, some suggest that several media companies and professionals are adopting more transparent and ethical discourses and practices vis-à-vis their co-creating users (Balnaves et al. 2004, 193). This would indicate a growing focus in the media professions on creating and sustaining genuine links between modern organizations and the different individuals and groups in society that deal with them. However, the question of power remains: in a situation where the largest media companies dismantle their production operations into a flexible global network of temporary affiliations in order to focus more on controlling distribution and access, in a context of increasingly precarious labor conditions for media workers, and given the complete lack of legal frameworks to protect the co-creating consumer, one cannot escape the observation that all of this does not seem to play into the hands of all stakeholders equally.

Conclusion

If the media industries in the broadest possible sense are key sites of the struggles over meaning and symbolic exchange in global society, it becomes essential to understand the working lives of the people within the creative industries. It is in media industries that Simon Cottle (2003) describes how "a growing army of media professionals, producers and others work in this expanding sector of the economy, many of them in freelance, temporary, subcontracted and underpaid (and sometimes unpaid) positions … They are also often at the forefront of processes of organizational change including new flexible work regimes, reflexive corporate cultures, and the introduction of digital technologies, multimedia production and multi-skilled practices" (3). In their ways of working and being at work, media professionals embody all the themes of social, cultural, and technological change in the liquid modern times as expressed in this chapter and throughout this book. To some extent the different elements of convergence culture have opened up the creative process in

the media for technological, cultural, and economic interventions, particularly with respect to the flexibilization of work and the creative autonomy of media professionals regarding their audiences and co-creating users. The cultural field of media production, when seen from an individual worker's perspective, is clearly not a sovereign sphere, devoid of external pressures, influences, and constraints. However, it should also not be seen as a domain of activity wholly determined, standardized, and controlled by the structure and organization of industry, nor by the increasingly prosuming activities of people using media. It is through the daily interaction of creativity, commerce, content, and connectivity that media practitioners give active meaning to their work and professional identity, which in turn shapes the meaning and significance of the way media industries function and evolve.

Notes

1 See www.alexa.com/site/ds/top_sites?ts_mode=global&lang=none.
2 See http://deuze.blogspot.com/2006/11/remote-control-journalism.html.
3 Source: http://journalism.nyu.edu/pubzone/weblogs/pressthink/2006/06/27/ppl_frmr.html.
4 Source: www.pewinternet.org/PPF/r/166/report_display.asp.
5 Source: http://yhoo.client.shareholder.com/ReleaseDetail.cfm?ReleaseID=174993.
6 Source: www.oecd.org/dataoecd/57/14/38393115.pdf.
7 Source: www.forrester.com/Research/Document/Excerpt/0,7211,42057,00.html.
8 Source: www.economist.com/surveys/displaystory.cfm?story_id=6794282.
9 See for example for the US media job market, www.iwantmedia.com/layoffs.html.

Websites accessed July 14, 2008.

References

Aoki, K. (1993) Adrift in the intertext: authorship and audience "recoding" rights. *Chicago-Kent Law Review* **68**, 805–38.

Atton, C. (2002) *Alternative Media*. Sage, London.

Bagdikian, B. H. (2000) *The New Media Monopoly*. Beacon Press, Boston.

Balnaves, M., Mayrhofer, D., and Shoesmith, B. (2004) Media professions and the new humanism. *Continuum: Journal of Media & Cultural Studies* **18**, 191–203.

Bauman, Z. (2002) *Society Under Siege*. Polity Press, Cambridge.

Benkler, Y. (2006) *The Wealth of Networks: How Social Production Transforms Markets and Freedom*. Yale University Press, New Haven.

Blair, H., Culkin, N., and Randle, K. (2003) From London to Los Angeles: a comparison of local labour market processes in the US and UK film industries. *International Journal of Human Resource Management* **14**, 619–33.

Bruns, A. (2005) *Gatewatching: Collaborative Online News Production*. Peter Lang, New York.

Bustamante, E. (2004) Cultural industries in the digital age: some provisional conclusions. *Media, Culture & Society* **26**, 803–20.

Canclini, N. G. (2001) *Consumers and Citizens: Globalization and Multicultural Conflicts*. University of Minnesota Press, Minneapolis.

Chan-Olmsted, S. and Chang, B. H. (2003) Diversification strategy of global media conglomerates: examining its patterns and determinants. *Journal of Media Economics*, **16**, 213–33.

Coe, N., Hess, M., Henry, Y. W., Dicken, P., and Henderson, J. (2004) "Globalizing" regional development: a global production networks perspective. *Transactions of the Institute of British Geographers* **29**, 468–84.

Cornelissen, J. (2003) Change, continuity and progress: the concept of integrated marketing communications and marketing communications practice. *Journal of Strategic Marketing* **11**, 217–34.

Cottle, S. (ed.) (2003) *Media Organization and Production*. Sage, London.

Deuze, M. (2004) What is multimedia journalism? *Journalism Studies* **5**, 139–52.

Deuze, M. (2006) Participation, remediation, bricolage: considering principal components of a digital culture. *Information Society* **22**, 63–75.

Deuze, M. (2007a) Convergence culture in the creative industries. *International Journal of Cultural Studies* **10**, 243–63.

Deuze, M. (2007b) *Media Work*. Polity Press, Cambridge.

Du Gay, P. and Pryke, M. (eds.) (2002) *Cultural Economy: Cultural Analysis and Commercial Life*. Sage, London.

Garnham, N. (2000) *Emancipation, the Media, and Modernity*. Oxford University Press, Oxford.

Hartley, J. (2007) "There are other ways of being in the truth": the uses of multimedia literacy. *International Journal of Cultural Studies* **10**, 135–44.

Hesmondhalgh, D. (ed.) (2006) *Media Production*. Open University Press, Maidenhead.

Jenkins, H. (2004) The cultural logic of media convergence. *International Journal of Cultural Studies* **7**, 33–43.

Jenkins, H. (2006) *Convergence Culture: Where Old and New Media Collide*. New York University Press, New York.

Jenkins, H. and Deuze, M. (2008) Convergence culture. *Convergence: The International Journal of Research into New Media Technologies* **14**, 5–12.

Jeppesen, L. B. and Molin, M. J. (2003) Consumers as co-developers: learning and innovation outside the firm. *Technology Analysis & Strategic Management* **15**, 363–83.

Keen, A. (2007) *The Cult of the Amateur: How Today's Internet is Killing Our Culture*. Random House, New York.

Lash, S. and Urry, J. (1994) *Economies of Signs and Space*. Sage, London.

Leadbeater, C. and Miller, P. (2004) *The Pro-Am revolution: How Enthusiasts are Changing Our Society and Economy*. Demos, London.

Leckenby, J. and Li, H. (2000) From the editors: why we need the journal of interactive advertising. *Journal of Interactive Advertising* **1**. At www.jiad.org/vol1/no1/editors/index.htm, accessed February 14, 2008.

McFall, L. (2004) The culturalization of work in the "new economy": a historical view. In Jensen, E. T. and Westenholz, A. (eds.) *Identity in the Age of the New Economy: Life in Temporary and Scattered Work Practices*. Edward Elgar, Cheltenham, pp. 9–33.

McKercher, C. (2002) *Newsworkers Unite: Labor, Convergence and North American Newspapers*. Rowman & Littlefield, Lanham.

McLuhan, M. (1994) *Understanding Media: The Extensions of Man*, reprint edn. MIT Press, Cambridge.

Manovich, L. (2005) *Remixability*. At www.manovich.net/DOCS/Remix_modular.doc, accessed February 14, 2008.

Outing, S. (2005) The 11 layers of citizen journalism. *Poynter Online*. At www.poynter.org/content/content_view.asp?id=83126, accessed February 14, 2008.

Power, D. and Scott, A. (eds.) (2004) *Cultural Industries and the Production of Culture*. Routledge, London.

Rodriguez, C. (2001). *Fissures in the Mediascape: An International Study of Citizen's Media*. Hampton Press, Cresskill.

Rossiter, N. (2007) *Organized Networks: Media Theory, Creative Labour, New Institutions*. Nai, Rotterdam.

Scott, A. (2000) *The Cultural Economy of Cities: Essays on the Geography of Image-Producing Industries*. Sage, London.

Shafer, J. (2005) Media deconcentration. *Slate* [Online]. At http://slate.com/id/2115066, accessed February 14, 2008.

Silverstone, R. (2006) *Media and Morality: On the Rise of the Mediapolis*. Polity Press, Cambridge.

Sotamaa, O. (2005) Creative user-centred design practices: lessons from game cultures. In Haddon, L., Mante-Meijer, E., Sapio, B., Kommonen, K.-H., Fortunati, L., and Kant, A. (eds.) *Everyday Innovators: Researching the Role of Users in Shaping ICTs*. Springer, Dordrecht, pp. 104–16.

Svensson, G. (2005) The spherical marketing concept: a revitalization of the marketing concept. *European Journal of Marketing* **39**, 5–15.

Terranova, T. (2000) Free labor: producing culture for the digital economy. *Social Text* **18**, 33–57.

Throsby, D. (2001) *Economics and Culture*. Cambridge University Press, Cambridge.

Toffler, A. (1981) *The Third Wave*. Pan Books, London.

Tunstall, J. (ed.) (2001) *Media Occupations and Professions*. Oxford University Press, Oxford.

Turner, B. (2003) McDonaldization: linearity and liquidity in consumer cultures. *American Behavioral Scientist* **47**, 137–53.

Turow, J. (2005) Audience construction and culture production: marketing surveillance in the digital age. *The Annals of the American Academy of Political and Social Sciences* **597**, 103–21.

Von Hippel, E. (2005) *Democratizing Innovations*. MIT Press, Boston.

Part III

Methodologies and Models

....

Editors' Introduction

·····································

How might one actually conduct media industry analysis? What tools and resources are available to the researcher initiating such work? What potential challenges or obstacles might one encounter along the way? This section indicates the varied approaches that might be taken by scholars operating from a media industry studies perspective. The authors in this section map out some of the most recent directions being taken in media economics, regulation and the law, critical cultural policy studies, cultures of production, and audience analysis.

Philip M. Napoli begins by showing the complicated position of media economics in the academy. At the same time that media economics often has not been taken seriously by traditional economists, it also has been dismissed by media studies scholars. Yet, he argues, the distinctive nature of media products warrants greater attention from both camps. Napoli indicates some of the key ways in which media are different from other products – including their competing markets of advertisers and consumers – and suggests some of the potential ramifications of their singular status. These examples underscore the value of combining cultural and political analyses with economic analysis. As Napoli emphasizes, not only do economic factors directly impact the types of texts the industry creates, but many policy decisions are based primarily on input from media economists.

John McMurria's chapter on regulation and the law also looks at the challenges of cross-disciplinary applications of policy scholarship. Illustrating how US laws and policies have been impacted by the dominance of a legal liberalist perspective, McMurria makes a case for the contributions of three other approaches: political economy, institutional analysis, and critical cultural citizenship. He argues that critical cultural citizenship, in combination with political economic and institutional analyses, best serves those interested in the pursuit of social justice. Case studies of specific moments in US regulatory history show how each approach can be applied. These case studies illustrate how the critical cultural citizenship perspective, in particular, exposes value judgments made on the basis of race, class, gender, and nation. Along with offering a means by which to reframe past policy decisions, the critical cultural citizenship approach might challenge the neoliberal views shaping contemporary regulations.

Neoliberalism is a focal point for Toby Miller's essay as well. Miller asserts that two of the main ways that scholars have considered the interaction between governments and media industries in recent years – through the prisms of cultural policy and creative industries analysis – have led them to become complicit with neoliberal aims. He traces how approaches originally intended to make the humanities "useful" have in fact led to a betrayal of cultural studies' progressive goals. Those who embrace the "creative class" rhetoric are seduced by misleading statistics and overblown public relations from the industry and government. He asserts that the concerns that motivated cultural studies in the past – including labor inequalities and cultural imperialism – remain every bit as pressing today. As an alternative to creative industries and cultural policy studies, he turns to critical cultural policy studies. Through a case study of Hollywood–government relations, he indicates how scholars might go about using such an approach.

For John Thornton Caldwell, the best way to understand how the industry works is by looking closely at the "work worlds" of media professionals. In contrast to the "top-down" approach favored by most traditional political economists, he lays out a "bottom-up" approach, which he calls a "cultural studies of film/television production." The complexities of the industry become apparent by exploring how practitioners represent themselves and their work to each other, the press, and the public. By integrating textual analysis, interviews, ethnographic field observation and economic/industrial analysis, Caldwell suggests how to more fully understand the power struggles taking place in the post-Fordist media landscape. Caldwell's model for undertaking research consists of three registers of "deep industrial practices," which he illustrates through specific examples and photographs. His use of photographs functions as a key methodological intervention supporting his argument that film and television studies scholars need to expand their ideas of what they define as "texts." Caldwell contends that the artifacts, organizations, events, and people associated with the production process can be analyzed as texts in the same way that traditional film and television programs are.

Finally, Joshua Green and Henry Jenkins propose a new model for understanding the relationship between industry and audiences. They explore how the rise of Web 2.0 – with its greater interactive possibilities via such applications as social networking and user-generated videos – has transformed the ways that producers and consumers interact. The authors argue that these changes necessitate bringing together previously segregated literatures on audience studies and media industries. They proceed by combining the "convergence culture" approach developed in the US with work on the "creative industries" and "produsage" coming from Australia. In addition, they apply E. P. Thompson's idea of the "moral economy" to frame their discussion of the social, cultural, and emotional transactions occurring between producers and consumers. As Green and Jenkins show with the use of vivid examples, at times the stakes are very high as conflicts arise over issues such as intellectual property rights and appropriate compensation for work. Struggles also ensue between different corporate and individual stakeholders over the precise forms media texts should take. The co-authors conclude by proposing how the various players might reach a détente in their relationship and thereby best flourish in the new media landscape. In addition to suggesting yet another forward-thinking model for the analysis of industry, text, and audience, Green and Jenkins also outline future challenges for all of the stakeholders invested in contemporary media production and consumption.

12

Media Economics and the Study of Media Industries

....

Philip M. Napoli

An understanding of the economics of media is vital to a thorough understanding of the factors shaping the evolution, behavior, content output, and, ultimately, the impact of the media industries. As much as media industries are cultural and political entities, they also are economic entities, and an understanding of the economic constraints and incentives under which they operate, and of the basic economic characteristics of the products in which they deal, can provide valuable insights into a wide range of dimensions of media industry behavior.

Certainly, for most students and scholars, it is often the political and cultural dimensions of media industries that are the most compelling and that raise the most intriguing research questions. However, investigations of these questions should be sufficiently grounded in the basic economics of media industries – particularly given that an increasing proportion of the media sector around the world is becoming privatized and commercialized. Understanding the economic dynamics underlying the production, distribution, and exhibition of media content, as well as the dynamics underlying the buying, producing, and selling of media audiences, can lead to more well-rounded research on media industries, regardless of its disciplinary point of origin.

As research is increasingly making clear, the economic and the political/cultural dimensions of

media industries are not completely separate fields of inquiry. Indeed, much of the most compelling research in media economics taking place today is taking a more integrated approach toward both the economic and non-economic dimensions of media industries. For instance, recent research has shown that the product characteristics of different types of newspapers can lead newspaper readers to forego their local paper in favor of subscribing to the national edition of the *New York Times*. This, in turn, can have dramatic political repercussions, as those readers who defect from their local paper to the *Times* actually seem to become less likely to vote in local elections (George & Waldfogel 2006). As a study such as this illustrates, the competitive dynamics within a particular media industry sector can have dramatic political implications. Similar research has even suggested that the introduction of the Fox News channel into media markets can affect citizens' voting behavior (DellaVigna & Kaplan 2006). On a related topic, recent media economics research also has begun to explore the controversial notion of "media bias" (see Sutter 2001; Groseclose & Milyo 2005) and has suggested that the political slant (i.e., "bias") of media outlets may be able to be explained through an understanding of the product preferences of the consumers in which the individual media outlets operate (Gentzkow & Shapiro 2006).

Looking beyond politics to the cultural dimensions of media industries, recent research has shown how the availability of specialized content serving the interests of minority communities appears tightly tied to the demographic composition of the media markets in which the minority communities are located. Thus if minority audiences represent a relatively small proportion of the community, they are often very poorly served by their local media in terms of having content available to them that addresses their particular interests (Waldfogel 2003). Economic research has even examined the underlying market incentives that lead television programmers to provide violent programming. This research has illustrated that the sector of the TV audience most highly valued by advertisers (men and women in the 18–34 age range) also happens to be the segment of the audience most attracted to violent programming. This is a phenomenon that creates powerful economic incentives for programmers to continue to push the boundaries in terms of violent programming, and to make increased quantities of such programming available, thereby increasing the likelihood of children's exposure to such programming (see Hamilton 1998).

As these examples suggest, media economics can contribute to a broader understanding of the behavior of media industries and can indeed help us answer questions with implications that may be cultural and/or political in nature, in addition to economic. In this regard, media economics represents a useful foundation of knowledge for a wide range of important scholarly inquiries into the behaviors of media industries, as well as into the broader political and cultural ramifications of these behaviors.

Media Economics as a Field: Background and Evolution

What is particularly striking about the study of media economics is that, until recently, it was an area of inquiry that was very much on the periphery of mainstream economics. This marginal status for media economics was likely the result of a number of factors. These include: 1) the fact that the economics of

media industries often do not conform very well to the standard theoretical assumptions and models typically employed by economists (this point will be discussed in greater detail below); and 2) that the media industries have been seen within the economics community as a somewhat marginal, frivolous area of focus. As one well-known economist has described the mindset of the economics discipline toward the media and entertainment industries, "[such] frivolous activities can hardly exert the intellectual pull of serious industries such as steel, pharmaceuticals, and computer chips" (Caves 2000, vii). This traditional disinterest in the media sector is particularly puzzling when we consider that entertainment is the second largest export in the US economy.

However, scholars in other disciplines (e.g., communications, media studies, sociology, and cultural studies) with a strong interest in media industries have maintained a fairly extensive tradition of examining the economic dimensions of media industries. It is interesting to note that the main journal devoted to the topic – the *Journal of Media Economics* – has historically published the work primarily of scholars in communications and media studies, with the work of relatively few economists (until recently) found within its pages. As a result, much of the literature falling under the umbrella heading of "media economics" does in fact address many of the kinds of subjects and issues reflective of the interests and concerns of scholars in communications and media studies – though much of this work likely would not be considered true economics research by many traditionally trained economists.

Within the communication/media studies tradition, the segment of the media economics literature that has perhaps historically been the most visible is the "political economy" literature that draws heavily from critical media studies. This body of literature owes much to the work of critical scholars such as Noam Chomsky (see Herman & Chomsky 2002) and Herbert Schiller (1981), among others. Work in this vein has focused on examining how media industries reflect and serve established corporate and governmental interests, and on how trends in media ownership, market dynamics, and regulatory structures can exacerbate these tendencies. As should be clear, this political economy tradition has tended to take an overtly critical stance toward many of the institutions of capitalism, a perspective that is, in many ways, counter to the perspective underlying much economics research.

In recent years, however, economists have devoted substantially more attention to the economics of media industries. The most likely explanation for this is the increased extent to which economic analysis is being asked for – and utilized – by those who make policies and laws related to media industries. The Federal Communications Commission, for instance, has relied increasingly on economic analyses to guide its decision-making over the past decade (Napoli 2004). Even the courts have shown an increased interest in integrating media economics research into their decision-making processes related to laws and policies that impact media industries (Napoli 2005). As a result, the demand for media economics research has increased, with this demand from the policymaking sector in some ways helping to validate scholarly attention to what has traditionally (if incorrectly) been considered a frivolous or marginal area of focus within the economics community. Also as a result, there has developed within the policymaking sector a tension between those who see an over-reliance on economic analysis and analytical frameworks and those who see an insufficient reliance on economics (see Entman & Wildman 1992; Napoli 2001). In any case, the field of media economics certainly has grown significantly in recent years, and continues to reflect contributions from scholars with a wide range of disciplinary backgrounds.

Perhaps the earliest body of research that helped to coherently define the field of media economics is what has come to be known as the "program choice" literature (see Steiner 1952; Rothenberg 1962; Beebe 1977). This body of literature sought to explain how radio (and later, television) audiences would allocate their attention across available programming options under different conditions (e.g., different numbers of channels and program offerings). It also sought to explain how programmers would choose to program their channels under different conditions (e.g., different distributions of consumer preferences, different numbers of channels,

and different ownership conditions). Like much media economics research, this research was motivated by specific policy issues being confronted by media policymakers. In the case of the program choice literature, the key underlying question involved the costs and benefits associated with having competitive or monopoly conditions in the provision of programming (for a thorough overview of this literature, see Owen & Wildman 1992). Throughout its history, the program choice literature has been critiqued for oversimplifying the complex dynamics of how audiences select the programming that they consume (see Owen & Wildman 1992; Napoli 2003). In this regard the literature is reflective of the larger challenge that has always confronted media economics research – namely, adequately accounting for the variety of ways in which the economics of media industries do not conform well to traditional economic models and simplifying assumptions.

The Distinctive Economics of Media Industries

The basic economic characteristics of media industries pose significant challenges to traditional economic approaches. Much of this has to do with the nature of the products that media industries manufacture and sell. Media industries (ad-supported media industries, in particular) are unlike most other industries in that they operate in what is perhaps best described as a "dual product marketplace" (see Owen & Wildman 1992; Napoli 2003). That is, most sectors of the media industry simultaneously seek to manufacture and sell two completely different products to two completely different sets of consumers – they sell content to audiences; and they sell audiences to advertisers. These two product markets are very tightly interrelated.

What does all of this mean? Consider, for instance, a basic cable network (such as ESPN or the USA Network), which seeks to have as many subscribers as possible. These subscribers are obtained by convincing local cable systems to carry the network. These systems in turn charge their subscribers a rate that includes a small per-subscriber charge for the basic cable network. A portion of these subscription charges are then passed along to the cable network, such that a basic cable network can earn anywhere from a few cents to a few dollars for every household in which the cable network is being received. This revenue stream therefore represents the sale of content (i.e., the cable network) to audiences (i.e., the cable subscribers), with the cable system serving as the intermediary.

This same basic cable network also has a second, equally important, market in which it operates. Specifically, this network also is constantly selling advertising time on its network to advertisers interested in reaching the precise audience that watches this particular network. In this market, the size and demographic composition of the network's audience determine how much advertising revenue the network is able to capture. The more people who view the network, the more the network is typically able to charge for a commercial spot. Similarly, the more demographically attractive the network's audience is to advertisers (advertisers have a strong preference, for instance, for audiences in the 18–34 age range), the more the network can charge for a commercial spot. In this market, therefore, it is the sale of audiences to advertisers that is the focus.

Thus we have a "content" market and an "audience" market in which many media firms operate simultaneously. Of course, some sectors of the media industry participate almost exclusively in the content market (think, for instance, of a premium cable network such as HBO that does not incorporate advertisements into its programming, or the theatrical exhibition or home video distribution of motion pictures), while others participate almost exclusively in the audience market (think, for instance, of a broadcast radio station that provides all of its programming for free, and relies entirely on advertising revenues). The majority of sectors of the industry rely on some combination of revenues from both the content and audience markets. For instance, daily newspapers sell advertising space to advertisers along with newspapers to consumers; magazines, satellite radio, many websites, and cable systems similarly operate simultaneously in both the content and audience markets.

Even sectors of the media industry that traditionally have focused on only one of these markets have begun to diversify. Thus for instance, we see motion picture studios engaging in increased product placement; and, of course, motion picture theaters now frequently run product advertisements in advance of the feature film. By such mechanisms, the motion picture industry is making inroads into the audience marketplace. Similarly, the broadcast television networks, which traditionally have relied almost exclusively on the sale of audiences to advertisers, are using new technologies such as the iPod and video-on-demand to sell their programming (often commercial-free) directly to the consumer.

It is also important to recognize that content providers in those industry sectors that derive virtually all of their revenue from the sale of audiences to advertisers (e.g., broadcast television and radio, free weekly newspapers) still must compete with content providers who sell their content to audiences at a price. Thus for example, NBC's ability to attract and sell audiences to advertisers is affected by the performance of HBO, even though HBO is not a participant in the audience marketplace. And so, a network such as NBC is actually in the unusual position of manufacturing one product (television programming) and then essentially giving it away in order to attract and sell another product (audiences). It is difficult to identify another industry, outside of media, that operates under such a business model.

Further economic complications arise when we examine the distinctive attributes of the two primary products in the media marketplace – content and audiences. As many economists have noted, media content is a fairly distinctive product, with a number of important distinguishing characteristics. For instance, the "public good" nature of media content has been the subject of extensive analysis (Waterman 1987; Owen & Wildman 1992; Werbach 2000). From an economic standpoint, a public good is described as a product that is not "used up" in consumption. A public good is a product that can be consumed over and over again without additional units having to be produced (e.g., an art exhibit or a park). As public goods, media products can be sold and resold indefinitely without incurring significant additional production costs. This is because the costs associated with producing media products are, as is the case with all public goods, primarily "fixed." That is, the bulk of the money spent in producing media products is associated with the "first copy costs" – costs that are incurred up front and that do not vary according to how many audience members ultimately consume the media product.

The costs associated with a television program such as *Grey's Anatomy* do not vary much, regardless of whether the program is watched by 1 million or 30 million people. Consider, in contrast, a shoe manufacturer that incurs additional costs for each pair of shoes sold. Of course, the more shoes manufactured and sold, the lower the per-shoe manufacturing cost is likely to be, given the economies of scale that the manufacturer is likely to achieve by purchasing raw materials in larger quantities. And so, in economics, the traditionally held theory is that the price for a product must at least equal its "marginal cost" (the cost associated with producing the next pair of shoes) in order for the business to remain viable.

This basic proposition is problematic when we are talking about public goods such as media products. Because virtually all of the costs associated with media products are "fixed," it is difficult to identify a particular marginal cost associated with the product. In fact, the case can be made that any consumer who values a media product at a value greater than zero can contribute to the profits of the firm that produced that media product. Consider, for instance, someone who is very excited to see the next *Batman* movie. This individual is likely to be perfectly willing to spend $10 (or even more) to see the movie as soon as it is released in theaters. But what about someone who is not that excited to see the next *Batman*? They might only be willing to spend $3 or $4 to see the movie. The movie studio would still like to capture that consumer's $3 or $4 (while also capturing the more excited consumer's $10). Returning to an example from a private good, such as shoes, we instead would find ourselves in a situation where the person willing to pay only $3 or $4 for the pair of shoes probably would not be paying enough to cover the costs of manufacturing the pair of shoes. The $3 or $4 customer is thus not a viable customer for the shoe manufacturer, but is a viable customer for the motion picture producer.

All the motion picture producer has to do is figure out a way to sell that customer the ability to watch the movie for $3 or $4 while still capturing $10 from all of those consumers willing to pay $10 to see the film. This has given rise to the well-known strategy of "windowing" media products – wherein different media platforms are used at different points in time as a form of "price discrimination" (i.e., separating out consumers based on their level of willingness to pay for a product; see Owen & Wildman 1992). Those willing to pay $10 to see *Batman* get to see the movie first when it is in the theaters. Those only willing to pay $3 or $4 must wait until the movie is available via video-on-demand. Even those willing to pay less than $3 or $4 will have an opportunity to see *Batman*, when it eventually shows up on premium cable, then later basic cable, and on down the windowing sequence.

Windowing is representative of the essential public good nature of media products in that different price points are set at different points in time to accommodate different levels of demand for the product. This simply cannot be done with private goods such as shoes, automobiles, or computers. Unlike media, these products have significant marginal costs. The costs of printing and distributing individual newspapers, or encoding movies on DVDs, are minuscule compared with the original costs of producing the news reporting contained within the paper, or of producing the film contained within the DVD. And, as more and more distribution of media content moves online, these marginal costs shrink even further. Electronic downloading of movies, music, news, or books reduces further the already small marginal costs associated with the production and distribution of media products – costs such as discs, paper, ink, and packaging (see Anderson 2006). And so, one of the fundamental (and fundamentally appealing, from a strategic standpoint) aspects of the economics of media content is that the content can be sold at many different price points and can thereby reach a much larger proportion of the overall potential market than can be achieved in other product markets – all without incurring significant additional costs.

Audiences are perhaps an even more unusual product than content. In selling audiences to advertisers, media firms essentially deal in human attention, and human attention represents a much more abstract, elusive, and intangible product than, say, steel, insurance, or legal services. How can human attention be put into sufficiently concrete form to be effectively bought and sold? Scholars of media industries have devoted a tremendous amount of attention to this fundamental question, as well as to the mechanisms that are employed to accomplish this, and their shortcomings (see Meehan 1984; Ang 1991; Napoli 2003).

Human attention resists the type of clear, straightforward definition and measurement that typify the transactions that take place in most other industries. It is generally easy for the buyer and seller of steel to agree on whether a ton of steel is being bought. The steel need only be weighed. But if you are an advertiser buying audiences, if you seek to buy 7 million males, 18–34 years old, and purchase this audience from one or more television networks, how do you determine whether you've actually received what you paid for? Generally, various forms of "ratings" data are used in this kind of transaction. A wide range of audience measurement firms (e.g., Nielsen Media Research for television, Arbitron for radio, Audit Bureau of Circulations for newspapers, Nielsen Net/Ratings and ComScore/Media Metrix for the Internet) work to effectively and reliably measure audience attention across different media, and to package these measurements in ways that facilitate the efficient functioning of the "audience marketplace," in which buyers and sellers all feel reasonably confident that they know enough about the characteristics of the product being bought and sold (see Napoli 2003). The numbers provided by these measurement firms essentially become the currency in these markets.

Unfortunately, these numbers are rough approximations, at best, of who is actually reading, watching, or listening to what. Different measurement firms often produce very different portraits of who is consuming what, as slight differences in methodology can produce very different outcomes. Indeed, it is important to recognize that, for the most part, the measurement of media audiences is conducted by observing the behaviors of relatively small samples of the overall population of media consumers

(see Napoli 2003). For the numbers derived from these samples to provide a reasonable representation of the behavior of the population as a whole, the measurement process must be incredibly rigorous, the samples must be meticulously generated, and the audience members taking part must be diligent and thorough in their participation. Otherwise, the audience data are not likely to accurately reflect the behaviors of the population as a whole and advertisers will become skeptical as to whether their ad dollars are being effectively spent.

Into this very tenuous state of affairs, new technologies are constantly being introduced (DVRs, handheld devices such as iPods, etc.) that dramatically complicate the process of accurately measuring audience behavior. Yet perhaps unlike any other market, the market for media audiences functions on the basis of a product that does not really exist in any kind of tangible or verifiable form. Audiences are, instead, a statistical abstraction created from measurement practices that are constantly struggling to keep pace with the changing media environment – and, as many critics would argue – these practices are not effectively keeping up with changes (see Ang 1991; Napoli 2003).

Audiences also are highly perishable. That is, unlike media content, which – as noted above – can be sold and resold indefinitely (Owen & Wildman 1992), the shelf life for media audiences is exceptionally short, lasting only for the duration of time that a media product is consumed (see Napoli 2003). For this reason, audiences have been described as "very fleeting products: they become obsolete almost instantly" (Ang 1991, 61). Therefore, audiences need to be sold before they are even produced. Thus in some cases, media outlets sell their audiences months in advance of the content being distributed. For instance, broadcast networks sell much of their commercial inventory for the upcoming television season (which begins in the fall) throughout the spring and summer via the "upfronts."

Of course, for this kind of marketplace to operate effectively, these transactions must be based on reasonably accurate and reliable predictions as to the size and composition of audiences that are going to consume the content. This means, that, unlike most products, audiences are bought based on predictions regarding the quantity (audience size) and quality (audience demographics) of the product to be produced. Unfortunately for advertisers and content providers, another distinguishing characteristic of audiences is that they are highly unpredictable (Bielby & Bielby 1994; Caves 2000; Gitlin 2000; DeVany 2004). This is due in large part to the fact that, unlike most other products, the audience is not one over which producers (i.e., content providers) have much control (see Berry & Waldfogel 1999). Content is made available to audiences in the hopes of attracting them. However, the content provider has relatively little ability to control the size and composition of the audience that ultimately consumes the content. Considering these difficult conditions, it is perhaps not surprising that a significant amount of research has sought to better understand the factors that help explain – and thus predict – the behavior of media audiences (see Bielby & Bielby 1994; DeVany 2004). Despite these efforts, throughout various sectors of the media industry, it is not uncommon for content that was expected to be a huge hit to flop miserably, or for content with little expectation of success to unexpectedly become a hit (Bielby & Bielby 1994). In the mid-1990s, for instance, television industry pundits were very optimistic about a new Chicago-based hospital drama, titled *Chicago Hope*, while giving a similar, competing drama, *ER*, very little chance of making it past the first season.

As should be clear, from an economic standpoint, media industries are unlike most other industries – and these differences bear directly on how these industries are structured and behave. In this regard, a thorough understanding of the distinctive economics of media industries serves as a useful tool for gaining insights into a wide range of dimensions of media industry behavior.

Using Media Economics to Understand, Study, and Critique Media Industries

The distinctive economic characteristics of the product markets in which media industries operate are particularly important in that they can help explain many of the behavioral patterns that frequently are identified and discussed by media scholars and critics. For instance, the oft-noted tendency of media organizations to constantly rely on established and proven genres, formulas, or properties, rather than producing original or innovative content can be seen as a reflection of the industry's inability to effectively gauge and predict audience preferences. Reliance on past successes becomes the closest thing to a risk-reducing strategy that industry decision-makers have at their disposal (see Bielby & Bielby 1994). And, given the combination of high production costs and the unpredictability of consumer response, virtually all sectors of the media industry are very high risk enterprises.

Similarly, the public good nature of media content compels many of the behavioral patterns that have been identified (and frequently criticized) by media industries scholars. The tendency to consistently re-use, repeat, and repurpose existing media content, rather than producing new content, long has been a defining trait of media industries (see Negroponte 1996; Kompare 2005). Most media outlets – particularly "new media" – depend heavily on content already produced for other media. Most cable networks produce relatively little original programming, and what little original programming they do produce is repeated over and over throughout any given week. Much of the most popular content online is originally produced for other media, whether it be television, radio, newspapers, or movie theaters/DVD. This, of course, is the essence of the "windowing" strategy discussed earlier. However, here it is taken beyond price discrimination to also serve as a way to provide content at the lowest possible cost (often referred to as "repurposing"). That is, from a content provider's standpoint, it is often the case that previously produced content can be obtained for far less than the cost of producing original content. Therefore, many cable networks choose to focus on providing reruns of broadcast network programming, or Hollywood movies, rather than filling their schedule with new content. Old episodes of *Law & Order* or *Sanford & Son* generally can be obtained for far less than the cost of producing even the most inexpensive forms of original programming.

In addition, if such properties are chosen wisely, they can be comparably successful in attracting audiences.

This dimension of the economics of media content also helps explain the common phenomenon of "one-way flows" of media content (Wildman 1994). As many analysts of media industries have noted, US media products tend to flow through media markets around the world – often proving much more successful than domestically produced content in many countries (Miller et al. 2005), while US media audiences consume relatively little foreign-produced media content. A number of explanations for this phenomenon have been put forth, ranging from conscious efforts by US media firms and governmental agencies to influence foreign governments and cultures, to the inherent fascination that other cultures have with US culture, to the well-known "cultural imperialism" argument (see Wildman 1995).

An economic approach to one-way flows suggests that the phenomenon may simply result from the higher production budgets of US media products, which make them inherently more appealing to international audiences than domestically produced content (Wildman 1994). Because of the unique pricing characteristics associated with public goods discussed above, these US media products often can be obtained for less than the cost of original, domestically produced content. As a result, US media products become appealing options for both foreign content providers and foreign audiences. This pattern reflects the broader, more generalized tendency for media products to flow from large markets to small markets, as the larger content investment that accompanies the greater revenue potential of large markets makes this content inherently more appealing to audiences in the smaller markets (Wildman 1994).

As these few examples indicate, the application of economic tools and concepts to the study of the behavior of media industries can provide useful insights that can contribute to well-rounded understandings of these industries and their behaviors, as well as to those of the audiences who consume their products. In this regard, scholars and students with an interest in developing a deeper understanding of media industries – regardless of their disciplinary background or particular areas of research interest – likely

can benefit from the work being conducted in the media economics field.

Conclusion

Media industries possess a number of distinctive economic characteristics, and an understanding of these characteristics can provide useful insights into a wide range of dimensions of the behavior of media industries and their audiences/consumers – helping us to understand patterns in production, distribution, and consumption of media products. Analysts of media industries, regardless of their disciplinary background, can be very well served by incorporating an understanding of the basic underlying economics of these industries.

As the field of media economics continues to develop, it is likely to remain highly interdisciplinary in nature, particularly in terms of economic analytical tools and concepts increasingly being applied to questions that would historically have been considered outside the realm of traditional economics. Examples of recent efforts to integrate issues of economics into political and cultural studies of the media include work on the nature of the relationship between media market characteristics and political participation (DellaVigna & Kaplan 2006; George & Waldfogel 2006), the nature of media bias (Gentzkow & Shapiro 2006) and the effect of media organization behavior on the behavior of politicians and the political knowledge of the citizenry (Snyder & Stromberg 2006). At the same time, scholars from outside the economics discipline (e.g., from communication and media studies, cultural studies, etc.) are likely to continue to engage in a wide range of politically and/or culturally oriented inquiries that also address the economic dimensions of media industry behavior (e.g., Gitlin 2000; Napoli 2003; Miller et al. 2005). Ideally, this will help to ensure that the field of media economics maintains a strong focus on analyzing media industries not only as economic entities, but as political and cultural entities as well.

In this regard, media economics seems particularly integral to the development of media industry studies. The study of media industries is proving itself to be a highly interdisciplinary field in its own right, attracting scholars and students from both the humanities and the social sciences. Indeed, such interdisciplinarity would seem to be essential for developing a well-rounded understanding of an industry as complex and unique as the media, and with such profound potential for political and cultural influence.

References

Anderson, C. (2006) *The Long Tail: Why the Future of Business is Selling Less of More*. Hyperion, New York.

Ang, I. (1991) *Desperately Seeking the Audience*. Routledge, New York.

Beebe, J. (1977) Institutional structure and program choices in television markets. *Quarterly Journal of Economics* **91**, 15–37.

Berry, S. T. and Waldfogel, J. (1999) Free entry and social inefficiency in radio broadcasting. *RAND Journal of Economics* **30**, 397–420.

Bielby, W. T. and Bielby, D. D. (1994) "All hits are flukes": institutionalized decision-making and the rhetoric of network primetime program development. *American Journal of Sociology* **99**, 1287–313.

Caves, R. E. (2000) *Creative Industries: Contracts Between Art and Commerce*. Harvard University Press, Cambridge.

DellaVigna, S. and Kaplan, E. (2006) The Fox News effect: media bias and voting. Paper presented at the 4th Workshop on Media Economics, Washington DC. At http://elsa.berkeley.edu/~sdellavi/wp/foxvote06-03-30.pdf, accessed February 8, 2008.

DeVany, A. (2004) *Hollywood Economics: How Extreme Uncertainty Shapes the Film Industry*. Routledge, New York.

Entman, R. M. and Wildman, S. S. (1992) Reconciling economic and non-economic perspectives on media policy: transcending the "marketplace of ideas." *Journal of Communication* **41**, 5–19.

Gentzkow, M. and Shapiro, J. M. (2006) Media bias and reputation. *Journal of Political Economy* **114**, 280–316.

George, L. M. and Waldfogel, J. (2006) The *New York Times* and the market for local newspapers. *American Economic Review* **96**, 435–47.

Gitlin, T. (2000) *Inside Prime Time*. University of California Press, Berkeley.

Groseclose, T. and Milyo, J. (2005) A measure of media bias. *Quarterly Journal of Economics* **120**, 1191–237.

Hamilton, J. T. (1998) *Channeling Violence: The Economic Market for Violent Television Programming*. Princeton University Press, Princeton.

Herman, E. S. and Chomsky, N. (2002) *Manufacturing Consent: The Political Economy of the Mass Media*, reprint edn. Pantheon, New York.

Kompare, D. (2005) *Rerun Nation: How Repeats Invented American Television*. Routledge, New York.

Meehan, E. (1984) Ratings and the institutional approach: a third answer to the commodity question. *Critical Studies in Mass Communication* **1**, 216–225.

Miller, T., Govil, N., McMurria, J., Maxwell, R., and Wang, T. (2005) *Global Hollywood 2*. British Film Institute, London.

Napoli, P. M. (2001) *Foundations of Communications Policy: Principles and Process in the Regulation of Electronic Media*. Hampton Press, Cresskill.

Napoli, P. M. (2003) *Audience Economics: Media Institutions and the Audience Marketplace*. Columbia University Press, New York.

Napoli, P. M. (2004) Media economics and media policy: the good and the bad. Paper presented at the Latin American Meeting of the Econometrics Society, Santiago, Chile. At www.fordham.edu/images/undergraduate/communications/media%20economics%20and%20media%20policy.pdf, accessed February 8, 2008.

Napoli, P. M. (2005) The broadening of the media policy research agenda. Paper presented to the Social Science Research Council. At http://programs.ssrc.org/media/publications/PhilipNapoli.1.Final.doc, accessed February 8, 2008.

Negroponte, N. (1996) *Being Digital*. Vintage, New York.

Owen, B. M. and Wildman, S. S. (1992) *Video Economics*. Harvard University Press, Cambridge.

Rothenberg, J. (1962) Consumer sovereignty and the economics of TV programming. *Studies in Public Communication* **4**, 45–54.

Schiller, H. (1981) *Who Knows? Information in the Age of the Fortune 500*. Ablex, Norwood.

Snyder, J. M. and Stromberg, D. (2006) Media markets' impact on politics. Paper presented at the 4th

Workshop on Media Economics, Washington DC. At http://americandemocracy.nd.edu/speaker_series/files/SnyderPaper.pdf, accessed February 8, 2008.

Steiner, P. O. (1952) Program patterns and preferences and the workability of competition in radio broadcasting. *Quarterly Journal of Economics* **66**, 194–223.

Sutter, D. (2001) Can the media be so liberal? The economics of media bias. *Cato Journal* **20**, 431–51.

Waldfogel, J. (2003) Preference externalities: an empirical study of who benefits whom in differentiated-product markets. *RAND Journal of Economics* **34**, 557–68.

Waterman, D. (1987) Electronic media and the economics of the first sale doctrine. In Thorne, R. and Viera, J. D. (eds.) *Entertainment, Publishing and the Arts Handbook*. Clark Boardman, New York, pp. 3–13.

Werbach, K. (2000) Syndication: the emerging model for business in the Internet era. *Harvard Business Review* **78**, 85–93.

Wildman, S. S. (1994) One-way flows and the economics of audiencemaking. In Ettema, J. S. and Whitney, D. C. (eds.) *Audiencemaking: How the Media Create the Audience*. Sage, Thousand Oaks, pp. 115–41.

Wildman, S. S. (1995) Trade liberalization and policy for media industries: a theoretical examination of media flows. *Canadian Journal of Communication* **20**, 367–88.

13

Regulation and the Law
A Critical Cultural Citizenship Approach

· ·

John McMurria

This essay identifies four methodological approaches to media regulation and the law including legal studies, institutional analysis, political economy, and critical cultural citizenship. It then advocates a critical cultural citizenship approach through utilizing this methodology to assess the emergence of radio, broadcast television, cable television, and digital media. Attention is placed on constructs of cultural citizenship within the broader socioeconomic and cultural contexts of an expert class concerned with the emergence of mass culture in the 1920s, the postwar local television station allocations process as a response to mass culture anxieties, the taste hierarchies that promoted consumer choice using cable wires, and the libertarian roots of digital media deregulations. This history of electronic media regulation reveals a transformation in public service ideals from a Progressive/New Deal era committed to universal service and the paternalistic care of a susceptible national broadcast citizenry to a neoliberal era culminating in the Telecommunications Act of 1996, which equates public service with industry deregulation, market competition, and individual consumer choice. For a media industry studies committed to the broader project of social justice, calling attention to constructs of cultural citizenship questions how regulation and the law evoke registers of power across categories of class, race, gender, and nation. It also asks how regulatory frameworks

within the media industries have contributed to, or contested, the broader neoliberal political movement.

Four Approaches to Media Regulation
· ·

Because many of the elected officials and appointed administrators that populate regulatory arenas have formal legal backgrounds, *legal studies* has had a significant impact on policy decision-making. Despite a range of specialties and diverging approaches to legal studies, most law schools, legal journals, and courts of law share a broad commitment to legal liberalism. Derived from classical liberal theories of subjectivity, this orientation to the law considers individuals as autonomous and selfish rather than social and collective, separates individual subjective values from knowable objective facts, and embraces a rule-based, pragmatic, antitheoretical, case-law oriented approach to the legal process. As such, legal liberalism favors universal, abstracted individual rights over historically particular group rights, the quantitative methods of applied science and microeconomics over political economy and the sociocultural and historical methods of the humanities, and legal precedent and timeless norms over the dynamics of historical and cultural specificity (Kelman

1987; Pritchard 2006). Legal liberalism in media law is principally focused on assessing regulation through First Amendment jurisprudence (Parsons 1987; Powe 1987). Standard media law textbooks adhere to legal liberalism in focusing almost entirely on court opinions and their First Amendment contexts, providing little socioeconomic or cultural context for the shift of free speech concerns away from the public's rights of information access to corporations' private rights of profit accumulation (Carter et al. 2004; Ross 2004; Pember & Calvert 2006).

Regulation treats different media technologies with varying First Amendment protections, from the most strictly protected press to the more regulated broadcasters, under justifications that the airwaves are considered a scarce public resource and their ubiquitous reach necessitates protecting unsuspecting citizens from obscenity and indecency. Though marginalized in legal arenas, critical legal studies and critical race theory have questioned the contradictory assumptions of legal liberalism through arguing that individuals cannot be separated from social contexts or subjective values from objective facts, particularly when considering the power relations that persist across social categories of class, gender, sexuality, and race (Kelman 1987; Streeter 1990; Crenshaw et al. 1996; Brown & Halley 2002; Classen 2004). For example, African American and Latino organizations have argued that there is a direct correlation between subject position, viewpoint diversity, and media ownership within historical conditions of racial discrimination, in contrast to legal liberal reasoning that concludes no such correlation can be empirically proven (Williams 1996; Center for International Media Action 2003; Horwitz 2005).

An *institutional approach* to media regulation considers the politics and everyday decision-making procedures within legal and regulatory institutions (Le Duc 1973; Krasnow et al. 1982; Baughman 1985; Galperin 2004). Institutional analyses consider the regulatory process to involve competing interest groups, from corporate lobbyists to public interest organizations (Napoli 2001a). Liberal legal principals often guide institutions such as the Federal Communications Commission (FCC) that favor "objective" microeconomic studies supporting

deregulation over the "subjective" testimony of creative workers, advocacy groups, and concerned citizens who support public interest oversight (Blevins & Brown 2006). Most social science-based communication research is directed toward understanding or influencing the institutional decision-making process (Braman 2003). Though providing insights into the regulatory process and guidance for strategic interventions, these institutional approaches remain bound by the "inside-the-beltway" legal liberal consensus (Streeter 1996, 113–62).

A *political economy* approach to media regulation and the law considers ownership structures and the capitalist ideologies that sustain them (Calabrese & Sparks 2004). For critics including Robert McChesney (2000), the free-market ideologies characteristic of the Telecommunications Act of 1996 have not produced competition but rather have facilitated the growth of large, integrated media conglomerates such as Time Warner, Disney, and News Corp that control a variety of media outlets including television stations, newspapers, magazines, film studios, cable systems, and websites. These profit-seeking commercial giants favor the free-market viewpoints that allow them to grow and create a depoliticized, mass entertainment culture that exploits violence and sex for the lowest-common-denominator audience. Political economic approaches to global media policies locate systemic power relations between the Global North and South and the empowerment of transnational corporations (Raboy 2002). To address the corporate control of the media, political economists advocate public-funded alternatives.

Rather than counterpose a capitalist commercial media against a public-funded alternative, a *critical cultural citizenship* approach considers regulation and the law as "a site for the production of cultural citizens," with commercial and public media offering "a series of rationales for particular types of conduct" (Lewis & Miller 2003, 1). Advertiser-supported commercial media promote consumer-oriented citizenship in which individual interests, cultural preferences, and social needs are best met through purchasing commodities in a free-market economy. Public interest media rationales promote good citizenship via commitments to particular cultural values and authorized behavior in the name of national heritage, collective belonging, an informed citizenry, a stable society, decency, local identities, and/or democratic participation. Critical approaches to these rationales for conduct consider the ways in which they operate to produce compliant self-governing citizens for sustaining particular cultural, social, and economic relations within capitalist liberal democracies, and how they discriminate or exclude across social and cultural registers of class, gender, sexuality, race, and nation. These boundary-defining rationales for citizenship work through particular value hierarchies, such as those that dismiss commercial media as "least common denominator" or that support public-funded systems to promote cultural "uplift" – each propagates elite values that reproduce unexamined class, gender, and race relations under the sign of proper citizenship (Miller 1998; Ouellette 2002; Miller 2006). A critical cultural citizenship approach seeks to understand the broader historical shift away from the collective forms of citizenship within the social welfare society to the ascendancy of consumer citizenship within the neoliberal polity (Calabrese & Burgelman 1999).

To varying degrees, the institutional analysis, political economy, and critical cultural citizenship approaches question legal liberal assumptions of apolitical, reasoned, and objective rulemaking by identifying the politics of institutions, the capitalist ideologies that inform debate, and the governing value systems that define cultural citizenship. However, because critical cultural citizenship considers the rights and obligations of societal membership that are necessarily activated through state and market institutions, as well as the cultural inscriptions that provide textures of meaning within and across these institutions, it necessitates combining institutional and political economic methodologies with those of cultural studies, which understands culture as the fabric of everyday life and as a contested site for producing and challenging social and economic inequalities (During 1999). To illustrate the methodological orientation of a critical cultural citizenship approach to media, a critical assessment of the emergence of the new media technologies of radio, broadcast television, cable television, and

digital media is provided below. Each of the four case studies that follow demonstrates how a focus on constructs of cultural citizenship engages with the other three methodological approaches to regulation and the law while attention to cultural value hierarchies illuminates otherwise unexamined power relations and provides a more productive conceptual framework for challenging legal liberal assumptions and the neoliberal consensus that has come to dominate media regulation.

The Expert Class, Cultural Hierarchies, and the Emergence of Broadcasting

Unlike the publicly financed or state-controlled broadcasting systems established in most regions outside the US, in 1934 the US Congress created the FCC to regulate an advertising-sponsored, commercial broadcasting system (Smith & Patterson 1998). For Robert Horwitz (1989), the commercial system of broadcasting derives from Progressive-era concepts of government–corporate relations in infrastructure industries that were thought essential to the public interest, and to the smooth operations of an increasingly national, corporate economy. From the Interstate Commerce Commission (1887) to the FCC, Congress created federal agencies to guide the corporate development of these industries. The "public interest" and protections of free speech were thought best served through "safeguarding the commerce function" of these industries rather than investing the state with a more substantial role (1–15, 47–64). Thomas Streeter (1996) calls these regulatory principles "corporate liberal" because they justified corporate organization as technologically necessary and entrusted administrative experts in federal agencies with a "functional" and "paternalistic" mandate to safeguard the public interest (31–58). Secretary of Commerce Herbert Hoover exemplified these corporate liberal principles in presiding over a series of radio conferences in the early 1920s that established the regulatory framework for the 1934 Act. Although Hoover thought overly intrusive advertising over the "public airwaves" was distasteful, he supported a growing Fordist economic consensus that prioritized rising consumer demand to keep mass-produced goods rolling off the increasingly industrialized production lines. For Hoover, radio advertising would serve as such a stimulant. The radio conferences culminated in temporary legislation in 1927 that favored high-powered national and regional "clear channels" with superior technical facilities, almost all of which were owned by the NBC and CBS networks, and re-assigned nonprofit and educational groups to lower-power stations on shared, inferior frequencies (Streeter 1996, 84–104). Stations that catered to particular interests such as WEVD in New York (named after socialist Eugene Victor Debs), the Chicago Federation of Labor's station or religious stations were dismissed as "propaganda stations" (Krattenmaker & Powe 1994, 22–25).

A broadcast reform movement comprised of labor unions, religious groups, educational organizations, and intellectuals generated a critique of advertising-supported broadcasting, particularly between 1927 and 1934. Despite the often elite cultural biases that framed these critiques, such as those of educators and cultural critics who described popular commercial radio as catering to "people of low intelligence" and the "hotcha element" that "threaten the very life of civilization," Robert McChesney argues that this reform movement represents "the sole instance in which the structure and control of a major mass medium were subject to anything close to legitimate political debate in US history," and an important historical precedent to inform current struggles to challenge the status quo of commercial media (McChesney 1993, 3–6; 94–120).

A critical cultural citizenship approach to early radio regulation considers these institutional and political economic contexts for the emergence of a commercial structure for broadcasting but takes more seriously the hierarchies of taste that separate the so-called "hotcha element" from the elite class of reformers. The national consumer economy supported by corporate liberals gave pause to prominent academics including Harold Lasswell, John Dewey, and Walter Lippman, who perceived a shift from a society steeped in the traditional binding ties of family, homogeneous neighborhoods, and

interpersonal interaction toward a "mass" society where individuals became increasingly detached from each other in fragmented, heterogeneous, urban environments, and therefore more susceptible to the "propaganda" influence of mass media (Czitrom 1983, 93–112; Simpson 1994, 17–20). Also, middle-class progressive reformers became increasingly concerned about the cultural influence of mass media. Jane Addams advocated the super-vised recreation of young people in part to protect against the "overwhelming temptation of illicit and soul-destroying pleasures" of the movies (Jowett et al. 1996, 26). Protestant reformers worried most about how tawdry amusements enticed working-class immigrants, many of whom were Jews and Catholics, away from a Protestant ethic of austere work and moral rectitude (Nasaw 1993, 174–85). And when jazz recordings dominated record sales by the early 1920s, progressive reformers such as the General Federation of Women's Clubs organized to "annihilate jazz" because it was created by "barbaric people to stimulate brutality and sensuality" (Hilmes 1997, 47). As Susan Douglas has written, general interest magazines in the early 1920s promoted radio programs that "should elevate musical tastes, and should promote contemplation and the ability to discriminate between the worthy and the base" (Douglas 1987, 313).

The educational alliances that most forcefully advanced alternatives to commercial broadcasting in this period expressed similar concerns about the rise of popular commercial radio derived from African American musical traditions and working-class cul-tural sensibilities. In 1934, the National Committee on Education by Radio sought to deploy "radio as a cultural agency" to combat the prevalence of "jazz of a debased sort with 'crooning'" and other popular commercial radio (Tyler 1934, 6; 96; 99). Corporate liberal federal agency regulators of commercial broadcasting shared similar elite cultural values, such as dissuading broadcasters from airing "recorded music" at a time when jazz dominated record sales (Kahn 1984, 57–69). Support for well-financed, high-powered, "quality" commercial stations in "the public interest" meant promoting a radio cul-ture that rose above crass commercialism to recon-cile middle-class cultural tastes with support for a burgeoning consumer society. Between corporate liberals invested in expert guidance over commercial media and an organized reform community motivated by cultural uplift fell the amateur radio operators, working classes, immigrants, and African Americans who had little or no representation in regulatory arenas. Thus, rather than the historical precedent of a reform movement challenging the status quo of commercial media, the lesson might be that historical or contemporary frameworks that counterpoise culturally debased commercial media against uplifting public alternatives obfuscate the discriminatory rationales of cultural citizenship that each constructs.

Local Service Stations, Mass Culture Frustrations, and the Emergence of Television

To facilitate the immediate growth of television and to stimulate the postwar economy, in 1945 the FCC established technical standards for RCA's production-line-ready patented black and white television sets using the limited VHF spectrum instead of opting for the more protracted launch of a CBS and Zenith-backed color TV standard using the more expansive UHF spectrum (Boddy 1990, 31–45). But with only 13 TV frequencies on the VHF band, substantial interference ensued. Thus the FCC froze new station allocations in 1948 until the commissioners devised a local community station-centered allocations plan in 1952 that set aside spectrum in the VHF *and* UHF bands to optimize the number of local stations nationwide, including 1,319 UHF set-aside station allocations and spectrum for educational stations. But the FCC's plan failed to consider the population densities that were required to sustain a local advertising-supported station and it also did not consider the prevailing economics of network television that privileged national programs and affiliate contracts for big city markets (Sterling & Kittross 1990, 294–304). Further, consumers lacked access to UHF tuners on RCA's VHF-ready consoles. Thus by 1956 only 156 UHF commercial stations were on the air (Boddy 1990, 54). Without

resources for programming, educational TV stations fared even worse, as just 19 of 200 educational stations were operating by 1956 (Shayon 1956, 373).

From an institutional and political economic perspective, early television regulations represented a compromise between capitulations to powerful industry players, such as RCA's interest in a VHF standard, and the creation of space for more local stations on the UHF band. But the economically irrational local allocations plan also exposed contradictions between the FCC's concessions to commercial institutions structured around advertising sponsorship within a national television economy and the FCC's vision for television as a technology for local community expression. The FCC's localism ideals were shared by a broad spectrum of sociologists, academics, and cultural critics who expressed concern over the impact of mass culture and the national consumer society that television helped spawn. Sociologists designed studies to empirically gauge how mass society had transformed local culture, including the Middletown studies of the 1920s and 1930s (Lynd & Lynd 1929; Lynd & Lynd 1937), the Yankee City series published in 1941 (Warner & Lunt 1941), and studies titled *Small Town in Mass Society* and *Eclipse of Community* in the 1950s (Vidich & Bensman 1958; Stein 1960). Sociologist David Riesman's widely read *The Lonely Crowd* lamented the loss of an "inner-directed" individualism of the "age of production," to an "outer-directed" character of conformity within an "age of consumption" (Riesman 1950, x–xi; 20). Cultural critics such as Dwight MacDonald (1957) lamented the usurpation of "folk culture" by a "mass culture" that was "fabricated by technicians hired by businessmen." These cultural critics shared with other intellectuals what Jackson Lears has described as a "tendency to perceive mass consumption and conformity as the defining characteristics of postwar American society" (Lears 1989).

Evidence of these mass culture anxieties is found in the FCC's 1946 Blue Book report on local broadcast radio stations. The report criticized local radio stations for airing popular jazz recordings and an overabundance of daytime soap operas rather than live local classical music, revealing particular raced, gendered, and classed priorities for local cultural expression. Also, empirical radio audience surveys exposed a perceptual distance between social scientists and "the people" they surveyed. For example, the influential empirical research methodologist Paul Lazarsfeld, who consulted on the Blue Book, conducted a radio audience study released in 1946, concluding that "the large majority of the people in this country are pleased with radio as it is," yet because a minority of well-educated viewers was less satisfied with radio, "in cultural matters the experts who see a problem in its broader contexts should get a preferential hearing" (Lazarsfeld & Field 1946, vii–viii; 69). These "objective" empirical studies also revealed racial biases. The numerous radio and television audience studies conducted by Lazarsfeld and others at the Bureau of Applied Research at Columbia University from the 1940s through the 1960s considered income, education, gender and religion as meaningful categories of social distinction, but none identified race, assuming the normative whiteness of those interviewed (Lazarsfeld & Field 1946; Lazarsfeld & Kendall 1948; Steiner 1963).

To conclude, the four regulatory approaches emphasize different aspects of early television regulation. An institutional approach highlights the decision-making processes of the FCC that balanced corporate interests with commitments to localism. A political economic approach reveals that RCA, advertisers, and the national networks benefited most from the standards and allocations process, while educational stations struggled because they lacked funding for programming. Legal liberalism considers the localism principles of television regulation to be rational, normative ideals passed on through judicial precedent, and that policymakers should be vigilant in definitional clarity so that "beliefs and ideology" do not infect the principles (Napoli 2001b). The cultural citizenship approach takes seriously the contradictions between the FCC's institutional/ideological support for the national advertising-sponsored, network-centered television system and its economically irrational local allocations plan. This approach resists separating normative principles from social and cultural contexts to expose the racial, gender, and class biases of mass culture critiques that mourned lost local community ideals and FCC reports that faulted local radio stations

for failing public interest standards. This expert class embraced cable television as a new technology for transcending mass broadcast culture.

Cable Television, Consumer Choice, and the Neoliberal Polity

When Congress created the legal framework governing broadcasting in 1927, lawmakers identified the airwaves as scarce public property and prioritized general public interest, advertising-supported stations that insulated viewers from "propaganda" and "offensiveness." But since the late 1940s when cable operators began to distribute broadcast television, and soon thereafter original programming, regulators have debated the property status of cable. In 1958 the Senate proposed a bill that considered cable a public medium equal to over-the-air broadcasting, applying broadcast public interest rules to cable operators. In the 1960s many state and municipal regulators treated cable as a public utility with similar universal service requirements of electricity and water. And in the 1970s the Nixon and Ford administrations recommended that cable be regulated as a common carrier with similar universal service requirements to telephone service (Parsons 1987). While each of these regulatory frameworks attributed a strong public property status to cable television, when Congress wrote the first federal laws for cable in 1984, they explicitly stated cable operators were not to be subjected to the public interest rules of broadcasters or to the universal service provisions of public utilities or common carriers (Parsons & Frieden 1998). Though Congress gave cities authority over the franchising process and rights to require public, government, and leased access channels, federal regulation considered TV cables private wires not scarce public information conduits, viewers were paying individual consumers not collective publics, and cable operators were private companies with strict First Amendment protections, not public trustees with universal service mandates.

This privatization of cable was informed by a broader political shift in the late 1970s toward deregulation; at the time, classical liberal economists championed laissez-faire market policies as solutions to stagflation, world trade organizations reduced trade barriers for the internationalization of capital, and conservative political leaders dismantled social welfare programs (Harvey 2005). The Reagan administration's FCC chairman Mark Fowler famously promoted this neoliberal order in treating television like any other free-market commodity – a "toaster with pictures" (Fowler & Brenner 1982). But the emergence of neoliberal regulatory policies has earlier cultural origins in debates over pay-TV, as was evident in four congressional pay-TV hearings between 1956 and 1969. Those supporting pay-TV, including New Deal liberals associated with Americans for Democratic Action (ADA), television critics, performing arts institutions, educators, and elected officials, shared the cultural perspective that commercial television represented the degraded tastes of a mass audience. These pay-TV advocates believed that given a choice to pay for television, many viewers would likely choose more "sophisticated" programs such as televised Broadway plays, ballet, symphonic music, opera, and university lectures. Opposed to pay-TV were veterans' associations, women's groups, senior citizens, civil rights leaders, labor unions, and local officials who criticized this unjust move to privatize a public medium by defending the cultural value of popular commercial television and the rights of low-income citizens to access affordable quality television. However, pay-TV proponents argued that unlike the audience-maximizing commercial broadcasters that catered to the "lowest common denominator," individual viewer payments would work like "ballots" to ensure a broader spectrum of tastes were accounted for. In conflating the right to vote with the privilege to pay, these pay-TV advocates no longer conceived TV viewers as citizens with equal rights to receive information and entertainment over the public airwaves, but as individual consumers with rights to purchase television from competing providers within a free-market economy (McMurria 2007).

In addition to these elite proponents of pay-TV, by the late 1960s social scientists and nonprofit foundations became interested in broadband interactive cable technologies. Through these more capacious communications pipes, these cable advocates envisioned more channels for programs that catered to specific tastes and a technology to aid communication within marginalized communities. These "Blue Skies" enthusiasts encouraged the FCC to lift its 1966 freeze on cable development in major cities to unleash cable's two-way capacity to address urban poverty and racial inequality just as African Americans violently protested their desperate conditions in major cities across the US (Sloan 1971; Smith 1972; Streeter 1997). In the early 1970s, nonprofit foundations conducted experiments on two-way cable, often under the direction of Cold War social scientists with training in military defense systems, offering job information, health and child care, distance education, and opportunities for citizen participation in local community affairs (Light 2003, 163–230). The sponsors of these studies believed that the urban protests were partially sparked by a lack of opportunity to more actively participate in civic life. When two-way cable experiments proved too costly to implement on a wide basis, these broadband cable evangelists supported lifting cable rules that protected local broadcast stations so that the commercial cable industry could develop two-way cable capacities.

Two-way cable never materialized as an effective social service technology, yet the deregulatory impulses ignited by the "Blue Skies" social scientists continued. A year prior to Congress' 1984 Cable Act that largely treated cable operators as private companies with strict First Amendment protections, the prominent social scientist Ithiel de Sola Pool described cable as a "technology of freedom" and advocated to "reduce the public control" of cable and other electronic forms of communications through extending the First Amendment freedoms of print to all media in the "electronic era" (Sola Pool 1983, 8; 166–68; 232).

To conclude, this knowledge class – from pay-TV enthusiasts who promoted a more refined television culture to social scientists and foundations that advocated deregulating broadband cable to solve inner city crises – shared a faith that deregulated electronic media could elevate tastes and address structural and race-based inequalities. However, movies and sports rather than Shakespeare reined in pay-TV, and urban decay rather than renewal continued as broadband cable developed in the cities. Nonetheless, these electronic media enthusiasts enabled, in part, broader neoliberal transformations that reconceived viewing publics as consumers and reduced public interest mandates to those facilitating competitive markets. This cultural citizenship approach to cable television reframes institutional and political economic approaches that fault the FCC for protecting broadcasters to the detriment of pay-TV and cable development (Gershon 1990; Hilmes 1990, 130; Sterling & Kittross 1990; Parsons & Frieden 1998; Mullen 1999). It also questions a legal liberalism limited to understanding case law as an attempt to "balance" the First Amendment rights of cable operators with those of viewers (Parsons 1987). These neoliberal discourses of a consumer citizenship proliferate within the contexts of the emergence of digital media technologies.

Digital Media, Participatory Culture, and the Cybertarian Society

The "Blue Skies" enthusiasm that sparked cable deregulations and neoliberal forms of cultural citizenship reveals one particular cultural history of the neoliberal framework that shaped the 1996 overhaul of the 1934 Communications Act. Another emerged out of the revolutionary prognostications of networked computing technologies. Fred Turner traces how one form of this digital utopianism sprang from a 1960s counterculture informed by a cybernetics systems worldview and a back-to-the-land communal movement that came together in Stewart Brand's *Whole Earth Catalog* in 1968 (Turner 2006). Brand conceived the *Catalog* for the young, affluent, white counterculturalists who rejected political activism in favor of a quest to find psychic wholeness, self-sufficiency, and freedom from social and class hierarchies in "frontier" communes far from urban race riots and anti-war demonstrations. The *Catalog* included consumer products for living off the land and served as a network forum for the technocentric theories and designs of Marshall McLuhan and Buckminster Fuller, the avant-garde performance art of John Cage and Robert Rauschenberg, and the "Acid Trips" conceived by

author Ken Kesey. All were inspired by the cybernetics visions of Norbert Weiner, who understood society as a system of interlinking messages much like organisms and machines. Though the communes did not last, Brand began to broker a series of encounters between counterculturalists and the developing computer industry in Silicon Valley that over time "helped redefine the microcomputer as a 'personal' machine, computer communication networks as 'virtual communities,' and cyberspace itself as the digital equivalent of the western landscape into which so many communards set forth in the late 1960s, the 'electronic frontier'" (Turner 2006, 6).

The Whole Earth network of counterculturalists and computer technology entrepreneurs migrated online in 1985 through the Whole Earth 'Lectronic Link (the WELL) and formed the Global Business Network in 1987 that included corporate leaders interested in networking systems. In 1993 former *Catalog* editor Kevin Kelly started *Wired* magazine, which brought together countercultural visionaries such as Esther Dyson, John Perry Barlow, and George Gilder, along with high-tech stock analysts and right-wing politicians who shared an enthusiasm for a "digital revolution" that promised a decentralized, egalitarian, and free-market libertarian society. Though systems theory, countercultural communalism, and the electronic frontier offered a worldview for a non-hierarchical society of equals, the white patriarchal communes relegated women to subservient roles just as they escaped the racial struggles in cities in parallel with suburban white flight. The electronic network of visionaries existed as an exclusive club of mostly affluent white men in an immaterial "cyberspace," who promoted a neoliberal politics that rejected the material redistributive functions of a New Deal and Great Society welfare state (Turner 2006).

Another movement that emerged within Silicon Valley coalesced around ideals of open source software and the Internet as a "commons," a term from common law that designates certain resources be held in common, such as city streets and parks. Richard Stallman, a researcher at MIT, created the Free Software Foundation in 1985 to develop software code that was open for others to improve. Stallman and the Finnish computer science student Linus Torvalds each developed important components of the GNU/Linux open source operating system. Legal scholars Lawrence Lessig and Yochai Benkler have given wider expression to this free software movement by extending these values of open access beyond the software or *code* layer of the Internet, to the *physical* components of transport (wires, airwaves) and reception (computers, cell phones), and the *content* layer of audiovisual creations (Lessig 2001; Benkler 2006). A "commons" approach advocates nonproprietary control at each level and conceives creativity as a process of reshaping cultures that have come before, necessitating robust fair-use provisions for copyright (Boyle 1996; Litman 2001). The Creative Commons movement has fought lobbying from cable providers, Hollywood studios, and recording companies to "enclose" the open architecture of the Internet and constrict the fair appropriation of creative works (Aufderheide 2002). For example, while phone lines are open to all Internet service providers (ISPs) under common carrier rules that have existed for over a century, making possible the neutral "end-to-end" open architecture of the Internet, in 2002 the FCC ruled that cable broadband service was not a common carrier and thus could discriminate against competing ISPs to favor its own service and corporate clients (Benkler 2006). The most vigorous efforts to enclose information and creativity have been at the content layer, where Congress extended copyright terms to 95 years for corporate-owned material and life-plus-70 years for human authors. The courts have narrowed fair-use exemptions for noncommercial copying and made any digital sampling unlawful (Benkler 2006). Opponents of these trends have established a Creative Commons license that allows creators to choose a variety of less restrictive protections, including no restrictions on copying with simple attribution to the original author (Lessig 2001).

While the Creative Commons movement has organized critical resistance to the enclosures that threaten an open Internet, it has also constructed idealized visions of society based on the revolutionary promises of a "networked information economy" that invoke the hierarchies of cultural value of postwar mass society critics and the libertarian ethos of digital utopianism. Benkler offers the most elaborated framework for this vision in *The Wealth of Networks*, where he argues that if unconstrained by big government and corporate power, the networked information economy "holds great practical promise: as a dimension of individual freedom; as a platform for better democratic participation; as a medium to foster a more critical and self-reflective culture; and, in an increasingly information-dependent global economy, as a mechanism to achieve improvements in human development everywhere" (Benkler 2006, 2). Whereas government regulations during the "industrial information economy" preserved the power of Hollywood, the recording industry, and broadcasters to shape opinion and "program toward the inane and soothing," government regulations in the "networked information economy" should be minimized to allow "non-market" and private voluntary modes of "social production" to bloom, such as the 50,000 volunteers who monitor the collaboratively authored Web encyclopedia Wikipedia. These voluntary modes of production promise a more "transparent" and "malleable" "folk culture" (13–23). Drawing from classical liberal theories of freedom based on the potential for autonomous, rationally self-aware individuals to maximize their life choices, Benkler looks to the "connected personal computer" to realize the essence of a universal humanity that "in terms of human freedom and development must transcend the particular traditions, both liberal and illiberal, of any single nation" (16–28, 70–74). Therefore the particular history of racial discrimination in the US or colonialism worldwide is less relevant than the availability of free information resources that trickle down to the "less well off" to "improve equality of opportunity" (13–14).

Though Benkler identifies important new modes of participatory social relations in the networked information economy, in extrapolating a broader theory of social justice from an information technology-centric perspective on society – guided by classical liberal universalistic assumptions about individual freedom – this version of digital utopianism fortifies a neoliberal consensus that supports free-market economies, volunteerism, and self-help to address social needs, rather than the redistributive programs of the social welfare state (Duggan 2003). It also downplays the role of new information technologies in establishing a post-Fordist global economy based on the flexible, decentralized modes of capitalist accumulation, international divisions of labor, and service-centered growth that has resulted in increased income inequalities worldwide (Harvey 2005). Such neoliberal policies as the Telecommunications Act of 1996 have left the US ranked 16th in worldwide broadband penetration in 2005, behind countries including South Korea and Canada, which have gone beyond ensuring an open architecture for an Internet commons by implementing widespread digital literacy programs, investing in infrastructure and subsidizing universal broadband service in low-income areas to address the uneven development of what Murdock and Golding have called the social, cultural, and economic capitals that propagate the digital divide (Murdock & Golding 2004; Frieden 2005; Jin 2005).

Thus a critical cultural citizenship approach to digital utopianism reveals the links between the embrace of a more participatory Internet culture and a libertarian and neoliberal politics. This cultural approach extends institutional and political economic histories of the 1996 Telecommunications Act that focus on how legislators favored corporate campaign contributors over the public interest groups that rallied around "open platforms" and a "public lane" on the information highway (Aufderheide 1999, 43–53). These three frameworks provide important economic, social, and cultural contexts that are absent in liberal legal histories of media deregulation (Emeritz 1996).

Conclusion

With attention to the broader socioeconomic and cultural currents that informed constructs of cultural citizenship within media regulatory arenas, this essay has considered the hierarchies of taste advanced by an expert class during the rise of broadcasting, the class, gendered, and racial assumptions of postwar localism goals in television, the embrace of cable technologies to uplift television culture and solve structural racism, and the cybertarian politics that accompanied the digital utopianism of networked computer technology. This critical cultural citizenship approach can inform institutional and political economic methodologies. While cronyism, administrative capture, party politics and capitalist ideologies impact FCC decisions, so do the cultural sensibilities of the professional class that informs regulatory decision-making. Political economy's critique of the capitalist ownership alliances of commercial media can also question the tasteful, white, middle-class norms that have historically constituted public-funded alternatives. If advanced within regulatory circles, together these three approaches can destabilize the assumptions and rationalizations of a legal liberalism that insists on the normative objective procedures that treat citizens as autonomous individuals rather than members within a more complex social fabric, and that brackets particular power relations across social categories of class, race, gender, and nation. Finally, the cultural citizenship approach to regulatory history presented here identified a correlation between the cultural aspirations of an administrative class eager to transcend mass culture under a banner of expanding democratic participation, and enthusiasm for neoliberal policies to free new technologies to do so. Thus the project of social justice should not only be concerned about how new media technologies can be regulated to provide wider democratic participation, but how beliefs that a participatory media can liberate the people have supported a broader neoliberal politics that reproduces power relations and social stratification.

References

Aufderheide, P. (1999) *Communications Policy and the Public Interest: The Telecommunications Act of 1996.* Guilford Press, New York.

Aufderheide, P. (2002) Competition and commons: the public interest in and after the AOL-Time Warner merger. *Journal of Broadcasting & Electronic Media* **46**, 515–31.

Baughman, J. L. (1985) *Television's Guardians: The FCC and the Politics of Programming, 1958–1967.* University of Tennessee Press, Knoxville.

Benkler, Y. (2006) *The Wealth of Networks: How Social Production Transforms Markets and Freedom*. Yale University Press, New Haven.

Blevins, J. L. and Brown, D. H. (2006) Political issue or policy matter? The US Federal Communications Commission's third biennial review of broadcast ownership rules. *Journal of Communication Inquiry* **30**, 21–41.

Boddy, W. (1990) *Fifties Television: The Industry and its Critics*. University of Illinois Press, Urbana.

Boyle, J. (1996) *Shamans, Software, and Spleens: Law and the Construction of the Information Society*. Harvard University Press, Cambridge.

Braman, S. (ed.) (2003) *Communication Researchers and Policy-Making*. MIT Press, Cambridge.

Brown, W. and Halley, J. (eds.) (2002) *Left Legalism/Left Critique*. Duke University Press, Durham.

Calabrese, A. and Burgelman, J. (eds.) (1999) *Communication, Citizenship, and Social Policy: Rethinking the Limits of the Welfare State*. Rowman & Littlefield, Lanham.

Calabrese, A. and Sparks, C. (eds.) (2004) *Toward a Political Economy of Culture: Capitalism and Communication in the Twenty-First Century*. Rowman & Littlefield, Lanham.

Carter, T. B., Franklin, M. A., and Wright, J. B. (2004) *The First Amendment and the Fourth Estate: The Law of Mass Media*, 9th edn. Foundation Press, Westbury.

Center for International Media Action (2003) *Media Policy Action Directory*. Brooklyn, NY. At www.mediaactioncenter.org/files/directory_booklet2.pdf, accessed July 25, 2008.

Classen, S. D. (2004) *Watching Jim Crow: The Struggles Over Mississippi TV, 1955–1969*. Duke University Press, Durham.

Crenshaw, K., Gotanda, N., Peller, G., and Kendall, T. (eds.) (1996) *Critical Race Theory: The Key Writings that Formed the Movement*. New Press, New York.

Czitrom, D. J. (1983) *Media and the American Mind: From Morse to McLuhan*. University of North Carolina Press, Chapel Hill.

Douglas, S. (1987) *Inventing American Broadcasting, 1899–1922*. Johns Hopkins University Press, Baltimore.

Duggan, L. (2003) *The Twilight of Equality? Neoliberalism, Cultural Politics, and the Attack on Democracy*. Beacon Press, Boston.

During, S. (ed.) (1999) *The Cultural Studies Reader*, 2nd edn. Routledge, London.

Emeritz, B. (1996) *The Telecommunications Act of 1996: Law and Legislative History*. Pike & Fischer, Silver Spring.

Federal Communications Commission (1946) *Public Service Responsibilities of Broadcast Licensees*. GPO, Washington DC.

Fowler, M. and Brenner, D. (1982) A marketplace approach to broadcast regulation. *Texas Law Review* **60**, 207–57.

Frieden, R. (2005) Lessons from broadband development in Canada, Japan, Korea, and the United States. *Telecommunications Policy*, 595–613.

Galperin, H. (2004) *New Television, Old Politics: The Transition to Digital TV in the United States and Britain*. Cambridge University Press, Cambridge.

Gershon, R. A. (1990) Pay cable television: a regulatory history. *Communications and the Law* **12**, 7–12.

Harvey, D. (2005) *A Brief History of Neoliberalism*. Oxford University Press, New York.

Hilmes, M. (1990) *Hollywood and Broadcasting: From Radio to Cable*. University of Illinois Press, Urbana.

Hilmes, M. (1997) *Radio Voices: American Broadcasting, 1922–1952*. University of Minnesota Press, Minneapolis.

Horwitz, R. (1989) *The Irony of Regulatory Reform: The Deregulation of American Telecommunications*. Oxford University Press, New York.

Horwitz, R. (2005) On media concentration and the diversity question. *Information Society* **21**, 181–204.

Jin, D. Y. (2005) Socioeconomic implications of broadband services: information economy in Korea. *Information, Communication & Society* **8**, 503–23.

Jowett, G. S., Jarvie, I. C., and Fuller, K. H. (1996) *Children and the Movies: Media Influence and the Payne Fund Controversy*. Cambridge University Press, Cambridge.

Kahn, F. J. (1984) *Documents of American Broadcasting*. Prentice-Hall, Englewood Cliffs.

Kelman, M. (1987) *A Guide to Critical Legal Studies*. Harvard University Press, Cambridge.

Krasnow, E. G., Longley, L. D., and Terry, H. A. (eds.) (1982) *The Politics of Broadcast Regulation*, 3rd edn. St. Martin's Press, New York.

Krattenmaker, T. G. and Powe, L. A., Jr. (1994) *Regulating Broadcast Programming*. AEI Press, Washington DC.

Lazarsfeld, P. F. and Field, H. H. (1946) *The People Look at Radio*. University of North Carolina Press, Chapel Hill.

Lazarsfeld, P. F. and Kendall, P. L. (1948) *Radio Listening in America*. Prentice-Hall, New York.

Lears, J. (1989) A matter of taste: corporate cultural hegemony in a mass-consumption society. In May, L. (ed.) *Recasting America: Culture and Politics in the Age of Cold War*. University of Chicago Press, Chicago, pp. 38–57.

Le Duc, D. R. (1973) *Cable Television and the FCC: A Crisis in Media Control*. Temple University Press, Philadelphia.

Lessig, L. (2001) *The Future of Ideas: The Fate of the Commons in a Connected World*. Random House, New York.

Lewis, J. and Miller, T. (2003) *Critical Cultural Policy Studies: A Reader*. Blackwell, London.

Light, J. S. (2003) *From Warfare to Welfare: Defense Intellectuals and Urban Problems in Cold War America*. Johns Hopkins University Press, Baltimore.

Litman, J. (2001) *Digital Copyright*. Prometheus Books, Amherst.

Lynd, R. and Lynd, H. (1929) *Middletown: A Study in Contemporary Culture*. Harcourt Brace, New York.

Lynd, R. and Lynd, H. (1937) *Middletown in Transition*. Harcourt Brace, New York.

McChesney, R. W. (1993) *Telecommunications, Mass Media, and Democracy: The Battle for the Control of US Broadcasting, 1928–1935*. Oxford University Press, New York.

McChesney, R. W. (2000) *Rich Media, Poor Democracy: Communications Politics in Dubious Times*. New Press, New York.

MacDonald, D. (1957) A theory of mass culture. In Rosenberg, B. and White, D. M. (eds.) *Mass Culture: The Popular Arts in America*. Free Press, Glencoe, pp. 59–73.

McMurria, J. (2007) A taste of class: pay-TV and the commodification of television in postwar America. In Banet-Weiser, S., Chris, C., and Freitas, A. (eds.) *Cable Visions: Television Beyond Broadcasting*. New York University Press, New York, pp. 44–65.

Miller, T. (1998) *Technologies of Truth: Cultural Citizenship and the Popular Media*. University of Minnesota Press, Minneapolis.

Miller, T. (2006) *Cultural Citizenship: Cosmopolitanism, Consumerism, and Television in a Neoliberal Age*. Temple University Press, Philadelphia.

Mullen, M. (1999) The pre-history of pay cable television: an overview and analysis. *Historical Journal of Film, Radio and Television* **19**, 39–56.

Murdock, G. and Golding, P. (2004) Dismantling the digital divide: rethinking the dynamics of participation and exclusion. In Calabrese, A. and Sparks, C. (eds.) *Toward a Political Economy of Culture: Capitalism and Communication in the Twenty-First Century*. Rowman & Littlefield, Lanham, pp. 244–60.

Napoli, P. M. (2001a) *Foundations of Communications Policy: Principles and Process in the Regulation of Electronic Media*. Hampton Press, Cresskill.

Napoli, P. M. (2001b) The localism principle in communications policymaking and policy analysis: ambiguity, inconsistency, and empirical neglect. *Policy Studies Journal* **29**, 372–387.

Nasaw, D. (1993) *Going Out: The Rise and Fall of Public Amusements*. Basic Books, New York.

Ouellette, L. (2002) *Viewers Like You: How Public TV Failed the People*. Columbia University Press, New York.

Parsons, P. (1987) *Cable Television and the First Amendment*. Lexington Books, Lexington.

Parsons, P. R. and Frieden, R. M. (1998) *The Cable and Satellite Television Industries*. Allyn & Bacon, Boston.

Pember, D. R. and Calvert, C. (2006) *Mass Media Law*, 2007–8 edn. McGraw-Hill, New York.

Powe, L. A., Jr. (1987) *American Broadcasting and the First Amendment*. University of California Press, Berkeley.

Pritchard, D. (2006) A new paradigm for legal research. In Reynolds, A. and Barnett, B. (eds.) *Communication and Law: Multidisciplinary Approaches to Research*. Lawrence Erlbaum, Mahwah, pp. 43–59.

Raboy, M. (2002) *Global Media Policy in the New Millennium*. University of Luton Press, Luton.

Riesman, D. (1950) *The Lonely Crowd: A Study of the Changing American Character*. Yale University Press, New Haven.

Ross, S. D. (2004) *Deciding Communication Law: Key Cases in Context*. Lawrence Erlbaum, Mahwah.

Shayon, R. L. (1956) Educational television suffers a second defeat. In Elliott, W. (ed.) *Television's Impact on American Culture*. Michigan State University Press, East Lansing, pp. 373ff.

Simpson, C. (1994) *Science of Coercion: Communication Research and Psychological Warfare, 1945–1960*. Oxford University Press, New York.

Sloan Commission on Cable Communications (1971) *On the Cable: The Television of Abundance*. McGraw-Hill, New York.

Smith, A. and Patterson R. (eds.) (1998) *Television: An International History*, 2nd edn. Oxford University Press, Oxford.

Smith, R. L. (1972) *The Wired Nation: Cable TV, The Electronic Communications Highway*. Harper & Row, New York.

Sola Pool, I. de (1983) *Technologies of Freedom: On Free Speech in an Electronic Age*. Harvard University Press, Cambridge.

Stein, M. (1960) *Eclipse of Community*. Harper, New York.

Steiner, G. A. (1963) *The People Look at Television: A Study of Audience Attitudes*. Knopf, New York.

Sterling H. and Kittross, J. M. (1990) *Stay Tuned: A Concise History of American Broadcasting*, 2nd edn. Wadsworth, Belmont.

Streeter, T. (1990) Beyond freedom of speech and the public interest: the relevance of critical legal studies to communications policy. *Journal of Communication* **40**, 43–63.

Streeter, T. (1996) *Selling the Air: A Critique of the Policy of Commercial Broadcasting in the United States*. University of Chicago Press, Chicago.

Streeter, T. (1997) Blue skies and strange bedfellows: the discourse of cable television. In Spigel, L. and Curtin, M. (eds.) *The Revolution Wasn't Televised: Sixties Television and Social Conflict*. Routledge, New York, pp. 221–42.

Turner, F. (2006) *From Counterculture to Cyberculture: Stewart Brand, the Whole Earth Network, and the Rise of Digital Utopianism*. University of Chicago Press, Chicago.

Tyler, T. F. (ed.) (1934) *Radio as a Cultural Agency*. National Committee on Education by Radio, Washington DC.

Vidich, A. and Bensman, J. (1958) *Small Town in Mass Society*. Princeton University Press, Princeton.

Warner, W. L. and Lunt, P. S. (1941) *The Social Life of a Modern Community*. Yale University Press, New Haven.

Williams, P (1996) Metro Broadcasting, Inc. v. FCC: regrouping in singular times. In: Crenshaw, K., Gotanda, N., Peller, G., and Kendall, T. (eds.) *Critical Race Theory: The Key Writings that Formed the Movement*. New Press, New York, pp. 191–200.

14

Can Natural Luddites Make Things Explode or Travel Faster?
The New Humanities, Cultural Policy Studies, and Creative Industries

. . . .

Toby Miller

A hundred, fifty, even twenty years ago, a tradition of culture, based on the Classics, on Scripture, on History and Literature, bound the governing classes together and projected the image of a gentleman. (J. H. Plumb)[1]

I propose a constructive alternative to the Great Society, which I have chosen to call "A Creative Society" … to discover, enlist and mobilize the incredibly rich human resources of California [through] innumerable people of creative talent. (Ronald Reagan)[2]

Creative class ideas have generated headlines like "Cities Need Gays To Thrive" and "Be Creative or Die." They have also been slated, attacked and written off by a mob of angry academics, wonks and other pundits. (Max Nathan)[3]

This chapter engages ways of analyzing and intervening in the media industries that derive from attempts to create a practical, progressive, and profound new humanities. I go back to the period between the mid-1950s and 1960s of anxieties about the impact of big science, new technology, and industrial organization on everyday life and aesthetic pursuits. I argue that the humanities prefigured the coming crisis of de-industrialization, and continue to adapt to it. Subsequent transmogrifications into cultural policy studies and creative industries discourse have enabled and responded to the end of what was once a grand bifurcation between the arts and the sciences – at some cost. I suggest that a renewed critical cultural policy studies should be used to analyze media industries.

Exploding Binaries
. . . .

In 1956, C. P. Snow coined the term "Two Cultures" in a magazine article that became a lengthy pamphlet the following year. Snow wrote the piece to understand his divided self: "by training … a scientist: by vocation … a writer."[4] Fearing that "the whole of western society is increasingly being split into two polar groups,"[5] he perceived the "Two Cultures" as those who quoted theater versus those who quoted thermodynamics.[6] Snow could move from South Kensington to Greenwich Village and encounter the same discourse. Each site had "about as much communication with MIT as though the scientists spoke nothing but Tibetan."[7] Artists and humanists were disarticulated from agricultural and industrial change, "as if the natural order didn't exist."[8] Because "literary intellectuals, are natural Luddites … very little of twentieth-century science has been assimilated into twentieth-century art." But there was an opportunity for the "clashing point" of these discourses "to produce creative chances."[9]

Snow's provocation drew an irritated response from the literary critic F. R. Leavis, whose publishers feared Snow would sue[10] after reading that: "Not only is he not a genius, he is intellectually as undistinguished as it is possible to be."[11] More temperately, the historian J. H. Plumb (1964) lamented, "Quips from Cicero are uncommon in the engineers' lab" and "Ahab and Jael rarely provide a parable for biologists" (7). Plumb and his kind had reason to be worried. The humanities in UK, like the liberal arts in the US, had long formed "the core of the educational system and were believed to have peculiar virtues in producing politicians, civil servants, Imperial administrators and legislators" because they incarnated and indexed "the arcane wisdom of the Establishment." But "the rising tide of scientific and industrial societies, combined with the battering of two World Wars" had "shattered the confidence of humanists in their capacity to lead." Plumb saw just two options, as per Snow: adaptation "to the needs of a society dominated by science and technology, or retreat into social triviality" (7). For Graham Hough (1964), the humanities must embrace "a world dominated by industry and science and large organizations," or be consigned to "the never-never-land of the organic society with those happy peasants Dr. Leavis [and] Richard Hoggart" due to the irrelevance of disciplines that "do not make anything explode or travel faster" (96).

On the other side of the Atlantic, Barry Goldwater, Ronald Reagan, and other far-right conservatives were railing against "Great Society" liberalism, which promised an end to poverty and discrimination through state intervention. Their disastrous defeat at the 1964 presidential election, seemingly the death rattle of the right, was soon followed by Reagan winning the governorship of California. The idea of a "Creative Society" was central to a campaign rhetoric that birthed today's neoclassical, neoliberal idea of technology unlocking the creativity lurking in individuals, permitting them to become happy and productive in ways that elude corporate and governmental dominance – and discourage collective organization.

Between Hough and Reagan, critic and governor, these cats were onto something. The latter-day emergence of cultural policy studies and creative industries discourse answers the persistent dilemma of making the humanities relevant, while the creativity lobby buys into human-capital doctrines of neoliberalism. Both elements make things explode and travel faster, whether via first-person shooter games or cultural search engines. How did this happen?

Cultural Studies and Cultural Policy Studies

Cultural studies began as a rejection of the traditional humanities' high aesthetic prejudices. Its first three decades, until the 1990s, were characterized by semiotic insurrectionism, with the progressive reader of texts a pacific but vibrant semiotic guerrilla. The next challenge was to engage the public sphere. This represented an articulation with its own past, via the foundational figure of Hoggart. Soon to become the inaugural director of the Centre for Contemporary Cultural Studies, he published his first and most famous book, *The Uses of Literacy: Aspects of Working Class Life* (1957) the same year as Snow's polemical pamphlet. In many ways, Hoggart's work generated the shift envisaged by Hough. And it connected with Snow, whose fine phrase "the corridors of power" described lobbying. Hoggart testified in defense of *Lady Chatterley's Lover* at Penguin Books' renowned pornography trial, and the company subsequently endowed the Birmingham Centre. He became part of a tradition known in the UK as "the great and the good." It has counterparts in the UN's Eminent Persons Groups, Royal Commissions, and joint bodies convened by otherwise rivalrous think tanks in the US, for example the AEI (American Enterprise Institute) Brookings Joint Center for Regulatory Studies. The idea is to blend popular visibility, political bipartisanship, professional expertise, and public interest in bodies that deliberate on matters of policy without the burden of party loyalty or corporate responsibilities. Hoggart served on the UK's Pilkington Committee on Broadcasting and similar inquiries into the arts, adult education, and youth services[12] and went on to become a United Nations Educational, Scientific and Cultural Organization (UNESCO) culturecrat.[13]

But the first academic formation of cultural policy studies began in the 1970s, at some distance from cultural studies, in the positivistic social sciences. It developed through the Association of Cultural Economics; conferences on economics, social theory, and the arts; and evaluations of policies and programs undertaken at various colleges and institutes. Publications such as *Arts and Education Policy Review*, the *Journal of Arts Management, Law, and Society*, and the *Journal of Cultural Economics* address the arts–academic service to state and capital, dressed up as objectivity.

By contrast with empiricist social science, cultural studies has a more overtly political drive, articulated to social movements and cultural workers' rights. Stuart Cunningham (1992) suggested 15 years ago that:

> Many people trained in cultural studies would see their primary role as being critical of the dominant political, economic and social order. When cultural theorists do turn to questions of policy, our command metaphors of resistance and opposition predispose us to view the policy making process as inevitably compromised, incomplete and inadequate, peopled with those inexpert and ungrounded in theory and history or those wielding gross forms of political power for short-term ends. (9)

He called for cultural studies to displace its "revolutionary rhetoric" with a "reformist vocation," drawing new energy and direction from "a social democratic view of citizenship and the trainings necessary to activate and motivate it" (11). This "engagement with policy" would avoid "a politics of the status quo," because cultural studies' ongoing concern with power would ground it in radicalism. Angela McRobbie (1996) called cultural policy "the missing agenda" of cultural studies, offering a program for change (335). Jim McGuigan (2004)

welcomed this turn, provided that it retained radical insights by connecting to public debate and citizenship rights (21).

This policy trend within cultural studies, which in many ways picked up on Hoggart's example, took off in late 1980s Australia. It involved both locals and a number of scholars who had left the UK, so it had strong ties to more conventional, established protocols of cultural studies. Apart from Cunningham, key figures included Tom O'Regan, Tony Bennett, David Saunders, Ian Hunter, and Colin Mercer. (I worked with them in the two cities where the tendency took firmest hold, Brisbane and Perth.) Their objects of analysis were the media, museums, copyright, pornography, schooling, and cultural precincts. Their methods – archival research, questionnaires, and Foucauldian theory – emphasized the foundational nature of government in the creation of the liberal individual (understood not as per US politics, but rather US education, i.e., a person open to new ideas delivered in a rational form and reasoned manner). In Latin America, similar engagements materialized in the work of Néstor García Canclini (1995), *inter alios*. In the UK, cognate practice was underway at the Greater London Council (Lewis 1983, 1985, 1986, and 1990). Everything seemed to be in accord with Hoggart's heritage, and the yet more radical inspiration of Antonio Gramsci, with culture a terrain of struggle for hegemony. In the words of the venerable German socialist rallying cry, this would be a "Long March of the Institutions" (Mansfield 1990).

Things Traveling Faster

How did cultural policy studies slide into creative industries discourse? The new turn has reacted to the prevailing political economy. The First World recognized that its economic future lay in finance capital and ideology rather than agriculture and manufacturing, and the Third World sought revenue from intellectual property rather than minerals and masses. Changes in the media and associated knowledge technologies over this period have been likened to a new Industrial Revolution or the Civil and Cold Wars. They are touted as routes to economic development as much as cultural and political expression. Between 1980 and 1998, annual world exchange of electronic culture grew from US $95 billion to US $388 billion. In 2003, these areas accounted for 2.3 percent of Gross Domestic Product across Europe, to the tune of €654 billion – more than real estate or food and drink, and equal to chemicals, plastics, and rubber. The Intellectual Property Association estimates that copyright and patents are worth US $360 billion a year in the US, putting them ahead of aerospace, automobiles, and agriculture in monetary value. And the cultural/copyright sector employs 12 percent of the US workforce, up from 5 percent a century ago. PriceWaterhouseCooper predicts 10 percent annual growth in the area globally (Dreher 2002; McChesney & Schiller 2002; UNCTAD 2004, 3; European Commission 2007).

The British Academy (2004), the peak national body of the great and the good in the human sciences, notes that: "Whereas the dominant global industries of the past focused on manufacturing industry, the key corporations today are increasingly active in the fields of communications, information, entertainment, leisure" (14–16, 18–19). US economic production in particular has been adjusting away from a farming and manufacturing base to a cultural one, especially in foreign trade. It now sells feelings, ideas, money, health, insurance, and laws – niche forms of identity, aka culture. The trend is to harness the cultural skills of the population to replace lost agricultural and manufacturing employment with jobs in music, theater, animation, recording, radio, TV, architecture, software, design, toys, books, heritage, tourism, advertising, fashion, crafts, photography, and cinema (Towse 2002; UNESCO 2002). The US National Governors' Association argues that "innovative commercial businesses, non-profit institutions and independent artists all have become necessary ingredients in a successful region's 'habitat'" (quoted in Tepper 2002). Right across the US, municipal, regional, and state funding agencies are dropping old funding and administrative categories of arts and crafts, and replacing them with the discourse of the creative industries. The same thing is happening in Europe, Latin America, Africa, and Asia. In 2006, Rwanda convened a global conference on the "Creative Economy" to take the social healing engendered by culture and commodify it. Brazil houses the United Nations Conference on Trade and Development (UNCTAD) and the United Nations Development Program's International Forum for Creative Industries. Even India's venerable last gasp of Nehruvianism, its Planning Commission, has a committee for creative industries, and China "is moving from an older, state-dominated focus on cultural industries … towards a more market-oriented pattern of creative industries" (UNCTAD 2004, 7; Ramanathan 2006). They are in thrall to the idea that culture is an endlessly growing resource – in UNCTAD's words, "Creativity, more than labor and capital, or even traditional technologies, is deeply embedded in every country's cultural context" (3).

In the case of the media, a great deal of technology, content, and personnel emerge from universities. This has offered humanities intellectuals already interested in cultural policy – for reasons of cultural nationalism or in opposition to corporate culture – the opportunity to peer at the heart of power. They have shifted their discourse to a copyright-inflected one, focusing on comparative advantage and competition rather than heritage and aesthetics. Neoliberal emphases on creativity have succeeded old-school cultural patrimony.

So the British Academy (2004) invokes cultural studies in the search to understand and further the "creative and cultural industries" (viii). The UK Arts and Humanities Research Council places a high priority on cultural policy studies.[14] The Australian Research Council, which initially supported a major cultural policy initiative under the Gramscian-turned-Foucauldian Bennett, now funds a Centre of Excellence for Creative Industries and Innovation run by a lapsed poet and Girardian (Cunningham) and a hitherto semiotic romantic (John Hartley).[15] Even the prosaic National Research Council of the US National Academies, which would surely never endorse such checkered pasts, explains that the electronic media play "a crucial role in culture," offering "personal, social, and educational benefit" and "economic development" (Mitchell et al. 2003, 1).

Economically, the media have become the leading edge of many export industries; politically, they are central to democratic communication and the parliamentary process; and culturally, they incarnate and encourage social trends. The US Social Science Research Council (SSRC) surveys the scene in this way:

> Changes in the technologies and organizational structure of the media are transforming public life – in the US and around the world. These changes affect not only the forms of delivery of media content – digital broadcasting, the Internet, and so on – but more fundamentally the ways in which we understand the world, communicate with each other, and participate in public life. Advances in digital technologies, the concentration of media ownership, the privatization of communications infrastructures, and the expansion of intellectual property regimes are underlying features of this transformation – both its causes and effects, and global in reach. What do these developments mean for a democratic society? What does a rich democratic culture look like under these conditions and how can we achieve it?[16]

Ties have strengthened across Snow's two cultures. Computing applications to narrative and art, and vice versa, are well known to professors, from engineering to dance. As Thomas Pynchon (1984) put it, looking back on the "Two Cultures" a quarter of a century later, "all the cats are jumping out of the bag and even beginning to mingle" (1). Faculty at opposite ends of the campus write the same codes, analyze the same narratives, go to the same parties, take the same drugs, and sleep with the same people.

This is not the interdisciplinarity so often crowed about in the humanities – interdisciplinarity without multiple languages, without numbers, without ethnography, without geography, without experiments. This is something much more challenging. The new humanities, the creative industries humanities, responds to a great appeal, a grand passion of the age, where, in Pynchon's memorable words, "even the most unreconstructed of Luddites can be charmed into laying down the old sledgehammer and stroking a few keys instead" to line up with technocrats (41) – where technocrats are artists and critics. Many of these maneuvers are in thrall to Richard Florida (2002) and his business school acolytes, who seek out a "creative class" that they claim

is revitalizing postindustrial towns through a magic elixir of tolerance, technology, and talent, as measured by same-sex households, broadband connections, and higher degrees. True believers in this putative liberation from corporate domination and cultural uniformity argue for an efflorescence of the creative sector via new technology and small business (Cunningham 2002). A new world supposedly makes consumers into producers, frees the disabled from confinement, encourages new subjectivities, rewards intellect and competitiveness, links people across cultures, and allows billions of flowers to bloom in a post-political cornucopia. It's a kind of Marxist/Godardian wet dream, where people fish, film, fuck, and finance from morning to midnight. The mass scale of the culture industries is progressively overrun by the individual talent of the creative sector (Dahlström & Hermelin 2007).

Creative industry academics have become branded celebrities. They descend on welcoming burghers eager to be made over at public expense by professors whose books appear on airport newsstands rather than cloistered scholarly shelves (Gibson & Klocker 2004). These carpet-bagging consultants have sidestepped the historic tasks laid out by the left. Prone to cybertarianism, they are often gullible MIT-like/lite subscribers to digital capitalism and the technological sublime. There are three major groups: Richard Floridians ride around town on their bicycles to spy on ballet-loving, gay-friendly, multicultural computer geeks who have moved to deindustrialized, freezing rust/rusting freeze belts; true-believer Australian creationists criticize cultural policy studies as residually socialistic and textual; and Brussels bureaucrats offer blueprints to cities eager to be made over by culture and tolerance in search of affluence. A makeover is underway "from the rusty coinage of 'cultural industries' to the newly minted 'creative industries'" (Ross 2007, 1).

In part, this is the interdisciplinarity that Snow favored. But he also fought for ordinary people "lost in the great anonymous sludge of history" where life, he said (troping Thomas Hobbes) "has always been nasty, brutish and short" (1987, 26–27; 42). In his commentary on Snow, Pynchon defended old-style Luddites. Far from protesting new technology, they opposed well-established machinery that had shed jobs over two centuries. Ned Lud was no "technophobic crazy." He recognized that men who did not do productive work controlled the lives of those who *did* work. His concerns matter still.

Today's discourse of creative industries ignores such critical issues as the precariat/immaterial labor, high-tech pollution, and cultural imperialism, not to mention the need to understand industries rather than celebrate them. For instance, the high-technology service and cultural industries of the "new" economy supposedly represent clean business. The Australian Council for the Humanities, Arts and Social Sciences' submission to its national Productivity Commission refers to a "new post-smokestack era of industry" (CHASS 2006) – a post-manufacturing utopia for workers, consumers, and residents with residues of code, not carbon. Yet the Political Economy Research Institute's 2004 *Misfortune 100: Top Corporate Air Polluters in the United States* has media owners at numbers 1, 3, 16, 22, and 39 (Boyce 2004). Media production relies on the exorbitant water use of computer technology, while making semi-conductors requires the use of hazardous chemicals, including some known carcinogens. Waste from discarded electronics is one of the biggest sources of heavy metals and toxic pollutants in the world's trash piles. The accumulation of electronic hardware causes grave environmental and health concerns, stemming from the potential seepage of noxious chemicals, gases, and metals into landfills, water sources, and e-waste salvage yards. Much e-cycling is done by pre-teen young girls, who pick away without protection at discarded First World televisions and computers (California alone shipped about 20 million pounds of electronic waste in 2006 to Malaysia, Brazil, South Korea, China, Mexico, Vietnam, and India). They are looking for precious metals to sell, with the remains dumped in landfills (Puckett & Smith 2002; Shabi 2002; Shiva 2002; Lee 2007).

Or consider the labor of designing electronic games. Worker issues include power on the job, pensions, healthcare, and credits. They may make millions for a corporation, but no one knows their names. Big publishers develop exploitative labor practices as their power increases via the destruction or purchase of small businesses. In 2004, ea_spouse

anonymously posted (on *LiveJournal*) a vibrant account of grotesque exploitation experienced by her fiancé and others at Electronic Arts (EA), which makes *The Sims* and John Madden games. She eloquently ripped back the veneer of joyous cybertarianism from the industry, noting that EA's claim to blend aesthetics and technology, as per the company's name and trademark ("Challenge Everything") belied both its treatment of workers and its products. Regarding labor: "To any EA executive that happens to read this, I have a good challenge for you: how about safe and sane labor practices for the people on whose backs you walk for your millions?" Regarding texts: "Churning out one licensed football game after another doesn't sound like challenging much of anything to me; it sounds like a money farm" (ea_spouse 2004). Then she detailed the exploitation: a putatively limited "pre-crunch" is announced in the run-up to releasing a new game. A 48-hour week is required, which supposedly obviates the need for a real "crunch" at the conclusion of development; the pre-crunch goes on beyond its deadline; a 72-hour work week is mandated; illness and irritability strike; and a crunch *is* announced – everyone must work 85- to 91-hour weeks, with the occasional Saturday evening off, and no overtime or leave. So many errors are made from fatigue that time is needed to correct them. Turnover among engineers runs at 50 percent. Yet *Fortune* magazine ranks EA among the "100 Best Companies to Work For." It is #91 among corporations that "try hard to do right by their staff" as measured by the Great Place to Work® Institute in San Francisco. EA describes itself to *Fortune* as "a one-class society," and its Vice-President of Human Resources offers the following astonishing dictum: "Most creativity comes at one of two times: When your back is up against the wall or in a time of calm."[17] *Fortune* delights that workers can "refresh their energy with free espresso or by playing volleyball and basketball." In 2007, the firm ranked #62 in the magazine's "List of Industry Stars" (Levering et al. 2003; *Fortune* 2007).

This is the ugly face of the creative sector – for those supposedly atop its cresting wave. Such conditions represent a key switching point in an "hourglass" economy, with increased inequality. Union protections that classically applied to media workers in the US are displaced by a transfer of insecure conditions from the old arts sector, in the name of flexibility and "fun stuff." People are pushed into the precariat: jobs are part-time and multiple, risk is intense, and disparities in income extreme. Cybertarian statistics, which "orbit, halo-like, around creative industry policy, do not measure such things" (Ross 2007, 7). Concerns about labor seem passé to mavens who testify that the number of billionaires in their thirties involved in the creative industries indexes "an open economy and an open society" (Potts 2006, 339). Some might regard their emergence as a sign of class politics structured in dominance.

It makes sense to track the clever work that propagandists of the creative industries undertake as part of their desire for power. It makes sense to see how intellectual property operates, and acknowledge the cultural components of consumption and hence of many economic sectors. But to believe the rhetoric? The first country to adopt neoliberal creative industries discourse was the US, via Reagan's "creative society," starting four decades ago and providing today's bestselling pop-academic tomes (Caves 2000; Florida 2002). What has been the outcome of a fully evolved fantasy about small business and everyday creativity as motors of economic growth? Crumbling bridges, dangerous freeways, dysfunctional levees, 3 million people homeless, inadequate schooling, an electricity grid that barely functions, 50 million people without healthcare, and politics run by pharmaceutical firms, health insurance, tort law, finance capital, oil corporations, arms manufacturers, tobacco companies, and gun owners – operating very creatively.

UNESCO's Global Alliance for Cultural Diversity (2006) heralds creative industries as a portmanteau term that covers the cultural sector but goes further, beyond output and into that favorite neoliberal canard of process. But the claim that what is made in a sector of the economy does not characterize that sector, that "creativity" is not just an input but an industry's defining quality, is misleading. This bizarre shift in adjectival meaning makes it possible for anything profitable to be catalogued under "creative." The term lacks precision. It doesn't work for

independent statisticians and others who must "create" workable categories; more precise efforts at definition significantly diminish the claims made for the sector's economic contributions (Alanen 2007; Department for Culture, Media and Sport 2007; Galloway & Dunlop 2007). A boosterist sleight of hand places the humanities at the center of economic innovation by pretending that it encompasses corporate and governmental information technology (which is where real money is made and real power exercised – and not, sorry, by small business entrepreneurs) (Garnham 2005). It's obvious that big firms rarely innovate. This is not news. But it's inaccurate to regard that fact as a shift in the center of gravity. The cultural industries remain under the control of media conglomerates and communications firms. Who owns www.last.fm and www.myspace.com? (Viacom and News Corp.) Which websites are most read for news? (TV networks and wire services). We must ask whether creative industries discourse amounts to "recycling audio-visual cultural material created by the grassroots genius, exploiting their intellectual property and generating a standardized business sector that excludes, and even distorts, its very source of business," to quote *The Hindu* (Ramanathan 2006). The beneficiaries of innovations by "talented amateurs" are, once again, corporations (Marcus 2005; Ross 2007).

There is minimal proof for the existence of a creative class or that "creative cities" outperform their drab brethren economically. Companies seek skills when deciding where to locate their businesses – but skills also seek work. City centers only attract those who are young and not yet breeding. The centrality of gay culture in the Floridian calculus derives from assuming same-sex households are queer (but university dorms and sorority/fraternity houses are not quite there). Even if this were accurate, many successful cities in the US roll with reaction (consider Houston, Orlando, or Phoenix). The idea of urbanism incipient in US demographic statistics includes the suburbs (which now hold more residents than do cities) so that, too, is a suspect figure in terms of the importance of downtown lofts to economies. There is no evidence of an overlap of tastes, values, living arrangements, and locations between artists and accountants, despite their being bundled together in the creative concept; nor is it sensible to assume other countries replicate the massive internal mobility of the US population. Finally, other surveys pour scorn on the claim that quality of life is central to selecting business campuses, as opposed to low costs, good communications technology, proximity to markets, and adequate transportation. A European Commission evaluation of 29 "Cities of Culture" disclosed that their principal goal – economic growth stimulated by the public subvention of culture to renew failed cities – has itself failed. Glasgow, for instance, was initially hailed as a success of the program; but many years after the rhetoric, there has been no sustained growth. In 2008, Liverpool became an official City of Culture, having allocated £3 billion in public funds to an arts program, a museum, galleries, a convention center, a retail outlet, renewed transportation, rebuilt waterfront, and every good thing. This was premised on regeneration through culture, but skeptics asked, "Is that a foundation strong enough to sustain a lasting economy? Or ... pyramid selling" (Nathan 2005)? Bureaucrats and consultants make desperate claims to distinguish cities creatively (Bristol lays claim to Cary Grant as a native son) even as the data for London illustrate that the creative industries rely on the health of the finance sector. The upshot of creative industries discourse is that market objectives have over-determined cultural ones. Creative cities are creative ways of euphemizing gentrification for the urban middle class (Hoggart 2005, 168; Miller 2005; Linklater 2006; Oakley 2006; Bell 2007; Freeman 2007; Huijgh 2007; Peck 2007; Ross 2007).

Critical Cultural Policy Studies

In the 1960s, Hoggart posed the following question, even as he championed the expansion of cultural studies into the popular and the practical:

> What is one to make of a medieval historian or classicist who finds nothing odd – that is, nothing to be made sense of, at the least, if not opposed – in the sight of one of his new graduates going without second thoughts into, say, advertising; or of a sociologist or

statistician who will undertake consultant work without much questioning the implications of the uses to which his work is put? (100)

Thirty years later, Virginia Postrel wrote a *Wall Street Journal* op-ed, welcoming cultural studies as "deeply threatening to traditional leftist views of commerce ... lending support to the corporate enemy and even training graduate students who wind up doing market research" (1999, A18).

The question for us is: what sense of the public interest informs contemporary cultural policy studies and creative industries discourse? *Kultur Macht Europa* issued a sterling declaration following its Fourth Federal Congress on Cultural Policy in 2007 about protecting cultural workers as well as proprietors under copyright and other laws, and ensuring diverse media textuality as well as infrastructure. We see similar tensions played out in the Jodhpur Initiative for Promoting Cultural Industries in the Asia-Pacific Region, adopted in 2005 by 28 countries (*Jodhpur Initiatives* 2005). Such concerns should also animate scholarly analysis. And there *are* counterexamples to inspire an alternative view. Across Latin America, media studies has adopted a more critical cultural focus than creative industries discourse, as per the Consejo Latinoamericano de Ciencias Sociales (Costa et al. 2003). Cultural studies at the Universidad Nacional Costa Rica offers a trans-Central American perspective on cultural change through the media.[18] Ecuador's Universidad Andina Simón Bolívar focuses on cultural analysis and production through the lens of subalternity, transterritoriality, and local social identities, with an emphasis on cultural policy.[19] Many scholars and activists committed to critical cultural policy studies, such as George Yúdice (2002) in Miami, Stefano Harney (2002) and Kate Oakley (2004 & 2006) in London, David Bell (2007) in Leeds, and Justin Lewis and his collaborators (2005) in Cardiff beaver away, weathering slings and arrows from the comfortably pure ultra-left for engaging with commerce and the state, and sending a few of their own toward those who unproblematically embrace such links.

So what's in the toolbox of a critical cultural policy studies that is practical but retains some skepticism, as opposed to an amiable creative industries lobby that sees sweetness and light wherever it turns? How might critical cultural policy studies contribute to understanding the media industries, as opposed to regurgitating the anodyne rhetoric of publicity departments, industry mavens, government consultants, and business journalism hacks? I have some general suggestions, which I apply to the case of US screen drama.

The core elements to analyzing the media through critical cultural policy studies are:

- documents from public bureaucracies (international, national, regional, state, and municipal governments) and private bureaucracies (corporations, lobby groups, research firms, nongovernment organizations, and unions);
- debates (congressional/parliamentary, press, lobby group, activist, and academic);
- budgets (where media industries draw their money);
- laws (enabling legislation and legal cases about labor, copyright, and censorship);
- history (what came before and what is new);
- people (who is *included* and who is *excluded* from cultural policy and the media); and
- pollution (the environmental costs of these sectors).

Some core Internet sources are given in Appendix 14.1. The journals listed in Appendix 14.2 will keep you abreast of academic debates in policy-related media areas. Appendix 14.3 contains a list of relevant professional associations.

You can also read surveys of critical cultural policy studies (Miller & Yúdice 2002; Lewis & Miller 2003). Recent histories that bring the relationship between communications and cultural policies into sharp relief include books by Bob McChesney (2007) and Dan Schiller (2007).

Statistics are at the core of analyzing any industry: how many people there are, what they make, what it sells for, who buys it, and so on. In very large countries with wealthy populations, it is very tempting to look to domestic numbers, laws, and trends and effortlessly extrapolate from them to divine what culture is, what people like, and so on. This makes it all the more important for analysts to relativize their own experience, rather than universalize

it. UNESCO promulgated a *Framework for Cultural Statistics* in 1986 that remains the standard. Revised on a piecemeal basis, it will probably be replaced by 2009. Meanwhile, the UN's *International Flows of Selected Cultural Goods, 1994–2003* and *Statistics of Films and Cinemas*, the Latinobarómetro, Eurostat, and Eurobarometer are helpful, along with the European Commission's 2006 *White Paper on a European Communication Policy* and 2007 *European Agenda for Culture in a Globalizing World*. More and more major organizations are putting together policy information on the cultural/media/creative industries, such as the Motion Picture Association of America,[20] the National Governors' Association,[21] Americans for the Arts[22] (consult its National Arts Policy Database and creative industries data city-by-city), the World Intellectual Property Organization[23] (which has its own Creative Industries Division and a 2003 *Guide on Surveying the Economic Contribution of the Copyright-Based Industries*), the National Association of Television Program Executives,[24] and the Convenio Andrés Bello.[25] Good ways of staying current include subscribing to online digests, such as the Benton Foundation's service,[26] daily headlines from the Free Press,[27] and Americans for the Arts' list-serv. Be sure to look at non-English language and international sources as well as the dominant ones, or your analysis will betray its provincialism.

Sadly, in the case of the US, most media industries information is proprietary. Tiny but informative research reports sell for thousands of dollars. A further problem is that in the US, unlike most other nations, the fantastical claim is repeatedly made that there is no such thing as cultural policy, or that it exists in live performance and the plastic arts but not the popular media. This laughable canard persists, despite all evidence to the contrary (Miller & Yúdice 2002; Lewis & Miller 2003). So one needs to be particularly inventive to find out the truth, especially when investigating Hollywood, a veritable citadel of cultural policy secreted behind an illuminated sign of private enterprise. Of all the places seeking generation or regeneration through state strategy designed to stimulate industries, California should be the last on the list, given its claims to being at the very heart of laissez-faire. Yanquis take this as an article of faith, and pour scorn on European media subvention in favor of a mythology that says Hollywood was created because of the desire to tell stories that bound the nation together and, less altruistically, to make money by fleeing the unions and frost of New York's Lower East Side for the Southland's unorganized labor and bountiful sun.

The rhetoric of private enterprise is so powerful that even those who directly benefit from the way that public–private partnerships drive Californian screen drama willfully deny that corporate capital and state aid animate the industry. To transcend that rhetoric, we must follow the money, asking how film and TV are actually financed. Where is the evidence? In movie and TV credits, trade magazines, legal disputes that go to court and necessitate disclosure, balance sheets and annual reports of public film authorities, industry analyses by for-profit research firms (if you can afford them), books about how to shoot offshore or finance your movie with taxpayers' money, and occasional papers or protests from unions or activists. Hollywood relies on the state in a myriad of ways, some of them barely visible. It uses foreign sources of state money, about 200 publicly funded film commissions across the US,[28] Pentagon services, and ambassadorial labor from the Departments of State and Commerce. I shall address these serially, drawing on earlier work (Miller et al. 2005).

If it's German money from the 1990s or the early twenty-first century funding a film, the chances are that it came from tax breaks available to lawyers, doctors, and dentists. If it's French money, it might be from firms with state subvention in other areas of investment, such as cable or plumbing. If a TV show or movie is shot in Canada, public welfare to attract US producers is a given. If it is made in any particular state of the US, the credits generally thank regional and municipal film commissions for cross-subsidy of everything from hotels to hamburgers. State, regional, and municipal commissions reduce local taxes, provide police services, and block public wayfares. Accommodation and sales tax rebates are available to Hollywood producers almost universally across the country. The California Film Commission reimburses public personnel costs and permit and equipment fees, while the state government's "Film California First Program" has covered everything from free services through to wage tax credits.

On the war front, Steven Spielberg is a recipient of the Defense Department's Medal for Distinguished Public Service, Silicon Graphics designs material for military and cultural uses, and virtual-reality research veers between soldierly and audience applications, much of it subsidized by the Federal Technology Reinvestment Project and Advanced Technology Program. The University of Southern California's Institute for Creative Technologies uses military money and Hollywood directors to test out homicidal technologies and narrative scenarios. The governmental-screen industry link is clearly evident in the way that film studios sprang into militaristic action in concert with Pentagon preferences after September 11, 2001, and even became a consultant on possible attacks. Why not form a "White House–Hollywood Committee" while you're at it, to ensure coordination between the nations we bomb and the messages we export? (There is one.) The industry even argues before Congress that preventing copyright infringements is a key initiative against terrorism, since unauthorized copying funds transnational extra-political violence. And with the National Aeronautics and Space Administration struggling to renovate its image, who better to invite to lunch than Hollywood producers, so they will script new texts featuring the agency as a benign, exciting entity?

When it comes to plenipotentiary services, since the 1920s and 1930s, Hollywood lobbyists have regarded the US Departments of State and Commerce as message boys. The State Department undertakes market research and shares business intelligence. The Commerce Department pressures other countries to import screen texts with favorable terms of trade. Negotiations on so-called video piracy have seen Chinese offenders face severe penalties, even as the US claims to monitor human rights there. Protests by Indonesian filmmakers against Hollywood that draw the support of their government see Washington threaten retaliation via industrial sanctions. In the mid-1990s, a delegation to Hanoi of congressmen who fought in the American war in Vietnam ushered in film scouts, multiplex salespeople, and Hollywood films on TV. And the US pressures South Korea to drop screen quotas.

Finally, it is worth seeing how closely the fiscal fortunes of Hollywood are linked to the complexion of the government. After the 2000 election, Wall Street transferred money away from Silicon Valley/Alley and Hollywood and toward manufacturing and defense as punishments and rewards for these industries' respective attitudes during the election and subsequent coup. Energy, tobacco, and military companies, 80 percent of whose campaign contributions had gone to George Bush Minor in the 2000 elections, suddenly received unparalleled transfers of confidence. Money fled the cultural sector, where 66 percent of campaign contributions had gone to Al Gore Minor. There was a dramatic shift toward aligning finance capital with the new Administration – a victory for oil, cigarettes, and guns over film, music, and wires. The former saw their market value rise by an average of 80 percent in a year, while the latter's declined by between 12 and 80 percent (Schwartz & Hozic 2001).

Conclusion

The binary of the arts versus the sciences with which I began no longer matters. Those two cultures are blending. Today, we need a politics that is not in thrall to capital, creationism, or consultancy. Otherwise we are left with Billy Bragg's lament in "Tear Down the Union Jack" for the displacement of "the great and the good" by "the greedy and the mean" in "England.co.uk." But cultural policy, particularly in its folkloric arts-and-crafts/wine-cheese-and-trees manifestation, can appear dilettantish and dull. What can it offer alongside creative industries' promise of "technological enthusiasm, the cult of youth, branding and monetization fever, and ceaseless organizational change" (Ross 2007, 2)? Applying critical cultural policy studies to the media industries offers the social movement dynamism of cultural studies and the industrial acuity of political economy, as opposed to the cybertarian mythology of creative industries discourse. Getting to know cultural policy and intervening in it is an important part of participating in politics, because resistance goes nowhere unless it takes hold institutionally. That must be the crux of critical cultural policy work on the media – social movement access and governmental articulation, not subvention of corporations.

Notes

Thanks to Justin Lewis, Rick Maxwell, Inka Salovaara Moring, and the editors for their comments.
1 Plumb (1964), p. 7.
2 R. Reagan (1966) The creative society. Speech at the University of Southern California, 19 April. Available online at www.reaganlibrary.com/reagan/speeches/creative.asp.
3 Nathan (2005).
4 Snow (1987), p. 1.
5 Ibid., 3.
6 Ibid., 15.
7 Ibid., 2.
8 Ibid., 14; 23.
9 Ibid., 16; 22.
10 Ibid., 57.
11 Leavis (1972).
12 Hoggart (1973), pp. 182–96; Hoggart (2005), p. 207.
13 Hoggart (2005) looks back on the Pilkington Committee as one of his proudest moments: "A proof of its force came when a wealthy man, financially interested in the establishment of commercial television, publicly burned the report in a garden bonfire, with like-minded friends in attendance" (208).
14 See www.ahrb.ac.uk.
15 See www.arc.gov.au.
16 Source: www.ssrc.org/programs/media.
17 Fortune (2007).
18 See www.una.ac.cr.
19 See www.uasb.edu.ec.
20 See www.mpaa.org.
21 See www.nga.org.
22 See www.americansforthearts.org.
23 See www.wipo.int.
24 See www.natpe.org.
25 See www.cab.int.co.
26 See www.benton.org.
27 See www.freepress.net.
28 See www.filmcommissionhq.com.
Websites accessed July 14, 2008.

References

Alanen, A. (2007) What's wrong with the concept of creative industries? *Framework: The Finnish Art Review* **6**. At www.oecd.org/dataoecd/52/52/37794008.pdf, accessed July 14, 2008.

Bell, D. (2007) Fade to grey: some reflections on policy and mundanity. *Environment and Planning* **A39**, 541–54.

Boyce, J. (2004) *The Misfortune 100: Top Corporate Air Polluters in the United States*. Political Economy Research Institute, Amherst.

British Academy (2004) *"That Full Complement of Riches": The Contributions of the Arts, Humanities and Social Sciences to the Nation's Wealth*. Oxford University Press, Oxford.

Canclini, N. G. (1995) *Hybrid Cultures: Strategies for Entering and Leaving Modernity*. University of Minnesota Press, Minneapolis.

Caves, R. (2000) *Creative Industries: Contracts Between Art and Commerce*. Harvard University Press, Cambridge.

CHASS (2006) [Council for the Humanities, Arts and Social Sciences] *CHASS Submission: Productivity Commission Study on Science and Innovation*. CHASS, Canberra.

Costa, M. V., Silveira, R. H., and Sommer, L. H. (2003) Estudos culturais, educação e pedagogía. *Revista Brasileira de Educação* **23**, 36–61.

Cunningham, S. (1992) *Framing Culture: Criticism and Policy in Australia*. Allen & Unwin, Sydney.

Cunningham, S. (2002) From cultural to creative industries: theory, industry, and policy implications. *Culturelink*, 19–32.

Dahlström, M. and Hermelin, B. (2007) Creative industries, spatiality and flexibility: the example of film production. *Norsk Geografisk Tiddskrift – Norwegian Journal of Geography* **61**, 111–21.

Department for Culture, Media and Sport (2007) *The Creative Economy Programme: A Summary of Projects Commissioned in 2006/7*. DCMS, London.

ea_spouse (2004) EA: the human story. *LiveJournal*. At ea-spouse.livejournal.com/274.html, accessed January 18, 2008.

Dreher, C. (2002) What drives US Cities. *Hamilton Spectator*, 20 July.

European Commission (2006) *White Paper on a European Communication Policy*. At http://ec.europa.eu/communication_white_paper/index_en.htm, accessed January 18, 2008.

European Commission (2007) *A European Agenda for Culture in a Globalizing World*. At http://ec.europa.eu/europeaid/infopoint/conferences/2008/01-15_culture_en.htm, accessed January 18, 2008.

Florida, R. (2002) *The Rise of the Creative Class and How it's Transforming Work, Leisure and Everyday Life*. Basic Books, New York.

Fortune (2007) The list of industry stars. 19 March.

Freeman, A. (2007) *London's Creative Sector: 2007 Update*. Working Paper 22, Greater London Authority, London.

Galloway, S. and Dunlop, S. (2007) A critique of definitions of the cultural and creative industries in public policy. *International Journal of Cultural Policy* **13**, 17–31.

Garnham, N. (2005) From cultural to creative industries: an analysis of the implications of the "creative industries" approach to arts and media policy making in the United Kingdom. *International Journal of Cultural Policy* **11**, 15–29.

Gibson, C. and Klocker, N. (2004) Academic publishing as "creative" industry, and recent discourses of "creative economies": some critical reflections. *Area* **36**, 423–34.

Global Alliance for Cultural Diversity (2006) *Understanding Creative Industries: Cultural Statistics for Public Policy-Making*. UNESCO, Paris.

Harney, S. (2002) *State Work: Public Administration and Mass Intellectuality*. Duke University Press, Durham.

Hoggart, R. (1957) *The Uses of Literacy: Aspects of Working Class Life*. Chatto & Windus, London.

Hoggart, R. (1973) *Speaking to Each Other*. Vol. 1: *About Society*. Penguin, Harmondsworth.

Hoggart, R. (2005) *Mass Media in a Mass Society: Myth and Reality*. Continuum, London.

Hough, G. (1964) Crisis in literary education. In Plumb, J. H. (ed.) *Crisis in the Humanities*. Penguin, Harmondsworth, pp. 96–109.

Huijgh, E. (2007) Diversity united? Towards a European cultural industries policy. *Policy Studies* **28**, 209–24.

Jodhpur Initiatives (2005) *Asia-Pacific Creative Communities: A Strategy for the 21st Century*. UNESCO, Bangkok.

Kultur Macht Europa (2007) Culture powers Europe. 7 June.

Leavis, F. R. (1972) *Nor Shall My Sword: Discourses on Pluralism, Compassion and Social Hope*. Chatto & Windus, London.

Lee, M. (2007) Our electronic waste is piling up overseas. *San Diego Union-Tribune*, 19 June, p. A1.

Levering, R., Moskowitz, M., Harrington, A., and Tzacyk, C. (2003) 100 best companies to work for. *Fortune*, 20 January, p. 127.

Lewis, J. (1983) *Cable and Community Programming*. Greater London Council, London.

Lewis, J. (1985) *The Audience for Community Radio*. Greater London Council, London.

Lewis, J. (ed.) (1986) *A Sporting Chance: A Review of the GLC Recreation Policy*. Greater London Council, London.

Lewis, J. (1990) *Art, Culture, and Enterprise: The Politics of Art and the Cultural Industries*. Routledge, London.

Lewis, J. and Miller, T. (eds.) (2003) *Critical Cultural Policy Studies: A Reader*. Blackwell, Malden.

Lewis, J., Inthorn, S., and Wahl-Jorgensen, K. (2005) *Citizens or Consumers? What the Media Tell Us About Political Participation*. Open University Press, Maidenhead.

Linklater, M. (2006) I don't want to spoil the party …. *The Times*, 8 November, p. 21.

McChesney, R. W. (2007) *Communication Revolution: Critical Junctures and the Future of Media*. New Press, New York.

McChesney, R. W. and Schiller, D. (2002) *The Political Economy of International Communications: Foundations for the Emerging Global Debate Over Media Ownership and Regulation*. United Nations Research Institute for Social Development, Geneva.

McGuigan, J. (2004) *Rethinking Cultural Policy*. Open University Press, Maidenhead.

McRobbie, A. (1996) All the world's a stage, screen or magazine: when culture is the logic of late capitalism. *Media, Culture & Society* **18**, 335–42.

Mansfield, A. (1990) Cultural policy theory and practice: a new constellation. *Continuum* **4**. At wwwmcc.murdoch.edu.au/ReadingRoom/4.1/Mansfield.html, accessed July 14, 2008.

Marcus, C. (2005) *Future of Creative Industries: Implications for Research Policy*. European Commission Foresight Working Documents Series, Brussels.

Miller, T. (2005) La reconstrucción cultural del centro de Manhattan tras el 11 de septiembre. In Karam, T. (ed.) *Mirada a la Ciudad Desde la Comunicación y la Cultura*. Universidad Autónoma de la Ciudad de México, Mexico, pp. 227–51.

Miller, T. and Yúdice, G. (2002) *Cultural Policy*. Sage, London.

Miller, T., Govil, N., McMurria, J., Maxwell, R., and Wang, T. (2005) *Global Hollywood 2*. British Film Institute, London.

Mitchell, W. J., Inouye, A. S., and Blumenthal, M. (eds.) (2003) *Beyond Productivity: Information Technology, Innovation, and Creativity*. National Research Council of the National Academies, Washington DC.

Nathan, M. (2005) *The Wrong Stuff: Creative Class Theory, Diversity and City Performance*. Centre for Cities, Institute for Public Policy Research Discussion Paper 1, London.

Oakley, K. (2004) Not so cool Britannia: the role of the creative industries in economic development. *International Journal of Cultural Studies* **7**, 67–77.

Oakley, K. (2006) Include us out: economic development and social policy in the creative industries. *Cultural Trends* **15**, 255–73.

Peck, J. (2007) The creativity fix. *Fronesis* **24**. At www.eurozine.com/articles/2007-06-28-peck-en.html, accessed August 20, 2008.

Plumb, J. H. (1964) Introduction. In Plumb, J. H. (ed.) *Crisis in the Humanities*. Penguin, Harmondsworth, pp. 7–10.

Postrel, V. (1999) The pleasures of persuasion. *Wall Street Journal*, 2 August, p. A18.

Potts, J. (2006) How creative are the super-rich? *Agenda* **13**, 339–50.

Puckett, J. and Smith, T. (eds.) (2002) *Exporting Harm: The High-Tech Trashing of Asia*. Diane Publishing, Darby.

Pynchon, T. (1984) Is it OK to be a Luddite? *New York Times Book Review*, 28 October, pp. 40–1.

Ramanathan, S. (2006) The creativity mantra. *The Hindu*, 29 October, p. 7.

Ross, A. (2007) Nice work if you can get it: the mercurial career of creative industries policy. *Work Organisation, Labour and Globalisation* **1**, 1–19.

Schiller, D. (2007) *How to Think About Information*. University of Illinois Press, Urbana.

Schwartz, H. M. and Hozic, A. (2001) Who needs the new economy? At http://archive.salon.com/tech/feature/2001/03/16/schwartz/index.html, accessed July 8, 2008.

Shabi, R. (2002) The E-waste land. *Guardian*, 30 November, p. 36.

Shiva, V. (2002) *Water Wars: Privatization, Pollution, and Profit*. South End Press, Boston.

Snow, C. P. (1987) *The Two Cultures and a Second Look: An Expanded Version of the Two Cultures and the Scientific Revolution*. Cambridge University Press, Cambridge.

Tepper, S. J. (2002) Creative assets and the changing economy. *Journal of Arts Management, Law, and Society* **32**, 159–68.

Towse, R. (2002) Review. *Journal of Political Economy* **110**, 234–7.

UNCTAD (2004) [United Nations Conference on Trade and Development] *Creative Industries and Development*. Eleventh Session, São Paolo. UNCTAD, Geneva, TD(XI)/BP/13.

UNESCO (1986) [United Nations Educational, Scientific and Cultural Organization] *Framework for Cultural Statistics*. UNESCO, Paris.

UNESCO (2002) *Culture and UNESCO*. UNESCO, Paris.

UNESCO (2005) *International Flows of Selected Cultural Goods*. UNESCO Institute for Statistics, Montreal.

UNESCO (2007) *Statistics of Films and Cinemas*. UNESCO, Paris.

WIPO (2003) [World Intellectual Property Organization] *2003 Guide on Surveying the Economic Contribution of the Copyright-Based Industries*. At www.wipo.int/meetings/en/doc_details.jsp?doc_id=18410, accessed January 18, 2008.

Yúdice, G. (2002) *El Recurso de la Cultura: Usos de la Cultura en la Era Global*. Editorial Gedisa, Barcelona.

Appendix 14.1

Core Internet Sources

AfricaMediaOnline, www.africamediaonline.com
Alternative Law Forum, www.altlawforum.org
Arts Management Network, www.artsmanagement.net
Asian Media, www.asiamedia.ucla.edu
Asia Media and Information Center, www.amic.org.sg
Audiovisual Observatory, www.obs.coe.int
Basel Action Network, www.ban.org
Centre for Cultural Policy Research, www.gla.ac.uk/ccpr
Council of Europe Cultural Policy, www.coe.int
Creative Commons, http://creativecommons.org
Cultural Democracy, www.culturaldemocracy.net
Cultural Policy & the Arts National Data Archive, www.cpanda.org
Culture Statistics Observatory, www.culturestatistics.net
Digital Divide Network, www.digitaldivide.net
European Commission Education Audiovisual & Culture Executive Agency, http://eacea.ec.europa.eu
Fairness in Accuracy and Reporting, www.fair.org
Feminists for Free Expression, www.ffeusa.org
Free Software Foundation, www.fsf.org
Fund for Women Artists, www.womenarts.org
Global Public Media, http://globalpublicmedia.com
International Federation of Arts Councils and Culture Agencies, www.ifacca.org
Observatory of Cultural Policies in Africa, http://ocpa.irmo.hr
Pew Charitable Trusts Cultural Policy, www.pewtrusts.com
Sarai, www.sarai.net
UNESCO, www.unesco.org/culture
Urban Institute Arts and Culture Indicators Project, www.urban.org

Appendix 14.2

Some Key Journals

Asian Journal of Communication
Asian Media
Canadian Journal of Communication
Columbia VLA Journal of Law and the Art
Communication Abstracts
Communication Law and Policy
Communications
Comunicaçao e Sociedade
Comunicaço & Politica
Convergence: The International Journal of Research into New Media Technologies
Cultural Sociology
Entertainment and Sports Law Journal
Entertainment Law Review
Eptic: Revista de Economía Politica de las Tecnologías de la Información y Comunicación
European Journal of Communication
European Journal of Cultural Studies
Federal Communications Law Journal
Feminist Media Studies
Fordham Intellectual Property
Gamasutra
Games & Culture
Global Media and Communication
Global Media Journal
Historical Journal of Film, Radio & Television
Information, Communication & Society
International Communication Gazette
International Journal of Communication

International Journal of Communications Law and Policy
International Journal of Cultural Policy
International Journal of Cultural Studies
Journal of Broadcasting & Electronic Media
Journal of Communication
Journal of Communication Inquiry
Journal of International Communication
Journal of Media Economics
Journal of Media Sociology
Journal of Radio Studies
Journalism
Journalism & Mass Communication Quarterly
Journalism History
Journalism Studies
Loyola Entertainment Law Journal
Mass Communication & Society
Media & Entertainment Law Journal
Media Development
Media History

Media International Australia
Media Law and Practice
Media, Culture & Society
Middle East Journal of Culture and Communication
New Media & Society
NORDICOM Review of Nordic Research on Media and Communication
Poetics
Political Communication
Public Opinion Quarterly
Revista Electrónica Internacional de Economía Política de las Tecnologías de la Información y de la Comunicación
Screen
Television & New Media
Transnational Broadcasting Studies
Visual Anthropology
Visual Anthropology Review
Women's Studies in Communication

Appendix 14.3

Professional Associations

American Association for Public Opinion Research
American Journalism Historians Association
Asociación Latinoamericana de Investigadores de la Comunicacion
Association for Chinese Communication Studies
Association for Education in Journalism and Mass Communication
Association of Internet Researchers
Broadcast Education Association
Chinese Communication Association

Cultural Studies Association
European Consortium for Communications Research
European Society for Opinion and Marketing Research
Global Communication Research Association
International Association for Media History
International Association for Media & Communication
International Communication Association
Media, Communications & Cultural Studies Association
National Communication Association
Society for Cinema and Media Studies
Southern African Communication Association
Union for Democratic Communications

15

Cultures of Production
Studying Industry's Deep Texts, Reflexive Rituals, and Managed Self-Disclosures

....

John Thornton Caldwell

I would say that our company is kind of a "tribal" thing. Once you are in, and get the secret tattoos – we're then in there as a family operation … The core group that we have is intensely loyal. When work is slow, they'll come in anyway. And we'll find 'em working on the computers, or screwing around on the stuff. They're there because they want to be. It's not just a paycheck issue. I'm old school. You just gotta love the work. (CGI and visual FX supervisor John Fleet)[1]

Film artists tell stories first with their minds, not their gear. However, even though people know that, they still make gear-based distinctions, because gear does matter. One of the most important things about gear is that it can define who can and who cannot compete on the production, and increasingly on the distribution side of media. (Cynthia Wisehart, editor, Millimeter)[2]

What are media scholars to make of talk by production workers, like the statement above, arguing that production companies are "secret societies" fueled by nonprofit affection for the craft "family"? Or that production workers "think" with their "gear," even as they legitimize themselves by the way that they publicly display tools on the set?[3] To show what production "is really like," directors like Bryan Singer publicly "open up" and hype their shoots as "theater" to web users worldwide,[4] while spin-control executives counter: "It's gotten more and more difficult, if not impossible, to cover up what went on the set when crew members can go from the day's work to pounding out gossip on the Internet."[5] Jaded producers add to the complaints that production is a leaky "world of gossip [where] information flows like a river down a mountain."[6] Media industry scholars face many challenges, but one of them is clearly *not* a lack of information about media industries. The question instead becomes: how does one intelligently unravel the many cultural, conceptual, economic, corporate, social, professional, and interpersonal strands of self-disclosure that are constantly thrown at viewer and scholar alike as part of industrial habit?

To address such a question, this chapter outlines the parameters of what might be termed the "cultural studies of film/television production." It considers

innovative research on the cultures, social organization, work practices, and belief systems of film/
video workers as an alternative to and extension of
traditional political economic analysis and industrial
film historical research. This chapter proposes using
ethnographic, sociological, critical, and industrial
methodologies as part of an "integrated cultural-
industrial study," and is based on the author's multi-
sited fieldwork in Los Angeles from 1995 to 2005
(primarily among below-the-line workers).[7] One
goal of my research, and the method that it entails,
is to enable readers to think more holistically not
just about the results of institutional activities in the
corporations, or film/television production forms
onscreen (what film industry scholars and critics typically focus on), but about *off-screen* media production
work worlds. Such worlds don't just "produce" popular culture, film, or television, a much studied perspective for over seven decades. Work worlds are
important cultural expressions and sociological
activities in their own right. They are composed of
professional communities and subcultures that
undertake many of the activities that other social
groups do: 1) to forge and remake their identities;
2) to legitimate their significance and value to
neighboring industrial communities; and 3) to interact
ritualistically in ways that allow them to survive
change and prosper.

The shift in perspective proposed here unsettles
academia's penchant for making "industry" one
thing, a monolith, rather than acknowledging that
"the" industry is comprised of numerous, sometimes
conflicted and competing socio-professional communities, held together in a loose and mutating alliance by "willed affinity." Such affinities only survive
until the next destabilizing threats emerge from new
technologies and changing economic conditions
that regularly unsettle longstanding craft conventions, job descriptions, and the very logic of the production chain itself. Times of great technological
and economic unruliness, like those today, do not
simply spur creativity and innovation. They also
systematically unsettle and "stress" workers and craft
groups. The organizations that represent these
stressed workers (the IATSE unions, The Society of
Operating Cameramen/SOC, the Motion Picture
Editors Guild/MPEG, the American Society of

Cinematographers/ASC, and others) typically
respond to institutional and industrial stresses in
public with a flurry of new "critical" and aesthetic
"theorizations" about how the industry works, what
it means, and why the group in question should
remain central in its future. This kind of (sometimes
desperate) "industrial film theorizing" helps maintain, regulate, and sanction the lived communities –
and existing job descriptions – that make up film
and television.

In one sense, my research aims to complement the
top-down macrosocial perspectives favored by, say,
political economists, with a from-the-ground-up
study of the microsocial cultural practices of worker
groups. This approach situates agency in the social
interactions, conceptual tactics, and cultural expressions of workers, not just in the corporate organization and economic strategies of the studios and
networks. The conglomerates do not simply manufacture content. Screen content results from a loosely
organized and dispersed arena of socio-professional
and intercultural contestation that unfolds within
the conglomerates. Accessing these phenomena is
complicated by the obsessively proprietary nature of
media corporations today. Yet many points of access
are indeed available, as I hope to show in the pages
that follow. The shift proposed here places additional demands on scholars and researchers, especially on those who may have been trained in
archival study, historical research, and/or close
formal analysis (as I was). The shift to "human subjects
research" makes training and grounding in ethnographic method far more important than it has been
in media political economy research or film industry
historical scholarship.

An Integrated Cultural–Industrial Methodology: Artifacts and Cultural Practices in Production Studies

Cultural studies of production, of the sort I am
framing here, place film and television studies in
dialogue with several interrelated disciplines, including sociological cultural studies,[8] the sociology of
work,[9] interpretive anthropology and performance

studies,[10] institutional theories of art,[11] political economy,[12] and new technology research.[13] Understanding production talk as cultural sense-making and self-ethnography requires more carefully and comprehensively considering the practices, expressions, and self-representations of producers, crew members, and technicians. The next few pages introduce how reflexive talk, trade artifacts, and craft rituals by these workers can be viewed as rich, coded, cultural self-portraits in their own right.

My research utilizes an integrated cultural-industrial method of analysis. My approach is synthetic, and examines data from four registers or modes of analysis: 1) the textual analysis of trade and worker artifacts; 2) interviews with film/television workers; 3) ethnographic field observation of production spaces and professional gatherings; and 4) economic/industrial analysis.[14] I attempt whenever possible to keep these individual research modes "in check" by placing the discourses and results of any one register (textual, ethnographic, interviews, and political economy) in critical tension or dialogue with the others. This method of cross-checking proves useful when interrogating production practices where, for example, the rhetoric of studio press kits do not jive with explanations provided by production craftspeople; or when demo tapes used to market equipment conveniently elide or gloss over labor issues raised through more macroscopic industrial analysis or spin; or when sunny disclosures in interviews with producers are contradicted by cost-saving new technologies that displace and stress production workers. Although perhaps larger than the traditional "toolkit" employed in textual or stylistic film analysis, the integrated methodology used here still very much fits within a critical film and media studies tradition. In some ways, my approach also responds to anthropologist George Marcus' proposal for "situated, multi-locale" field studies that integrate microsociological cultural analysis with macrosociological political economic frameworks.[15] In other ways, my approach follows Paul Willis' (1981) call to find and articulate examples of critical theory embedded within the everyday of workers' experiences, that is, through the pursuit of a kind of indigenous cultural theory that operates outside of academia.[16] I have been particularly drawn to this idea of "theorizing from the ground up," as an alternative to conventional approaches.

My research is also less about finding an "authentic" reality "behind the scenes" − an empirical notion that tends to be naïve about the ways that media industry realities are *always* constructed − than it is about studying the industry's own self-representation, self-critique, and self-reflection. This approach is less informed by traditional anthropology and its functionalist explanations than it is by the "interpretive" anthropology of Clifford Geertz. Both methodologies depend on fieldwork, but Geertz builds his model on hermeneutics rather than an explanation of direct social function. Geertz states: "The culture of a people is an ensemble of texts, themselves ensembles, which the anthropologist strains to *read over the shoulders* of those to whom they properly belong."[17] Following philosopher Paul Ricouer, Geertz argues that the ethnographic problem is not about "social mechanics" but about "social semantics," which for him means systematically treating "cultural forms ... [as] texts, as imaginative works built out of social materials."[18] Like Geertz, my research aims to "look over the shoulder" of film and television workers in terms of the "interpretive" nature of their practices. But I also hope to suggest, beyond this, how these industrial "critical" or "theorizing" artifacts, rituals, and mediated forms of reflexivity express an emerging but unstable economic and social order in Hollywood.

Filmmakers constantly dialogue and negotiate their cultural identities through a series of questions that we traditionally value as part of media and film studies − including questions about what film/video is, how film/video works, how the viewer responds to film/video, and how film/video reflects or forms culture. Yet filmmakers (unlike theorists) seldom systematically elaborate on these questions in lengthy spoken or written forms. Instead, a form of embedded theoretical "discussion" in the work world takes place in and through the tools, machines, artifacts, iconographies, working methods, professional rituals and narratives that film practitioners circulate and enact in film/video trade subcultures. Rather than simply accepting and legitimizing a studio executive's generalizations from interviews about how film/television works or what it means, therefore, such explanations should be grounded within the kinds of contexts schematized in this chapter (the material, symbolic, and representational practices of production workers).

My response to the coded and inflected nature of overt practitioner explanations in interviews or trade accounts is to consider them alongside a more systematic study of what I term the "deep industrial practices" of film/video production. My research seeks to describe the contexts in which embedded industrial sense-making and trade theorizing occurs, and categorizes artifacts and rituals into three registers: fully embedded, semi-embedded, and publicly disclosed "deep texts." The research in my book, *Production Culture: Industrial Reflexivity and Critical Practice in Film and Television*, is grounded within this tripartite methodological scheme. I introduce each of these registers, and discuss eight symptomatic examples of them through visual and photographic documentation, in the pages that follow.

Fully embedded deep texts

Attention to fully embedded deep texts is crucial to any effective production ethnography (table 15.1a). This strata is largely cut off from the public and commercially enacted or *circulated by production personnel within the relatively bounded, proprietary worlds of work*. Although the information contained in cinematographers' demo tapes or producers' pitch sessions can sometimes leak out into the public, the primary function of these artifacts and rituals is intra-guild, intra-association, or interpersonal interaction and dialogue, all of which are dynamics involved in the formation and maintenance of groups. Thus these fully embedded practices serve to facilitate relations inside of specific production groups.

The film/TV production world operates through a meticulously cultivated system of assisting and mentoring. The networks and practices of assisting and mentoring don't just help individuals move ahead organizationally or career-wise. They also create a collective knowledge database, along with industry standards and conventions for efficient craftwork. Camera crews, like the one in figure 15.1 directed by DP Lazlo Kovacs, ASC, do not just

Table 15.1 Deep textual practices and rituals

a. Fully embedded deep texts and rituals
(bounded professional exchanges; facilitates *intra-group* relations)
- Demo tapes and comp reels
- Pitch sessions
- Machine interface design
- Equipment iconography
- How-to manuals for production technologies
- Trade and craft narratives and anecdotes
- On-the-set crew pedagogy and work behavior
- Union and guild workshops
- Association/member newsletters
- Corporate retreats

b. Semi-embedded deep texts and rituals
(professional exchanges with ancillary public viewing; facilitates *inter-group* relations)
- Electronic press kits (EPKs)
- Advertiser "upfronts"
- Trade shows
- Trade publications
- Internship programs
- Technical bake-offs and reveals
- "How to make it in the industry" panels

c. Publicly disclosed deep texts and rituals
(professional exchanges for explicit public consumption; facilitates *extra-group* relations)
- Making-of documentaries
- DVD director tracks, and "extras"
- Docu-stunts during "sweeps" weeks
- Online websites (TV/dot-com interactions)
- Studio and network supported fan conventions
- Screening "Q&As"
- Televised show business reports
- Viral videos on YouTube.com and MySpace.com

distribute and segregate tasks in a clockwork-like Fordist manner. They also "distribute cognition" across segregated craft subspecialties, and interactively function as what sociologist Bruno Latour (1979) would term "actor-networks." Scholarly media studies of production miss their mark if they disregard these forms of socio-professional relations, incremental on-the-set interactions, and forms of collective or distributed cognition. Not only do workers demonstrate agency within the conglomerates, they also deploy workaday forms of critical analysis through mentoring communications and

Figure 15.1   On-the-set worker behavior. DP Lazlo Kovacs, ASC, animates longstanding, conventionalized "actor-networks" to achieve collective effects (photo © J. Caldwell)

assisting habits. In this way, they constantly provide meta-commentaries on productions and the corporations that make them. Scholars just need to learn how to listen to this "helpful" daily exchange of trade and worker hand-holding and chatter.

Worker tools are far from inert. As discussed above, they are cultural representations in their design and use. They are also instigators of subcultural craft expression among the workers who use, debate, and contend over them. Here (figure 15.2), technology-driven post-production work is depicted among workers – in promotional self-portraits – as anatomical self-loathing and stress-induced tissue fatigue. Faced with this kind of trade image and "evidence," to whom should a media studies scholar give more credibility? A producer optimistically promoting his "digital boutique" in interviews published in the self-dealing trades; or worker icons like this Telenium trade image, that underscore the human stress and anxiousness of the "digital sweat-shop" in profound and unsettling ways? Scholars should consider neither of these individual registers – verbal producer self-disclosures or visual worker self-representations – as unmediated gateways to

what is "really" going on in post-production. Rather, researchers should consider both registers, along with other methodologies – such as ethnographic observation and the economics of labor – to keep the results and explanations of any one register in check and credible.

Semi-embedded deep texts

A second broad category of workaday industrial theorizing can be understood as "semi-embedded" textual activities (table 15.1b). These practices function as forms of symbolic communication *between media professionals*, and help to facilitate "inter-group" relations. Yet these texts and rituals are simultaneously designed to spur and stimulate ancillary discussion and eventual awareness in the public sphere of the consumer as well. These "semi-embedded" deep texts travel further from specific or local working subcultures. That is, they typically function to bring generalizing discussions of the nature and meaning of film production from one corporate media company or craft group to another. Whereas the fully embedded practices discussed earlier are

PURE POWER

THE BIG FAT, NASTY POST HOUSE.

1.877.TELENIUM
www.telenium.com

Telenium™

LITTLE JIMMY CAN EAT 26 CHEESESTEAKS AND EDIT ALL NIGHT LONG.

Figure 15.2   Worker technical icons. Telenium: Big, Fat, Nasty Post House (photo of promo poster © J. Caldwell)

intra-group in nature, semi-embedded practices are inter-group since they function as go-betweens that facilitate institutional dialogue and (sometimes) contracting between media corporations and trade associations. Even if the ultimate objective is to promote or market a studio or network's film to the viewing public, the deep texts in this second category succeed only if they are persuasive in maintaining or forging new relationships between the makers of content and media journalists (through EPKs), advertisers (through upfronts), affiliates (through affiliate meetings), clients and buyers (through trade shows), and new personnel (through making-it panels and internships).

As discussed earlier, technologies function as loaded cultural artifacts. Yet while the interface design and use of production tools are "fully embedded" within production culture, staged demonstrations by technicians for other technicians (like the one in figure 15.3, featuring Cirque de Soleil aerial performers flying past the "Super-Technocrane" in Los Angeles in 2001) also function as "semi-embedded" practices that sometimes "leak out" to broader industrial and consumer audiences. In preemptive inter-group technical demonstrations at specialized production trade shows like this one, proprietary technologies stimulate "imagined worlds" for potential users. Through them, that is, workers suspend

Figure 15.3   Trade show technical demos (photo © J. Caldwell)

disbelief to imagine: 1) how hypothetical onscreen images might look; and 2) how the users themselves would look and function as they utilize and choreograph the demonstrated and theatricalized production tool. Such staged intra-group trade rituals and performances mirror the fact that film/video productions themselves unfold as staged forms of social performance on the set.

Scholars tend to focus either on the industrial conditions, the end results of film/television onscreen, or the ultimate uses of film/television by audiences. Much more attention needs to be focused on the long and complicated journeys that story ideas take through the socio-professional networks that manage, develop, and cultivate them over time. These journeys inevitably involve and require negotiation through a series of rule-governed, conventionalized socio-professional rituals, like fully embedded pitch sessions, and semi-embedded shootouts and technical bake-offs. The photographs here (figure 15.4) document "HD speed-dating for professionals" in LA. In this highly choreographed ritual, "high-definition" content development is stimulated and managed by staging a rapid succession

of five-minute socio-professional "hook-ups" with strangers. "Soft sell" is a necessary competence in much of film/TV, and these kinds of organized rituals, evoking LA's "singles scene," aim to kick-start the glacially slow industrial shift to HD (high-definition film/video, or HDTV). Despite the origins of media studies scholarship in textual analysis, effects research, and industrial history, media field research should always be sensitive to the "human touch" operative in instances like this one. After all, professional interpersonal rituals permeate screen content development.

As if the Darwinian struggle for survival in production were not difficult enough, various trade groups stage public gladiatorial-like contests between workers looking to gain greater visibility. Here (figure 15.5), with the announcement, "Rub elbows with industry colleagues," LA Center Studios hosts and stages weekend "shoot-outs," in which workers and aspirants from various companies leasing space on the lot compete to make short films in 2.5 days. Such cultural activities – evoking a hypermanic film festival ethos – attempt to artificially build community across the otherwise anonymous

Figure 15.4   HD speed-dating for industry professionals
(photo © J. Caldwell)

Figure 15.5   Worker shoot-outs and bake-offs
(photo © J. Caldwell)

workforces of competing companies. Just like "pitchfests," "HD speed-dating," and producer "boot-camps," shoot-outs produce a tremendous amount of "free" creative product on-the-cheap, even as the rituals transform and sometimes spotlight anxious, unknown workers into erstwhile artists. The vast and excessive oversupply of labor in LA makes these hyperactive, desperate group cultural

activities a useful and pervasive form of cheap concept R&D labor for the industry.

The film and television industries mount a series of high-profile collective rituals throughout the year. Such gatherings make the lived textures of how business within the conglomerates is carried out available to scholars. If speed-dating, discussed above, facilitates "soft sell" deal-making, then bringing the stars and big-guns out to the heartland is a form of "hard sell" at the syndication markets. Here (figure 15.6) onscreen talent and "booth babes" are flown in from LA to wow local broadcast station owners and quickly close deals and sales for next year's programming. The volatile post-Fordist world of film and television production depends on

Figure 15.6 Syndication markets (photo © J. Caldwell)

successful relationship- and consensus-building, which enables industrial partners to amortize costs and outsource risks. Trade shows and markets are the charged sites in which these tasks are broached and bartered. Such events are also "liminal" rituals and spaces within which practitioner groups suspend the day-to-day grind of work in order to collectively re-imagine a common future or contested present.

Any effective industry study must start with a pre-eminent question: where does film and television trade knowledge and information come from? Industrial knowledge constantly churns out from production companies, studios, and networks, but the process by which this happens is seldom transparent, direct, or self-evident. For example, to combat the destabilizing threats of crew workers' "leaky storyworlds," the studios and networks

mount all-out initiatives to preemptively "leak" their own preferred behind-the-scenes narratives. Corporate handlers and publicists lead journalists around by the nose at "press junkets," tightly orchestrated "set visits," and incestuous annual story-sharing courting rituals like the TCA (Television Critics Association) meetings.[19] Some trade writers refer to their profession as a kind of "whoring." Actually watching publicity unfold in these ways makes one far less inclined to take each day's breathless entertainment "news" at face value.

Publicly disclosed deep texts

The third and final broad set of practices in this model are self-consciously directed at the viewing public, yet must be recognized as textually inscribed or embedded nevertheless (table 15.1c). Publicly disclosed deep texts include making-of documentaries, DVD director tracks and "extras," docu-stunts during "sweeps" weeks, online websites (TV/dot-com interactions), studio and network-supported fan conventions, and show business reports (such as *Access Hollywood, Entertainment Tonight*). These kinds of "meta-texts" or "para-texts" on television might all be characterized as genres intended for public (rather than industrial) consumption. While increased viewership is an obvious goal of each of these genres, audience engagement works primarily by providing "access" to the ways that practitioners work, think, and talk about how they work and think. This kind of industrial theorizing is publicly performed for the ostensible benefit of the viewer (the person watching the DVD "bonus track" or the cable TV "making-of") lucky enough to have been given access to those "inside" the production process. Yes, these industrial meta-texts look in some respects like texts or programs that circulate on the very "surface" (the screens) of mass culture. Yet the public contact made available by industrial meta-texts is typically focused on the embedded theorizing process itself (for example, how a director or CGI artist conceptualizes a scene in a Pixar movie rather than the mere presentation of the scene itself). This industrial self-disclosure via meta-text, therefore, is an explicit act of "extra-group" (production–audience) engagement. As such, it proves to be a far

Figure 15.7   Behind-the-scenes programming: *Gay Hollywood* (photos of video frames © J. Caldwell)

more open-ended form of industrial theorizing and critical debate (no matter how scripted) than the previous two categories of intra-group and inter-group deliberation outlined above.

"Behind-the-scenes" programming (making-ofs, show-biz reports, and producer/writer/director commentaries on DVDs) blanket the multi-channel spectrum. The effusiveness of these "self-disclosures" challenges ethnographers and media studies scholars to carefully demarcate and consider exactly what their research can and should learn about the same phenomena. One example of behind-the-scenes programming is AMC's *Gay Hollywood*, a caution-ary, tabloid-film-studies, making-it-in-Hollywood tale (figure 15.7). A fundamental (even if consciously unintended) message emerges through the episodes: even if, like the on-camera subjects here, you have degrees from elite private universities (Stanford) and top film schools (USC), prime-time acting credits, international premieres (Sundance), and have been featured in over 150 other film festivals,

you're still a nobody in this town, destined, without a kitchen, to wash your dishes in the bathtub near your toilet, before you ever "make it." Lesson to the heartland and aspirants/fans: everybody starts at the bottom, and humiliation marks the endless, alienat-ing journey. This kind of ostensible "transparency" and self-disclosure, therefore, is much less about what "making-it" in the industry is actually like, than what the industry's obsessive programming gatekeepers *want* aspirants to think the industry is like.

"The industry" does not have clean "insides" and "outsides" that scholars can clearly identify or easily locate. Some of the most interesting markers of pro-duction culture activity and expression can be found by scholars, in fact, in the endless intermediate con-centric zones that separate and connect the cultures of production and the cultures of consumption. The image in figure 15.8 depicts a professional–public "table-read" of a script by the producers and cast of Imagine Entertainment's *Arrested Development*. Struggling for greater audience share, and desperate

Figure 15.8   "Table-read" and Q&A. *Arrested Development's* writers' room as semi-public theater (photo © J. Caldwell)

for series renewal on Fox after its first season, the production staged or "outed" this dramatization of the actors' and writers' typical prep day in order to create more buzz in public. Themes of collectivity ruled the design of the presentation as well as the Q&A discussions that followed, which supposedly detailed the inner workings of the show's writers' room in 2004. The intermediary spaces of industry – like table-reads, creative team Q&As, and producer publicity stunts – are well worth researching. Even a cursory look at these tactical spaces and rituals shows that they should not be taken *as* the industry, but rather as *contested sites* of cultural negotiation, marketing and economic give-and-take.

Conclusion

Media scholarship must better attend to the affective dimensions, visual practices, and theorizing claims that industry now makes about itself for the benefit of others. That is, scholars must first recognize and acknowledge that they are attempting to engage with and interpret an industry that already constantly interprets and scrutinizes itself with both embedded

and onscreen meta-criticisms. Looking closely at the artifacts and deep texts within the three registers schematized in this chapter suggests just how complex and varied are the ways that contemporary film/video corporations and their personnel broach, barter, discuss, employ, explain, and contest ideas about the nature and meaning of film/television.

Even though my research focuses on very local forms of knowledge and expression, I *am* ultimately interested in how the cultural activities of production workers described in this chapter fit within and animate the new realities of post-Fordism, neoliberal economic markets, flexible and outsourced labor practices, multimedia convergence, and multinational, corporate conglomeration. Scholars miss a great deal if they claim to understand these sorts of broader industrial and economic trends without also examining very local work, critical practices, and aesthetic "theories" employed and debated throughout the production chain, by craftsmen, practitioners, poorly paid mentees, overworked assistants, assistants to assistants, and unpaid interns. Scholars seem far more inclined to talk about the predatory designs of Rupert Murdoch's conglomerate than these off-the-radar seasonal workers who actually make film and television, locked as they ostensibly are in their own acute but Balkanized industrial turf battles. Such workers frequently provide capable and prescient critical analyses and ideological deconstructions, in symbolic form, of the conglomerates that employ them through inspirational trade stories, aspirational craft icons, consensus-building group demonstration rituals, partisan technical bake-offs, frantic camera shoot-outs, and quasi-spiritual "how to make it in the industry" seminars. Even a cursory recognition of such things suggests that it is time to stop looking, solely, at corporate and financial news in the film and television trades (which are always cooked, skewed, or unreliable) or government and regulatory issues (which overestimate film and television as control phenomena), in order to better understand the material and human conditions of production work itself. Without these very local production work-worlds, government and industry would be merely absentee landlords.

Notes

Photographs used in this chapter are by John Caldwell, copyrighted in 2008, and are reprinted here by permission of the author. Over 70 other photographs of this sort are included for analysis in my book *Production Culture: Industrial Reflexivity and Critical Practice in Film and Television*.

1   These are from spoken comments by VFX artist and supervisor John Fleet, recorded by John Caldwell in Los Angeles, June 2000.
2   Wisehart (2004), p. 9.
3   Ibid.
4   From director Bryan Singer's director's blog, www. bluetights.net, posted online while on location for *Superman Returns*, as quoted in "Dear Diary: Action!," *Time*, April 4, 2005.
5   Quote from Laurence Mark, co-producer, *Jerry Maguire*, explaining need for studio damage control in response to leaked stories and gossip as quoted in Harmetz (2000), p. 6.
6   Quote from Tom Sherak, an executive at Revolution Studios, as quoted in Harmetz (2000), p. 6.
7   The present chapter is in some ways an abstract of the methodology I employ in much greater depth in *Production Culture* (2008) and "Convergence Television" (2004).
8   The literature review in these next two paragraphs has been revised and adapted from my chapter, "Cultural Studies of Media Production" (2006). Key sources in sociological cultural studies include: Willis (1981); Lipsitz (1997); Seiter (1999); Davila (2001); Mayer (2003, 2008).
9   See Hirsch (1972), DiMaggio & Hirsch (1976), DiMaggio (1982), McRobbie (1998), Hochschild (2003), and Ross (2004).
10 See Geertz (1983), Clifford (1986), Turner & Bruner (1986), Geertz (1991), and Dornfeld (1998).

11 See Becker (1973).
12 See Schiller (1999), Miller et al. (2001), Hesmondhalgh (2003), and Schwoch (2008).
13 See Latour & Woolgar (1979, 1986), Latour (1988), and Agre (1997).
14 Newcomb & Alley (1983), Gitlin (1983), D'Acci (1994), Levine (2001), and Lotz (2007) all provide especially good examples of industry research that involves either on-set observations or interviews – rare methods in critical scholarship given rigid control of access to productions by producers. Another key book is Born (2004) *Uncertain Vision: Birt, Dyke and the Reinvention of the BBC*, which together with her earlier essay (2002) provides useful precedents for fieldwork.
15 See Marcus (1986).
16 See Willis (1981). I am especially interested in finding out how cultural forms are forged by worker resistance and accommodation within corporate media culture. While there is some overlap in the technical trades with Willis' picture of white male masculinity, I find very different forms of irony and self-consciousness that sometimes ill-fit with Willis' ideas of class "resistance."
17 This is how Geertz (1991) summarizes his approach in his influential ethnographic account, "Deep Play: Notes on the Balinese Cockfight."
18 Ibid., 266. Geertz develops this idea and methodological proposal from the work of Ricouer (1970) and from Frye (1964).
19 The TCA's own website, http://tvcritics.org, acknowledges its incestuous relations with the corporate conglomerates that constantly attempt to manage critics and journalists: "Set visits and other remote activities … may be coordinated not by individual presenters but by corporate partnerships inspired by industry consolidation." Website accessed August 20, 2008.

References

Agre, P. (1997) *Computation and Human Experience.* Cambridge University Press, Cambridge.

Becker, H. (1973) *Art Worlds.* University of California Press, Berkeley.

Born, G. (2002) Reflexivity and ambivalence: culture, creativity and government in the BBC. *Cultural Values* **6**, 65–90.

Born, G. (2004) *Uncertain Vision: Birt, Dyke and the Reinvention of the BBC.* Secker & Warburg, London.

Caldwell, J. (2004) Convergence television: aggregating form and repurposing content in the culture of conglomeration. In Spigel, L. and Olsson, J. (eds.) *Television After TV: Essays on a Medium in Transition.* Duke University Press, Durham, pp. 41–74.

Caldwell, J. (2006) Cultural studies of media production: critical industrial practices. In White, M. and Schwoch, J. (eds.) *Questions of Method in Cultural Studies.* Blackwell, Malden, pp. 109–53.

Caldwell, J. (2008) *Production Culture: Industrial Reflexivity and Critical Practice in Film and Television.* Duke University Press, Durham.

Clifford, J. (1986) On ethnographic allegory. In Clifford, J. and Marcus, G. (eds.) *Writing Culture: The Poetics and Politics of Ethnography.* University of California Press, Berkeley, pp. 98–121.

D'Acci, J. (1994) *Defining Women: Television and the Case of Cagney and Lacey.* University of North Carolina Press, Chapel Hill.

Davila, A. (2001) *Latinos Inc.: The Marketing and Making of a People.* University of California Press, Berkeley.

DiMaggio, P. (1982) Cultural entrepreneurship in nineteenth-century Boston. Part 1: The creation and organization of an organizational base for high culture in America. *Media, Culture & Society* **4**, 33–50.

DiMaggio, P. and Hirsch, P. M. (1976) Production organization in the arts. *American Behavioral Scientist* **19**, 735–52.

Dornfeld, B. (1998) *Producing Public Television, Producing Public Culture.* Princeton University Press, Princeton.

Frye, N. (1964) *The Educated Imagination.* University of Indiana Press, Bloomington.

Geertz, C. (1983) *Local Knowledge: Further Essays in Interpretive Anthropology,* 3rd edn. Basic Books, New York.

Geertz, C. (1991) Deep play: notes on the Balinese cockfight. In Mukerji, C. and Schudson, M. (eds.)

Rethinking Popular Culture: Contemporary Perspectives in Cultural Studies. University of California Press, Berkeley, pp. 239–77.

Gitlin, T. (1983) *Inside Prime Time.* Pantheon, New York.

Harmetz, A. (2000) They're rumors, not predictions; the gossip's in overdrive: the production is out of control. But just because there's trouble on the set doesn't mean there will be trouble at the box office. *Los Angeles Times,* 29 October, Calendar, p. 6.

Hesmondhalgh, D. (2003) *The Cultural Industries.* Sage, Thousand Oaks.

Hirsch, P. M. (1972) Processing fads and fashions: an organization-set analysis of cultural industry systems. *American Journal of Sociology* **77**, 639–59.

Hochschild, A. (2003) *The Managed Heart: Commercialization of Human Feeling.* University of California Press, Berkeley.

Latour, B. (1988) Mixing humans and non-humans together: the sociology of a door closer. *Sociology* **35**, 298–310.

Latour, B. and Woolgar, S. (1979) *Laboratory Life: The Construction of Scientific Facts.* Princeton University Press, Princeton. (Second edition published 1986.)

Levine, E. (2001) Toward a paradigm for media production research: behind the scenes at *General Hospital. Critical Studies in Media Communication* **18**, 66–82.

Lipsitz, G. (1997) *Dangerous Crossroads: Popular Music, Postmodernism, and the Poetics of Place.* Verso, London.

Lotz, A. (2007) *The Television Will Be Revolutionized.* New York University Press, New York.

McRobbie, A. (1998) *British Fashion Design: Rag Trade or Image Industry?* Routledge, London.

Marcus, G. (1986) Contemporary problems of ethnography in the modern world system. In Clifford, J. and Marcus, G. (eds.) *Writing Culture, The Poetics and Politics of Ethnography.* University of California Press, Berkeley, pp. 165–93.

Mayer, V. (2003) *Producing Dreams, Consuming Youth: Mexican Americans and Mass Media.* Rutgers University Press, New Brunswick.

Mayer, V. (2008) Soft-core in TV time: the political economy of a cultural trend. *Critical Studies in Mass Communication* **22**, forthcoming.

Miller, T., Govil, N., McMurria, J., and Maxwell, R. (2001) *Global Hollywood*. British Film Institute, London.

Newcomb, H. and Alley, R. S. (1983) *The Producer's Medium: Conversations with Creators of American TV.* Oxford University Press, New York.

Ricouer, P. (1970) *Freud and Philosophy.* Yale University Press, New Haven.

Ross, A. (2004) *No Collar: The Humane Workplace and its Hidden Costs.* Temple University Press, Philadelphia.

Schiller, D. (1999) *Digital Capitalism.* MIT Press, Cambridge.

Schwoch, J. (2008) *Global TV: New Media and the Cold War, 1946–69.* University of Illinois Press, Urbana.

Seiter, E. (1999) *Television and New Media Audiences.* Oxford University Press, Oxford.

Turner, V. W. and Bruner, E. M. (1986) *The Anthropology of Experience.* University of Chicago Press, Urbana.

Willis, P. (1981) *Learning to Labor: How Working Class Kids Get Working Class Jobs.* Columbia University Press, New York.

Wisehart, C. (2004) To digital or not. *Millimeter,* March, p. 9.

16

The Moral Economy of Web 2.0
Audience Research and Convergence Culture

....

Joshua Green and Henry Jenkins

> *The central principle behind the success of the giants born in the Web 1.0 era who have survived to lead the Web 2.0 era appears to be this, that they have embraced the power of the web to harness collective intelligence …* The lesson: Network effects from user contributions are the key to market dominance in the Web 2.0 era. (*O'Reilly 2005*)

> *<dsully> please describe web 2.0 to me in 2 sentences or less.*
> *<jwb> you make all the content. they keep all the revenue. (Bash.org)*

Throughout the 1980s and 1990s, fans were emblematic of audience resistance (Fiske 1989; Jenkins 1992), understood as actively appropriating and transforming mass media content as raw materials for their own cultural productions. Mass media depicted fans as living in the shadows of mass culture (if not the basements of their parents' suburban split-level houses), and media companies saw their tastes and concerns as "unrepresentative" of the general population. By the early twenty-first century, fans have been redefined as the drivers of wealth production within the new digital economy: their engagement and participation is actively being pursued, if still imperfectly understood, by media companies interested in adopting Web 2.0 strategies of user-generated content, social networks, and "harness-[ing] collective intelligence" (O'Reilly 2005).

This new talk about "putting the We in the Web" (Levy & Stone 2006) was initially embraced as granting consumers greater influence over the decisions that impacted the production and distribution of culture. By 2007, contradictions, conflicts, and schisms have started to appear within the Web 2.0 paradigm around the imperfectly aligned interests of media producers and consumers.

Consider, for example, FanLib.com, a start-up company that included established media players such as *Titanic* producer Jon Landau and entertainment lawyer Jon Moonves as advisors, and former Yahoo CMO Anil Singh as chairman (Jenkins 2007a). FanLib began by hosting officially sponsored fan fiction competitions around *The L Word* and *The Ghost Whisperer*. Soon, the company sought to become a general interest portal for all fan fiction, actively soliciting material from leading fan writers, deciding not to solicit prior approval from the studios and production companies. The company's executives told fans they wanted to promote and protect fan fiction writing and informed initial corporate investors that they would teach fans how to "color within the lines." When fans stumbled onto the corporate pitch online, there was an intense backlash that spread across blogs, LiveJournals, and various social networking sites.

Fans raised a number of objections. The company wanted to profit from content fans had historically circulated for free (and adding insult, they refused to share the generated revenues with the fan authors). This debate revealed a rift between the "gift economy" of fan culture and the commodity logic of "user-generated content." At the same time, the company promised to increase the visibility of once cloaked fan activities, thus heightening the legal risk that media producers would put the entire community under closer legal scrutiny. (Previously, there had been an unofficial truce between fans and producers: most producers were not going after fan fiction sites as long as they did not intend to make money out of what they created.) Yet FanLib.com denied that it bore any legal responsibility to defend fan writers against cease-and-desist letters from studios and networks. All of this fit within a growing debate about whether corporate distribution of user-generated content constitutes a form of unpaid outsourcing of creative labor, contributing to the downsizing of internal production teams (Scholz & Lovink 2007). These fans refused to be the victims of corporate exploitation, quickly and effectively rallying in opposition to FanLib and using their own channels of communication to inflect damage on its nascent brand. At the same time, FanLib.com did attract more than 18,000 participants (personal correspondence with Chris Williams, March 2008), including both those new to the world of fan fiction and thus not part of existing communities and those who, for whatever reason, felt disenfranchised from the existing fan fiction groups (Li 2007).

This example shows how media companies are being forced to reassess the nature of consumer engagement and the value of audience participation in response to a shifting media environment characterized by digitization and the flow of media across multiple platforms, the further fragmentation and diversification of the media market, and the increased power and capacity of consumers to shape the flow and reception of media content. The result has been a constant pull and tug between top-down corporate and bottom-up consumer power with the process of media convergence shaped by decisions made in teenagers' bedrooms and in corporate boardrooms.

Mass media are increasingly operating in a context of participatory culture, but there is considerable anxiety about the terms of participation. Some media producers adopt what we are calling a collaborative approach, embracing audience participation, mobilizing fans as grassroots advocates, and capitalizing on user-generated content. Others adopt a prohibitionist posture. Frightened by a loss of control over the channels of media production and distribution and threatened by increasingly visible and vocal audience behavior, some companies tighten control over intellectual property, trying to rein in the disruptive and destabilizing impact of technological and cultural change. Most companies are torn between the two extremes, seeking a new relationship with their audiences that gives only as much ground as needed to maintain consumer loyalty.

This essay focuses on the resulting reworking of the "moral economy" that shapes the relations between producers and consumers. "Moral economy" refers to the social expectations, emotional investments, and cultural transactions that create a shared understanding between all participants within an economic exchange. The moral economy that governed old media companies has broken down and there are conflicting expectations about what new relationships should look like. The risks for companies are high, since alienated consumers have other options for accessing media content. The risks for consumers are equally high, since legal sanctions can stifle the emerging participatory culture.

To understand this debate, we must bridge between the historically separate spheres of audience studies and industry research. Industry research – at least within academic circles – has taken a top-down approach, emphasizing the power of media companies and the impact of the decisions they make upon the culture; audience research has historically taken a bottom-up approach, emphasizing audience interpretation and cultural production read in cultural rather than economic terms. The result has been two conflicting claims about the current state of our culture: one emphasizing media concentration and the narrowing of options; the other emphasizing the expansion of grassroots participation. This essay proposes to read these two trends against each other and in doing so, provoke a conversation between two sets of literatures – one derived from business research, the other derived from cultural and media studies. This conversation, in our case, is a literal one, since many of the ideas here emerged from work done through the MIT Convergence Culture Consortium, which facilitates regular dialogues between academics and industry insiders.[1] This conversation also reflects the increased focus on social and cultural factors, even among tech industries, as people come to grips with the implications of Web 2.0. This conversation might also be understood in global terms as this article combines work done by American researchers interested in "convergence culture" with that done by Australian researchers focused on "creative industries" and "produsage." Historically, both audience research and industry studies have concentrated on single media industries rather than examining trends that cut across different media sectors and platforms. Our contention is that this research increasingly needs to adopt a comparative or transmedia approach because of the increased flow of media content and audiences across every available platform and the speed with which developments in one media sector impact thinking in every other corner of the entertainment industry.

Produsers and Other Participatory Audiences

> The term multiplier may help marketers acknowledge more forthrightly that whether our work is a success is in fact out of our control. All we can do is to invite the multiplier to participate in the construction of the brand by putting it to work for their own purposes in their own world. When we called them "consumers" we could think of our creations as an end game and their responses as an end state. The term "multiplier" or something like it makes it clear that we depend on them to complete the work. (McCracken 2005)

Push-button publishing, citizen journalism, and pro-amateur creative activities dominated early conceptions of the ways digitization would change media production. Newer, so-called "Web 2.0" companies integrate participatory components into their business plans. These activities run from feedback forums and beta-tests to inviting audiences to produce, tag, or remix content. Online services regularly collected under the banner of "Web 2.0" such as photosharing site Flickr, social networking sites MySpace and Facebook, and video uploading sites such as YouTube and Veoh, have built entire business plans on the back of user-generated content. Software companies engage users as beta-testers and co-creators of content (Banks 2002). Marketing departments build puzzles, scavenger hunts, and interactive components into websites and mixed-media campaigns to generate buzz around branded entertainment properties. Technological, cultural, and marketplace changes make such tactics a necessity.

Henry Jenkins (2006a) describes many of these changes in *Convergence Culture: Where Old and New Media Collide*. Convergence is understood here not as the bringing together of all media functions within a single device but rather as a cultural logic involving an ever more complex interplay across multiple channels of distribution. This convergence is being shaped both by media conglomerates' desires to exploit "synergies" between different divisions and consumer demands for media content where, when, and in what form they want it. Networked communities, as Pierre Levy (1997) has suggested, represent an alternative source of knowledge and power, intersecting but remaining autonomous from the transnational reach of consumer capitalism and the sovereignty of nation-states over their citizens. Web 2.0 companies incorporate and embrace (in Tim O'Reilly's (2005) terms, "harness") this collective intelligence rather than allowing it to exist as an independent source of consumer power and critique. The "remixability" of media content, shared platforms for the distribution of grassroots media, and the social networks that have grown up around media properties are reshaping audience expectations about the entertainment experience. Convergence culture brings with it a reconceptualization of the audience – how it is comprised, how it is courted, what it wants, and how to generate value from it.

There are many new labels for "the people formerly known as the audience" (Rosen 2006). Some call them (us, really) "loyals" (Jenkins 2006a), stressing the value of consumer commitment in an era of channel zapping. Some are calling them "media–actives" (Frank 2004), stressing a generational shift with young people expecting greater opportunities to reshape media content than their parents did. Some are calling them "prosumers" (Toffler 1980), suggesting that as consumers produce and circulate media, they are blurring the line between amateur and professional. Some are calling them "inspirational consumers" (Roberts 2004), "connectors" or "influencers," suggesting that some people play a more active role than others in shaping media flows. Grant McCracken (2005) calls them "multipliers," stressing their role in proliferating the values and meanings that get attached to particular brands. Each label describes audience practices related to, but significantly different from, the construction of the active audience within media and cultural studies' discussions in the 1970s and 1980s. To talk about participatory audiences now is to talk about how differently abled, differently resourced, and differently motivated media producers work in the same space. Consumption in a networked culture is a social rather than individualized practice.

Describing the productive consumption within collaborative projects such as the Wikipedia and online news sites, Axel Bruns (2007a; 2007b) introduces the concept of the "produser," a "hybrid user/producer" (2007a) involved in "the collaborative and continuous building and extending of existing content in the pursuit of further improvement" (2007b). Produsers contribute to the iterative improvement of goods and services, whether explicitly, in the form of online news sites (e.g., Slashdot, Digg) or knowledge projects (e.g., Wikipedia), or perhaps without their conscious knowledge, as happens when user purchase decisions contribute to Amazon's recommendation services.

Bruns (2007b) outlines four characteristics of produsage, describing a system built on community logics of re-use and permission rather than commercial logics of ownership and restriction. Produsage relies on the belief that with enough size and diversity, the community can achieve "more than a closed team of professionals." This community is flexibly organized and affords fluid participation. Not only do users move between status as producers and consumers, they participate as much as they are able to, depending on their skill, time, desire, interest, and knowledge. This fluidity reflects the ad hoc basis of

collective intelligence and the ways participatory audiences self-organize to achieve complex tasks. It also means the community is invested in the re-use and continued development of the "unfinished artifacts" it produces. Rather than commercial products, the fruits of produsage are open to iterative development and redevelopment. As such, produsage privileges what Bruns describes as "permissive regimes of engagement," where artifacts are licensed under copyright schemes that allow community redevelopment but prohibit commercial uses, especially those that close off these development rights.

Just as Bruns' category of the produser suggests a blurring of the role of producer and user, these trends also suggest a blurring of the historic distinction between fan and "average" consumer. As the web has made fan culture more accessible to a larger public and as digital tools have made it easier to perform such activities, a growing proportion of the population now engages in what might once have been described as fannish modes of consumption. Describing pyramids of participation, some commentators note that the most labor intensive activities are still performed by a self-selected few, while more casual modes of participation extend to a larger population (Horowitz 2006; Koster 2006).

While Bruns links produsage to collaborative news gathering, citizen journalism, and the Free and Open Source Software (FOSS) movement, these core characteristics also describe fan behaviors around branded entertainment. Robert Kozinets (2007) uses the term "wikimedia" production to describe the behavior of *Star Trek* fan filmmakers, who, in backyards, basements, and homemade studios, have been creating and distributing unofficial "episodes" using high-quality equipment and state-of-the-art special effects. *Star Trek: New Voyages*, for example, hopes to complete the original Enterprise's intended five-year mission (cut short after three seasons) while others raise questions not addressed on the air (including, for example, satisfying a longstanding but never fulfilled promise of explicitly queer characters). Kozinets compares this production process, where fans add not only to the original text but also correct, comment on, and contribute to other fan productions, to the collaborative process that is generating Wikipedia, a user-built online encyclopedia.

Wikimedia is the application of an open source model to branded entertainment – often operating outside but in dialogue with the processes that generate commercial culture (Kozinets 2007, 198).

These "collaborative media creators," like produsers, are motivated by a desire to enrich the community of fellow fans. In doing so, Kozinets argues they are also promoting the *Star Trek* brand, strengthening and prolonging its market value. Looking toward the future, these amateur productions are also providing a training ground from which writers, directors, and producers of any future *Star Trek* series might be recruited. Something similar occurred around the British television series, *Doctor Who*, which was off the air for more than a decade but rebounded, in part, based on talent recruited from the fan community (Jenkins 2006d; Perryman 2008). Several of these fan media productions have involved active collaboration with the original creators (actors, writers, and technical crew) from the official *Star Trek* franchise. Kozinet's description of *Star Trek* fan cinema challenges the ways that fans have been depicted both within the political economy tradition (as passive consumers of mass-generated content rather than as active participants in cultural production and circulation) and within the cultural studies tradition (as autonomous or resistant subcultures rather than as collaborators with commercial shareholders).

The Value of Engagement and Participation
• •

> Corporations will allow the public to participate in the construction and representation of their creations or they will, eventually, compromise the commercial value of their properties. The new consumer will help to create value or they will refuse it … Corporations have a right to keep copyright but they have an interest in releasing it. (McCracken 1997)

At the most basic level, the distribution and publicity mechanisms of networked computing renders visible the often "invisible" labor fans perform in supporting their favorite properties. Fans act as "grassroots intermediaries," shaping the circulation of media content

at a moment when the industry is concerned about market fragmentation. The result has been a revaluing of fan loyalty and participation based on "affective economics" (Jenkins 2006a). Older audience measurements were based on the concept of "impressions," counting the number of eyeballs watching a particular program at a particular time. Scaling up via samples said to be statistically significant, this counting determined the potential number of people exposed to advertisements. An impressions model assesses the frequency of exposure and contexts where ads are placed. Over time, "impressions" have been supplemented by demographic measurements, seeking more precise information about the kinds of viewers watching particular programs, given that different "demos" hold different value for different brands.

These same companies now search for signs of audience activity and "engagement." For example, research done by Initiative Media found that less than 10 percent of the viewers of most network television shows regard the program to be a favorite, while some shows – especially cult programs – are regarded as top choices by as many as 50 percent of their viewers (as described in Jenkins 2006a). The research, further developed through a close study of viewers of *American Idol*, suggests that viewers watching a favorite series were twice as likely as more casual viewers to pay attention to advertisements, less likely to switch channels during commercial breaks, and had significantly higher brand recall. Almost half of loyal *American Idol* viewers search the web for more information about the show and thus had more extensive exposure to affiliated brand messages. The researchers advised their industry clients that a show with a high level of engagement may be a better investment than a program with higher overall ratings but only superficial audience interest.

Under this model, the value of consumer loyalty is still being read primarily in relation to traditional consumption roles: watching television programs and purchasing advertised products. Other companies push further, developing feedback mechanisms that tap consumers' individual and collective insights to refine the production process. In his book *Democratizing Innovation*, Eric Von Hippel (2005) describes how manufacturers have enabled low-cost innovation by closely engaging with their "lead users." The earliest adopters frequently adapt products to their particular needs and interests. By incorporating these "lead users" into the design process, Von Hippel argues, companies can discover new and unanticipated uses for their products or locate untapped markets. Von Hippel talks about the emergence of an "innovation commons" as companies monitor social networks for user insights. "Crowdsourcing" constitutes a more formalized version of the innovation commons: companies such as Threadless, iStockphoto, and InnoCentive solicit design ideas from their consumers, using their online community to weight their attractiveness, and sharing revenue with the amateur creators whose products the companies produce and distribute (Brabham 2008).

While Von Hippel writes about manufacturing processes, similar practices occur within the creative industries. Historically, fan cultures have most often involved what the industry regarded as "fringe viewers" who fell outside of the desired demographic – for example, the most active reworking of program content came from female fans of action-adventure series or adult fans of children's culture (Ford et al. 2006). Increasingly, more sophisticated companies pay attention to such "surplus" consumers because they represent ways of extending their potential market. Modest shifts in the program content, for example, spending more time on a beloved secondary character or adding more serial elements, can broaden interest while spin-off products sometimes directly target these consumers. Similarly, some video game companies (Jenkins 2006a) allow player access to development tools, resulting in a "mod" culture where amateur designers produce and circulate "skins" for characters, new levels of game play, or animated films (machinima). Mods provide a low-cost, minimal risk way of determining what refinements might generate consumer interests. Minimally, these practices extend the shelf life of the original products (since the amateur content can only be played with the original software) and in some cases, these companies have hired these amateur designers or contracted to distribute their mods as part of official expansion packs (Camper 2005).

Harnessing productive fans is not always so straightforward. Raph Koster, the man in charge of the development of the multiplayer game, *Star Wars Galaxies*,

incorporated the fans of George Lucas' science fiction saga as clients in the design process, making early specs for the game available via the web (Squire & Steinkuehler 2006; Jenkins 2006a). Koster's early courtship of these fans resulted in an immediate fan base when the game launched, but power struggles within the company (Jenkins 2006b) resulted in significant deviations from the recommended policies. Retooling the game in hopes of expanding its market, the company alienated the original players without generating new interest. Von Hippel (2005) acknowledges that the earliest adopters are not necessarily representative of the larger market and thus their insights need to be weighed carefully in predicting market interest. Moreover, incorporating users into the design process requires trust; companies risk alienation and backlash when they pull back from what consumers perceive as commitments.

In other cases, fans play curatorial roles. For example, American fans of Japanese anime grab content that has not yet been imported, circulating copies through an underground circuit with their own amateur subtitles. While some companies might shut down such "piracy," the Japanese companies watched this black market closely but allowed it to continue. These "fan-subbing" practices are credited with identifying properties with American appeal and educating consumers about unfamiliar genres (Leonard 2005; Jenkins 2006a). Commercial distributors often draw heavily on titles with fan bases established through underground circulation. In many cases, fans have stopped circulating their amateur versions to ensure a viable market (Hatcher 2005). Sam Ford and colleagues (2007) argue something similar has occurred among fans of American wrestling, where the underground circulation of wrestling tapes indicated a market for the World Wrestling Entertainment's archives.

Accordingly, *Wired* magazine editor-in-chief Chris Anderson's (2006) idea of the "long tail" has become a major preoccupation within the creative industries. Drawing on examples such as Amazon, Netflix, and iTunes, Anderson argues that rather than focusing primarily on a small number of expensive properties with generalized viewership, media producers should produce and distribute lower-cost materials that may appeal to a range of niche audiences. While most physical stores can only stock those titles that quickly move units, online distribution can sustain a vast backlist. Anderson argues that the "long tail" of storehouse titles will collectively generate greater revenue than the most popular titles. Anderson's model suggests profit from niche markets depends on lowering promotional expenses (by relying more heavily on "buzz" from impassioned and empowered consumers) and distribution costs (through online exchanges). MySpace represents a good example of how this process works: the social network site is a favorite among bands – big and small – who want to identify and get information out to their most hardcore fans; here fans form "friend" groups, whose music they like, and then pass cuts along to their friends. Bands, in turn, use their sites to get word out about concerts or allow fans to sample new releases. Similar ideas have been embraced by independent media producers of all kinds. For example, the producers of the independent film, *Four Eyed Monsters*, have used a range of different Web 2.0 platforms to generate public awareness of their production (Jenkins 2007b). They have, for example, encouraged potential viewers to register their interest in seeing the film. As they identify sufficient numbers of interested viewers in any given locale, they solicit exhibitors, demonstrating a ready market in their area.

If media companies were monitoring fan conversations, they still did not necessarily understand what they were hearing. In mid-2006, New Line Cinema responded to online anticipation for B-grade horror-thriller *Snakes on a Plane*. Based on fan feedback, the film went back into production six months after principal photography had concluded to re-shoot scenes to up the film's rating to an R (from PG-13) and add dialogue that emerged from fan discussions. Most famously, star Samuel L. Jackson delivered the line, "I've had it with these motherfucking snakes on this motherfucking plane," which originated in a popular Internet parody. Taking a hands-off approach to fan use of *Snakes* intellectual property (IP), the studio showcased mash-up trailers, artwork, and t-shirts through the official website and relied heavily on the buzz rather than critics' previews or expensive marketing campaigns to "open" the movie. This online buzz generated its own interest, both online and off, setting up high box-office expectations.

When it failed to deliver a blockbuster opening, *Snakes* was quickly declared a bomb. This measurement of achievement, however, seems a narrow assessment of its success. While domestic box office did not match inflated expectations, the energy around the property created by grassroots intermediaries produced pre- and post-opening revenue streams in the form of marketing, merchandising, and ad-sales opportunities that a B-grade film like *Snakes* might not be expected to generate, and, as Jenkins (2006c) notes, a significant measure of the film's success will come further down the tail as *Snakes* succeeds or fails to generate more revenues as it is released on DVD or shown by campus film societies. The media confused the Internet fan following for a focus group, expecting it to scale out across the general population, rather than trying to understand the committed niche audience it attracted. Accounting for its success as a cultural phenomenon requires a more nuanced mode of measurement than box-office revenue.

In each of these examples, companies are reappraising the value of fan engagement and participation – in some cases, openly collaborating with fans and in others, allowing fans some free space to repurpose their content toward their own ends. Yet each also suggests potential conflicts since fan and corporate interests are never perfectly aligned.

Prohibitionists and the Moral Economy

> Our entire cultural economy is in dire straights … We will live to see the bulk of our music coming from amateur garage bands, our movies and television from glorified YouTubes, and our news made up of hyperactive celebrity gossip, served up as mere dressing for advertising. (Keen 2007)

Despite the apparent long-term necessity of the entertainment industry reshaping its relations with consumers (both in the face of new technological realities that make preserving traditional control over content difficult and because new models of consumer relations stress collaboration with users), media executives remain risk-averse. Andrew Currah

(2006) argues that the reluctance of studio executives to risk short-term revenue gains accounts for their reticence to experiment with alternative content distribution models despite a growing bank of data that suggests some forms of legal file sharing would be in the industry's long-term best interests. Many executives at public companies are paid to draw incremental increases in revenue from mature markets rather than to adopt more long-ranging or entrepreneurial perspectives. New ventures might violate agreements media producers maintain with big-box retailers, decrease revenues from established markets (DVD, PPV), or spoil the balance of release windows and the geographic management of content distribution. According to Currah (2006, 461–3), the executives best placed to authorize such changes are not likely to be around to see the long-range benefits and thus they opt for the stability and predictability of the status quo.

Both industry leaders and creative workers worry about a loss of control as they grant audiences a more active role in the design, circulation, and promotion of media content; they see relations between consumers and producers as a zero-sum game where one party gains at the expense of the other. For the creative, the fear is a corruption of their artistic integrity, according to what Mark Deuze (2006) calls an editorial logic (where decisions are governed by the development and maintenance of reputations within the professional community). For the business side, the greatest fear is the idea that consumers might take something they made and not pay them for it, according to a market logic (where decisions are governed by the desire to expand markets and maximize profits). A series of lawsuits that have criminalized once normative consumer practices have further inflamed relations between consumers and producers.

If the hope that consumers will generate value around cultural properties has fueled the collaborationist logic, these tensions between producers and consumers motivate the prohibitionist approach. If the collaborationist approach welcomes fans as potential allies, the prohibitionist approach sees fans as a threat to their control over the circulation of, and production of meaning around, their content. Consumers are read as "pirates" whose acts of repurposing and recirculation constitute theft. The prohi-

bitionist approach seeks to restrict participation, pushing it from public view. The prohibitionist response needs to be understood in the context of a renegotiation of the moral economy that shapes relations between media producers and consumers.

The economic and social historian E. P. Thompson (1971) introduced the concept of "moral economy" in his work on eighteenth-century food riots, arguing that where the public challenges landowners, their actions are typically shaped by some "legitimizing notion." He explains, "The men and women in the crowd were informed by the belief that they were defending traditional rights and customs; and in general, that they were supported by the wider consensus of the community." In other words, the relations between landowners and peasants, or for that matter, between contemporary media producers and consumers, reflect the perceived moral and social value of those transactions. All participants need to feel that the involved parties behave in a morally appropriate fashion.

Jenkins (1992) introduced this concept of "moral economy" into fan studies, exploring the ways that fan fiction writers legitimate their appropriation of series content. Through their online communication, fan communities develop a firm consensus about the "moral economy"; this consensus provides a strong motivation for them to speak out against media producers who they feel are "exploiting" their relationship or damaging the franchise. The growing popularity of illegal downloads among music consumers, for example, reflects the oft-spoken belief that the record labels are "ripping off" consumers and artists alike through inflated prices and poor contractual terms. The controversy surrounding FanLib spread so rapidly because the fan community already had a well articulated understanding of what constituted appropriate use of borrowed materials. Fans objected to profiting from fan fictions both because they saw their work as gifts that circulated freely within a community of fellow fans, and because they believed rights holders were more apt to take legal action to shut down their activities if money was changing hands (Jenkins 2007a).

In a review of the concept of the "moral economy" in the context of a discussion of digital rights management, Alec Austin and colleagues (2006) write, "Thompson's work suggested that uprisings (or audience resistance) was most likely to occur when powerful economic players try to shift from existing rights and practices and towards some new economic regime. As they do so, these players seem to take away 'rights' or rework relationships which were taken for granted by others involved in those transactions." A period of abrupt technological and economic transition destabilizes relations between media producers and consumers. Consumers defend perceived rights and practices long taken for granted, such as the production and circulation of "mix tapes," while corporations try to police behaviors such as file sharing, which they see as occurring on a larger scale and having a much larger public impact. Both sides suspect the other of exploiting the instability created by shifts in the media infrastructure.

This moral economy includes not simply economic and social obligations between producers and consumers but also social obligations to other consumers. As Ian Condry (2004) explains, "Unlike underwear or swim suits, music falls into the category of things you are normally obligated to share with your dorm mates, family, and friends. Yet to date, people who share music files are primarily represented in media and business settings as selfish, improperly socialized people who simply want to get something – the fruits of other people's labor – for free." Industry discourse depicting file sharers (or downloaders, depending on your frame of reference) as selfish does not fully acknowledge the willingness of supporters to spend their own time and money to facilitate the circulation of valued content, whether in the form of a "mix tape" given to one person or a website with sound files that can be downloaded by any and all. Enthusiasts face these costs in hopes that their actions will generate greater interest in the music they love and that sharing music may reinforce their ties to other consumers. Condry says he finds it difficult to identify any moral argument against file sharing that young people find convincing, yet he has been able to identify a range of reasons why people might voluntarily choose to pay for certain content (to support a favorite group or increase the viability of marginalized genres of music). The solution may not be to criminalize file

sharing but rather to increase social ties between artists and fans.

Contemporary conflicts about intellectual property emerge when individual companies or industries shift abruptly between collaborationist and prohibitionist models. Hector Postigo (2008) has documented growing tensions between game companies and modders when companies have sought to shut down modding projects that tread too closely on their own production plans or go in directions the rights holders did not approve. Because there has been so much discussion of the economic advantages of co-creation, modders often reject the moral and legal arguments for restraining their practice.

Some recent critics of Web 2.0 models deploy labor theory to talk about the activities of consumers within this new digital economy. The discourse of Web 2.0 provides few models for how to compensate fan communities for the value they generate. Audience members, it is assumed, participate because they get emotional and social rewards from their participation and thus neither want nor deserve economic compensation. Tiziana Terranova (2000) has offered a cogent critique of this set of economic relationships in her work on "free labor":

> Free labor is the moment where this knowledgeable consumption of culture is translated into productive activities that are pleasurably embraced and at the same time often shamelessly exploited ... The fruit of collective cultural labor has been not simply appropriated, but voluntarily channeled and controversially structured within capitalist business practices. (Terranova 2000)

On the other end of the spectrum fall writers like Andrew Keen (2007), who suggests that the unauthorized circulation of intellectual property through peer-to-peer networks and the free labor of fans and bloggers constitute a serious threat to the long-term viability of the creative industries. Here, it is audience activity that exceeds the moral economy. In his nightmarish scenario, professional editorial standards are giving way to mob rule, and the work of professional writers, performers, and media makers is being reduced to raw materials for the masses who show growing contempt for traditional expertise and disrespect for intellectual property rights. Keen concludes his book with a call to renew our commitment to older models of the moral economy, albeit ones that recognize the new digital realities: "The way to keep the recorded-music industry vibrant and support new bands and music is to be willing to support them with our dollars – to stop stealing the sweat of other people's creative labor" (Keen 2007, 188).

Terranova and others see the creative industries as damaging the moral economy through their expectations of "free" creative labor, while Keen sees the media audiences as destroying the moral economy through their expectations of "free" content. The sunny Web 2.0 rhetoric about constructing "an architecture for participation" papers over these conflicts, masking the set of choices and compromises that need to be made if a new moral economy is to emerge.

Final Thoughts

Rebuilding this trust relationship requires embracing, rather than resisting, the changes to the economic, social, and technological infrastructure we have described. The prohibitionist stance adopted by some companies and industry bodies denies the changed conditions in which the creative industries operate, trying to force participatory culture to conform to yesterday's business practices. While prohibitionist companies want to maintain broadcast-era patterns of control over content development and consumer relations, they hope to reap the benefits of the digital media space. NBC enjoyed the viral buzz that came with fans sharing the *Saturday Night Live* clip "Lazy Sunday" but issued a take-down notice to YouTube to ensure the only copies available online came from NBC's official site (within the proximity of their branding material and advertising) (Austin et al. 2006). The network's prohibition of file sharing reflects NBC's discomfort with YouTube drawing advertising revenue from consumer circulation of its content. While perhaps completely defensible within broadcast-era business logic, the decision ignored the ways that the spread of this content generated viewer interest in the broadcast series. For the network, the primary if not sole value of the content was as a commodity that could collect rents from

consumers and advertisers alike. In attempting to re-embed "Lazy Sunday" within the distribution logics of the broadcast era, locking down both the channel and context of its distribution, NBC also attempted to re-embed the clip within an older conception of audience impressions. Many viewers responded according to this same logic – skipping both commercials and content in favor of producers who offered them more favorable terms of participation.

Navigating through participatory culture requires a negotiation of the implicit social contract between media producers and consumers, balancing the commodity and cultural status of creative goods. While this complex balance has always shaped creative industries, NBC struck down their fans in order to resolve other business matters, such as their relationships with advertisers and affiliates, sacrificing the cultural status of creative goods for their commodity value. The alternative approach is to find ways to capitalize on the creative energies of participatory audiences. Mentos' successful management of the Mentos and soda videos that emerged online in 2006 represents a more collaborative approach. Noticing a fad around dropping Mentos mints into bottles of soda and filming the resulting eruption, Mentos permitted, supported, and eventually promoted the playful use of their intellectual property. Mentos could have issued cease-and-desist notices to regulate their brand's reputation, as FedEx did after a college student built a website featuring his dorm furniture made out of free FedEx boxes (Vranica & Terhune 2006). Instead, Mentos capitalized on the cultural capital its product had acquired, collaborating with audiences to construct a new brand image. Engaging and promoting fan engagement offers media companies a more positive outcome than attempting the wack-a-mole game of trying to quash grassroots appropriation wherever it arises. Doing so also brings corporations into direct contact with lead users, revealing new markets and unanticipated uses.

The renegotiation of the moral economy requires a commitment on the part of participatory audiences to respect intellectual property rights. We see the potential of rebuilding consumers' goodwill when anime fans cease circulating fan-subbed content when it is made commercially available or when gamers support companies that offer them access to modding tools. Collaborationist approaches recognize and respect consumer engagement while demanding respect in return. Working with and listening to engaged consumers can result in audiences who help to patrol intellectual property violations; though their investment may not be measured according to the same market logics as the production and distribution companies, fans are likewise invested in the success of creative content. In doing so, media companies not only acknowledge the cultural status of the commodities they create, they are also in a position to harness the passionate energies of fans.

Note

1   The Consortium is supported by MTV Networks, Turner Broadcasting, Yahoo! Inc., GSD&M's Idea City, and Fidelity Investments. These partners are provided with first access to research, in-house briefings, and white papers in return for their support. The Consortium also fields speakers in a variety of corporate and academic venues, and sponsors the Futures of Entertainment conference, which is accessible to the public. Podcasts of conference sessions are available at: www.convergenceculture.org/futuresofentertainment, accessed August 20, 2008.

References

Anderson, C. (2006) *The Long Tail: Why the Future of Business is Selling Less of More.* Hyperion, New York.

Austin, A., Jenkins, H., Green, J., Askwith, I., and Ford, S. (2006). Turning pirates into loyalists: the moral economy and an alternative response to file sharing. Report prepared for the members of the MIT Convergence Culture Consortium, Cambridge.

Banks, J. (2002) Gamers as co-creators: enlisting the virtual audience: a report from the net face. In Balnaves, M., O'Regan, T., and Sternberg, J. (eds.) *Mobilising the Audience.* University of Queensland Press, St. Lucia, Queensland, pp. 188–212.

Brabham, D. (2008) Crowdsourcing as a model for problem solving: an introduction and cases. *Convergence: The International Journal of Research into New Media Technologies* **14**, 75–90.

Bruns, A. (2007a) Produsage, generation C, and their effects on the democratic process. *Media in Transitions 5: Creativity, Ownership, and Collaboration in the Digital Age.* MIT Press, Cambridge. At web.mit.edu/comm-forum/mit5/papers/Bruns.pdf, accessed May 4, 2007.

Bruns, A. (2007b) Produsage: towards a broader framework for user-led content creation. *Creativity & Cognition Conference: Seeding Creativity: Tools, Media, and Environments*, Washington DC. At http://en.scientificcommons.org/21225069, accessed May 4, 2007.

Camper, B. (2005) Homebrew and the social construction of gaming: community, creativity and legal context of amateur game boy advance development. Thesis, Comparative Media Studies Program, MIT, Cambridge.

Condry, I. (2004) Cultures of music piracy: an ethnographic comparison of the US and Japan. *International Journal of Cultural Studies* **7**, 343–63.

Currah, A. (2006) Hollywood versus the Internet: the media and entertainment industries in a digital and networked economy. *Journal of Economic Geography* **6**, 439–68.

Deuze, M. (2006) Media Work and Institutional Logics. *Deuzeblog.* At http://deuze.blogspot.com/2006/07/media-work-institutional-logics.html, accessed June 20, 2007.

Fiske, J. (1989) *Understanding Popular Culture.* Routledge, New York.

Ford, S., Jenkins, H., and Green, J. (2007) Fandemonium: a tag team approach to enabling and mobilizing fans. Report prepared for the members of the MIT Convergence Culture Consortium, Cambridge.

Ford, S., Jenkins, H., McCracken, G., Shahani, P., Askwith, I., Long, G., and Vedrashko, I. (2006) Fanning the audience's flames: ten ways to embrace and cultivate fan communities. Report prepared for the members of the MIT Convergence Culture Consortium, Cambridge.

Frank, B. (2004) Changing media, changing audiences. Remarks at the MIT Communication Forum, Cambridge. At http://web.mit.edu/comm-forum/

forums/changing_audiences.html, accessed June 13, 2007.

Hatcher, J. S. (2005) Of otakus and fansubs: a critical look at anime online in light of current issues in copyright law. *Script-ed* **2**, 514–42.

Horowitz, B. (2006) Creators, synthesizers and consumers. *Elatable*, 17 February. At www.elatable.com/blog/?p=5, accessed August 20, 2008.

Jenkins, H. (1992) *Textual Poachers: Television Fans and Participatory Culture*. Routledge, New York.

Jenkins, H. (2006a) *Convergence Culture: Where Old and New Media Collide*. New York University Press, New York.

Jenkins, H. (2006b) So what happened to *Star Wars Galaxies*? *Confessions of an Aca-Fan*, 21 July. At www.henryjenkins.org/2006/07/so_what_happened_to_star_wars.html, accessed September 13, 2006.

Jenkins, H. (2006c) Snake eyes. *Confessions of an Aca-Fan*, 24 August. At www.henryjenkins.org/2006/08/snake_eyes.html, accessed September 12, 2006.

Jenkins, H. (2006d) Triumph of a time lord: an interview with Matt Hills. *Confessions of an Aca-Fan*, 28 September. At www.henryjenkins.org/2006/09/triumph_of_a_time_lord_part_on.html, accessed October 8, 2006.

Jenkins, H. (2007a) Transforming fan culture into user-generated content: the case of FanLib. *Confessions of an Aca-Fan*, 22 May. At www.henryjenkins.org/2007/05/transforming_fan_culture_into.html, accessed June 14, 2007.

Jenkins, H. (2007b) Four eyed monsters and collaborative curation. *Confessions of an Aca-Fan*, 19 February. At www.henryjenkins.org/2007/02/four_eyed_monsters_and_collabo.html, accessed June 27, 2007.

Keen, A. (2007) *The Cult of the Amateur: How the Democratization of the Digital World is Assaulting Our Economy, Our Culture, and Our Values*. Doubleday, New York.

Koster, R. (2006) User-created content. *Raph Koster's Website*, 20 June. At www.raphkoster.com/2006/06/20/user-created-content, accessed August 20, 2008.

Kozinets, R. (2007) Inno-tribes: *Star Trek* as wikimedia. In Cova, B., Kozinets, R., and Shankar, A. (eds.) *Consumer Tribes*. Elsevier, London, pp.194–211.

Leonard, S. (2005) Progress against the law: anime and fandom, with the key to the globalization of culture. *International Journal of Cultural Studies* **8**, 281–305.

Levy, P. (1997) *Collective Intelligence: Mankind's Emerging World in Cyberspace*. Plenum Trade, New York.

Levy, S. and Stone, B. (2006) The new wisdom of the web. *Newsweek*, 3 April, pp.46–53. At www.newsweek.com/id/45976, accessed August 20, 2008.

Li, X. (2007) Fanfic, Inc.: another look at FanLib.com (1 of 2). *C3 Weekly Update* [Internal newsletter of the Convergence Culture Consortium], 7 December.

McCracken, G. (1997) *Plenitude: Culture by Commotion*. Periph, Fluide, Toronto.

McCracken, G. (2005) "Consumers" or "multipliers": a new language for marketing? *This Blog Sits at the Intersection of Anthropology and Economics*, 10 November. At www.cultureby.com/trilogy/2005/11/consumers_or_mu.html, accessed June 27, 2007.

O'Reilly, T. (2005) What is Web 2.0? Design patterns and business models for the next generation of software. *O'Reilly*, 30 September. At www.oreillynet.com/pub/a/oreilly/tim/news/2005/09/30/what-is-web-20.html, accessed June 27, 2007.

Perryman, N. (2008) Doctor Who and the convergence of media: a case study in "transmedia storytelling." *Convergence: The International Journal of Research into New Media Technologies* **14**, 21–39.

Postigo, H. (2008) Video game appropriation through modifications: attitudes concerning intellectual property among modders and fans. *Convergence: The International Journal of Research into New Media Technologies* **14**, 59–74.

Roberts, K. (2004) *Lovemarks: The Future Beyond Brands*. Powerhouse Books, New York.

Rosen, J. (2006) The people formerly known as the audience. *PressThink*, 27 June. At http://journalism.nyu.edu/pubzone/weblogs/pressthink/2006/06/27/ppl_frmr.html, accessed June 8, 2007.

Scholz, T. and Lovink, G. (eds.) (2007) *The Art of Free Cooperation*. Autonomedia/Institute for Distributed Creativity.

Squire, K. D. and Steinkuehler, C. (2006) The genesis of "cyberculture": the case of *Star Wars Galaxies*. In Gibbs, D. and Krause, K. L. (eds.) *Cyberlines: Languages and Cultures of the Internet*, 2nd edn. James Nicholas, Albert Park, Australia, pp. 177–98.

Terranova, T. (2000) Free labor: producing culture for the digital economy. *Social Text* **63**, 33–58. At www.electronicbookreview.com/thread/techno-capitalism/voluntary, accessed August 20, 2008.

Thompson, E. P. (1971) The moral economy of the English crowd in the eighteenth century. *Past and Present* **50**, 76–136.

Toffler, A. (1980) *The Third Wave*. Collins, London.

Von Hippel, E. (2005) *Democratizing Innovation*. MIT Press, Cambridge.

Vranica, S. and Terhune, C. (2006) Mixing Diet Coke and Mentos makes a gusher of publicity. *Wall Street Journal*, 12 June. At http://online.wsj.com/public/article/SB115007602216777497-1mzdx_pOFlMB-wo9UAiqbsgY6MZ0_20060619.html?mod=blogs, accessed August 20, 2008.

Part IV

The Future: Four Visions

....

Editors' Introduction

....

This collection concludes with four distinctive outlooks on what the future of media industry studies might be. Despite their differing perspectives, each author underscores the importance of reassessing the ways we think, teach, and write about the media industries in the age of digital convergence. Throughout, there is a recognition that we are in the midst of a transitional, transformative moment in terms of the industrial structures, business models, narrative strategies, and relations between corporate interests and individual audience members/citizens/consumers/users. The ways that scholars ask questions, formulate new theories, design research programs, and connect to industry professionals are also in flux. All of the authors in this section recognize the possibilities new media forms offer for blending cultural and economic analysis in innovative ways.

The overarching tone in these essays is one of cautious optimism. The optimism comes from the perception that new media forms enable more democratic modes of communication, a rebalancing of power relations, renewed audience agency, and expanding notions of industrial parameters and definitions. However, there is also a note of caution here, as each contributor recognizes a number of ethical and moral issues likely to arise as business models continue to solidify.

John Hartley begins the section by challenging a number of longstanding assumptions about media industries scholarship. As a central figure in the formation of television studies, cultural studies, and "creative industries" scholarship, Hartley's take on the future is shaped by his rich background. In his essay, he indicates key ways in which work on the creative industries might intersect with media industry studies as it further develops. From his viewpoint, the rise of new, interactive media forms provides a means by which scholars can continue to move beyond the "culture industry" model formulated by the Frankfurt School so long ago. He problematizes the notion of "industry" itself, suggesting that the word's links to older conceptions of mass production and mass consumption help perpetuate outdated, linear-oriented sender–receiver models of communication. Instead, he argues for the value of thinking in terms of "social network markets," a phrase that transfers more authority and control to the "critical-creative citizen-consumer."

From Hartley's position, the increasing popularity of user-generated media represents a shift away from a supply model and centralized power structures and toward a demand model geared for knowledge acquisition. This model, in turn, not only presents the possibility of "new forms of polity, citizenship, and participation," but also the promise of greater digital literacy worldwide. He is careful to note, however, that this is an "emerging" model, not one that is dominant at this moment.

David Hesmondhalgh, a central architect of the "cultural industries" model, assesses the strengths and limitations of three prominent approaches that previously have been employed in the study of the media industries. In surveying what he describes as the "negative" examples of cultural economy, creative industries analysis, and the "Schiller–McChesney" version of political economy, he identifies core components of what media industry studies should be. He asserts that, as the discipline of media industry studies continues to develop, it needs to utilize social theory in the pursuit of empirically oriented analyses. Aware of the early and crucial stage at which media industry studies finds itself, Hesmondhalgh notes how important it is for scholars to have a strong historical foundation as well as an appreciation of the complexities and contradictions inherent in commercial media. These traits will keep researchers from being reductive in their analyses – analyses that should, he adds, further the goals of social justice.

In the following chapter, Jordan Levin offers a view from inside the media industries. Given his recent transition from "old" media (as CEO of the former WB broadcast network) to a prominent figure in the world of "new" media (as CEO of Generate), he is well positioned to speak first-hand about the rapid transformations shaping the contemporary landscape of entertainment. Levin considers the opportunities and challenges facing those working in the media industries today and maintains that media industry studies has the potential to provide a "sober and critically informed baseline" from which to assess the converging media environment. According to Levin, scholarly interventions during this time of dramatic change are best positioned from a perspective of interdisciplinarity, with equal emphasis placed on both the artistic and the commercial elements of media.

The book concludes with an essay by Peabody Awards director Horace Newcomb. In his position as an intermediary between the industry and the academy – as well as through his previous experiences as a scholar and screenwriter – Newcomb has interacted with the industry in multiple ways. These diverse experiences contribute to his call for specificity and clarity when researching and writing about the media industries. Echoing a recurring theme throughout this book, Newcomb maintains that the media industries defy broad generalizations and monolithic claims, and encourages scholars to be precise about "who" and "what" they are discussing when writing about "the industry." He makes the case for revisiting and refining past discussions of the relationship between structure and agency, with greater attention paid to the place that individuals have in the processes of cultural production.

Additionally, in arguing for "synthetic media industry research," Newcomb elaborates on ideas conveyed by many others in this collection: namely, that those shaping the boundaries of this nascent discipline retain a strong awareness of the fluidity, choices, and processes involved in making and distributing media texts. Whether as teachers and researchers of the media industries or as students and future employees of these industries, we find ourselves in a unique moment, one in which we can pause, closely evaluate, and critically assess contemporary changes – and, in the process, consider the potential interventions we might make to facilitate the outcomes we desire.

17

From the Consciousness Industry to the Creative Industries
Consumer-Created Content, Social Network Markets, and the Growth of Knowledge

John Hartley

Media Industry Studies: All Change?

According to *Time* magazine, 2006 was a tipping point; the year of "you" as in YouTube, the year of consumer-created content.[1] If this was a new reality for the media industries, what did it mean for "media industry studies"? I would argue that the field is overdue for a consumer makeover. For too long it has been dominated by top-down, ideologically motivated political economy approaches that have preserved the media effects paradigm ("what do media do to audiences?") well beyond its use-by date. In studies of media industries, too much attention has been paid to providers and firms, too little to consumers and markets. But with user-created content, the question first posed more than a generation ago by the uses and gratifications method and taken up by semiotics and the active audience tradition ("what do audiences do with media?") has resurfaced with renewed force. What's new is that where this question (of what the media industries and audiences did with each other) used to be individualist and functionalist, now, with the advent of social networks using Web 2.0 affordances, it can be re-posed at the level of systems and populations as well.

There is also new hope for integrating the study of economic and cultural systems and processes, which historically have been addressed by different academic disciplines. Now there is a chance to bring together, perhaps for the first time in a thoroughgoing way, the political economy and text/audience traditions; to unify the study of economic and cultural values in process of formation and change.

The industriousness of myriad creative users suggests that self-made media content has already disrupted the expert paradigm that dominated media production during the broadcast era. Is this a portent for industry in general? If so, then the YouTube generation is modeling the future of innovation and growth across the economy; and beyond into cultural and community contexts. In that case, "media industry studies" would provide a general public service if it were to devote itself to understanding emergent systems and values, both cultural and economic; if it focused on analyzing the process and dynamics of change directly. Such changes are leading the field beyond the study of "media power" toward that of the "growth of knowledge."

However, there remains a strong trace of ideological stand-off in much work on media industries: the pro-business spruikers of innovation (e.g., Beinhocker 2006; Leadbeater 2006) versus the anti-capitalist skeptics (Schiller 1989, 1992; Garnham 1990; McChesney & Nichols 2002, etc). Continuing problems carry through from the industrial or expert paradigm to the consumer or social network paradigm, and new problems demand urgent attention. These include both monopolistic tendencies (e.g., one supplier of content) and monopsonic tendencies (e.g., one buyer of labor) among existing and new media corporations; and the growing issue of "free labor" – the work put in by consumers and users as well as the conditions of employment in "media industries" (Terranova 2000). Nevertheless, such problems are not well understood using a technology of critique (as it were) that is based on *industry*; what is needed instead is one attuned to *information*. But taking this step changes the critical rules. As Tiziana Terranova (2004) puts it: "The cultural politics of information is no radical alternative that springs out of a negativity to confront a monolithic social technology of power. It is rather a *positive feedback effect* of informational cultures as such" (19).

The standard "critical" stance – "negativity to confront monolithic … power" – reminds us that the glass of media participation remains stubbornly half-empty. But it fails to account for how it came to be half-full. Critical analysis need not take sides, whether the slogan is Google's "You can make money without doing evil,"[2] or News Corp's simpler – and here I paraphrase – "Let's monetize that!" To dismiss both new media developments and their marketization is not only "critical" short-sightedness, it is also "industrial" suicide, as Peter Chernin, president and chief operating officer of News Corp pointed out to his industry colleagues:

> There are huge rewards for those who innovate, and death to those who do not … The knee-jerk reaction is to take pot-shots at what you don't understand. To dismiss user-generated content as crap and blogs as unauthoritative is not only unproductive but a waste of time. (Advanced-television.com 2007)[3]

So media industry studies needs a critical makeover, one that is forced upon it by changes in the external environment, both intellectual and industrial. It needs curiosity about change and growth, not an insistence on (rigid) structure and (residual) power.

Industry: Reality or Metaphor?

The problem lies not with the laudable effort to *study* "industries," but with the term "industry" itself.

In common with language in general, the social sciences and the humanities share a long history of borrowing metaphors from other domains to identify and describe their own object of study. Industry is one such term. However, like other metaphors of organizational scale – capitalism, society, culture, globalization – the name itself does not describe a necessary empirical fact on the ground. You can't stub your toe on an industry. Perhaps this is why in economics, a discipline that does have ambitions toward scientific and mathematical exactitude, "industry" is a derived term not a natural category. Firms produce goods or services, while "industries" are abstract aggregations of agents, prices, commodities, firms, transactions, markets, organizations, technologies, and institutions (Potts et al. 2008, MS 2). "Industry" is often used even more loosely, interchangeably with business, trade, market, or even community, as in "do you work in the industry?"[4] This doesn't mean that the term is useless or a lie; it means that it must be used with care, carrying with it a full trail of analytical explanation. But instead, media studies imported it as self-evident and as real, with connotations that endowed vertically integrated industrial corporations not only with moral qualities (chiefly evil), but also with exorbitant or "fabulous powers," as Ian Connell (1984) pointed out a generation ago. As a result, "the industry" – i.e., the media – is frequently described as having properties it cannot possess (e.g., consciousness), which in turn are soon personalized into barons, moguls, and assorted bêtes noires – Hearst, Berlusconi, Murdoch … Citizen Kane … stage villain. In general, the metaphor of industrial-scale agency carries with it connotations of power, control, hidden agendas, and the objectification of the consumer-audience, often provoking moralistic or ideological misgivings about wealth creation per se.

Industry is a modern term. Pre-modern and traditional societies did not have a word for it. It is borrowed from the Latin for "diligence," of the kind frequently attributed to ants. It originated in early modern English (in the 1500s) to describe individual actions: "intelligent or clever working; skill, ingenuity, dexterity, or cleverness in doing anything" (*Oxford English Dictionary*). In the nineteenth century it was applied metaphorically to large-scale systematic productive work and manufacture (as in "Captains of Industry"; an "Industrialist"); and in the twentieth century it was applied metaphorically again, to any "profitable practice" – the Shakespeare industry, the abortion industry – or to the industrialization of a country (these examples are from the *OED*).

This extrapolation, from individual "studied diligence" to the Industrial Revolution and thence to "organized exploitation," brought with it a model of a system. "Industry" henceforth required more than individual industriousness. The *system* couldn't work without spare money (capital), specialization (division of labor), new sources of energy (coal; steam), faster communications (railways; Reuters), machinery (cotton jenny), scale (manufactories; cities), an organized and disciplined labor force (the proletariat), and increasingly affluent consumers (their wives). Individual craftsmen were reduced to "labor," their value to that of "hands," and work itself from handiwork to repetitive routines, as satirized in Charlie Chaplin's *Modern Times* (1936). The twentieth century was marked by continuing ideological adversarialism (class war) in intellectual as well as industrial life, and so the concept of "industry" as a system never traveled far without this baggage. It was just such a vision of industrialization that was in the minds of those intellectuals, critics, and sociologists who contemplated what was called the "consciousness *industry*" and the "*industrialization* of the mind" (Enzensberger 1974); or the "*manufacture* of consent" (Herman & Chomsky 1988). When it came to "the media," therefore, it was almost inevitable that industry meant not "studied diligence" in the production and dissemination of meaningful representations, but "organized exploitation" on a society-wide scale, using bias, manipulation, and ideology rather than creativity, innovation, and dialogue.

Most of what goes on in the media "industries" is not captured in the industrial idea of the "production of goods." This is another extended metaphor. Media "content" is not a "good"; consumption is not what media audiences do. Consumption is in fact a pre-industrial, agricultural metaphor appropriate to foodstuffs, which are literally consumed. Cultural or symbolic "goods," like music, screen narratives, or printed stories, remain alive for indefinite reconsumption

(Garnham 1987; Lotman 1990). Furthermore, the "industry" label is not accurate for the myriad small or micro-businesses that drive the creation of novel content. Many performers and freelancers are more like itinerant traders than industrialists – Terranova (2004) dubs the open source movement "Internet tinkers." They operate in a market where the real "consumer" to date has been none other than the pre-Internet monopsonic "media industries." Musicians sell to record labels; moviemakers to film distributors; TV producers to networks. Creatives are organized into a market that services giant corporations. One result of this is a persistent tendency among the general public to treat creative intellectual property (IP) as a public good, resulting in the fascinating and still far from settled struggles over copyright, digital rights management, file sharing, plagiarism, and piracy on a mass scale.

The constellation of small independent traders selling creative services and "content" to distributors is often named metonymically after the district where the market is clustered: Hollywood, Tin Pan Alley, Wardour Street, Fleet Street, Silicon Valley, etc. Actually getting the general public to believe that there is such a thing as the media industry, say in the form of "Hollywood" (a derivative entity, having no real existence as such), by continuously "imagining" or "inventing" it in the textual form of news, previews, insider gossip, branding, and the like, takes a fair amount of corporate marketing and government effort, as John Caldwell (2006) has pointed out. With Web 2.0, more people are asking whether creativity itself, and also entrepreneurship, are well served by filtering consumer demand through such lumbering metaphors, or whether it might be possible to reconfigure the relationship between producer and consumer on more equal terms. In practice, that means reinventing the market, which is going on now.

From Industry to (Social Network) Markets

Despite the ill-fitting metaphors, the commonsensical idea of "industry" suited mass-circulation press and broadcasting well enough, because it was easy to imagine mass communication itself by using yet another metaphor, one that united abstract ideas like "communication" and "industry" with a real thing like wire. Thus industrial production and communication have both been imagined as one-way, with meanings and "content" proceeding along the value chain as signals do along a cable, as in Claude Shannon's (1948) foundational model that served the field for 50 years. However, the rise of interactive technologies during the Clinton presidency, and the extensive sharing of self-made media thereafter, meant that we could see how contemporary technologies and media might be used for two-way and peer-to-peer social network communication. Instead of an industry doing things *to* people, here was a market where things are done *by* people. Instead of being represented by the media, or being subjected to the media's own representations, people could self-represent. Transmission went both ways. Popular audiences began to revert from their "industrial" or passive status as the "objects" of mass communication to their original "communicative" status as its agent. They were the source not the destination of mediated meanings (Hartley 2008).

To account for this, an alternative model of communications was already at hand. The idea of the distributed network was independently developed by the Anglo-Welsh computer pioneer Donald Davies, who came up with the term "packet switching,"[5] and the Polish-American electrical engineer Paul Baran (1964), leading to the earliest visualization of the Internet (Barabási 2002, 143–5). The change in perspective from Shannon to Baran was important. It shifted attention away from a command system based on centralized control. This had perhaps unwittingly encouraged a kind of colonialist or imperialist view of industry, where consumers are atomized "subjects" or effects of causes located elsewhere, "always already" (in the paranoid lingo; Althusser 1971) positioned in a structure where they have no generative capability of their own; they were effects of power. Instead of this, in a coordinated market, consumers could be imagined as being able to "make a deal" – to agree on an exchange that may also require a continuing relationship – based on some level of calculation of advantage to themselves,

as well as paying money or attention to the provider. It is a two-way transaction (dialogue) in a complex network of choices (meaning system).[6]

During the industrial era, profit was generated by investment in the means of production (the Fordist/Taylorite factory system). Even in this period, the media were not standard "industries," because the locus of power and profit in the "culture industries" was not production but distribution (Garnham 1987). Since the dispersal of massive computing power into the consumer environment from the 1990s onward, however, distribution itself has transformed. Even though the TV and media giants are still active, and audiences still watch much more TV than they make for themselves, the "broadcasting model" of one-way communication, *from* a powerful central agency *to* dispersed and mutually disconnected passive consumers, is giving way at unprecedented pace to a "broadband model." Here consumers are linked in social networks, and productive energy can come from anywhere in the system. Thus what *Time* magazine called "a story about community and collaboration on a scale never seen before" – the story of "you"[7] – is modeling new forms of polity, citizenship, and participation for the economic/cultural system as a whole.

The Creative Industries Concept

Whether user-created content is critiqued as a corporate ruse or celebrated as an opportunity for "digital democracy" – whether you see a glass half-empty or half-full – the fact remains that the rise of self-made media poses important questions for media industry studies. A rethink of the metaphor of "industry" is in order, to include all the agents involved in the system, not just inherited corporate structures. It is also time to abandon the assumption that causation and communication flow one way only, and to take seriously the agency of the critical-creative citizen-consumer within an overall system in which major enterprises are also at work.

The place where this rethink seems to have progressed most energetically in recent years is in the new field of "creative industries" (Hartley 2005). The issues raised in the attempt to identify and explain the creative industries are of significance to media industry studies, because the creative industries are located at the very place where new values, both economic and cultural, new knowledge, and new forms of social relationship are emergent, and where they are in process of society-wide adoption and retention, often through market mechanisms. It may even be argued that the "creative industries" are the empirical form taken by innovation in advanced knowledge-based economies, in which case their importance – like that of the media – exceeds their scale as a sector of the economy. It extends to their role as a general enabling social technology. This would place *creative innovation* on a par with other enabling social technologies like the law, science, and markets. Where the media (in the guise of "cultural industries") were regarded as the social technology of ideological control in the modern industrial era, the creative industries may be regarded as the social technology of distributed innovation in the era of knowledge-based complex systems.

However, such a role was not clear from the outset. The idea of the "creative industries" had to evolve in practice. Moreover it seems to be evolving "sideways" as well as through time; it replicates across several different domains, for instance the arts, the media, and information systems. Successive phases have generated a characteristic economic model and policy response in each domain (Cunningham et al. 2008), see table 17.1.

Unlike biological evolution, but like the evolution of culture (Lotman 1990), earlier forms do not suffer extinction. They are supplemented not supplanted by their successors. Their co-presence can be ordered dynamically, along the lines proposed by Raymond Williams (1973) for culture itself, which

he saw as both "ordinary" (population-wide not "high culture") and as "whole way of life" (a system not a value). His dynamic schema was: residual, dominant, and emergent culture. Thus:

- Creative industries as art – generates a negative economic model. Here creativity is a domain of market failure. Art requires subsidy from the rest of the economy. The policy response is therefore a "welfare" model. This corresponds to a "residual" dynamic of culture.
- Creative industries as media and industry – generates a neutral economic model. Media and industries require no special policy attention other than "competition" policy. This corresponds to "dominant" culture.
- Creative industries as knowledge (both market and culture) – generates a positive, or an "emergent" economic model. Here the creative industries are indeed a special case, because they can be seen as the locus for evolutionary growth at the fuzzy boundary between (cultural) social networks and (economic) enterprise, where markets play a crucial role in coordinating the adoption and retention of novelty as knowledge. They require "growth" and "innovation" policy. This corresponds to "emergent" culture (Potts & Cunningham 2008).

The positive (3) or emergent (4) models of a creative economy have only recently been identified and theorized, and are not yet properly "crunched" in terms of statistical testing. Thus the growth and innovation policy responses themselves remain for the time being emergent approaches to the place and significance of creative innovation in a social totality characterized by growth, dynamism, change,

Table 17.1 The "creative economy": evolving sideways (co-present concepts and models of creative industries)

Creative form	Art, Individual	Media, Industry	Knowledge, Market/Culture
Model of culture	Residual	Dominant	Emergent
Economic model	(1) Negative	(2) Neutral	(3) Positive
			(4) Emergent
Policy response	"Welfare"	"Competition"	"Growth"
			"Innovation"

Table 17.2 The "creative industries": evolving through time (successive phases)

Phase	Form	Value-add	Innovation/change agent
Enlightenment/Modernism	Art/Reason	Individual talent	Civic humanism
Industrialization	Media	Industry scale	Cultural industries
Creative Industries 1 (1995–2005)	Industry	IP outputs	Creative clusters
Creative Industries 2 (now)	Market	Inputs (economy)	Services
Creative Industries 3 (emergent)	Knowledge culture	Human capital (workforce/user)	Citizen-consumers

and technologically enabled networks on a global scale. If this approach is on the right track, however, it shows that the very term "industry" is bound to a rapidly obsolescing paradigm, which is associated with a particular economic model and policy response, neither of which is appropriate for current circumstances. Here, instead of "industry," a better term is "market," in which agents with considerable freedom of choice or flexibility of action make a deal in which something is exchanged (money, attention, connectivity, ideas) for mutual benefit.

After a long, slow build-up, going back to the Enlightenment (Hartley 2005, 6–26), the "creative industries" burst upon the scene in the 1990s. Since then they have evolved much faster, going through three distinct phases (table 17.2). Each phase shows how a different cultural/economic form is thought to add value in a different way, with a different conceptualization of the agents of change and dynamism in the system. The concept of creative industries co-evolved with the practice, so the refinement of the model has been as much lived as theorized: it is the product of experience and benefits from the feedback effects of learning.

Phase 1: Industry, outputs, clusters

The creative industries were first mapped by the UK government's Department of Culture, Media and Sport (DCMS). In this first phase, attention was focused on the term "industry" itself, referring to firms whose *outputs* could be construed as creative:

The creative industries are those industries that are based on individual creativity, skill and talent. They are also those that have the potential to create wealth and jobs through developing intellectual property.

The creative industries include: Advertising, Film and video, Architecture, Music, Art and antiques markets, Performing arts, Computer and video games, Publishing, Crafts, Software, Design, Television and radio, Designer fashion.[8]

There has been continuing disagreement about what should be included. It has arisen from problems of scale (global corporations and sole traders in the same category); coherence (what is the unity of "product" among different creative industries?); scope (potential arbitrariness about what is included and what excluded); economic impact (creativity is dispersed across economic sectors, regions, occupations); and finally, the tendency to neglect the productive role of consumers, users, and non-market agencies. Rather than solving these problems conceptually, however, policymakers plumped for Michael Porter's cluster theory, seeking to identify "cultural quarters" (Roodhouse 2006; but see Oakley & Knell 2007), especially in deindustrializing cities that were redeveloping from centers of production to centers of consumption (tourism, retail, administration, and leisure).

It was also argued that creative industries were growing faster than other sectors, claiming extra dynamism for those associated with digital technologies. UK estimates made them worth £112.5 billion in 2001. Variously defined, the creative industries were said to be nearing 10 percent of the economy in the UK (2006),[9] and $819 billion or 6.56 percent of GDP in the US (2005).[10] In the UK they contributed more than 4 percent of export income and provided jobs for over 2 million people.[11] Estimates put the world market at over $3.04 trillion (2005). By 2020, according to WIPO, the UN's intellectual property agency, this sector will be worth $6.1 trillion.[12]

Phase 2: Market, inputs, services

In the second phase, attention widened from creative outputs to the economy as a whole, in order to identify the extent to which creative *inputs* were adding value to firms not otherwise regarded as creative, especially in the *services* sector, for instance government, health, education, tourism, financial services, etc. Creative disciplines, such as design, performance, production, and writing, add value to such services. However, it is hard to isolate and quantify the value added, not least because of the way that industry-based economic statistics are collected and organized. Recent estimates suggest that one-third of those in creative occupations are "embedded" in other sectors (Higgs et al. 2008).

Phase 3: Knowledge culture, human capital, citizen-consumers

The third phase is convergent with the extension of digital media into popular culture. The rise of so-called *user-created content* (OECD 2007) has drawn attention to the extent to which innovation, change, and growth are attributable not to firms alone, but also to *socially networked consumers*, and to non-market activities or "scenes" that escape traditional economic categories entirely. This phase challenges the closed industrial system of professional expertise, favoring instead the growth of "complex open networks" in which creative IP is shared, not controlled.

Creative Industries: Tested to Destruction?

First-player advantage for DCMS meant that its "cluster" definition captured the attention of policymakers around the world (more slowly in the US). Early adopters included many in the Asia-Pacific region, including Hong Kong, Taiwan, Singapore, Australia, New Zealand, and city governments such as Shanghai and Beijing in Mainland China. They adapted the DCMS template to regional realities. Among the best of these is Desmond Hui's report for Hong Kong (CCPR 2003).

Having captured everyone's attention without being conceptually robust, the "cluster" model required refinement. A sophisticated attempt was made by NESTA (National Endowment for Science, Technology and the Arts), which rejected the original DCMS definition in order to reinstate the industry metaphor: the creative industries seen as "industrial sectors rather than as a set of creative activities based on individual talent" (NESTA 2006). The NESTA model "clustered" the creative industries by the type of activity and organization characteristic of firms. It did not identify such clusters with specific geographic locations such as London.

Although the NESTA approach combines phases 1 and 2 by adding "service providers," the limitations of the word "industry" only become clearer. The creative industries remain firmly in the dominant or neutral economic model for which "competition" policy is the only real recourse.[13] It is hard to claim any exceptional status for them beyond their importance to global cities. Under this definition, they remain an esoteric niche of enterprises unified only by drawing a big circle around incommensurate but overlapping activities:

- media content;
- "experiences" (content you can walk into, like concerts, galleries, parks);
- "originals" (unscalable arts and crafts); and
- creative services (inputs to other firms; or facilities for rent).

It is hard to extend that idea to the economy in general. However, the political pressure to generalize from "creative industries" to "creative economy" was already apparent. The culture minister, Tessa Jowell, announced in 2005 that:

> Every industry must look to become a creative industry, in the broadest sense of the word … The increasing array of new and exciting ways to access creative content clearly demonstrates that industry is responding to the needs and expectations of consumers. But these are not just creative industries issues. They are issues for everyone who has a stake in the future of our knowledge economy.[14]

This remained UK policy after the change to Gordon Brown's government – you may even say in the teeth of their own evidence:

> Today there is growing recognition of the subtle but important linkages between the vitality of the creative core, the creative industries beyond and creativity in the wider economy – although uncovering their exact extent is made very difficult because of a paucity of evidence and data.[15]

Supply to Demand

Since they stem from the same policymaking environment, a static model of the economy, and a "residual" definition of art, the DCMS and NESTA approaches conceptualize the economy and artistic creativity alike in terms of the *provider*; even as they evolve from phase 1 (clusters) to phase 2 (services), and even as they recognize "the evolution of experience-searching, so-called "apex" consumers … and co-creation with consumers" (Hutton 2007, 96). Despite this gesture, there is no room for consumers *inside* the model. Industry continues to mean the supply side of firms or institutions or artists, with no attention to consumers, users, or creative individuals, who are seen as an effect of decisions taken by those further up the supply chain, or closer to the "core," with little causal agency of their own. This provider mentality is supported by the "residual" model of art,[16] see figure 17.1.

Instead of this, it is now possible to propose a *demand* model of creativity in an evolutionary model of the economy. This sees creative culture in terms of the growth of knowledge among the entire population, not merely among industry or artistic experts. Instead of being the *objects* of causal sequence, consumers, users, and citizens become its *subject*, navigating as agents, not being pushed around as passive effects, see figure 17.2.

This model pushes out toward the future, not the past; it is an "emergent" model of innovation. Here creativity may be located as part of "human capital." The provider/demand diagrams are of heuristic value only, of course: in reality the arrows always go both ways, see figure 17.3.

Social Network Markets

Seen this way, the evolution of the creative industries does allow us to make a significant conceptual advance; one based on evolutionary economics (Beinhocker 2006), and taking seriously the dynamics of change and innovation, the emergence of

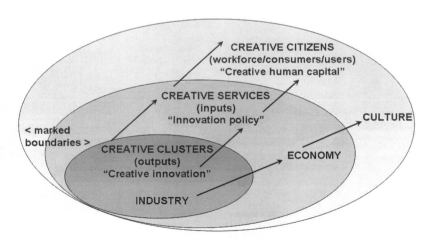

Figure 17.1 Provider model of creative causation

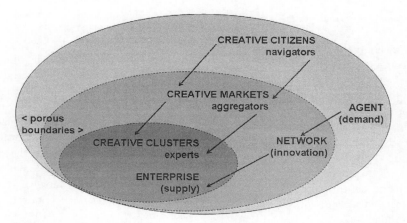

Figure 17.2 Demand model of creative causation

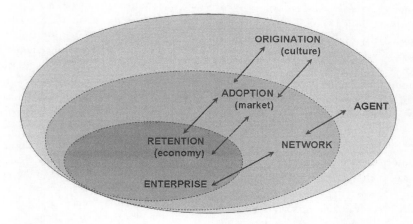

Figure 17.3 Interactive model of knowledge growth

order in complex systems, and the possibility that both economic and cultural "behavior" may be explained using game theory and complexity theory (see Dopfer & Potts 2007). In this environment, the object of the exercise is to understand the *origination, adoption, and retention of knowledge*, not simply to critique the activities of firms. Indeed, focusing on "industry" has been part of the problem. A better term than "industry" is "market," specifically "social network markets" (Potts et al. 2008). For one thing, it shifts causal sequence from a supply-driven to a demand-driven dynamic. A demand-led model of creative citizen-navigators requires a reformulation of the familiar "value chain" approach to cultural

production, which typically follows a one-way Shannonian logic of causation, like this:

1 producer (creation) and production (manufacture);
2 commodity (e.g., text, IP) and distribution (via media);
3 consumer or audience (but see Pratt 2004).[17]

Instead what is needed is:

1 agents (*origination*), who may be individuals or firms, characterized by choice, decision-making and learning;

2   networks (*adoption*), both real (social) and virtual (digital);
3   enterprise (*retention*), market-based organizations and coordinating institutions (Potts et al. 2008).

And instead of linear causation, what is needed is a dynamic and productive interrelationship among agents, networks, and enterprise; all are engaged in the mutual enterprise of creating values, both symbolic and economic. This is a complex open system in which everyone is an active agent, not a closed expert value chain controlled by "industry." Individuals originate ideas; networks adopt them; enterprises retain them.

This is the concept of the creative industries as a social network market, the special property of which is that *individual choices are determined by the choices of others within the network.* This is not a difficult concept to grasp; essentially it is Richard Lanham's (2006) "economics of attention." A social network market is at work whenever you read a review or heed "word of mouth" before trying a film, restaurant, or novelty of any kind. It operates when you value fashion over intrinsic worth. It explains celebrity culture; tastes and identities are formed on the basis of the choices of others. It underlies "aggregator" social network enterprises on the Internet such as Facebook, MySpace, even YouTube and Amazon, all of which operate by networking individual choices.

Social networks are a valuable adaptive mechanism for dealing with uncertainty, risk, and novelty at the macro-scale of populations and systems, even while they are driven by micro-scale individual choices. They occupy the border between established markets (economy) and non-market dynamics (culture), especially via Web 2.0 applications and creative expression. And they work both ways: just as individual consumers decide on this basis what to do, wear, see, or even be, so producers respond to the choices of others in deciding where to invest (hence the sequel industry). And neither "agents" nor "enterprise" discriminates between producers and consumers, which is of crucial importance in the fast-growing area of user-created content, consumer-led innovation, and self-made media. People can make enterprises out of enthusiasms. One moment you're a fan; next you're signing autographs.

Creative Destruction

Internationally, the essentially European (national public policy; culture) idea of creative industries has collided with the American (global free trade; intellectual property). In the process, the industrial concept of the consumer has been complicated by the network idea of the user. Now, computational power and individual consumers can both be theorized as agents of causation and change, and people's "noncommercial" activities – their culture, knowledge, choices, and social networks outside of the economy as such – need to be taken into account, for it transpires that this is where growth, innovation, and dynamism originate in the evolution not only of the economy but also of knowledge. Here then is a way to *harness the creative energies of all the agents in the system*, and a mechanism – the social network market – to coordinate their creative and communicative choices and activities on a global scale.

The Organization for Economic Co-operation and Development (OECD) has reported on the extent of disruptive renewal or "creative destruction" instigated by consumers in this process:

> User-created content is already an important economic phenomenon despite its originally noncommercial context. The spread of UCC and the amount of attention devoted to it by users appears to be a significant disruptive force for how content is created and consumed and for traditional content suppliers. This disruption creates opportunities and challenges for established market participants and their strategies. (OECD 2007, 5)

Indeed, consumers are not only the origin of traditional "demand" for products and services that established industries are geared up to supply, they also challenge the very business models underpinning those industries:

> New digital content innovations seem to be more based on decentralized creativity, organizational innovation and new value-added models, which favor new entrants, and less on traditional scale advantages and large start-up investments. (OECD 2007, 5)

The OECD has listed the sociocultural "impact" of user-created content as follows:

- altered economics of information production;
- democratization of media production;
- user autonomy, increased participation, and increased diversity;
- collaborative, sharing information, ideas, opinions, and knowledge;
- more diverse array of cultural content;
- diversity of opinion, free flow of information, and freedom of expression;
- challenges – inclusion, content quality, and security and privacy; digital divide, cultural fragmentation, individualization of the cultural environment. (OECD 2007, 6)

The impact of user-created content and emergent social network markets on policy has not been fully explored but should not be underestimated. It affects decisions across many areas, including the vexed question of IP law, because a social network market model is much more tolerant of "piracy" and IP-sharing than is an industry model. Indeed, a country like China may be at a competitive advantage by not having a provider-skewed IP regime. It can get on with promiscuous borrowing and shaping of ideas from wherever they come, just as was the case for the emergent industrial economy in the modernizing West. However, as large-scale creative enterprises coalesce in China, the pressure for IP reform will intensify, even though small-scale traders continue to benefit from a "ducking and weaving" model of regulation. A midway position here may be the Creative Commons movement, associated with Lawrence Lessig, which seeks to find ways to share IP as well as to monetize it (see Leiboff 2007). Beyond the legal framework, the UCC/social network market model also affects science and technology policy, industry policy, employment policy, and education policy. Doubtless it ought to influence taxation policy too, but that's too hard for me.

The Growth of Knowledge: A Future for Media Industry Studies?

Looking to the future, it is worth asking whether the recent mass propagation of creative *digital literacy*

as part of emergent social network markets may be enabling a further evolutionary step-change in the growth of knowledge. "Ordinary people" (formerly known as non-economic or passive audiences) need to be able to access social network markets as both agents and enterprises, to share their own expertise and to develop new networked expertise ("collective intelligence"), such that they too, as well as professional experts, *contribute to the growth of knowledge*. This ability needs to be propagated via population-wide education (formal and informal), and accounted for in economic modeling. It requires that consumer-created content is seen as more than mere self-expression and communication (leisure entertainment). Digital literacy can generate new forms of "objective" description and argumentation (Popper 1975); new forms of journalism and new works of the imagination, in which individual consumers are agents in a network, not subjects spiked on the end of advertisers' "hypodermic" communications. Their individual and collective agency is productive of human knowledge, not simply of corporate takings.

Now of course this is already happening, but it is not well integrated into models of mediated communication, or policy settings on creative industries, which are still too tied to "Industry" versus "Art" (respectively) rather than to integrated knowledge. Instead of ideological stand-off, consumer-led innovations need to be understood coherently as emergent knowledge in a complex open system, even while commercialized experiential self-expression (e.g., in computer games) looks at first sight like the very opposite of "knowledge" as we know it (i.e., as seen from the perspective of print-based modernity). If pushed beyond an adolescent "look at me" stage, digital literacy can assist not only in self-expression and communication, but also in the development of knowledge in an open innovation network. Consumer-created content is an excellent means for recruiting new participants into that adaptive network, and for lifting general levels of digital literacy and popular expertise. It may be modeling for the coming century the role – if not the methods – of public schooling in the earlier period of print literacy.

The development of social network markets and user-created content should not be seen as an end in itself, then, as if knowledge of the personal is all that is necessary for people outside existing professional elites. It is no advance to reinforce the barriers between popular and expert culture; "science" for producers; "self" for consumers – or worse still, "truth" for the experts, and Stephen Colbert's "truthiness" for the audience. The consequences of doing that are already part of the crisis confronting contemporary societies. People feel cut off from expert systems, including both science and entertainment, and are more skeptical than ever about "objective knowledge," whether it is presented as science or news. Not only are the claims and products of scientific research often rejected or delayed in the court of public opinion – GM foods, nuclear energy, climate change, bioscience – but even the modern commitment to rationality and the open society are undermined from within by resurgent religiosity (including New Age spiritualism), "me"-culture, and a moralizing politics of fear.

The need is not to separate "science" (description and argumentation) and "popular culture" (self-expression and communication) further from one another but to invest in holding them together. This is something that creative social networks and social network markets can do, as long as creative digital literacy is propagated on a population-wide basis. The shift from broadcast to interactive media has begun to democratize the publication of self-expression. This is already complicating the entire edifice of "representation" in both symbolic and political communication, because people can now "represent" themselves via self-made media. They are no longer satisfied with deferring to professional representatives; they want direct voice, action, creative expression – and, increasingly, knowledge. Creative industries are the generative engine of emergent knowledge.

If the history of print literacy is anything to go by, democratizing digital literacy will unleash presently unthought-of innovations; these may be as remarkable over time as have been the products of print realism, which include science, the novel, and journalism. It is important to include within any account of creative innovation the *emergent* means for growth within the system as a whole. These now include rather than

exclude the general public, many of whom are already joining the life of science by contributing directly to the evolution of knowledge. Among the many examples might be Wikipedia (and variants); "oral" history on the web including digital storytelling and photographic archiving on Flickr; Google Sky (zoom from your house to the universe); SETI (Search for Extra-Terrestrial Intelligence); computer games for problem-solving;[18] and critical discussion of science versus creationism on YouTube. The "long tail" means that there are infinitely more examples; what is rarely done in critical media industry studies is to take these seriously as part of democratized digital media and population-wide social network markets.

The next stage in the evolution of the creative industries is to return the concept to the place where it began – "creative industriousness," evenly available among the human population, but this time coordinated, scaled, and technologically enabled in such a way that social networks can harness the creative imagination of all the agents in the system, which itself can be used for growing knowledge as well as for self-expression. Industry policy, therefore, ought to be directed toward the propagation of digital literacy and participation, and not remain narrowly focused on the firms that service it. If "human capital" is the most important resource for a creative economy, it follows that education is an important component in the policy mix. However, taking a lesson from the way that entertainment media do it, education too must be "demand-led," organized as much through entertainment, media, and consumption (use) as through formal schooling. The desire to enjoy creative content within a social network is the mechanism through which learning occurs. These social networks are given life by individual desires, daydreams, mischief-making, and play. Self-indulgence by myriad teenagers – extending to whole populations – forms the enabling infrastructure for new knowledge. So a final question on the topic of the future of the media industries is this: what achievements will be enabled by the combination of creative industries, social network markets, mediated entertainment, and universal digital literacy? Let's find out.

Notes

1 Stengel, R. (2006) Now it's your turn. *Time*, 25 December, p. 8.
2 Google's slogan is available online at www.google.com/corporate/tenthings.html.
3 This news item appeared ten days after Chernin was reported to have earned $34m that financial year – more than Rupert Murdoch. See www.guardian.co.uk/media/2007/sep/07/citynews.business.
4 See http://johnaugust.com/glossary.
5 See Davies' obituary. At www.guardian.co.uk/Archive/Article/0,4273,4024597,00.html.
6 Choice includes recognizing weakness and loss in a transaction that nevertheless results in a gain for the weaker party: for instance, academic authors often choose to sign over copyright in their work to a publisher in order to get published. They relinquish rights to gain readers.
7 Stengel (2006), p. 8.
8 See www.culture.gov.uk/3084.aspx.
9 See www.hm-treasury.gov.uk/budget/budget_06/bud_bud06_speech.cfm.
10 See www.iipa.com/pdf/2006CopyrightIndustries ReportPressReleaseFINAL01292007.pdf.
11 See www.culture.gov.uk/4848.aspx.
12 Seewww.unescobkk.org/fileadmin/user_upload/culture/Cultural_Industries/Singapore_Feb_05/WIPO-Session_3.ppt.
13 Its "provider" perspective leads NESTA to advocate a stronger IP regime, which is antithetical to the "sharing knowledge" priorities of user-led innovation.
14 See www.culture.gov.uk/reference_library/minister_speeches/2097.aspx.
15 See www.culture.gov.uk/what_we_do/Creative_industries/creative_economy_programme.htm, accessed February 2008: page since removed, but see also www.cep.culture.gov.uk/index.cfm?fuseaction=main.viewBlogEntry&intMTEntryID=3104, accessed July 15, 2008.
16 For example as used by David Throsby for his economics of culture, see Hutton (2007), pp. 96, 109; Throsby (2001).
17 Pratt (2004) gives a creative industries value chain with four links, none involving consumers:

  1 creation/content origination;
  2 manufacture (of prototypes and production instruments);
  3 distribution and mass production;
  4 exchange (exhibition and retailing).

18 For example, see http://worldwithoutoil.org.
Websites accessed July 15, 2008.

References

Advanced-television.com (2007) News Corp boss urges innovation, 17 September. At www.advanced-television.com/2007/Sep17_Sep21.htm, accessed July 15, 2008.

Althusser, L. (1971) *Lenin and Philosophy and Other Essays*. Monthly Review Press, New York.

Barabási, A. L. (2002) *Linked: The New Science of Networks*. Perseus, Cambridge.

Baran, P. (1964) *On Distributed Communications*. Vol. 1: *Introduction to Distributed Communications Networks*. Rand, Santa Monica.

Beinhocker, E. (2006) *The Origin of Wealth: Evolution, Complexity and the Radical Remaking of Economics*. Harvard Business School Press, Boston.

Caldwell, J. T. (2006) Critical industrial practice: branding, repurposing, and the migratory patterns of industrial texts. *Television & New Media* **7**, 99–134.

CCPR (2003) [Centre for Cultural Policy Research] *Baseline Study on Hong Kong's Creative Industries*. University of Hong Kong for Central Policy Unit HKSAR, Hong Kong.

Connell, I. (1984) Fabulous powers: blaming the media. In Masterman, L. (ed.) *Television Mythologies: Stars, Shows, Signs*. Boyars, London, pp. 88–93.

Cunningham, S., Banks, J., and Potts, J. (2008) Cultural economy: the shape of the field. In Anheier, H. K. and Isar, Y. R. (eds.) *The Cultural Economy*. Sage, Newbury Park, pp. 15–26.

Dopfer, K. and Potts, J. (2007) *The General Theory of Economic Evolution*, 3rd edn. Routledge, London.

Enzensberger, H. M. (1974) *The Consciousness Industry: On Literature, Politics and the Media*. Seabury Press, New York.

Garnham, N. (1987) Concepts of culture: public policy and the culture industries. *Cultural Studies* **1**, 23–38.

Garnham, N. (1990) *Capitalism and Communication: Global Culture and the Economics of Information*. Sage, London.

Hartley, J. (ed.) (2005) *Creative Industries*. Blackwell, Malden.

Hartley, J. (2008) The "supremacy of ignorance over instruction and of numbers over knowledge": journalism, popular culture, and the English constitution. *Journalism Studies* **9**, 679–91.

Herman, E. S. and Chomsky, N. (1988) *Manufacturing Consent: The Political Economy of the Mass Media*. Pantheon, New York.

Higgs, P., Cunningham, S., and Bakhshi, H. (2008) *Beyond the Creative Industries: Mapping the Creative Economy in the UK*. NESTA, London.

Hutton, W. (2007) *Staying Ahead: The Economic Performance of the UK Creative Industries*. DCMS, London.

Lanham, R. (2006) *The Economics of Attention: Style and Substance in the Age of Information*. Chicago University Press, Chicago.

Leadbeater, C. (2006) *We-think: The Power of Mass Creativity*. At www.wethinkthebook.net/book/home.aspx, accessed July 15, 2008.

Leiboff, M. (2007) *Creative Practice and the Law*. Thomson Legal and Regulatory, Sydney.

Lotman, Y. (1990) *Universe of the Mind: A Semiotic Theory of Culture*. Indiana University Press, Indianapolis.

McChesney, R. W. and Nichols, J. (2002) *Our Media, Not Theirs: The Democratic Struggle Against Corporate Media*. Seven Stories Press, New York.

NESTA (2006) *Creating Growth: How the UK Can Develop World Class Creative Businesses*. NESTA, London.

Oakley, K. and Knell, J. (2007) *London's Creative Economy: An Accidental Success?* The Work Foundation, London.

OECD (2007) *Participative Web: User-Created Content*. Working Party on the Information Economy. At www.oecd.org/dataoecd/57/14/38393115.pdf, accessed July 15, 2008.

Popper, K. (1975) The rationality of scientific revolutions. In Harré, R. (ed.) *Problems of Scientific Revolutions*. Oxford University Press, Oxford, pp. 72–101.

Potts, J. and Cunningham, S. (2008) Four models of the creative industries. *International Journal of Cultural Policy* **14**(3), 233–47.

Potts, J., Cunningham, S., Hartley, J., and Ormerod, P. (2008) Social network markets: new definition of the creative industries. *Journal of Cultural Economics* **32**(3), 167–85.

Pratt, A. C. (2004) Creative clusters: towards the governance of the creative industries production system? *Media International Australia* **112**, 50–66.

Roodhouse, S. (2006) *Cultural Quarters: Principles and Practice*. Intellect Books, Bristol.

Schiller, H. (1989) *Culture, Inc.: The Corporate Takeover of Public Expression*. Oxford University Press, New York.

Schiller, H. (1992) *Mass Communications and American Empire*, 2nd edn. Westview Press, Boulder.

Shannon, C. E. (1948) A mathematical theory of communication. *Bell System Technical Journal* **27**, 379–423; 623–56.

Terranova, T. (2000) Free labor: producing culture for the digital economy. *Social Text* **18**, 33–57.

Terranova, T. (2004) *Network Culture: Politics for the Information Age*. Pluto, London.

Throsby, D. (2001) *Economics and Culture*. Cambridge University Press, Cambridge.

Williams, R. (1973) Base and superstructure in Marxist cultural theory. *New Left Review* **1/82**, 3–16.

18

Politics, Theory, and Method in Media Industries Research

·····································

David Hesmondhalgh

In the mid-1990s, I attended an interview for a university position to research and teach about the media industries. At an informal meeting before the interviews, one of the other candidates claimed, with beguiling but alarming frankness, that he had applied for the job because he wanted to work at the university concerned, but didn't understand how anyone could possibly be interested in such an outdated topic.

It was by no means unusual to hear remarks of this kind about media industries analysis at the time – though not, admittedly, from those who wanted to be paid to teach the subject. Intellectual and political fashion favored post-structuralism, postmodernism, Giddensian sociology, and cultural studies. In a backlash against the supposed "productivism" of Marxism and critical theory, these areas were showing great interest in cultural consumption. Those still drawn to the study of media industries were for the most part aware that their area was out of fashion; and, as is often the case in such situations, they tended to portray this as evidence of their commitment to truth and/or good sense over modishness. Many of them responded by either furiously attacking or coldly ignoring these new concepts and theories. The result was too often a dialogue of the deaf. Instead of useful synthesis, debate was often characterized by excessive generalization, simplification, and attacks on straw figures. Various shorthand ways of describing intellectual tensions became embedded

in media research and teaching: "political economy versus cultural studies," "modernism versus postmodernism," and so on. (Contrasts between "Media Studies 1.0" and "Media Studies 2.0" are the latest and most fatuous version of this.) Further simplification and confusion ensued.

However, behind the unhelpful shorthand formulations lurked a set of theoretical, political, and methodological questions of real significance to media studies. Given inevitable limitations on time and energy, should analysts prioritize production or consumption? Popular culture and entertainment media, or news and factual media? The formulation of media and cultural policy, or the everyday experience of media? How do we understand the relationship between economics and culture? To what extent should we conceptualize the social world as an independent reality to which we can gain independent, objective access? Should the politics underlying social research be based primarily on a politics of recognition or redistribution? If both, how to combine and reconcile them? How do we explain how things happen in society – what causes things to happen in the way that they do? The benefit of polemical debates – whether in print, in seminars, or in the bar – was that at least some of these issues were raised. The downside was that they were often raised in a simplistic manner, and the key questions got buried beneath the polemics.

Since its 1990s nadir, the study of media industries and production, often linked to an interest in media and communications policy, has undergone a considerable resurgence. This is clear from the increasing number of doctoral dissertations, journal articles, conferences, and research centers devoted to these topics in recent years. One reason is that the media industries continue to be such an important part of the social and economic landscape. Another is that national and regional governments have shown an interest in expanding the role of media business, often through "creative industries" and "cultural industries" policies. A third is that the media industries are changing as quickly as ever and there is a demand for analysis that attempts to make sense of the transformations being brought about by the Internet, digitalization, audience fragmentation, and new developments in intellectual property.

In such circumstances, it might be tempting for those involved in media production research to ignore theoretical, political, and methodological questions such as those listed above, and to see them as distractions from more urgent business – responding to another government report, organizing against a new policy initiative, submitting another funding application. This chapter is founded on the view that such a response would be a mistake. Only by carefully and painstakingly grounding its claims, and by paying attention to theoretical and methodological issues, will media industries research accrue the long-term intellectual credibility to maintain its recent momentum, and to build on it. At the same time, we must not lose sight of vital questions of social justice and of policy pragmatics. A more concise way to put this is that media industries research requires *a politics of cultural production informed by social theory and by empirical work*. In this chapter, I attempt to indicate what such a project might look like by highlighting some strengths and weaknesses in three types or groups of approach that have recently been of interest to media industries researchers: creative industries analysis, political economy (in fact, one particular type of political economy), and cultural economy.

Creative Industries Analysis

The first type of analysis I call "creative industries analysis" for the sake of brevity. However, the term

refers not only to research that employs the term "creative industries" but also to a wider set of approaches focusing on the role of creativity in modern economies and societies, where terms such as "creative economy" and "creative class" are just as likely to be heard. All these phrases have been, and continue to be, very widely used in government policy over the last decade and have spread across the globe, producing countless documents, committees, and plans.[1] What these various initiatives have in common is a concern to generate more wealth and employment by expanding the creative industries (or the creative economy, or the creative class). One reason, then, why the term "creative industries" is so relevant to media industries research in the twenty-first century is that it represents a significant development in government policy toward the media. Creative industries policy now operates alongside various long-familiar instruments of media policy such as content control (obscenity law, advertising regulation, etc.), spectrum licensing, and subsidy.

But what does the term "creative industries" actually mean? In some policy settings it has really been used to refer to "the arts" as defined in cultural policy since the mid-twentieth century. "Creative industries" is preferred in order to denote a new approach that focuses on the economic value of the arts rather than on their cultural, educational, or spiritual worth. Alternatively, and more commonly, in what is sometimes called "the UK model" (because of the British Labour government's influential creative industries policy and definitions), the traditional arts are grouped with the commercial media industries to comprise a sector that is then presented as one of the fastest-growing in advanced industrial economies, and therefore particularly ripe for further expansion. Not content with this, influential enthusiasts such as Richard Florida and John Howkins have moved definitions of creative activity well beyond the commercial media plus the arts. For Howkins (2001), the media are merely part of a broader "creative economy" consisting of all industries involved in the generation and exploitation of intellectual property including the massive science, engineering, and pharmaceutical sectors. Yet in spite of the deep conceptual confusions, these varying definitions have had a strange mutually reinforcing effect, leading to a veritable cult of creativity. What the various definitions share is a primary concern for economic returns over other aspects of symbol-making and human creativity. In its emphasis on the growing importance of the symbolic realm, creative industries policy can be seen as an offshoot of notions of the information society, adapted for the era of neoliberalism.

Nevertheless, the term "creative industries" brings some benefits. One is that it draws attention to relationships between commercial and noncommercial sectors of cultural production. However, the same was true of an older alternative term "cultural industries" and yet in Anglophone countries (notably the UK, Australia, and New Zealand), talk of creativity has now thoroughly displaced this older concept. Why the shift to "creative"? The word of course has many positive connotations, but also some business credibility derived from its adoption by management theorists and gurus. In the context of neoliberalism this made it preferable to "cultural industries," which for many analysts was tainted by a sense of old-fashioned leftism, derived partly from its history as a term of critique in the 1960s and 1970s but also from the adoption of "cultural industries" regeneration policies by left-wing councils in deindustrializing European cities in the 1980s.

The result is that an increasing number of researchers now write about "creative industries" rather than "media industries" or "cultural industries." Significantly, this includes some talented and energetic media studies analysts, for example John Hartley, Stuart Cunningham, and Terry Flew of the Queensland University of Technology. Unlike some neoclassical economists and policymakers who have adopted the term "creative industries" (e.g., Caves 2000), these researchers are fully aware of the importance of questions of power when it comes to media and culture, having cut their teeth on earlier debates between post-structuralists and Marxists. A strong influence on many of these researchers is a version of cultural studies that recognizes the importance and complexity of popular culture, but which also argues that cultural studies and cultural policy can be mutually enriching areas of intellectual and political activity (see Bennett 1998). Consequently, the creative industries researchers bring with them a grounding in cultural theory, but also a commendable willingness to engage with policymakers, and to seek to influence the way that policy is forged and enacted. In this respect, then, creative industries research might seem to offer not only a potential alternative to the way that neoclassical economics conceives of media production, but also a model of critical but pragmatic policy engagement.

However, there are reasons to think that creative industries analysis does not offer a good way forward for media industries research. The definitional problems referred to above have helped lead to many inflated estimates of the importance of the sector. Creative industries may be growing at above-average rates compared with other sectors, but they are unlikely to be the basis of significant economic growth in themselves, except perhaps in a few particular cities with high concentrations of media activity. (Alternatively, there are calls for yet more "mapping documents.") There is much loose talk about the value of "creativity" but little attempt to define it. Adopting the creativity rhetoric has allowed many arts and media policymakers to claim that their areas are increasingly central to the economic action in modern societies. The downside of this is that the media and the arts are no longer able to operate as specialist domains, with their own dynamics and their own distinct policy needs. As ministries of finance, trade and industry departments, and tourism agencies have become more interested in creative industries, the artistic and educational value of culture may have slipped further down the policy agenda. The creative industries are often considered prestigious because of the idea that they might offer lessons to other sectors about how to manage and produce innovation. Underlying this is a neoliberal emphasis on competitive efficiency and productivity. Even if individual policymakers and analysts have other goals, the political danger is that policy aimed at protecting quality, innovation, and the promotion of social justice actually becomes less prestigious and less well-resourced by attempting to smuggle these values in, disguised in the cloak of economics. The result is often that more resources are made available – for example, more money for museums and galleries – but with strings attached. Social, cultural, and artistic qualities are seemingly valued only when they can be converted into economic indicators (this has been a feature of media and cultural policy – including creative industries policy – under the Blair/Brown Labour regime; see Hesmondhalgh 2005).

The creative industries researchers are not unaware of these dangers. They argue in response that there are also possible advantages when media industries such as television become incorporated into creative industries policy. Yet for all their policy pragmatism, when creative industries researchers get round to addressing the benefits that might accrue from engagement with such policy, there is a ring of utopianism as resounding as in the left and paternalist policy regimes they seek to move beyond. Cunningham (2004), for example, argues that "hitherto marginal programming could be significantly upgraded," that "programming produced for and by regional interests might be as fundamental as the guarantee of a basic telephone connection to all," and that "programming inclusive of demographics" (such as content catering for young people and children) might be "as fundamental as free and compulsory schooling."

Other creative industries researchers have optimistically tied their research agenda to new conceptions of the roles that universities, arts and humanities education, and cultural studies might play in these changing conditions. Terry Flew (2004), for example, advocates a creativity-centered "new humanism" that would be directed neither toward training in a canon of great works nor the cultivation of anti-capitalism, but rather aiming to "impact upon the conduct of commercial enterprises, and the corporatizing public sector," and to "align social consciousness and cultural awareness with enhanced economic productivity." But what form such "social consciousness" might take remains curiously vague. As James Donald (2004) asks Flew in a thoughtful and eloquent response: "Is critique too outmoded to be redeemable? Has Cultural Studies become a subsidiary of the Business School?" Donald rightly points out that it is too simplistic to accuse the creative industries researchers of an attempt to "depoliticize" cultural studies and critical media research. But he spots an evasiveness about questions of political value that is present in a great deal of research published under the creative industries banner (see also Hartley 2005).

Political Economy

I want to turn now to another type of media industries analysis, which has also gained much attention in recent years, but which represents a very different research tradition and political trajectory. It is firmly rooted in political economy, in the Marxian and leftist traditions that creative industries researchers seek to move beyond. However, it is important to realize that political economies of the media and culture have taken a number of forms since they began to emerge in the 1960s and 1970s. In earlier work (Hesmondhalgh 2007) building on the valuable account of Vincent Mosco (1996), I distinguished between a mainly European tradition of political economy focused on a sociological analysis of the distinctive qualities of the cultural industries and a mainly US lineage that I called the Schiller–McChesney tradition, after its two most notable exponents, Herbert Schiller and Robert McChesney. This latter tradition has produced a formidable stream of publications over the decades, valuably tracking the continuing story of media concentration and conglomeration, and the ties between US politicians, policymakers, and media interests.[2]

This tradition has also been marked by its willingness to engage in campaigning and activism for media reform. Perhaps the most striking example of this was the role of Robert McChesney (and the Free Press campaigning group he helped found) in the 2003 campaign to overturn the Federal Communications Commission's attempt to reduce restrictions on media ownership concentration in the US. This culminated in the first Media Reform conference, held in November 2003, attended by nearly 2,000 people, including such luminaries of the US left as Jesse Jackson and Ralph Nader. This is politically engaged scholarship that puts to shame those in academia who share its concerns with questions of justice, equity, and the public good from the comfort of their office swivel chairs. McChesney has rightly worried in various publications that critical media research risks irrelevance unless it engages in public debate and activism of this kind. Is this then a model for a politics of cultural production informed by social theory and empirical work?

Certainly the engagement with strategic uses of power is preferable to the complacency about neoliberalism to be found in much media economics and in some creative industries analysis. But this kind of political economy work has its downside too.

One problem with the Schiller–McChesney tradition as a form of political economy analysis is that it provides little sense of the contradictions in capitalist media production. This is linked to an inadequate engagement with media texts, with the specificity of media content. If, as McChesney (1999) has claimed, "the real way to assess the content of the media system is to judge it in its entirety," then this raises at least two questions (32). What is the nature of the media system that is being assessed? And on what basis do we make such an assessment?

The short answer that political economy in general would give to the first question would usually be "capitalist media production." After all, one of the defining features of political economy is its concern with the relationships between capitalism and media. But in spite of explicitly locating themselves in this broader tradition, the key writers in the Schiller–McChesney tradition provide little help with some fundamental questions regarding capitalism. To give just one brief example of such a question: what general account of political economic and sociocultural change might most adequately underlie a good account of capitalist media? Would it be based on something approximating Marx's version? Or a revised Marxian version taking account of the widely acknowledged (and inevitable) blind spots in Marx's own writing? Or rather would the emphasis be on a more sociological account of the kind provided by, say, Weber and his heirs, which might emphasize capitalism as linked to broader processes of modernization and rationalization?

Whatever answers might be given to these questions, ultimately any serious analysis of capitalist media would *at some point* have to confront relationships between, say, capitalism and modernity, and indeed questions of historical explanation. But I have been unable to find any real encounter with these problems in anything approaching this form in the Schiller–McChesney tradition. Linked to this is the question of *evaluation*, of the assessment of capitalist media. In the words of one exponent of more

theoretically informed versions of political economy, a central issue in understanding media as modern institutions is "the general question of the nature of the capitalist mode of production and of the difficult balance to be struck … between its genuinely emancipatory and its dominating characteristics" (Garnham 2000, 41). Capitalist modernity, then, as characterized both by emancipation and by domination: how do we disentangle and interpret these tendencies in assessing modern media?

Again, key writers in the Schiller–McChesney tradition are silent on this historical problem. There is a great deal to criticize in contemporary media production, and Schiller, McChesney, and others have provided powerful critiques. But at some point within a relevant body of work, it will be necessary to face the question of how to compare the existing capitalist media system with other systems of cultural production that have existed historically. After all, there seems little doubt that the cultural experience of those of us living in contemporary capitalist societies is richer and more diverse than those living in pre-modern societies. As an example, anyone who enjoys music and has reasonable amounts of disposable income would find it literally impossible to find time to listen to all the music that is available, much of it beautiful, funny, skillful, and/or clever. I would argue that the same is true in Europe, North America, and Australasia (the regions I know best) of television (assuming a recorder of some kind), films on DVD, books, magazines, and comics.

Now, I think I would probably be the last person to deny that cultural production and circulation are marked by the injustice and inequality characteristic of modern societies in general, which certain tendencies in capitalist modernity constantly threaten to entrench and deepen. The formidable cultural resources unleashed by capitalism are – like most other domains of life, including food, drink, and shelter – much more available to the wealthy and the educated. There are also significant spatial inequalities. It is much more possible to hear American music in the Philippines than Philippino music in the US (outside marginalized and exploited migrant communities). This is the domination rather than the emancipation side of capitalist modernity. The point is that in certain forms of political economy, this former aspect is constantly emphasized at the expense of the latter. The temptation might be to stress domination over emancipation in order to avoid providing "an advertisement for the status quo" (McChesney 1999, 31) and to rally the troops in a quest for greater social justice. But if we are involved in academic work on media industries, as opposed to polemics (which have their place too) then we have an opportunity to register these complexities. Instead, work produced in the Schiller–McChesney tradition all too rarely seems to get round to any such direct confrontation with the really difficult problems surrounding how we understand capitalism, democracy, and the media, in spite of their identification with political economy; contradiction is simply not built into its research program. Behind this lack – it seems to me – lies a failure to engage with social theory, either in its classical or its modern forms. An understanding of capitalist culture as complex and contradictory would be just one gain from such an engagement.[3]

To address such complexities is not just a scholastic exercise, a modern version of Aquinas' reflections on whether there is excrement in heaven (though some modern academic debates about politics, economics, and the media are almost as unworldly as this). They are the basis of controversies concerning how major historical and social questions affect our work. Not every account needs to deal with such foundations. A research program will generally mix more theoretical and more empirical work. And there will be a wider division of labor, with some scholars within particular traditions and programs taking on more theoretical work and others undertaking more empirical work. Yet I would suggest that as well as failing to be adequately engaged with social theory and media theory, much work in the tradition of political economy I am discussing also fails to be *adequately empirical*. This may seem an odd claim, given the hundreds of sources footnoted and referenced in, for example, Herman and McChesney's *The Global Media* (1997). The main empirical method used is the combing and selective quotation of secondary sources, especially the trade press and more prestigious US newspapers and magazines. There is nothing wrong with this as a method. But ideally it requires explicit and regular discussion of the validity

and reliability of the sources used, and combination with other methods. In my view there is too little focus on methodology in the Schiller–McChesney tradition, and too little attention to the relationship between theory and empirical analysis.

This raises important issues for media industries research as a whole, concerning the relation between, on the one hand, "macro" analysis of prevailing trends across particular industries and sectors, and on the other hand, "micro" studies, such as sociological analysis of the production of particular texts. Other traditions of political economy have combined the two (e.g., Golding & Elliott 1979). But the Schiller–McChesney tradition strongly favors the former, and even in its overviews of the research terrain, rarely refers to such empirical studies. Herman (1995), a leading US writer in this tradition, has commented that organizational studies based on qualitative sociological methods "exaggerate the potential media professionals have for dissent and 'space'" (81). This may be true of particular studies, and Herman is right to stress that we need quantitative studies of media output (an occasional feature of the Schiller–McChesney tradition at best) but this is not an either/or choice. Micro studies need not be uncritical, as is shown by classic works such as that by Elliott (1972) or more recent studies such as Grindstaff (2002). A new generation of critical media sociologists has turned to ethnographic methods, and in my view this has the potential to enrich media industries research hugely.[4] The views that emerge in such studies nearly always contain more gradation than the chiaroscuro pictures painted by political economists in the Schiller–McChesney tradition. For some, this emphasis on complexity, contradiction, and fine detail ultimately means that such sociologists are unconsciously or otherwise complicit with the powerful. But it may also derive from the fact that, however much the world is marked by inequality and abuses of power, it is also a messy and complex place.

Cultural Economy

A third term, and associated strand of analysis, that has captured the interest of some media industries researchers in recent years has been "cultural economy."

The term is intended as an alternative to "political economy" and the main reason for replacing "political" with "cultural" is to emphasize the centrality of meaning, representation, discourse, and culture in economic practices (Du Gay 1997, 3). Like creative industries research, then, the cultural economy approach represents an attempt to bring cultural studies to bear on questions of production and more broadly economic life. But it also reflects the legacy of the post-structuralist wing of the "cultural turn" in social thought, associated with Stuart Hall, and manifest in cultural economy's attempt to deconstruct the dualistic thinking that it sees operating both in traditional humanist, conservative thought and in Marxian and "critical" approaches. In particular, any dualistic opposition of economics and culture, whether on the part of neoclassical economists or Marxists, is seen as deeply problematic (Du Gay & Pryke 2002). Indeed, the central goal of cultural economy as an approach in social theory appears to be a better understanding of the relationships between economics and culture (see Amin & Thrift 2004).

Another reason for replacing "political economy" with "cultural economy" for theorists who have attached themselves to the term is a desire to engage with debates about the degree to which modern economies are becoming "culturalized," either through the increasing economic importance of cultural industries, or the way that more and more goods and services can be conceived of as "cultural goods" because they are increasingly "aestheticized," and/or imbued with meanings, associations, and desires (Du Gay & Pryke 2002; cf. Lash & Urry 1994). In the case of Du Gay and Pryke at least, the response is a profound skepticism about any *general* "epochal" claims that increased culturalization has taken place. This is linked to a preference for the close "genealogical" studies advocated by Foucault (though it has to be said Foucault was also capable of being "epochal"). There is a strong sense that the relations between entities such as culture and economy can only be understood in specific contexts. This is post-structuralism with a strongly empirical bent, echoing new historicism in literary studies or actor network theory in sociology.

It is easy to see why the concept of cultural economy might be of potential interest to media production researchers. If the terms "economics" and "culture" have any abstractable meaning (and some writers who use the term "cultural economy" seem somewhat undecided about whether they do), then the media industries can easily be conceived as operating on the boundaries between them, providing a test case for their merging, or otherwise. What is more, cultural economy seems to have two advantages over the two other tendencies in media industries research examined above. It is more sophisticated theoretically than creative industries research and than the Schiller–McChesney tradition of political economy, and although it is only partly concerned with the media industries, cultural economy researchers have produced empirically or genealogically oriented studies of media production. These studies have been mostly confined to advertising (e.g., Nixon 2003) and are very limited in number. Yet the term "cultural economy" remains an intriguing one for many researchers interested in the relations between cultural production and economic or organizational processes, especially those who are skeptical about the benefits of any lingering traces of Marxism in cultural analysis. Its links to social and cultural theory also make it attractive.

Nevertheless, media production analysts might want to hesitate before adopting "cultural economy" in the hope of invigorating their research. In particular, we might question the degree to which its seemingly sophisticated probing of "culture" and "economy" has real analytical pay-off. As Ray and Sayer (1999) point out, "Those who have expressed scepticism about the [culture/economy] distinction are unable to stop referring to the cultural and the economic separately, which suggests that we still need it" (4). Economic life, Ray and Sayer argue, has always been and will always be profoundly cultural, but that does not mean that we cannot distinguish between economic and cultural processes – as long as we are clear what we mean by each (and ironically those who advocate cultural economy are usually less clear about this than their opponents).

Du Gay and Pryke's (2002) response to Ray and Sayer is that "actual cultural interests and capacities can only be formulated and assessed in the context of definite normative and technical regimes ... There is no need to assume that these regimes are founded on any prior, general analytical distinction" (9). But this is to misunderstand the way in which abstract terms such as "economic" and "cultural" are used as tools to make sense of society. Du Gay and Pryke, for example, have recourse in the passage I have just quoted to an abstract category known as "regimes." Their statement implies that they would put this "prior" concept of regime to work in the analysis of various social situations. In fact, it is impossible to do anything other than invoke such "prior, general" terms in *any* social analysis – and inevitably contrastive distinctions such as that between "culture" and "economy" will be part of this. There has to be some more specific argument why the distinction between "economic" and "cultural" is not a meaningful or a useful one, beyond an objection to the fact that it is "prior" and "general." I do not think that Du Gay and Pryke successfully make such an argument. After all, as long as we specify the terms, we can make reasonable distinctions between forms of activity that are *primarily* "cultural," such as painting a picture, and others that are *primarily* "economic," such as buying shares in a company listed on the Stock Exchange (and also activities that are *primarily* "political"). Certainly, many activities will not be easily categorized in this way, and such abstractions are going to have uncertain, porous boundaries. But the same is true of any term or distinction useful enough to think about anything other than the simplest phenomena.

The issue then is really how well or badly we separate culture from economy – and, as Warde (2002) points out, this is "almost entirely a function of the general models that we use to characterize societies" (186). Using distinctions such as economic/cultural (and others such as economic/political or political/cultural) can help us to develop historical explanations, such as differentiating and comparing different types of causes in explaining a particular historical development or situation.[5] It can also help us make normative judgments. This should not involve some absurd splitting, where the economic is "bad" and the cultural/artistic is "good." If we avoid such traps, then the distinction can enable us to observe, for example, whether television workers may, at particular times, be pressured by primarily economic imperatives (e.g., the need to make profit)

in carrying out their primarily cultural – meaning artistic or informational – work (such as putting together a news report or producing a television drama). The cultural economy approach is absolutely right to question certain simplified readings of the relations between culture and economy. But the danger is that they end up deconstructing the culture/economy pairing out of existence. This risks blocking off the pursuit of a number of important normative questions.

Toward a Politics of Cultural Production

In this chapter, I have sought to identify some problems with three tendencies or approaches in recent cultural analysis that have been the object of a certain degree of interest among media industries researchers. My strategy here could be construed as a negative one. By highlighting weaknesses, I might seem to be pouring cold water on some exciting analytical fires. My criticisms, I confess, arise out of a fear that researchers will be misled by the superficial attractiveness of these terms and approaches. However, more positively, my aim has been to allow a picture of a positive agenda for future media industries research to emerge, by contrast, from these criticisms. Let me now briefly attempt to summarize these positive elements and to build on them.

Creative industries analysis shows the benefits of pragmatic, policy-oriented research, and yet one that is not naïve about questions of cultural power. However, as a negative example, it shows that media industries research needs to be extremely skeptical with regard to claims about transformations in cultural production – especially those pertaining to the size of the relevant sectors. This also means a need for great care over definitions. Otherwise, researchers risk reproducing the loose rhetoric and hazy conceptions of policy entrepreneurs. It also shows that an adequate politics of cultural production needs to be explicit about the normative principles underlying its research. At crucial points, creative industries analysis is vague on this matter, and this means that it risks being complicit with a privileging of "wealth creation" over certain other aspects of life – including the artistic, informational, and expressive, a normative preference characteristic of much neoliberal thought.

The Schiller–McChesney tradition of political economy work is certainly not complicit with neoliberalism or with the negative tendencies in the modern capitalist media system. Its key researchers show an admirable dedication to activism in various forms, and to social justice and equality. Because one of the most worrying aspects of the modern media is that they can contribute to exacerbating economic, social, and cultural inequality, this is an important element of a politics of cultural production. Also welcome is political economy's focus on the importance of understanding capitalism as a way of understanding the modern media. However, the Schiller–McChesney tradition's blind spot regarding contradiction shows the importance of paying proper attention to historical and social-theoretical questions regarding the nature of capitalism, and its imbrications with (or, alternatively, its autonomy from) other aspects of modernity. Another major blind spot – its failure for the most part to provide or engage with properly conducted micro studies of everyday production contexts – is equally limiting. The recent surge in analysis of such everyday production offers a much more hopeful route for media industries analysis. So too do efforts to link the study of cultural production to the sociology of art and music (see Born 2008).

Cultural economy offers some of the theoretical sophistication and empirical analysis that the mainstream of political economy in the US lacks. But it risks sophistry in its excessive deconstruction of categories that have the potential to produce normative orientations for use in both theoretical and empirical research. In my view, a politics of cultural production needs to resist some of the theoretical temptations offered by "the cultural turn."

I began by stating my view that critical media industries research needs to be underpinned by an engagement with social theory, with empirical work (which means an engagement with methodological problems and dilemmas), and with a politics opposed to inequality and injustice. This is a compressed statement, and this chapter represents an attempt to expand and justify it. The components of this program might seem a big ask for media industries research, engaging with the broadest historical questions regarding the intertwining of economics and culture in capitalism, and at the same time undertaking micro studies of cultural production, and paying constant attention to the normative principles underlying research. I have not even mentioned the necessity to keep up with contemporary changes in the media industries.[6] And of course it is easier to make such statements than to apply the principles they contain. As I said earlier, not every account can deal adequately with such foundations. But that is why it is important to understand media research programs – including media industries research – as collaborative enterprises. Some researchers may focus on empirical work, some on theory, some on the normative political principles underlying research. The vital thing is to engage across these activities – an intellectual division of labor – and to attempt to find the best possible syntheses of these different tasks (my own attempt is in Hesmondhalgh 2007). My suggestion in this chapter is that the three research types or tendencies I have discussed do not represent the foundations for such a synthesis nor therefore for the future of media industries research.

Notes

1 In this respect, the US is something of an exception among advanced industrial countries. The tremendous strength of its media industries, combined with a tradition of limited public support for media and culture, has meant that the concept of "creative industries" looks exotic. US readers should note, however, that "creative industries" is certainly no longer a British, or a European phenomenon: it is transcontinental. In the US, the concept of the "creative class," with its links to urban regeneration, has gained much more purchase than "creative industries."

2 Whether this can viably be deemed a "tradition" is a question there is no space to discuss in detail here. In my view, there are clear characteristics shared by a

group of key political economists based in the US, notably Noam Chomsky and Edward Herman, as well as Schiller and McChesney. These shared characteristics, discussed above and in Hesmondhalgh (2007) are not nearly so apparent in the work of other political economy analysts (e.g., Nicholas Garnham or Graham Murdock). This is sufficient in my view to mark their work as a distinctive tradition within the political economy of culture.

3 Other gains would include clearer conceptions of structure and agency in relation to cultural production, and of the interrelations of macro and micro levels. This lack of engagement with social theory on the part of media studies is by no means confined to the Schiller-McChesney tradition of political economy. Many identify modern social theory as a whole with merely one strand of it, overly emphasizing poststructuralism or the work of Anthony Giddens. See Sibeon (2004) for one indication of the richness of contemporary social theory, and Garnham (2000) and the contributions to Hesmondhalgh and Toynbee (2008) for rare engagements from within media studies.

4 Some more recent studies, especially in the US, have tended to claim that such empirical "micro" studies of

media production are a feature of, or at least are encouraged by, cultural studies. In fact, cultural studies with a very small number of exceptions (see the discussion of cultural economy below) has neglected such close studies of media production. They are much more a feature of cultural and media sociology, for example the "production of culture" school.

5 As Warde (2002) shows, the culture/economy distinction can also help to formulate reasonable research questions. For example, we might ask whether the economy is being more affected by culture than previously, and this question can then be tested through empirical work. In making this statement, Warde recognizes the importance of very carefully defining what we mean by "culture" and favors a restrictive sense of the term as meaning "artistic practices." More general uses tend to render the debate over economy/culture relations meaningless.

6 This is an activity that I think sometimes takes over the working lives of some analysts. This is perhaps understandable but keeping up with the latest takeovers, technologies, and trends can distract from the bigger historical picture, and from theoretically informed empirical research on specific questions.

References

Amin, A. and Thrift, N. J. (eds.) (2004) *The Blackwell Cultural Economy Reader*. Blackwell, Oxford.

Bennett, T. (1998) *Culture: A Reformer's Science*. Sage, London.

Born, G. (2008) The social and the aesthetic: methodological principles in the study of cultural production. In Alexander, J. and Reed I. (eds.) *Meaning and Method: The Cultural Approach to Sociology*. Paradigm, Boulder, forthcoming.

Caves, R. E. (2000) *Creative Industries: Contracts Between Art and Commerce*. Harvard University Press, Cambridge.

Cunningham, S. (2004) The creative industries after cultural policy: a genealogy and some preferred futures. *International Journal of Cultural Studies* **7**, 105–15.

Donald, J. (2004) What's new? A letter to Terry Flew. *Continuum: Journal of Media & Cultural Studies* **18**, 235–46.

Du Gay, P. (1997) Introduction. In Du Gay, P. (ed.) *Production of Culture/Cultures of Production*. Sage, London, pp. 1–10.

Du Gay, P. and Pryke, M. (2002) Cultural economy: an introduction. In Du Gay, P. and Pryke, M. (eds.) *Cultural Economy: Cultural Analysis and Commercial Life*. Sage, London, pp. 1–19.

Elliott, P. (1972) *The Making of a Television Series: A Case Study in the Sociology of Culture*. Constable, London.

Flew, T. (2004) Creativity, the "new humanism" and cultural studies. *Continuum: Journal of Media & Cultural Studies* **18**, 161–78.

Garnham, N. (2000) *Emancipation, the Media, and Modernity: Arguments about the Media and Social Theory*. Oxford University Press, Oxford.

Golding, P. and Elliott, P. (1979) *Making the News*. Longman, London.

Grindstaff, L. (2002) *The Money Shot: Trash, Class, and the Making of TV Talk Shows*. University of Chicago Press, Chicago.

Hartley, J. (ed.) (2005) *Creative Industries*. Blackwell, Oxford.

Herman, E. S. (1995) Media in the US political economy. In Downing, J., Mohammadi, A., and Sreberny-Mohammadi, A. (eds.) *Questioning the*

Media: A Critical Introduction. Sage, London, pp. 77–93.

Herman E. S. and McChesney, R. W. (1997) *The Global Media: The New Missionaries of Corporate Capitalism*. Cassell, London.

Hesmondhalgh, D. (2005) Media and cultural policy as public policy: the case of the British labour government. *International Journal of Cultural Policy* **11**, 95–109.

Hesmondhalgh, D. (2007) *The Cultural Industries*, 2nd edn. Sage, London.

Hesmondhalgh, D. and Toynbee J. (eds.) (2008) *The Media and Social Theory*. Routledge, New York.

Howkins, J. (2001) *The Creative Economy: How People Make Money from Ideas*. Allen Lane, London.

Lash, S. and Urry, J. (1994) *Economies of Signs and Space*. Sage, London.

McChesney, R. W. (1999) *Rich Media, Poor Democracy: Communication Politics in Dubious Times*. University of Illinois Press, Urbana.

Mosco, V. (1996) *The Political Economy of Communication: Rethinking and Renewal*. Sage, London.

Nixon, S. (2003) *Advertising Cultures: Gender, Commerce, Creativity*. Sage, London.

Ray, L. and Sayer, A. (1999) Introduction. In Ray, L. and Sayer, A. (eds.) *Culture and Economy After the Cultural Turn*. Sage, London, pp. 1–24.

Sibeon, R. (2004) *Rethinking Social Theory*. Sage, London.

Warde, A. (2002) Production, consumption and cultural economy. In Du Gay, P. and Pryke, M. (eds.) *Cultural Economy: Cultural Analysis and Commercial Life*. Sage, London, pp. 185–200.

19

An Industry Perspective
Calibrating the Velocity of Change

....

Jordan Levin

Asking a media industry professional to write about media industry studies is a dicey proposition. For starters, you're asking someone who is used to unloading their thoughts in a constant stream of jagged and abrupt emails pounded out on their BlackBerries to actually take the time to think about what they are trying to say and then communicate those ideas in a cohesive manner. Said industry professional actually has to do this on paper, so to speak, rather than scribbling bullet points and models haphazardly on an oversized whiteboard. This unfortunate soul who has been recruited by the academic community to reveal the linguistic shortcomings of professionals in the media industry, as compared to the academics tasked with actually trying to make sense of what the pros are trying to say, has to do something relatively unheard of in the modern media age … they have to slow down, extract themselves from the bubble, and think.

They have to think not just about the present, but search the past and envision the future. This is no small task for a professional. The immediate is what they are consumed by at any given moment. The pressures placed on them by their corporate management, board of directors, and investors to prove their value on a quarterly basis allow little time to think about today, let alone yesterday or tomorrow. The rapid pace of change is all-consuming, making it more difficult for anyone in an executive seat to

come up for air, let alone reach a vantage point that affords a broader vista of our business.

Nor should one overlook just how much this medium, founded on creativity by visionary creators, has become a business. In an era of media consolidation, it is worth noting that only one media conglomerate's DNA is firmly connected to the work of a creative pioneer. That company is Disney. The remaining conglomerates' core roots are electronics, journalism, theatrical exhibition, cable distribution, appliances, and the occasional weapon of mass destruction. The age of media companies being run by independent visionaries determined to introduce the next great creative endeavor has long since passed. Deregulation led to consolidation. Vertical integration deemphasized the value of singular creative ideas in favor of supposed synergistic value. In an effort to manage risk more efficiently, businessmen were recruited to displace creative executives. As a result, the tone and tenor of conducting a creative enterprise hardened. Essentially, creativity became perceived as nothing more than a glorified commodity.

And yet as these companies now struggle to make all their disparate pieces work together, it is becoming increasingly clear that the central component, the core piece that drives everything else, is what it has always been: creative content. As such, the conglomerates have begun to leverage their production, marketing, and distribution hegemony to control and derive value from the flow of content. Creators have seen their independence compromised by what amounts to indirect collusion on the part of the conglomerates.

While the conglomerates' apparent stranglehold on the industry seems assured at this moment in March 2008, it is, in reality, nothing less than illusory. Their actions seem less an example of confident leadership than a final death grip applied with all the determination and remaining force of a fading oligarchy in the waning days of its power. A friend of mine, a successful feature film writer named John Rogers, has spent considerable time thinking about the larger trends affecting media. He has compared this period in the media industry to that of the Soviet Union in August 1991 – a time when hard-liners opposed to the concepts of perestroika (roughly translated into economic and political restructuring) and glasnost (openness) staged a coup that briefly displaced the progressive panache of Gorbachev with the repressive, traditional images of old, graying bureaucrats in lifeless, gray suits. Their seizing of power was futile and ultimately short-lived, for change was in the air, the will of the people strong, and the march of time inevitable.[1]

Within our present media landscape, similar progressive forces are at work that are restructuring the economic foundation of our industry and undermining the existing conglomerates' market dominance, not only changing how information is controlled, but perhaps even more significantly *who* controls the flow of information. While it is obvious that disruptive technologies are the catalysts for this transformative change, what is less apparent is who is driving this change and what constituency will be the ultimate beneficiary of this evolution. Just as the leadership of today's media conglomerates wrested control of the industry from the hands of its entrepreneurial founders and pieced together their individual achievements into larger holding companies of mass size and scale, along have come new market entrants determined to shape the face of media in the twenty-first century. Whether these competitors come in the form of Internet powerhouses like Google, telecommunications giants like the new AT&T, marketing communications companies like

WPP, or international competitors like Endemol, Fremantle, or ITV, all will face a new market reality: technology has empowered the individual consumer in a revolutionary fashion.

Power to the People

In 1984, Apple Computers announced the introduction of the breakthrough Macintosh personal computer and operating system, which served as the model for Microsoft's defining Windows operating system. To create awareness for this new product, Apple purchased a 30-second commercial spot in the Super Bowl and, in so doing, presented one of the seminal television commercials of all time. Directed by Ridley Scott, "1984" paid homage to George Orwell's novel of the same name and featured a dynamic, athletic, young woman emblazoned with Apple's colorful corporate logo. We see her running through the tunnels of a dystopian society chased by fascist guards to a meeting hall filled with lifeless citizens, hypnotized by the rhetoric of their authoritarian leader broadcast on a massive video screen. On reaching the center of the hall, the woman spins around in circles, releasing an Olympic hammer that strikes the image of Big Brother as he reaches the apex of his speech. The audience is showered in sparks and a burst of energy is released that liberates the citizens' souls.

While Apple viewed Microsoft as Big Brother back in 1984, more recently Apple has certainly relished playing David to the entertainment industry's Goliath. Watching that clairvoyant commercial anew, it is hard not to be struck by the subversive, revolutionary message as it relates to our present media age. To take the David analogy one step further, the stone that fells the giant just might be the iPod.

In January 2007, Steve Jobs announced that Apple Computer would change its corporate name to simply "Apple." As friend and former colleague Rusty Mintz noted, "No subtext necessary." In one simple move, Apple released itself from the restraint of labels, thereby anticipating the blur spreading across the media industry. In fact, as the recent launch of the iPhone demonstrated, Apple isn't just a computer company. It's a mobile company. It's a consumer electronics company. It's a digital distribution company. It's a product design company. It's a content company. It's a marketing company. It's a populist company. By simply dropping "computer" from its name, Apple instantly redefined its mission and confirmed for the world that we have entered the era of convergence.

I would argue that we are both witnesses to and participants in the largest, most fundamental transformation in the history of media since the advent of typeface, the moving image, and terrestrial broadcast transmissions. The change is far more significant than the transition from radio to television or movies from larger screens to smaller screens. The latter developments did not alter the fundamental narrative structures, the underlying hierarchy of power, or the core foundations of basic business models. What we are presently experiencing is the shift away from a top-down business model being imposed on consumers by the producers and distributors of media to a bottom-up business model emerging out of the consumption behavior of media users. The era in which a privileged few accessed tools to facilitate the publishing of content for distribution over exclusive distribution networks reaching the masses is being eroded by both efficient production tools and peer-to-peer communication that provides anyone with the ability to communicate their ideas to anyone else, anywhere, any time.

To reference John Rogers' earlier comparison with the Soviet Union, media companies built their businesses on an economic foundation most closely resembling communism or at the very least a cartel such as OPEC. Simply put, they controlled the production and distribution of media. They determined how, when, and where consumers were able to experience media. Limited production runs and fixed shelf space constrained the mass availability of the still image, written word, and musical note. If you wanted to see a moving image, for example, you could only see it at certain times in certain cinemas for a limited window. Before the home video marketplace was established, if you missed that film in the movie theater you would have to wait until it aired on free, broadcast television. With the advent of home video, you could rent or purchase that film to watch at your convenience, but

you needed to wait until the theatrical window had passed. Television offered the convenience of experiencing entertainment in the comfort of your home; however, you were forced to watch programs on the network's terms, not your own. If you wanted to catch an episode of your favorite show, you needed to do so when the network dictated. If you missed it, you would have to wait for a repeat.

To be fair, technology, or the limitation thereof, shaped the aforementioned model. The sheer cost of production and distribution limited these functions to companies with significant capital and industrial control. Emergent technologies are now facilitating the transition from a corporate-imposed to a consumer-controlled model. While it might not seem that simple, the bottom line is that consumers pay for content. To some extent, sponsors also fund content production by subsidizing direct consumer spending on content in exchange for the opportunity to deliver an advertising message to that audience. Nonetheless, even in this instance, consumers are still paying for the content by leasing their eyeballs to advertisers. Given the historic barriers of entry created by the access to and expense associated with production and distribution, both studios and networks became firmly entrenched as the conduit for consumers, advertisers, and creators to develop and maintain relationships with one another. Commerce was transacted between the three, with the studios and networks essentially serving as middlemen through the creation of a central marketplace. Ultimately, the studios and networks became the central source of funding for content production, clouding the fact that it is still consumers' dollars or eyeballs that are truly driving the underlying economics. As a result, the traditional media conglomerates have, in large part, been wary of fully embracing the unlimited potential these new technological tools offer for fear of undermining the enormous capital investment they've made in the current infrastructure. Yet the pace of change is accelerating at such a rapid clip that their efforts to adapt, regulate, and even in some cases, legislate emerging technology to their benefit have largely been futile. The ability for creators, advertisers, and consumers to circumvent the media conglomerates and more easily access one another has led to greater competition to satisfy consumers' evolving media consumption habits. Consumers used to have to seek out content, but the reverse is becoming increasingly true. Content needs to find consumers in order to succeed.

The emergence of so-called new media has prompted an increase in overall media consumption, but consumer choice is fragmenting mass media across multiple platforms. New technologies are gaining share at the expense of traditional media. The relative penetration and adoption rate of advanced tools for consumption such as DVRs, iPods, and high-speed Internet access is largely immediate compared to the rollout of the DVD or even slower rollout of VCRs, analog cable systems, and color television. The dominant media companies will face even greater uncertainty when the Digital Transition Act is enforced in the first quarter of 2009. Now consumers have finally been given the technological control they have so long desired to access what they want, when, where, and how they want it. To be blunt, the genie is out of the bottle. While the media conglomerates continue to wrestle the genie for their obligatory wishes, their inability to know what they want has ceded those wishes to that of the consumer.

As a result, the model has become inverted. Consumers have always wanted more and in recent years they have been able to take control. To reference the author Malcolm Gladwell (2000), we have reached what he identified as the proverbial "tipping point," or the point at which a little change has a big effect. As he observed in his book of the same name, behavior is contagious. Change is driven by the social connectivity of a small, but powerful group of influencers, or "exceptional people," whose early adoptive behavior catalyzes a movement. The resultant change does not happen gradually or incrementally, as many would expect, but rather at one critical moment, thereby tipping behavior from niche to mainstream. In regard to media, the digital revolution is making the present that moment.

Taking Responsibility

Disruptive technological innovations have lowered the traditional barriers of entry for production and distribution, empowering consumers with the ability to produce, distribute, and consume content on their terms. Such a seminal shift in control has forced the media industry to adapt to a truer capitalist model, in which a company's success or failure will be largely dependent on monetizing consumer behavior rather than imposing behavior on the consumer. The beginning of this new millennium is being marked by the transition from information being controlled by a few and distributed to the masses to a new era in which information will be more freely controlled and exchanged by everyday people around the globe within a more democratic, peer-to-peer, open ecosystem.

Not only is it imperative to recognize and mark this decisive moment in time, but it is critical to study the media industry of the past in order to gain a better understanding of the issues and opportunities presented by the media industry of the present and more importantly the future. It probably goes without saying that information is power. We have entered a global media communications age. The digital revolution is transforming our world with as much significance as the Industrial Revolution did over a century ago. Dismissing media industry studies as nothing more than the trivial dissection of popular movies and television shows, or the more cerebral social science of communication theory, is to overlook the underlying value information carries in the modern economy.

From the time I entered the College of Communication at the University of Texas at Austin in 1985 to my current work with both that distinguished institution and others, the academic community overall has largely regarded the study of media industries with a wary eye, belittling the passions of their peers as a naïve and unworthy fascination with disposable pop culture meant to satisfy the elective interests of an unsophisticated and entitled student body. Some parochial administrators fear the professional creep such studies might introduce into the rarified air of their ivory towers. Yet it is in this very entrenched and disparaging mentality that academia ironically most closely resembles the institutional arrogance of the media conglomerates themselves. Neither truly recognizes the tectonic power shift underfoot that is compromising their ability to shape the minds of their respective audiences with the influence and efficiency of the past. In large part, this is due to their lack of understanding of this specific discipline. Neither the academic community nor the media industry itself has sufficiently studied the forces that are shaping the present information age. Perhaps because the true study of the media industry cuts across so many academic disciplines, from the arts to communications or business to law, it has never been able to find a clearly defined home or a powerful enough sponsor from which to establish itself as a critical field of study. An interdisciplinary approach is needed to inject the study of the media industries with the profile and prestige necessary to significantly impact not just the academic community and media business but ultimately our society at large. I would argue that the stakes have never been higher, for without the proper historical and sociological context, our understanding of the forces shaping our culture will become more difficult as those forces become more complex.

Uncertainty Creates Opportunity

One needs to look no further for a flash point signaling an industry in deep turmoil than the labor unrest that has most recently challenged the entertainment business. Such strife has arisen primarily due to the inability of either the media companies or the creators themselves to articulate a clear business model for the emerging digital marketplace. Having given up too much of a stake in the once nascent home video business, the Writers Guild refused to make the same mistake twice. Hence nearly 20 years after their last work stoppage, the writers – by an overwhelming margin – authorized their guild to strike on the expiration of their contract with the AMPTP (the Association of Motion Picture and Television Producers) in late 2007. However, unlike the 1988 strike, the contemporary issues were much more complex and the answers far less clear. The resulting work stoppage is estimated to have cost the local economy $3 billion. Writers' individual losses will never personally be recouped. That is beyond

the point however. The general consensus among the writers was that they were not just fighting for themselves, but for future generations of creative talent. Even though the Directors Guild was able to craft a new agreement without having to invoke a strike, uncertainty remains over the upcoming labor renegotiations with the Screen Actors Guild. The overall inability of both the collective talent guilds and corporate leadership to identify a clear and confident path forward has given rise to a pervasive sense of fear and anxiety throughout the industry.

While the number of media companies represented by the AMPTP is fewer than in past negotiations, they are a far more powerful force in both size and scope as a result of their diversified holdings than anything the guilds have ever confronted. The inevitable and highly visible labor conflict emerged as a raw, emotional outburst, pitting individual artists against larger corporate interests. Yet those larger corporate interests now extend past Hollywood to Silicon Valley, Wall Street, Madison Avenue, and even around the world. The strength of the traditional media conglomerates is being disintermediated not just by Internet giants and technology powerhouses, but also by the shifting behavior of both consumers and advertisers newly empowered by technology.

It is ironic that these modern labor tensions have been set against the backdrop of an era wherein the individual consumers themselves have never exercised, nor desired, such collective power to shape media. It is not surprising that the writers effectively used the Internet to communicate their message to the external world through blogs and user-generated videos, but the support they in turn received from a global online community could not have been expected. While initially an industry contract dispute, the writers' strike is beginning to scale into a wider overall movement manifesting the larger fight between individuals and companies for control of the digital domain. In essence, empowered web denizens, fellow artists, and everyday individuals growing increasingly uncomfortable with the rising influence of larger institutions in their daily lives embraced the writers who were marching on the strike lines as foot soldiers in a more significant battle over personal expression, privacy, and control.

Essentially, this conflict raises the larger question: Who controls the media? Will it be the people or the conglomerates? We are a society ever more dependent on media. While the technological and capital barriers inherent in the broadcasting model necessitated that power reside in the hands of a few communicating to the masses, the digital model allows anyone to communicate with anyone else. Will the flow of ideas and the resulting discourse be truly open, free, and accessible to all, or will these ideas exist in appearance alone, with the larger underlying control ceded to a few powerful companies?

From Observation to Leadership

Clearly there is much at stake, but few have been able to articulate the deeper underlying issues or provide a contextual frame large enough to encompass the economic, social, creative, historical, and even political forces at work. The influence of media industry studies is essential during periods of disruption and transition in order to provide a sober and critically informed baseline for premeditated examination. Unlike many other academic disciplines, the intersection of competing market forces within this field of study makes a comprehensive understanding of present-day media issues a uniquely complex challenge. Weighing the larger impact and consequences of decisions made by leaders influencing the macro industry is necessary to ensure the proper balance between the micro interests of business, technology, society, the artist, and the consumer. Establishing media industry studies as not simply a respectable interdisciplinary field of knowledge, but one that is critical to mapping our future, must become a priority throughout academia, the media industry itself, and all of the constituencies it touches.

The need to embed media studies into the fabric of decision-making becomes more imperative as the velocity of change continues to accelerate throughout media. The utter collapse of the music industry, in a rather compressed period of time, serves as a warning to other sectors of the media industry that they must have a thoughtful strategy to overcome the inevitable inflection points they will be forced to confront. Could the record labels have foreseen a

future in which a popular group like Radiohead would reject working with the labels in favor of self-publishing and self-distributing their work directly to consumers? Perhaps not. Could the record labels have envisioned a future wherein technological progress facilitated Radiohead making more money by allowing their audience to name their price to download their new CD than they ever could have personally made on a hit release through the label system? To do so would have been to deny everything they believed in. Should the current media industry leaders be able to recognize their waning production, marketing, and distribution power arising from newer media models dependent on emerging digital technologies? Absolutely they should. The music industry at least had an excuse for blindly stepping into the void, having played the unfortunate role of the proverbial canary in the coal mine. However, as mentioned earlier, media professionals face intense pressure to increase margins on a quarterly basis and are, more often than not, rendered reactive when facing the challenges affecting their business. Asking those executives to rely on their own instincts, or the advice of either their strategic planning or business development divisions, mistakenly places the full responsibility for navigating the digital transition on their compromised shoulders.

A Community of Understanding

The future of the media industry must be guided by the collective influence of all constituencies dependent on the dynamic health and robust growth of this ever-expanding ecosystem. However, their respective visibility is limited by the scope of their peripheral understanding. The divide between Silicon Valley coders, Hollywood creators, venture capitalists, Madison Avenue admen, and corporate media executives is vast. All are heavily invested in seeing the media industry continue to grow, but each approaches planning and execution with a different set of assumptions and values. Only by introducing media industry studies into the fabric of the larger institutions shaping the field can we hope for these businesses, and ultimately society, to be able to collectively understand, and most importantly control, what will be the most pervasive influence of the twenty-first century.

The time to impose this discipline is now. The rising power of the individual consumer in not simply shaping new behavior and even newer business models, but in playing an active role in the creation of content itself, will no doubt be accelerated by prolonged labor conflict in Hollywood. The diminishing supply of original entertainment content on traditional linear screens will, at the very least, seed greater consumer acceptance of the Internet as a source for original content. More than likely, consumer dissatisfaction with the reduced entertainment choices on television will migrate disenfranchised audiences to original, made-for-Internet content. However, if original content is going to make a noticeable and lasting impact with consumers, narrative structures will have to adapt to reflect the strengths of digital media itself.

Marshall McLuhan noted that society organizes thought in a manner most reflective of the dominant medium of the era. As we shift from a passive, linear experience to a nonlinear, interactive medium, you can already begin to see the impact of digital media on younger consumers through their byte-sized discourse with one another and open source, multimedia expression of self. The rise of blogging, citizen journalism, and self-publishing has become second nature. What this means is that people are not simply consuming content, but generating content with scant awareness that they are contributing to the cumulative narrative text of the Internet.

It is likely that in order for storytelling to resonate with the children of the digital age it will have to initially reach and engage them where they share their personal stories. Portals, platforms, applications, and widgets along with sites and services such as MySpace, Facebook, Flickr, YouTube, Digg, del.icio.us, SayNow, Stickam, Slide, Tumblr, and Twitter facilitate the creation, sharing, and storage of users' lives and will increasingly become the frames across which stories are weaved. Content will begin to play the role of web integrator. Nonlinear narratives will live in three dimensions, engaging audiences through multiple portals and across the full range of a narrative's overarching metaverse. Each user will experience their own

beginning, middle and end to any given story depending on the timing, frequency, and duration of their personal engagement. Traditional storytelling and social media will begin to intersect. Communities of enthusiasts evolving around targeted content will play the roles of evangelist and viral marketer. User interaction will either directly or indirectly influence story and character development. Casual gaming will install a deeper customer base. Virtual worlds will nurture organic and evolving narrative organisms. Hive behavior may challenge the original intent of the creator. The network effect will drive both creative and commercial growth while the overall narrative process will become more fluid. Successful properties will expand across both linear and nonlinear platforms offering a ubiquitous, but highly personal, immersive experience adaptable to the expectations of the various media.

As a result, media will be more representative of our world as whole. Narrative expression will be increasingly unfiltered and begin to more naturally reflect the diversity of a medium unrestrained by geographical boundaries and racial, religious, gender, and class inequalities. The resulting liberation of media has the potential to free consumers from the restraints of the traditional gatekeepers and access the full breadth of what Chris Anderson (2006) has dubbed "the long tail." The power of visual images in shaping contemporary societies, or more specifically the crucial impact of television, cinema, the Internet, and advertising on public opinion, political affairs, and market strategies, has been defined as "videocracy."[2] However, this democratization of media also increases the opportunity for consumers to both manipulate and be manipulated by content. Look no further than the ease with which still images can be altered with the basic Photoshop application. Digital media has the power to instantly and efficiently make what was heretofore unreal, suddenly and convincingly real. As is oftentimes said of the new media frontier, it is, by any definition, the Wild West.

On the other hand, traditional media was, and still is, regulated. There exists a system of checks and balances to protect the public trust. No doubt the pressure placed on companies to exercise their incumbent power in the interest of the greater good has waned with the rise of increased competition, shifting political alliances, the speed of market change and the expansion of media platforms. As my colleague Ivana Ma has suggested, content, while seemingly a form of artistic expression, can also be viewed within a business sense as essentially an engagement tool.[3] Contextual entertainment could become the next evolution of contextual advertising – that is, web advertising that automatically targets users based on the content being viewed. Such a development would only further cross-pollenize entertainment and sponsorship, information and commerce. There used to be a safety net of sorts. In a landscape of unlimited choice, such safeguards are not realistically possible.

While consumers deserve to be agents of change empowered with new technologies to customize the production, distribution, and consumption of both professional and unprofessional content, they also need to be empowered with the knowledge to both understand, and ultimately control, the media they experience. Such need goes far beyond simple media education. The blurring of media and the symbiotic relationship between media and fundamental economic, social, and political forces requires a more rigid understanding of media's role in an increasingly complex and diverse society. Media industry studies offer the discipline required to establish an integral foundation from which to dialogue, confront change, and create opportunity. We are witnesses to a watershed moment in our culture. The legitimization of media industry studies will be the challenge and defining work of the current generation of academics and advocates of this field of study.

Notes
· ·

1   John Rogers, personal conversation.
2   See   www.urbandictionary.com/define.php?term= videocracy, accessed July 14, 2008.

3   Ivana Ma, personal conversation.

References
· ·

Anderson, C. (2006) *The Long Tail: Why the Future of Business is Selling Less of More.* Hyperion, New York.

Gladwell, M. (2000) *The Tipping Point: How Little Things Can Make a Big Difference.* Back Bay Books, New York.

20

Toward Synthetic Media Industry Research

....

Horace Newcomb

As I suspect is the case for many individuals in many different settings, I find myself almost overwhelmed each day as I open electronically delivered reports, newsletters, and trade publications related to media industries. Some of these are journals with long histories, such as *Broadcasting & Cable, Variety*, and the *Hollywood Reporter*. Others, *TVNewsday.com* or Cynthia Turner's *Cynopsis* (fragmented recently into *Cynopsis Digital, Cynopsis Kids*, and *Cynopsis Weekender*), are newly developed aggregators of articles found in these journals, combined with links to still other publications or collected information. This list does not include blogs, corporate sites, or other online resources that increase in number on what seems to be a daily basis. The availability of this much detail leads to my first question regarding media industry research: Which media industry?

When I open *Daily Variety*, and click on "News," I click again, out of habit, on TV as my first subcategory. After surveying the list of items I usually go to "Business," then to "International," though sometimes in different order. Often I find the same item listed under all three, a point certainly suggestive for research procedures and one to which I will return in other ways.

When I begin the day with *Broadcasting & Cable*, or *MultiChannel News*, or *Media Post*, some of the same items appear again. Comparing coverage of an item in these different publications returns me to the question: Which media industry? Stated differently, what does a particular event, decision, or development mean in the contexts of interest to different professional, industrial constituencies? How have writers and editors shaped these same items for their subscribers, or even presumed readers? What assumptions have they made with regard to the significance of the items within specific industrial contexts? Who needs to know what?

The "which industry" question, then, leads to another, one too often overlooked in media industry research: Whose media industry? When the question is addressed, it is often done so in a grand manner, examining consequences of ownership or policy. In terms of the possessive, "commercial" industries are poised counter to "public service" industries. Media industries addressing "citizens" are poised counter to those addressing "consumers." "Free services" are defined in distinction from "subscription" services. This list could be extended and for certain analytical purposes these definitional categories are richly productive. Here, however, I intend something different with the word "whose," and an example will provide a more precise application.

When this essay was begun, the Writers Guild of America (the WGA), with its two branches, West and East, was conducting a strike against the Association of Motion Picture and Television Producers (the AMPTP). The possessive query – whose? – can thus be defined in terms of these two powerful organizations, both central to any notion of media industries in the US and by extension, to others around the world. Issues are framed in some of the traditional terms of labor relations: wages, benefits, jurisdiction, earnings, contract duration, and so on. "Whose" here focuses on the struggle for control as defined in terms of creative activity on the part of writers and distribution on the part of the executives, with financial dispersal the focus of the struggle between them. (The issues are somewhat different for writers and distributors of feature films, but in this instance, from this vantage point, all writers are lumped into the same guild.) Without fresh content, the distributors must seek alternative strategies to maintain viewers. For the US television industry, this links their interests to those of advertisers, who depend on viewers to guarantee their clients access to potential consumers. And without access to the distribution systems of television and film, the writers find themselves unable to earn. The issues, of course, were much more refined in this case, focused on implications of newer forms of distribution such as DVDs and the Internet.

But I also want to complicate this description by pushing the notion of the possessive "whose" into more precise segments. Within the ranks of writers for television are those who also hold producer positions. In some cases the title of producer is largely an indication of a higher pay grade. In others it denotes specific duties. For the most successful writer-producers known as show runners, it blurs the lines of possession, authority, and control. Show runners are contractually obligated in most cases to perform duties over and beyond those of "staff writers," whose work is done on specific assignment and can be changed by the executive producer/show runner. Trade publications and reported word-of-mouth information indicated different degrees of commitment to the strike on the part of these groups. Groups of show runners took pains to publicly announce their total commitment to the strike and express their solidarity with other writers, walking picket lines under banners exhibiting this stance. But some reports suggested that powerful show runners worked through "back channels" with representatives of the AMPTP to smooth the negotiations to the point of ending the strike when it did.

Within both groups of writers there are still other distinctions. Most members of the WGA, for example, do not work on a regular basis. While the enhancements sought by the guild would benefit all writers who might work in the future, some have complained that going out on strike and losing money in the "present" when most striking writers would have earned very little during the same period is unfair. "Whose" television industry, then, is at stake?

The same point is made more forcefully by other labor unions. Most notable among them is the International Alliance of Theatrical Stage Employees (IATSE). Members of IATSE comprise a great many "below-the-line" workers. In the early stage of the writers' strike, the international president of IATSE, Thomas Short, wrote and distributed a strong letter of protest to Patric Verrone, president of the WGA West. The letter pointed out that more than 50,000 employees represented by IATSE could be affected by the strike action. His argument, restated as negotiations continued to be ineffective, represents yet another possessive involvement with the media industry. News and trade publications have also pointed frequently to the effects of the strike as they ripple through various service industries linked to the production of television and motion pictures. It could be said, then, that the "media industry" of the television writer is in many respects different from that of the carpenter or electrician who builds the set or the caterer who prepares meals for crew, staff, and cast. At the beginning of the negotiations, the Screen Actors Guild (SAG) generally supported the WGA action, in no small part because the contracts for each union "ripple" into one another; all would be affected by specific issues over which negotiations could fail in the construction of a new contract that would be agreeable. Indeed, the Directors Guild of America (DGA) entered into negotiations with the AMPTP while the writers remained on strike. The DGA reached an agreement, an event pushing the writers to come to a settlement. In the final stages of the WGA action, the DGA contract was used as both a model for a settlement and as leverage for the writers to move their own demands into a stronger position.

Yet even as this essay passed through stages of editorial preparation, events continued to change. Numerous other factors were involved in these matters. For instance, I have not mentioned the pressure applied by the cancellation of the Golden Globes Awards Ceremony or that felt throughout "the industry" to make sure the same decision was not made for the Academy Award presentations. The concerns were very practical. Estimates of financial losses in the Los Angeles area ranged as high as $123 million a week. After negotiations by both were concluded, the chief economist for the Los Angeles County Economic Development Corporation, Jack Kyser, estimated that between November 5, 2007 and early February 2008 the loss totaled $2.5 billion. As described in the *Hollywood Reporter*, "The figure includes lost wages from TV shows that were canceled and films that were put on hold as well as a plethora of support services, ranging from limo drivers to florists. Kyser suggested that the cancellation of the Golden Globes resulted in a $60 million shortfall for the community." The concerns reach even to the policy arena: "Kyser also noted that California grants no incentives for low-budget film productions," which are now common in many other states, "and with the state's budget deficit soaring, none can be expected anytime soon" (Guider 2008).

So far, these descriptions related to the identification – which media industry – and possession – whose media industry – have focused on major organizations and larger patterns of interaction. But questions in both areas also function with great intensity at the level of specific individual projects. Here is an example.

Through the years I have written a number of screenplays. I have been paid on occasion for this work and have been lucky to have worked with some experienced professionals in the process. Nothing I have written or co-written has ever been filmed. This is not unusual for screenwriters at any level in any segment of the media industries and those fortunate, as I have been, to have reliable income from other sources may continue their efforts with some comfort. My interest in following such pursuits stems from many sources, but one motivating factor is that the first original screenplay I co-authored was very nearly produced as a "major"

picture, making the process seem relatively easy as well as greatly enjoyable.

One collaborator, a media producer based in Austin, Texas, initiated the project. We had worked together in other settings and he asked that I collaborate with him and another writer (who also held an academic appointment at another university), to develop ideas. The story focused on television evangelists. The three of us had similar backgrounds in southern and southwestern Protestant religious groups. The individual who became my co-writer had conducted extensive research on televangelism and knew a number of well-known figures personally. The story was loosely based on actual events in which a prominent minister was discovered to be conducting an affair with an employee. Sometime later the employee and her husband were found murdered. No charges were brought but general suspicion was cast on the minister, who later died in an automobile crash that bore some marks of suicide.

A major factor was that our local producer was also professionally associated with a far more powerful producer based in New York. The individual had been a hugely successful talent agent, producer, and significantly, had developed numerous film financing operations throughout the world grounded in legitimate tax shelter "loopholes" in various tax codes (loopholes later closed). For personal reasons, the New York producer was very interested in a story that would criticize some aspects of Protestant evangelicals, while at the same time treating them knowledgeably and with respect rather than as crude stereotypes. The key issue in the story was power rather than sex or money.

We worked on the script for several years before accepting any payment in order to preserve our own "control" and "involvement." At one point we worked with a young Hollywood director who had recently completed an enormously successful movie. Though his previous work had been richly comedic, he was intrigued by our idea, which he described as "a preacher driving around with a pistol in his pocket." His office was decorated with original posters from John Ford films. The New York producer dismissed him as an inexperienced former actor, rejected him as a potential director, and went on to make a deal with a director of great and longstanding reputation, academy nominated, and based in New York. We worked off and on with this director for some time in both New York and Austin. He had negotiated a "pay or play" contract, meaning that he was paid (quite well) regardless of what happened with the project in the end.

One version of the end came in New York. The Austin producer and writers, the New York producer, and the director met at the director's home for a long story conference session. Throughout the day the New York producer and the director hammered at the script, each expressing *his own* specific ideas for what was needed to move on to production. It should be noted here that the New York producer did not yet have the involvement of a studio, the necessary element that would make production and distribution more likely for such a project. By the end of the day it was clear that the two had not reached agreement on the final version of the script that would give us direction on final rewrites.

The New York producer hailed a taxi and took the front seat. The three from Texas sat in the back. Driving in the lowering dusk toward mid-town Manhattan, the New York producer's words floated over the seat: "This is my movie, and if it's not made the way I want it to be made, it won't be made at all." It has not been made. The end is hardly ever the end with such projects, of course. Inquiries appear at odd times and interest comes and goes more than 20 years later.

Circumstances were substantially better for the director. In addition to his payment for our project, he had negotiated the desirable "two picture deal" with the New York producer. The contract provided that his other project would be made first. It was completed and distributed with the producer's assistance. The picture dealt with a sequence of important historical political events and though not commercially successful, it was a fine piece of work.

I do not cite this incident as evidence. It is not "fieldwork." It is not "ethnography," "auto" or otherwise. It "proves" nothing. Nor do I recount an anecdote, certainly not a personal one, to argue that media industry research should be nothing more than individual accounts. Rather, I intend to press the questions of "which" and "whose" media industries we study and how responses and analyses of

those specific questions must be compiled if we are to make progress in understanding media industries as important features of social and cultural experience.

The events I describe are examples of a project within a much larger process. The process itself is common, familiar, perhaps descriptive of the vast majority of major motion picture projects – those begun, developed, never produced. The more specific terms of the process stand out clearly. Beginning writers and a relatively inexperienced producer had enormous freedom and much encouragement to develop a specific story in personally defined ways. In long meetings they argued over and negotiated among themselves the details of narrative structure, scenes, lines, words, and actions. Frequent suggestions from other producers and directors helped shape the project, in some ways positively, others negatively, but always with a shared intention of creating an important story that could be made as a movie. The contracted director made significant contributions, respected the lived experiences of the writers, and gave great authority to the project. All involved relied heavily on the influence of the more experienced producer to secure top-level collaborators, which did happen. They also anticipated that he would secure a studio distribution deal. In this case his influence was not nearly as far-reaching as perhaps it once had been.

In this account the "which" is a fairly straightforward example of work in the Hollywood movie industry. It would have been significantly different had the Texas group attempted to raise funds to produce an "independent film," different and perhaps more successful. But the project would also have faced a different, but equally difficult path to completion and distribution. There are many "which-es" available at any time with any project. The question of "whose" media industry is more complicated. This group, like all writers, producers, and directors – as well as all the other professions engaged in making films and television – had and have different conceptions of "the industry," even of "our industry," as it is so often described.

Despite my simple example, these different perspectives, rooted in specific interests, are increasingly also the case with questions grounded in "which" and "whose" media industry will drive research. This is especially so now, when new technologies and consequent convergence, conflation, and widespread speculative investment seem to be bringing the industries closer together even as they complicate experiences. If the scholarly task is to back away, to gain sufficient analytical distance to determine relationships and commonalities among those industries, it remains necessary to acknowledge and understand the differences among them and among varieties of possessive involvement.

Put more bluntly, every media industry study is a case study.

This is so even for those studies operating deductively from the most general theories and claims. Practices such as capitalism, commercialism, or public service offer certain kinds of explanatory power. So too do "Hollywood" or "independent," "commercial" or "experimental." When applied in the analysis of companies or corporations, practices or policies, films or television programs, an actor's, director's, producer's, or entrepreneur's actions, they offer important information. But in the end they represent a "case" outlined and examined in terms of high levels of similarity and generalization – the "case" of media industries in capitalist organization, which, it should be noted, does not necessarily mean the same thing as the "case" of commercial industries or the "case" of "Hollywood film." Analysis here should be quick to recognize variation among the broad patterns and to challenge generalizations on this basis.

Beginning inductively, with specific individuals, examples, policies, historical circumstances, and so on, the emphasis will likely already be on distinction rather than similarity. Here, the problem for the analysis must be to remain open to precisely those similarities, those general theories, defined above as deductive beginning points to see that the specific "case" may relate to others in definable ways, that it may indeed be an "example" of larger patterns, tendencies, or modes of standardization.

Clearly, I have come round to very old arguments focused on the variable power and influence of structure and agency. Media industry research and analysis, however, demand more than rote acknowledgment of the ever-oscillating relationship between the two. Power, whether of capital accumulation

and control or of individual creativity, intimidation, or authority, operates differently depending on "which" media industry one studies and "whose" interests and definitions form the boundaries of that "industry."

Structure and agency do certainly remain constantly in play, from the plane of individual actions to the far more general planes such as labor negotiations. Structure and agency also work within individual decisions and within large organizations. The Writers Guild is a powerful organization dedicated to work on behalf of its individual members, providing for their economic well-being and protecting their individual work. It is also a structuring organization, demanding membership if one intends to do that work in the mainstream US media industries, and seeking to extend its authority into newer forms of media distribution. It is, then, both structure and agent. Its members engage it, negotiate its restrictive boundaries, change them with votes, and participate in collective action in hopes of individual benefit. Any analysis of this organization, its history, policies, or specific actions such as the 2007–8 strike, will be, finally, a case study.

Any method or approach outlined in this collection can be applied. Any history, audience study, textual, cultural, or political economic analysis will give us more general or specific information. The same questions – of economic control, individual experience, labor relations, distribution patterns, etc. – can be applied to various industries and settings. They can be applied vertically, tracing patterns within an industry, from the general concept ("Hollywood") to the individual film or television program. They can be applied horizontally, following specific questions across film to television to music and further. They can be studied diachronically or synchronically. And any of these analyses can, and most do, pursue one or the other focus, emphasizing similarity/structure or agency/difference.

Moving from any case, large or small, to any more systemic formation is extremely difficult. Yet the fact is, systemic or structural analyses are common in media industry research as explanations. Studies of specific projects ("cases" defined in more restrictive ways than I have suggested) are presented as "examples" that verify or "confirm" the effectivity of structures previously defined or merely assumed. Most such studies ground explanation in "levels" of influence and power. They acknowledge individual variations, but often cite them as examples of applications of structural power or, if they fall outside the patterns, as aberrations that also prove the case. I have avoided the use of "levels," but my aim has not been to imply that agency at the lower rungs is in any way more significant than accumulated structuring power at the top.

The problem is not which pole on the opposition is dominant, even when examining a particular instance. Rather, I want to focus on movement, fluidity, and choices, both strategic and tactical, in any situation. Analyses may explore how structures restrict, shape, encourage, or otherwise influence agency. They can also examine how agents engage structures in ways that accumulate and become new practices and techniques, how modifications move incrementally toward change, or how agents simply acknowledge, manipulate, and seek to subvert structures as so often happens in the processes of production. In either situation, however, the point is to recognize that the process studied is one of constantly shifting involvement and engagement of individuals and groups who are always exceptionally aware of both the structures in which they work and the degrees of agency they hold.

In large part because of the embedded "cultural" qualities of the "products," those who work in the media industries – from owners to caterers – do their work knowing full well that pushing the "system" at any point can alter relations throughout. What goes on in media industries is often much like a dance. Choosing any specific aspect for analysis places the researcher on the floor. One must know, or at the very least be aware of, the music and the appropriate steps, acknowledging at the same time that both music and movement are open to and in some ways expect or even demand improvisation. No screenwriter expects the work to go unchallenged by directors or actors or "development executives." No director expects to be free of producer or studio demands. Much of the work in the creative community, and perhaps much of the pleasure, lies in engaging the opposition, negotiating with "the enemy." It's always important to have someone to blame.

To emphasize this fluid state, one effective strategy for those who study such processes might be described as "synthetic media industry research." If every study is a case study, a central goal should not be to suggest that every individual instance proves the free exercise of agency, or to force all instances into conformity within an overarching explanation, but to determine relationships among cases. How, where and when do definitions and practices disappear, re-emerge, shift, and change? How have developments resulting from emerging technologies affected the music industry and how do fears and promises of similar developments affect film and television? How will the most recent WGA strike affect television, an especially apt question given studies examining how previous strikes altered programming, production, and viewer relations, expectations, and experiences? How does pressure emerging or applied at one point in one industry move across other industries? How have new technologies pushed policymakers to consider new social and cultural relations among media users and industries, if indeed policymakers have considered these matters at all? Where, in our analytical calculations, do we make a place for the significant and regular application of arrogance, pride, greed, experience, naïveté, novelty, failure, or pleasure, and so on, which so often appear as features of both structures and agents? And how do these "individual" characteristics work in relation to powerful structural features such as financial organization and existing technologies?

Such questions and problems may require more complex notions of "media systems and industries." But complexity and precise understanding are necessary because these industries remain central to social and cultural life and promise only to become more so as they become more tangled. New technologies for production and distribution enable many more citizens to take places in "the media industries." At the same time, the promise of huge financial reward leads to shifts of seismic magnitude at the highest structural levels. Attempts to create personal stories and perspectives occur simultaneously with attempts to establish control and to accumulate power and authority. Struggles to exercise influence in cultural, political, and economic life continue to become more complex. Put another way, the music becomes more intense, the dance steps more complicated. We may not be on the floor or the bandstand, but we are seated at the judges' table. If the academic study of media industries is to have any role in shaping better policies, better practices by those who work in media industries and those who teach them, and better understanding on the part of media users, it cannot rely on received generalizations or assumptions regarding how media industries operate. Before we raise the numbered cards, before we declare winners and losers, we have to know as much about the steps and the arrangements – and the improvisations – as possible.

Reference

Guider, E. (2008) Strike's toll on California: $2.5 bil. *Hollywood Reporter*, 20 February. At www.allbusiness. com/media-telecommunications/movies-sound-recording/7066303-1.html, accessed July 25, 2008.

Index